In the Name of Necessity

In the Name of Necessity

Military Tribunals and the Loss of
American Civil Liberties

Marouf Hasian Jr.

The University of Alabama Press
Tuscaloosa

Typeface: Perpetua

∞

The paper on which this book is printed meets the minimum requirements of American
National Standard for Information Sciences—Permanence of Paper for Printed Library
Materials, ANSI Z39.48-1984.

Library of Congress Cataloging-in-Publication Data

Hasian, Marouf Arif.
In the name of necessity : military tribunals and the loss of American civil liberties /
Marouf Hasian, Jr.
p. cm. — (Rhetoric, culture, and social critique)
Includes bibliographical references and index.
ISBN 0-8173-1475-X (cloth : alk. paper)
1. Courts-martial and courts of inquiry—United States. 2. Civil rights—United States.
3. Necessity (Law)—United States. 4. Military necessity. I. Title. II. Series.
KF7625.H37 2005
343.73'0143—dc22

2005005307

Contents

Acknowledgments

I have incurred many intellectual and emotional debts while writing this book, and I would like to thank the professionals, friends, and colleagues who helped me along the way: Karen Ashcraft, Ed Bennett, George Cheney, Ann Darling, Lisa Flores, Don McAngus, Marty Medhurst, Gordon Mitchell, Trevor Parry-Giles, Sally Planalp, Rick Rieke, and Helga Shugart. I would also like to thank Dean Robert Newman and the other administrators at the University of Utah who provided me with sabbatical support so that I could write this book. The courteous staff who work in the interlibrary loan department at the University of Utah's Marriott Library helped track down some invaluable materials.

My editor John Lucaites and the staff of The University of Alabama Press have provided me with invaluable criticism, and I have profited immensely from the advice of the anonymous reviewers who read drafts of this manuscript. My copyeditor, Dawn Hall, made many changes that significantly improved the final product.

Several of the chapters in this book contain material that was previously published in scholarly outlets, and I would like to thank the following journals for providing reprint permission: Chapter three is a revised version of a manuscript that was originally published in the *American Indian Cultural and Research Journal* in 2003 ("Cultural Amnesias and Legal Rhetoric: Remembering the 1862 United States–Dakota War and the Need for Military Commissions," volume 27, number 1), by permission of the American Indian Studies Center, UCLA © Regents of the University of California; a version of chapter five has been revised for the journal *Rhetoric and Public Affairs;* chapter six originally appeared in *Rhetoric and Public Affairs* ("Franklin D. Roosevelt, Wartime Anxieties, and the Saboteurs'

Cases," volume 6, number 2, Summer 2003; chapter seven will appear in a forthcoming issue of *Controversia,* a publication of the International Debate Education Association ("Victor's Justice: General Yamashita, and Collective Memories of American Military Tribunals"); and an earlier version of chapter eight, "The Legal and Public Debates over the Necessity of Bush's Military Order," was presented at the Presidential Studies Conference at Texas A&M University in the spring of 2004.

Several staff members at the Library of Congress helped me obtain the necessary permission for the reprint of the photograph of the Wirz hanging that appears at the beginning of chapter five (LC-B8171, 909971/CO, 7752). I would also like to thank Kate Wagner of the University of Maryland and the staff of the National Archives and Records Administration for the help that was provided in securing copies of some of the records of the military commissions on this trial.

In the Name of Necessity

I

Introduction

The Genealogical Origins of
Necessity and Military Necessity

A strict observance of the written laws is doubtless one of the highest
duties of a good citizen, but. . . . The laws of necessity, of self-preservation,
of saving our country when in danger, are of higher obligation.
—Thomas Jefferson, 1810

In the aftermath of the 9/11 attacks,[1] and the beginning of the war for
the "liberation" of Iraq,[2] many audiences around the world were asked to
remember that in times of war, military "necessities" have to take center
stage. Rick Atkinson and Thomas Ricks, for example, told readers of the
Washington Post that while the nation hoped this would be a short conflict,
we all needed to acknowledge the "military necessity of preparing a protracted, more violent and costly war."[3] During that same week, President
George W. Bush explained to Congress that Americans were holding more
than "600 enemy combatants at Guantánamo Bay," and that they were being treated "humanely, and, to the extent appropriate and consistent with
military necessity, in a manner consistent with the principles of the Geneva Conventions of 1949."[4]

These select usages of the term "military necessity" serve as illustrative
examples of the enduring influence of some key evocative terms within
our legal and public cultures. In this book, I want to provide a critical
rhetorical analysis that explores some of the historical and contemporary
reasons for the popularity of the terms "necessity" and "military necessity,"
and I want to analyze how these phrases are used in modern defenses of
military tribunals. In November of 2001, President Bush told a conference
of U.S. attorneys that some "non–U.S. citizens" may be planning to com-

mit mass murder, and that the dictates of the land's "national security interest" might mean that these enemies would have to be tried "by military commissions."[5] Since that time, many citizens, scholars, public commentators, jurists, and politicians have engaged in countless debates about the nature of due process and the constitutionality of these military tribunals. George Fletcher, for example, argued in the winter of 2004 that under the Third Geneva Convention, the Guantánamo detainees deserved to have some type of international status hearings in front of a "competent tribunal" that would replace the current American suspension of writs of habeas corpus.[6]

As I note throughout this book, the complex issues surrounding these tribunals are not simply matters that can be resolved through formalistic legal analyses that discover the "right" interpretation of key precedents, statutes, or military codes. In the wake of 9/11, we are living in a world where we are having to renegotiate the ways we think about legal justice and the spirit behind these laws. My research has convinced me that in the name of necessity too many Americans have unjustifiably embraced the idea that we can have military tribunals that provide full and fair trials. Even if we take into account some of the alleged problematics associated with the use of civilian courtrooms—extended delays, the potential lack of secrecy, the costs in terms of time and money, and the potential dangers that are faced by participants—we should not automatically assume that military tribunals provide the needed correctives. Before the "war on terrorism," many American officials wrote and talked about the problems associated with *foreign* uses of military commissions,[7] and many of these same officials lamented the fact that citizens in other countries had to deal with human rights violations, the absence of civilian oversight, and the rules of evidence that governed what some have called "kangaroo courts." Do we really believe that our "modified" military tribunal regulations will protect the rights of either U.S. citizens or noncitizens?

After analyzing the different generational arguments left to us by both critics and defenders of these military tribunals, I have been persuaded by the detractors of these proceedings that these trials are neither desirable nor necessary. In January of 2004, some of the military lawyers assigned to defend some of the detainees at Guantánamo Bay sent an appellate brief to the U.S. Supreme Court that included this warning, "those who fall into the [legal] black hole may not contest the jurisdiction, competency, or even the constitutionality of the military tribunals."[8] This situation has become so problematic that many defendants have lawyers arguing that any type of hearing is better than indefinite detention or solitary confinement. The recent publicity surrounding Abu Ghraib prison, and the disclosure that some members of the Justice Department and Defense Department were crafting legal justifications for coercive interrogations (again, in the name of "necessity") simply underscores the importance of having judicial review outside of the military's various chains of command.[9]

I share Michael Ignatieff's concern that we may be witnessing the erosion of the "human rights" discourse that became the "dominant moral vocabulary" we have been using since the end of the Cold War.[10] Obviously, the advent of 9/11 or the call for the tribunals are just some of the reasons that necessitarian vocabularies seem to once again resonate with so many audiences, but these events have served as key catalytic moments in our reassessment of many of our cultural, legal, and political values. I will argue that the necessity of war often gets confused with the need for tribunals, and that our decontextualization of seminal legal precedents exacerbates the problem. My rhetorical analysis of some key tribunal cases has led me to disagree with those critics who believe that trying "terrorists under a military commission is not inherently problematic."[11]

For centuries, many previous generations had talked and read about the vaunted Enlightenment principles of "freedom," "liberty," and "independence," but these contested terms have always been circumscribed by the need for the "survival" of civilizations, the maintenance of social "order," or the primacy of "public safety." Oftentimes, our inherited Anglo-American lexicons have discursive hierarchies that privilege those rhetorical clusters that have treated openness and freedom as the norm, and the restrictive idioms that are associated with communal "necessities" have been viewed as the exceptions that simply underscore the magnitude of our freedoms. While realists might contend that during wartime the calculus changes, we have inherited lexicons that have been used by those who have been suspicious of aggregated power. Justice Hugo Black, for example, voiced his belief that "military trials of civilians charged with crime, especially when not made subject to judicial review, are so obviously contrary to our political traditions" that they are a "radical departure from our steadfast beliefs."[12] Are these remarks persuasive in a world filled with anthrax, dirty bombs, and sleeper cells?

Justice Black may be exaggerating the obviousness of this libertarian tradition, and those who share these sentiments may be forgetting that our civilian and military histories are also filled with tales of broad executive power, the importance of having martial law, or the deference that has been given to military leaders during times of war. Now prudence seems to demand that the sons and the daughters who have been bequeathed these Enlightenment rhetorics may need to redraw the mythic line that exists between civilian and military governance.[13] Ratna Kapur might write about how any "military action resorted to under international law must meet certain legal requirements—including necessity, proportionality, and discrimination,"[14] but this does not prevent contentious communities from debating the meaning of those terms.

As I watched the collapse of the second of the Twin Towers on 9/11 with some of my colleagues, I realized that in the coming years many American communities were going to have to make some difficult decisions about the relinquishment of some taken-for-granted civil liberties. A major rhetorical inversion seemed to be taking place in the discourse of the times— some of our traditional freedoms could now be reconfigured as luxuries or even barriers. For example, President Bush admonished us to remember that the "danger to the safety of the United States" meant that it "would not be practicable to apply" in military tribunals the "principles of law and the rules of evidence generally recognized in the trial of criminal cases in the United States."[15] This type of legal logic has led to a situation where the symbolic dangers associated with terrorism can be tied to a host of public policy measures.[16]

In sum, we have become a necessitarian nation. In the name of "necessity" we close borders, condone more racial profiling, and put up with more intrusive governmental surveillance. We have been told that if Americans truly want to win their "war on terrorism," billions of dollars will have to be spent on homeland defenses, military armaments, and technological innovation. The day after the attacks on the Twin Towers, the U.N. Security Council adopted a resolution that indicated their "readiness to take all necessary steps to respond to the terrorist attacks of 11 September 2001 and to combat all forms of terrorism."[17] The U.S. Congress passed measures that empowered the president to use "all necessary and appropriate force against those nations, organizations, or persons he determines planned, authorized, committed, or aided the terrorist attacks."[18]

Several weeks later the Bush administration announced it had credible evidence that this was the work of Osama bin Laden and the al-Qaeda network, and the bombing of Afghanistan became a part of the indeterminate war against terrorism.[19] The potential existence of weapons of mass destruction in Iraq meant that there were even those who advocated that the American military needed to engage in preemptive attacks in situations where delay might bring disproportionate misery. Under Article 51 of the U.N. Charter, nations can invoke the right of self-defense against an "armed attack,"[20] and conversations about new forms of "military necessity" circulated in many venues during the beginning the second U.S.-Iraqi war.[21]

The pervasiveness of these types of necessitarian arguments helps us understand just why the idea of unilateral U.S. military tribunals resonates with so many audiences. During times of war, national leaders can persuasively argue that they need to use all of their inherent and constitutional powers so they can deal with extraordinary criminals, extraordinary times, and extraordinary situations. They are, after all, supposedly dealing with rogue states, hidden enemies, and never-ending battles. Unfortunately, notes political theorist Harvey Mansfield, the "elastic" nature of the concept of "necessity" means the term "can be stretched to include many things that aren't really necessary."[22]

Now that some tempers have cooled in the wake of 9/11, perhaps it is time for researchers and scholars to take a closer look at the rhetorical origins of this necessitarian state. Were the "measures" labeled as necessitous really as "unprecedented" as the "danger that called them into being?"[23] Even if we granted that we were at war because our commander in chief said we were at war, did the American president and his executive advisors really need all of the power they were requesting? Rather than simply accepting at face value the public or legal assertions that take for granted the existence of a priori necessities, we need critiques that investigate the rhetorical acts that helped create those apparent exigencies. Several years ago, modern Cassandras, with their commentaries on "catastrophic terrorism,"[24] had warned us that something like 9/11 might happen, but the experiential nature of these traumas simply underscores the importance of grappling with these complexities.

Contemporary American debates about "necessity" or "military necessity" become global concerns when U.S. forces extend the temporal and geographical frontlines in this "war" on terrorism. Many observers want a variety of terrorists to be tried in military tribunals,[25] and hundreds of captured fighters from around the world are now being held in detention centers in Cuba, Afghanistan, and Iraq. For example, commentators have written about how Jose Padilla ("the dirty bomber") and Saddam Hussein need to be tried by military, and not civilian authorities.[26] While some critics argue that these captured members of al-Qaeda or Taliban organizations need to be prosecuted in front of international courts,[27] defenders of the American commissions respond that the selective targeting turned this into a uniquely American affair. Most Americans may have accepted these types of arguments, but there are many international communities who symbolically link these tribunals with the specter of "victor's justice," legal "black holes," and American exceptionalism. I share the concerns of David Cole and James Dempsey, who argue that some of our antiterrorist policies sacrifice our civil liberties, while exacerbating the terrorist problem.[28]

Many critics of Bush's military policies began complaining about some of his executive actions in the fall of 2001, but the U.S. Department of Defense added fuel to the fire by releasing a proposed list of some twenty-four crimes that would be used by "tribunals conducting trials for adversaries captured in the campaign against terrorism and held by the military."[29] Some of these potential crimes included the willful killing of protected persons, attacks on civilians, the destruction of protected property, pillaging, taking hostages, and the employment of poisons or similar weapons. Defense Secretary Donald Rumsfeld has observed that these rules could also be applied to Iraqi suspects who might come into U.S. military custody.[30] As several members of the Second Circuit Court of Appeals observed in December of 2003, the Bush administration seemed to be arguing that we were now dealing with a very extensive "zone of combat" that justified the detention and possible trial of both citizens and noncitizen "enemy combatants."[31]

When Bush administration officials and supporters of these tribunals justify the use of extensive executive discretion, they use a host of related arguments that are tied to a nation's necessitarian rights of preservation—the supposed inherent rights of commanders in chief, congressional ratification of executive action, key judicial opinions (usually World War II decisions)—that underscore the importance of deference in times of war, international "rules of war," and statutory authority.[32] It will be my contention that none of these various rationales can withstand historical and judicial scrutiny, and that a balanced look at the rhetorical histories of many of these tribunals reveals the troubled nature of these military trials.[33]

As I note in the following chapters, there have been many generations of Anglo-Americans who have talked or written about the perceived differences between real and "feigned" necessities, and we need to keep these conversations in mind as we have public deliberations about the nature and scope of presidential power. Leaders may act as if necessities are self-evident, but the word "necessity" has always been a contested, ambiguous, and polysemic term that sometimes gained its rhetorical power by appearing to be a natural marker of some nondiscursive crisis or emergency. All of us know about the tragedies and traumas that are associated with the loss of life and property, but we often disagree about the extent or causes of these problems. The symbolic acts involved in the characterizations of empirical events as necessitous conditions are parts of complex rhetorical processes that bring together our material and discursive worlds. Given our adherence to the polysemic values that surround notions like "freedom" and "liberty," we do not always treat claims about "necessity" in the same way. As Kirk Davies recently observed, "our predilection for demanding 'our rights'" has meant that we are suspicious of those who ask for more authority in dealing with national emergencies or crises.[34] Yet there are times when we leave behind these suspicions, and we defer to the actions of presidents who may find it "impracticable to apply the rules of federal court."[35] Heather Maddox explains that

> Presidential powers during times of emergency, sometimes referred to as the Doctrine of Necessity, set the stage for a continued push and pull between the President and Congress in the arena of war

and foreign policy. . . . Combining executive power with executive purpose often results in complex problems and equally, if not more complex solutions. One's idea of how much power the President should have in acting by necessity, with national security interests in mind, are inescapably founded on individual views of foreign policy and international relations. This notion of necessity has in the past provided a "wild card" allowing the President to act outside the narrow proscriptions of the Constitution in certain circumstances.[36]

The strategic usages of this notion of necessity are both protean and formidable.

A variety of social, political, and economic policies, both here and abroad, has been promoted in the name of "necessity" or "military necessity." Kenneth Burke admonished us to remember that "freedom" and "necessity" were "God terms" that explained some of the "conditions" and "motives" that had to be "taken into account when one is planning an action."[37] Gregory Raymond has similarly intoned that there have been many "foreign policy undertakings" that were justified through the use of "a rhetorical strategy and form of argument that appeals to the exigencies of necessity."[38]

Even the most natural-looking "necessities" are in fact social constructs that have to be constantly argued for, and publicly defended. For example, whether a child growing up in New England needs to be vaccinated to protect the public health, safety, and welfare of neighbors is something that requires warranted assent, and ratification by select communities. The parents of the child might believe that the family has an inherent right to freedom of religion, and that coercive vaccination would constitute a violation of their religious beliefs.[39] Other members of the community might argue that the vaccination of the child has to be contextualized as an act requiring individual sacrifice that will benefit the entire community. "Necessities" are therefore never self-evident creations—we are all human agents who have to decide whether events such as earthquakes or mudslides are going to be framed as "man-made" or "natural" disasters. Michel Foucault once observed that the social construction of a "Need" involves political acts that have been "meticulously prepared, calculated and used."[40] For example, the attacks on the Pentagon and Twin Towers could have been characterized as domestic *crimes* rather than acts associated with an indefinite war on terrorism. At the same time, these acts could have been defined as violations of international law that justified the creation of international tribunals.

Even in situations where military experts and commanders have agreed about what constitutes a "necessity," they have often disagreed on just who should be empowered to announce the existence of this condition, or who should have the power to respond to the situation. These were topics that interested both elites and laypersons, because all types of governmental officials might use necessitarian arguments when justifying the restrictions that might be placed on one's spiritual, political, or economic liberties. For example, during the late sixteenth century, these types of claims were so familiar that one of John Milton's characters in *Paradise Lost* critiques the usage of "necessity, the tyrant's plea" in excusing "devilish deeds."[41] Milton elaborates by noting that this "fiend" tied "necessity" to "public reason," "honour," and "empire." His contemporaries were perhaps worried that sophistry might be used to confuse publics who might not know that an amorphous public "necessity" was used to hide the obvious existence of some God-given volition.

This typical example of Anglo-American discourse on "necessity" would be just one of the fragments to reappear in hundreds of future debates about the imposition of martial law, the need to suppress dissent, or the creation of military tribunals. Later in this chapter I provide a general overview of some of the historical usages of these ideas in military situations, but before I do that I would like to provide a brief overview of the critical legal perspectives framing this project.

Ideographic and Iconographic Analyses in the Study of Political and Legal Genealogies

For many interdisciplinary scholars who have looked into the historical or contemporary usages of "necessity" or "military necessity," the polysemic nature of these words is maddening, because now researchers are having to deal with layers of arguments and precedents that have accumulated with the passage of time. Our own selective argumentative histories and collective histories are often filled with discursive fragments that are survivals from bygone debates and social controversies. Asymmetrical power relationships, shifting evaluative hierarchies, and divergent interpretations of chronological events have influenced what we choose to remember, and what we choose to forget.

Many orthodox commentators who write about "necessity" often try to deal with these complexities by trying to sift through the "rhetoric" to get to the underlying "reality," and in the process of doing this they have to bracket out the material contexts and the contradictory meanings that may be associated with those terms. This formalistic approach that is based on a convergence or correspondence view of language and meaning assumes that legal principles and standards exist independent of rhetorical contestation. Commentators who adopt these traditional stances often allege that if we just peel off enough layers of the discourse surrounding the events, we can improve our clarity of vision and see the actual physical necessities that exist independently of the rhetoric. Audiences' *perceptions* of these necessities are then measured against some mythical, independent assessment of necessitous circumstances. Legal commentators can complain that the "declaration" of an emergency is not the same thing as an actual emergency, or that military authorities continued to maintain "martial law" long after the danger had passed. But they fail to mention that their own position is based on a competing rhetorical declaration.

These types of reductionist approaches that were popularized in legal communities during the nineteenth and twentieth centuries have the advantage of providing us with rules and standards that appear to be linear, consistent, universal and reasonable, but they ignore the contested nature of all of the fragments, narratives, and other figurations that influenced the creation of those legal markers in the first place.[42] "The law," notes Shoshana Felman, "perceived itself either as ahistorical or as expressing a specific stage in society's historical development."[43] Complex diachronic and synchronic debates that once provided the contexts for popularized maxims get left behind as modern-day commentators talk about obvious necessities or unquestionable military necessities. This conflates epistemic representations with ontological realities and blurs the lines that exist between social and material realities. Some empowered civilian and military leaders can use select precedents from particular historical situations as analogous instances that demanded our immediate attention. This can bring false analogies, hasty generalizations, and self-serving argumentation.

Within many of these formalistic or orthodox ways of thinking about legal duties and rights, necessitous circumstances are treated as a priori facts that inform the decisions made by the elites who have special training in the handling of those types of affairs. This is one of the reasons why we hear so much about civilian "deference" during times of war, or the need for discretion in the absence of written authorization. The very existence of the prior emergency, or the precedential value of the analogy, becomes a taken-for-granted part of a deductive argument. The "iron" laws of necessity are thus used to characterize both the situations and the responses to those situations.

From a critical rhetorical perspective, these analytic approaches invariably take texts out of contexts, and the commentaries written about the meaning of "necessity" become a part of sedimented rhetorics that surround these key terms. Those contextual tales that get left behind—what Peter Fitzpatrick calls "dangerous supplements"—are the temporary losers in jurisprudential debates about law, order, and the maintenance of authority.[44] Given the thousands of necessitarian debates that have taken place over hundreds of years, there are now many penumbral layers of sedimented meanings, and countless tropes and narratives that surround the core of all contested terms.[45] Multiple interpretative communities have battled for centuries over the meanings of these words, and when modern-day critics write about "necessity," they are making inherently political decisions.

This, however, is the not the dominant way many legal scholars or laypersons think about the relationship between legal discourse and "necessity." At the same time that some Anglo-American writers have naturalized the existence of emergencies, others have naturalized the role that legal "principles" play in constraining behavior during those events. These commentators often write about the historical importance of terms such as "precedent," "case law," and "judicial opinions," and they magnify the power of select judges, lawyers, or juries in regulating human affairs. Since at least the time of Christopher Langdell, these privileged interpretations have been collected in legal briefs, judicial opinions, and treatises that scientifically arrange facts, laws, issues, and conclusions.[46] For example, a person who believes in this type of legal formalism might hope the discovery (or consensual creation) of some key judicial interpretation of "necessity" or "military necessity" might prevent military commissions from overstepping their authority.

These types of traditional approaches, which either naturalize the emergencies or naturalize the legal principles that supposedly place constraints on empowered governmental agents, share the problem of trivializing the role public rhetorics play in the communal creation of our necessitous circumstances. The orthodox frameworks that highlight the words that appear in legislative bills or judicial opinion help valorize the role of "great" leaders, but they de-emphasize the roles that audience receptions, power relations, and cultural beliefs play in the social interpretations of our facts and conditions. The privileging of elite remarks in a post-9/11 world is a precarious endeavor, for as Elmer Mahoney once observed, our "history reveals that the [U.S.] Supreme Court, under the shield of military necessity, rather consistently upheld governmental repression of personal rights during periods of war."[47] Both liberal and conservative judges talk about the "deference" due American presidents.[48]

We therefore need an approach to rhetoric and law that looks at both texts and contexts, symbolic constructions and material constraints, vernacular and elite texts. No one jurist's views on "necessity" or "military necessity" should be controlling, and we need to go beyond simply claiming that some earlier court allowed an earlier presidency a great deal of latitude in dealing with emergencies. We need to be asking about the constitutive creation of that emergency, the duration of that alleged emergency, and the motivations of the social agents who are making decisions about proportionate responses in allegedly necessitous situations.

If we are going to be asked to relinquish some of our most cherished civil liberties in the name of "necessity," we ought to be able to explore the whole range of arguments that have been used by Americans in many generational debates about these controversial military tribunals. The only way we can really study this many arguments is by purposely blurring the traditional lines that exist between "legal" and "extrajudicial" ideas. This type of an approach needs to take into account the substantive role of rhetoric, without falling into the extremes of ignoring discourse, or valorizing the rhetorical power of privileged legislators or jurists. This

is no easy task, for this critical stance asks us to take seriously the arguments that may appear in newspapers, books, journals, novels, or the
Internet.

I will therefore be using a critical approach in my investigation of military tribunals that reviews how multiple audiences talked or wrote about
"necessity" or "military necessity." I want to provide readers with an understanding of the selective nature of these rhetorics, and I hope they get
a sense of the incredible mobility of some of these key terms. This means
paying attention to what gets said or what gets muted, and observing the
potential recycling of a host of libertarian and necessitarian arguments.
We need to frankly acknowledge that some claims, arguments, and issues
simply get glossed over or forgotten with the passage of time.

In order to carry out this task, I will be using what many communication
scholars have called an "ideographic" approach to political discourse.[49]
Michael McGee popularized the concept of the "ideograph," and this rhetorical type of analysis extends the work of those who suggest we take an
interactionist view of language. An ideograph has been defined as a key
evocative term or phrase that illustrates the political allegiances of an individual and a community in a major social, political, economic, or legal
controversy.[50] Examples of ideographs include words like "equality," "liberty,"[51] "freedom," "progress,"[52] "independence," "freedom of speech,"
or "law and order." These key terms can have either positive or negative
valence,[53] and they can gain or lose their rhetoricity.

Ideographs are important because they provide us with the residual
traces of how other diachronic or synchronic communities have interpreted particular facts, conditions, or situations. They gain their substantive meaning regardless of whether single authors like the way they are
being used and abused, because they have a way of becoming a part of elite
and vernacular vocabularies. These abstract value terms serve as powerful
argumentative warrants, and we have empirical evidence of the significance of these terms when we see the "social actions" that are taken in
their name.[54] Key ideographs gain their rhetoricity when they are used
with other political units in concrete situations. For example, in *Crafting
Equality,* Celeste Condit and John Lucaites explain why ideographs are just
some of the units of analysis that go into the creation of what they call a
"rhetorical culture":

By rhetorical culture we mean to draw attention to the range of linguistic usages available to those who would address a historically particular audience as a public, that is, a group of potentially disparate individuals and subgroups who share a common interest in their collective life. In this rhetorical culture we find that full complement of commonly used allusions, aphorisms, characterizations, ideographs, images, metaphors, myths, narratives, and topoi or common argumentative forms that demarcate the symbolic boundaries within which public advocates find themselves constrained to operate.[55]

Such an approach emphasizes the ways that speakers and communities make compromises when they interpret these various political units of analysis. Unlike more formalistic views of language and law, this type of perspective keeps track of convergent and divergent meanings in a host of complex political, social, or economic situations.

One of the key advantages of taking what could be called the "ideographic turn" is that this type of approach tries to take into account both the social agency of human actors and the social constraints that create the boundaries for these key ideographic units of analysis.[56] Such a perspective avoids the extremes of either valorizing political terms as hypostatized markers of democratic societies or treating the words as superfluous covers for economic or political substructures. Unlike Marxist approaches that view public discussions as merely the epi-phenomenal superstructures that surround a core of deterministic economic forces, an ideographic approach sees rhetoric as an "influential" rather than "causal" force in facilitating or inhibiting social change.[57] For example, the designation of an event as a "disaster" might involve the study of passive and active writings on that event, and the study of both "knowledge as disaster and knowledge disastrously."[58]

In this type of critical rhetorical analysis, audience perceptions are key parts of the cocreation of local knowledges and legal frameworks. An ideographic method assumes that people who believe in an ideology are not automatically dupes or inactive listeners—they are simply considered to be social actors who accept as legitimate one set of hierarchal values over another set of competing values.[59] Critics applying ideographic analyses assume that public discourses are social phenomena that need to be investigated. In the words of Dominick LaCapra, "documents are texts that supplement or rework 'reality' and not merely sources that divulge facts about 'reality.' "[60]

This ideographic approach has heuristic value because it helps us trace the actual way various communities voiced their concerns about salient political, social, or economic issues. Rather than looking for the ways that the "masses" failed to live up to some ahistorical or decontextual standard of rationality,[61] we would keep track of the pragmatic claims that were deployed in volatile situations. Anna Alonso has argued that communal knowledge is often based on the imaginative figurations that come from both official and popular discourses,[62] and if this argument has any merit, then we need to rethink the way we read some of our canonical texts. For example, Dr. Francis Lieber's famous code on the "Law of War" gained and lost rhetorical power, depending on how often it was deployed in generational debates about the desirability of Abraham Lincoln's military commissions (see chapters two and three).[63]

By themselves, ideographs are powerful indicators of human attitudes and values, but they gain in symbolic importance when they are combined with other units or analysis, or become parts of larger social narratives or legal myths. Our necessitarian ideas about military tribunals cannot help but be tied to the ways we think about "foreign" enemies, "combatants," "sleeper" cells, presidential power, military honor, and "national security." Each generation crafts its own lexicons, and the critics who take the ideographic turn participate in genealogical investigations that trace how these universalizing concepts were created in the first place,[64] or recirculate as "fragments" in other apparently finished texts.[65] Our legal archives— often treated as the repositories that preserve our "primary" materials— are themselves collections that include or exclude particular written and visual images.[66]

I should note here that I am not calling for an abandonment of analyses that dissect arguments that appear in legislative documents or judicial opinions. I am simply claiming that they should be viewed as small but influential parts of much larger conversations. For example, in our 2001 debates about the desirability or constitutionality of military tribunals, why did we constantly have to read about cases like *Ex parte Milligan*[67] and the World War II saboteurs' cases,[68] while we rarely heard about the trial of General Yamashita,[69] or the nineteenth-century hanging of thirty-eight Dakota Indians? Why did we read countless quotations from Supreme Court jurists talking about the importance of "military necessity," or the importance of judicial deference, but very little commentary on earlier public criticisms of these cases? Precedential fragments in the form of propositional logics became the key components in a host of truncated debates.

An ideographic analysis of this type of legal discourse would widen the lens of our inquiry so that we could study the arguments of both the winners and losers in many earlier controversies, and it would provide us with a much better understanding of how President Bush's recent Military Order[70] fits within several different rhetorical frameworks. The genealogical recovery of some of these rhetorical histories may also help us answer a host of intriguing political questions:

- How did earlier generations argue about "necessity" or "military necessity," and what did these historical audiences think about the nature and scope of American civil liberties?
- Have there ever been times when courts or legislatures questioned the wartime powers of a president, and do we have traces of any reasonable public critiques of these military commissions?
- Given the popularity of the Nuremberg trials, why do so many audiences accept the arguments that are used in defense of unilateral, American military tribunals?
- Who profits from the trial of particular defendants, the selection of forums, the location of the trials, the choice of the applicable rules of evidence, or the decisions that are made about public coverage of a particular proceeding?

All of these are key topoi that may influence the ways we think about our modern military tribunals.

In sum, a critical ideographic approach would ask readers to review the ways that rhetors and their audiences have *performed* particular instantiations of our "rules of law," and it would invite us to search for legal divergence in place of univocal convergence. Note, for example, the way Austin Sarat talks about the rhetorical dimensions of trial transcripts:

Each transcript gives potent evidence of the perspectivism and poly-
vocality of human experiences of point-counterpoint in which competing renditions of events, motives, possibilities sit side-by-side. . . .
One must be open to the process through which texts come to speak
to each other, through which readings bring remembrance of ideas,
insights, imaginings encountered elsewhere, in other texts . . . the
trial transcript . . . is at once an assertion of history against memory
and a particular kind of memorialization.[71]

We can of course apply what Sarat is saying about legal "transcripts" to any
number of judicial or legislative artifacts, because transcripts are not the
only types of archival materials that can be unpacked or interrogated.

With this in mind, I would like to provide an overview of some of the
discursive origins of both "necessity" and "military necessity."

A Brief Rhetorical History of the Anglo-American
Origins of Necessity and Military Necessity

Since time immemorial, the concept of "necessity" has fascinated communities of people who associated the word with ideas about fortune, conditions of need, and feelings of inevitability. In many Greek myths, Necessity was personified as the daughter of either Zeus or Chronos, and these
ancients placed her at a spindle wheel, weaving the trajectory of the plan-
ets.[72] For example, in *The Republic*, Plato pictured Necessity in his Vision of
Er, and he characterized her as the mother of the Moiroae. Some of these
tragic tales explained to audiences that Necessity was a part of a cyclical
world, filled with the mysterious forces of causation and determinacy.[73]

Yet many of these Hellenistic allegorical tales also provided human beings with some choice or leeway in the face of this deterministic fate, and
the study of "Necessity" purportedly provided Greek citizens with some
information about the natural or supernatural forces that shaped their
lives. The fabled character Prometheus was depicted as the light giver who
might help some rational beings leave the "realm of Necessity" through
the thoughtful use of fire.[74]

In the militaristic permutations of these Greek tales of necessity, soldiers and civil leaders were often portrayed as leaders who had to deal

with exigent circumstances. Thucydides, in the *History of the Peloponnesian War,* explains that in 432 B.C. some Spartan representatives traveled to the oracle at Delphi to ask if that city-state needed to go to war over the alleged Athenian violations of a peace treaty. After receiving what was interpreted as a positive response, the Spartans organized a meeting of the Peloponnesian League, where their allies the Corinthians explained that they had all "arrived at the moment of necessity."[75]

Many of these writers theorized that when human beings lost their power of volition, they became necessitous and potentially desperate creatures. In the *Timaeus,* Plato compares and contrasts the harmonious rule of the Demiurge, with the tyranny of Necessity. In the former situation, humans lived in a Paradise where they enjoyed all of the benefits of nature, while in the latter situation they lived in the midst of terrible convulsions that wreaked havoc among all the races.[76] The realities of needing some social and natural constraints clashed with the desire to be free of those restrictions. Many years later, Cicero commented on the fact that the Epicureans and the Stoics were attempting to reconcile the simultaneous existence of human free will and necessity.[77]

By the sixteenth and seventeenth centuries, political philosophers and theologians were conversing about the merits of mechanistic or Newtonian models of the universe. Some of these writers assumed that social hierarchies existed in nature, and that the members of these societies needed to think of themselves as pieces of a clock, working together harmoniously. Learning about natural necessities or political necessities was considered to be a liberating experience. For example, Thomas Hobbes explained that "Liberty and Necessity" were "consistent" parts of his world, because liberty needed to be operationalized as the "absence of externall Impediments."[78] In theory, if one learned the true causes of a particular phenomenon, then one's epistemic knowledge could contribute to the process of scientific or political reformation. Vico provided yet another permutation of these ideas when he noted that even poets needed to use their imaginative powers [*fantasia*] as they participated in the creation of nations, formal contracts, and legal codes. Art and science came together as citizens and leaders learned about the "necessities and utilities" of life.[79]

During this same period, judges who operated within legal spheres were hearing arguments about a variety of natural or social necessities—cases of extremity, of justifiable entry onto another's land, and the seizure of supplies so that they would not fall into the hands of one's enemies.[80] The judges in the *Case of Armes* (1597), for example, determined that the notion of "necessity" allowed people to "arm themselves to suppress Riots, Rebellions, or to resist Enemies, and to endeavour themselves to suppress or resist such Disturbers of the Peace, or Quiet of the Realm."[81] The British common law thus recognized that there were times when the King or Queen had subordinates who needed the type of discretion and power that would allow them to act in abnormal, emergency situations. The popular maxim that encapsulated this ideal—*Quod enim necessitas cogit defendit* [That which you know you need, defend]—supposedly gave guidance when court participants looked at "both the existence of the danger and the propriety of what was done to meet it."[82]

Within various political and legal realms, competing notions of "necessity" were deployed by the defenders and critics of the church, king, queen, or parliament. John Phillip Reid contends that during this period European audiences were hearing and reading about "tory" and "whig" variations of what it meant to demarcate the rights and responsibilities of citizens in times of war and peace.[83] A genealogical review of some of the discourse of the period reveals that by this time at least two polarized narratives framed the ways various generations thought about Anglo-Saxon "necessities."

- The *Tory* version of "necessity." Leaders believed that there were many times when a society is called upon to defend itself against riots, revolutions, and rebellions. Given the importance of royal prerogatives, it should be the King, Queen, or their subordinates who make decisions during necessitous times. Since this is an issue of survival, the military authorities should be given a great deal of discretion. In these situations, the "will" of those in authority will be of paramount importance.
- The *Whig* version of "necessity." There are relatively few times when a society has to worry about exigent circumstances. Parliamentary representatives are the ones who should be given the responsibility of determining if a "real" emergency exists, and how to respond to

that emergency. The "people" and their Parliamentary representatives should be the ones in charge of regulating the military. There is a great deal of difference between declaring that an emergency exists, and providing facts that support that declaration.

Clearly there would be many variants of these themes, but these basic templates supplied common lexicons that could be used in a host of European debates, where commentators wrote or spoke about the preservation of certain constitutional orders, parliamentary sovereignty, Crown obligations, the role of the judiciary, or the circumstances that warranted the imposition of "martial law." For example, Sir Matthew Hale, who was chronicling the recent English struggles taking place between the Crown and Parliament, would write in the 1670s that the signing of the 1628 Petition of Rights showed how "martial law" was "in truth and reality," not "a law," but an action that was based on the "necessity of government, order, and discipline."[84]

This type of interpretation reinforced the idea that "necessity" was some material essence or condition that could not be accurately represented in any written laws or social contracts. This meant that those who deployed the phrase needed to acknowledge both the existence of this inherent right and some of its potential dangers. This was especially true in military situations. In one of Hale's treatises, he left us with these fragments that would be copied for hundreds of years: "martial law . . . is rather indulged than allowed . . . and only in cases of necessity . . . in time of open war . . . [martial law] is not permitted in time of peace, when the ordinary courts are open."[85] This whiggish way of thinking about "open" courts was certainly popular during the Protestant Reformation, and these principles were considered foundational pieces of the unwritten English common law.

Political commentaries about necessitarian doctrines were often connected to theological arguments about an individual's place within a religious or social hierarchy. For example, conservative Tories could deploy royalist rhetorics that used familial metaphors to justify devotion to God's laws or royal prerogatives, and this often included commentaries that explained why decisions had to be made about the raising of armies or the collection of taxes. At the same time, moderate Whigs might claim that the wisest of merchants and government officials were the ones who avoided turning "rich, acute, diligent and laborious" nations into countries populated with "slow, idle, proud, and beggarly People."[86] More radical dissenters or levelers helped to popularize the idea that this talk of "necessity" was simply a "tyrant's plea," an excuse to avoid the protection of rights or the provision of goods to the masses. After all, who do you think ended up having to pay most of the taxes, or supplying the troops for royal or parliamentary wars?

This thick discursive tapestry, which was already embroidered with countless social, political, and economic strands of necessitarian arguments, became even more complex over time. The communities of people who lived through the Reformation had to worry about the deceptive powers of "rhetoric," and it was no easy task for anyone to be able to tell the difference between the true propagators of the faith, and the disciplines of Satan. Oliver Cromwell, in his speech before the First Parliament of the Protectorate, tried to reassure his audience that he was no threat to their ordered society:

> I would it had not been needful for me to have called you hither to have expostulated these things [concerning the militia, etc.] with you, and in such a matter as this! But necessity had no law. Feign necessities, imaginary necessities, are the greatest cozenage that men can put upon the providence of God, and make pretences to break known rules by. But it is as legal and as carnal and as stupid, to think that there ware no necessities that are manifest necessities, because necessities may be abused or feigned.[87]

Within this worldview, denizens who knew the difference between real and feigned necessities populated the best European societies. Victoria Kahn explains that for "many contemporaries, the danger of a Machiavellian appeal to success or superior force as a sign of providence was paralleled by the potentially Machiavellian invocation of necessity. This was not always an easy task. Just as it was difficult in practice to distinguish godly from ungodly force, so it was difficult—and for some, impossible—to discern the differences that existed between Cromwell's "appeals to necessity from 'necessity, the tyrant's plea.' "[88] Both elites and members of the public had to worry about clarion calls for standing armies, the dissolution of Parliaments, and the chaos that came from continuous warfare.

By the time of the Renaissance and the Enlightenment, most literate communities knew that the world was occupied by different "types" of people and various "stages" of states, and informed commentators wrote about the character attributes of those who were governed by "necessity" and those who used their rational faculties to escape nature's apparent restrictions. Individuals could search for personal improvement and perfection, while societies could either evolve or degenerate. Audiences at the time often read that without laws and benevolent military rule, societies regressed into primitive states of nature, ending the chances of survival for both the individual and that form of government.[89] As England's Lord Chancellor averred in 1762, "necessitous men [*sic*] are not, truly speaking, free men, but, to answer a present exigency, will submit to any terms that the crafty may impose upon them."[90] If a person was characterized as "necessitous," that person would always be the target of sophists, a threat to the yeomen who were the stalwarts of independent lands. Economic frames of analyses could therefore be tied to a host of religious, political, and legal prefigurations.

European critics of the British or French Revolutions were now supplied with several different national and mythological templates that could frame competing notions of where to draw the lines between ideographic "liberties" and "necessities." If they wanted to, they could concentrate on whiggish ideas about parchment rights, and they could congratulate themselves on having parliaments and constitutional documents that protected them from tyranny. Such commentaries led J. H. Plumb to conclude that "Freedom, Liberty, Right, Reason, Necessity; these were the great girders of abstraction upon which they build their treatises of philosophical liberalism."[91] There were few listeners who misunderstood the allusions being conjured up when one English parliamentarian in the 1780s waxed eloquently on the fact that "Necessity is the plea for every infringement of human freedom. It is the argument of tyrants; it is the creed of slaves."[92]

Americans were also mesmerized by the symbolic power of "necessity." In the "New" world, former colonists were complaining about the tyranny being imposed by King George's advisers, and in the 1776 Declaration of Independence they outlined these grievances:

He has erected a multitude of New Offices, and sent hither swarms of Officers to harass our people and eat out of their substance.

He has kept among us, in times of peace, Standing Armies, without the consent of our legislatures.

He has affected to render the Military independent of, and superior to, the Civil power.[93]

In many ways, the Declaration of Independence was a whiggish text that supposedly provided a bulwark that would protect Americans from Cromwellian dangers.

Yet some of the Founders were also appropriating some of the "tory" commentaries that were filled with necessitarian arguments. Stephen Lucas has written that during the eighteenth century the word "necessary" carried "strongly deterministic overtones," and that the "purpose of the Declaration" was to "persuade 'the opinions of mankind' that" it was " 'necessary' for 'one people' (the Americans) to separate from 'another' people' (the British)."[94] Several years later, the authors of the U.S. Constitution would try to rectify this situation by crafting a written document that gave the government only limited powers, including "necessary and proper" ones, but many of the Founders realized that no piece of parchment could cover all exigencies. When Thomas Jefferson thought that Aaron Burr's conspiracy of 1806–7 was threatening to divide the new nation, he ordered General James Wilkinson to stop this Southwestern separatist movement by proceeding under the rule that *inter arma silent leges* [in times of war, the laws are silent].[95] Hundreds of years later, Justice Rehnquist in his commentaries on the importance of the separation of powers would critique this same phrase.[96]

Given these labyrinthine commentaries on "necessity," many nineteenth-century treatise writers tried to simplify matters by finding the organizing "rules of law" that would help separate out civilian and military judicial norms, or real from false necessities. Writers during this period would craft arguments that extended some of the English common law ideas about "necessity" and "liberty," where the existence of an exigency created situations where humans had to act outside the boundaries of national and international rules of law. An assortment of scientific, legal, political, or cultural rationales could be used to buttress this claim. John Stuart Mill, for example, once observed that the word "Necessity . . . sometimes stands only for Certainty, at other times for Compulsion; sometimes for what cannot be prevented."[97] Hundreds of essays that talked about necessitarian principles and the scientific predictions that could be made about the inexorable forces of nature were written in popular magazines. "Necessity" thus survived in our elite and vernacular lexicons as a dangerous supplement, a term that could be used to remind citizens of the limits of human agency. Words like "liberty" and "equality" were viewed as pillars of liberal communities, but the shadowy limits of those ideals were never far from view.

Many defendants who appeared in Anglo-American civil courts took advantage of the evocative powers of these necessitarian doctrines by arguing that there were times when they themselves could not be held personally culpable for particular actions—nature or nurture sometimes brought catastrophe, chaos, and unpredictability. A very suspicious Lord Coleridge had to listen to the case of *The Queen v. Dudley,* where shipwrecked defendants had killed a cabin boy in order to survive in the open sea.[98] In this infamous case of cannibalism, Coleridge rejected the necessity defense, asking: "Who is to be the judge of this sort of necessity?" He was convinced that in cases like this there was "no safe path for judges to tread but to ascertain the law to the best of their ability and to declare it according to their judgment."[99] In theory, the lines between freedom of action and restrictive necessity had to be drawn on a case-by-case basis.

During this same century, American military leaders often remarked that they were empowered subalterns who represented their commander in chief, and courts had to look into the question of whether a particular factual pattern resembled the ones involving martial laws or military laws. In the 1870s, Justice Waite of the U.S. Supreme Court justified General Ben Butler's seizure of "contraband" in New Orleans and his use of military authority on the basis of precedents that seemed to show that "martial law is the law of military necessity," and that "it is to be administrated by the general of the army, and is in fact his will."[100] Critics might complain that this was "arbitrary," but Butler had to be "obeyed" because during wartime a general is dealing with a "theatre of the most active and important military operations."[101] Many defenders of President Bush's policies after 9/11 would recycle these very arguments and case precedents.

By the end of the nineteenth century, both England and the United States were dealing with a host of "colonies" or "territories," and the inheritors of select "tory" tales about "necessity" and "military necessity" could now talk of how "those agencies which were charged with the national defense" had to be given some "authority" on "the spot" that included measures that "in normal times would be *ultra vires.*"[102] Liberal critics might talk about individual rights or parliamentary regulation of these affairs, but these could be dismissed as unrealistic and sentimental critiques. For example, in an 1851 debate about the use of force in Ceylon, the Duke of Wellington claimed that once a general declared martial law in an area, he was only bound by the "rules and regulations and limits" of that general's "will."[103]

These imperial discussions of "necessity" complemented the domestic conversations about local rebellions and civil wars. In America, courts and commissions grappled with the question of whether Northern states could be turned into "war" zones when the civil courts remained open, and during the Sioux "uprising" of 1862 (chapter three) President Lincoln felt obliged to send in federal troops to help maintain order in the Northwestern Frontier. Four years later, the U.S. Supreme Court in *Milligan*[104] (chapter four) seemed to revive the idea that civil authorities should have the primary responsibility for assessing the legitimacy of necessitous pleas, but even during that time many state and local authorities treated this as an antiquated precedent that had little to do with the demands of modern warfare.[105] For many years, Northerners who wanted to "reconstruct" the South and keep a tight rein on the activities of the Ku Klux Klan used military commissions.[106]

By the beginning of the twentieth century, the protean nature of the concept of "necessity" meant that some members of Anglo-American judiciaries had already witnessed how the term had been used to justify the confiscation of cargo, the destruction of personal property to avoid aiding the enemy, or the obedience or disobedience of superior orders during wartime. Formalists, who believed in the evolutionary nature of the "rule of law," realized that the growing power of the military in Anglo-American affairs meant that there needed to be some appreciation of the parallel development of "military law." "By 1911," argues Gerald Crump, "military law had remained almost unchanged for 135 years."[107] Yet Norman Lieber, the U.S. Judge Advocate General, would confidently write in the *North American Review* that readers needed to realize there were now really "four" kinds of military "jurisdictions":[108]

1. "Military law," which involved the "legal system" of the "military establishment." This was supposed to explain how the Constitution provided some members of the military "grants" of power that were a part of the "municipal" law;
2. The military power that came from the "law of nations," where a military government had to deal with "hostile occupation" and "military power" had to be "exercised by a belligerent over the inhabitants of an enemy's territory";
3. "Martial Law," which was supposed to apply to the "army," was used when military power had to be "extended in times of war, insurrection, or rebellion over persons in the military service"; and
4. "Martial Law" had to be applied at "home," where "military power" was used to control "parts of the country" over "persons and things not ordinarily subject to it."[109]

These various logical distinctions make perfect sense from a formalistic perspective, but for countless generations a plethora of audiences mixed and matched arguments about martial law, military law, state necessities, rebellions, riots, insurrections, civil wars, and foreign invasions. At the same time that Lieber tried to separate out the "four" kinds of military jurisdictions, he could not help positing the notion that "martial law" came from the "application of the doctrine of necessity, founded on the right of national self-preservation."[110]

These formalistic discussions of "necessity" and "military law" inadvertently helped with the proliferation and popularization of these terms, and now just about any governor or civic leader could read about the discretion that came with the imposition of "martial law" or a declaration of an emergency. Early-twentieth-century judges promiscuously used the idea of "necessity" to rationalize the suppression of dissent, the crushing of labor activities,[111] the quarantining of foreign "others," and the pacification of "rebels" in places like the Philippines. The end of the American frontier, the arrival of millions of immigrants, the promotion of massive industrialization, and the spread of overseas ventures all contributed to a situation where both civil and military authorities had to become familiar with the appropriation of military lexicons. During this same period of time, interest in civilian control of the military waxed and waned, depending on how Americans felt about isolationism, the draft, the imposition of martial law in their own communities, or the use of military tribunals. For example, long before the passage of the Uniform Code of Military Justice (UCMJ) in 1950, General Samuel Ansell was calling for the "civilianization" of military law.[112]

For the next forty years, Anglo-American politicians and military officers argued back and forth about the desirability of this "civilianization."[113] After Pearl Harbor, the liberal inheritors of "whig" positions on these issues were hard pressed to explain why the commander in chief and his subordinates should not be given all the power they needed in dealing with the Axis powers. Those who fought the "good" war were convinced this was a conflict between fascist and democratic nations, and necessitarian arguments were refurbished to fit the exigencies of World War II. For example, "martial law" would be declared in Hawaii, and few doubted that this was a time of national emergency. Charles Fairman argued in the *Harvard Law Review* that Americans needed to follow the lead of their allies and alter the ways they thought about the *Milligan* precedent and military-civilian relationships:

> In the British Empire the present situation is quite otherwise. The Boer War saw the complete abandonment by the Judicial Committee of the Privy Council of the historic doctrine that where the courts are open martial law cannot prevail. This new view was consistently applied in the Irish Rebellion—and also by the Free State courts when they in turn had to consider the power of their own government to maintain itself. So long as war is raging the judiciary will assert no control over a commander. And with the restoration of peace an act of indemnity is invariably passed.[114]

An obviously envious Fairman wished that the American judges and lawyers would get their act together and realize that their British colleagues had a much more realistic way of looking at governmental usages of emergency powers. He was convinced that the 1914 Defence of the Realm Act, the 1920 Emergency Powers Act, and the British interpretations of these acts had contributed to a situation where a "kindred people" were persuasively arguing for a "new view of war power."[115] In chapters six and seven, I illustrate how various American presidents and their subordinates used these types of arguments to justify the expansion of their own executive powers during times of war.

In the aftermath of the Korean and Vietnam wars, many scholars began writing about how "military law" had progressed to the stage where it had its own traditions, its own rules and standards, and a system of justice that now rivaled its civilian counterpart. Alterations in the Code of Federal Regulations, for example, reflected some of the changes that had been suggested by military authorities who wanted clearer definitions of both "martial law" and "Necessity."[116] Edward Sherman certainly understated matters when he remarked that the "military has jealously guarded the distinctive aspects of its system of justice."[117] By 1987, in court cases like *Solorio v. United States,*[118] the members of the Supreme Court made it clear that they felt a person's military status was enough to vest a military court-martial with jurisdiction over the offender, "irrespective of any service connection to the offense."[119]

In less then two decades, we would be asking ourselves if the military court-martial rules could be applied in the military tribunal trials of "terrorists" and those who "harbored" terrorists. New variants of necessitarian tales were used in modern debates about the detention of foreigners, the trial of American citizens, the need for military secrecy, and the jurisdiction of U.S. federal courts. The older claims that melded together martial law and "military necessity" were now being deployed in more general military situations, and the war against terrorism involved many new battlefields. Kirk Davies, writing in the *Air Force Law Review* in 2000, made these eerie remarks:

> In 1998, Americans were exposed to the specter of martial law in the from of a hit movie, *The Siege*. The movie vividly depicted the after-

math of a terrorist attack on New York City where the government declared martial law and rounded up thousands of Arab-Americans and put them in internment camps. Unfortunately, some time in the future, life may imitate art and America's experience with martial law may extend outside the movie theatre into reality. It seems obvious that a number of anti-American groups exist both within and without our borders that would not hesitate to employ terrorism and other tactics that could result in upheaval and, perhaps anarchy within our country.[120]

Luckily, in the aftermath of 9/11, we have not seen any internment camps, but we are clearly a devastated nation that has been traumatized (see chapters eight and nine). The invasions of Afghanistan and Iraq only complicate the situation.

In the next few years, mounting public pressure will once again cause changes in the rhetorical lines that are drawn between civil liberties and national security interests. As the world looks on, we will be on center stage as American authorities write about the inevitability and legitimacy of military tribunals. A few jurists have complained about some provisions of Bush's Military Order, but the Pentagon has already selected some of the civilians, judge advocates, and military defense lawyers who will become performers in these new judicial dramas. Major John Smith told reporters for the *Washington Post* that the "commissions are set up to provide full and fair trials, while protecting sensitive information and taking into account the unique battlefield environment."[121] What does not get emphasized is the fact that the rules of evidence will allow in hearsay evidence that the trials can be held in secret, and that the entire appellate review process stays within the commander in chief's chain of command.

As readers peruse the following case studies, I hope they keep in mind how the selection of some of these procedural rules can impact the justice dispensed in these military tribunals. As we read about the trials and tribulations of Major André, the Dakota warriors, Milligan, Yamashita, and others, we can readily understand why many conservatives and liberals have qualms about the desirability and legality of more modern tribunals. While many critics are willing to admit there are some cases that justify the use of these commissions, I have yet to see any situation where civilian courts—or better yet, international tribunals—could not do a better job of dispensing individuated justice.

As we learn more about the arguments presented in these tribunals, I hope we do not forget that we may simply be hearing the latest version of the "tory" and "whig" templates that have framed our historical commentaries on constitutional rights and duties. In the name of necessity, will we be one of the generations that tears to shreds some of those vaunted Enlightenment ideas that have been a part of our Anglo-American cultures? Will we be able to find some negotiated compromises that will help us avoid the extremes of "gladiatorial ethics"[122] or tardy judiciary responses? Can a review of some key historical debates about military commissions and "military necessity" provide us with some insight into the promise and perils of these tribunals?

2

The Capture of Major André

By his countrymen he [André] was considered a martyr to his loyalty,
and by the Americans the hero of a romantic tale of unmerited fortune.
They forgot that he had been deep in a dastardly plot of treason against
a people long struggling in vain for liberty.

—James Paulding, 1835

$\mathbf{A}$t different historical junctures, as I noted in chapter one, various individuals and communities have been obsessed with the idea of balancing human volition and natural limitations, and the American colonists who lived through their own "revolution" were no exception.[1] The famous signing of the Declaration of Independence allowed for the crafting of discursive justifications for the formation of a new nation, but it would be the colonial actions on the field of battle that would test their mettle and their resolve. Several years after the beginning of the Revolutionary War, Elbridge Gerry noted some of the political upheavals taking place in a world where,

> The ministry of England advocates for despotism, and endeavoring to enslave those who might have remained loyal subjects to the king. The government of France [has become] an advocate of liberty, espousing the cause of protestants [*sic*] and risking a war to secure their independence. The king of England [is] considered by every whig in the nation as a tyrant, and the king of France [is] applauded by every whig in America as the protector of the rights of Man! . . . These, my friend, are astonishing changes.[2]

In theory, the beginning of the American Revolution would lead to the progressive establishment of a new nation, and the power of the military was considered to be an essential ingredient in the preservation of the United States of America.

In Enlightenment cyclical narratives, all human societies were constantly in a state of motion, degenerating or regenerating. Whether one believed in the laws of Newtonian physics or the organic process of societal change, studying the ancient Greeks and Romans showed how eternal vigilance and equipoise were needed in order to prevent the decay of even the best human civilizations. The colonists had to study the laws that regulated the natural and social worlds, so that "liberty" did not turn into "license," and feigned necessities did not take the place of real necessities. Americans who were familiar with both "tory" and "whig" ideologies understood that if they were going to stay together, they were going to have to develop the enduring type of "character" that could survive the temptations that could lead to individual corruption or national degeneracy.[3] George Washington, for example, worried that patriots were "accustomed to unbounded freedom," and he admonished them to remember that this was no time to "brook the Restraint which is indispensably necessary to the good order and Government of the Army."[4]

American colonialists hoped the continent of Europe would provide the fledgling nation with judicious examples of how rational governments dealt with military discipline and social order, and the balancing of rights and duties. Michael O. Lacey explains that while it is

> impossible to point to the first modern [military] commission, during the Reformation in Europe . . . at least one commander sought an alternative method for resolving the status of the unlawful belligerent. . . . [Gustavus] Adolphus was . . . among the first to institute the use of a panel of officers to hear law of war violations and make recommendations on their resolution. The use of the military commission was one of the many revolutionary reforms Gustavus Adolphus instituted for the successful enforcement of discipline and administration in his army. . . . The British adopted a similar system. . . . [and] The United States['] early military traditions were, in many respects, carbon copies of their former colonial masters, the British.[5]

Yet many American colonials also played the role of skeptics and openly criticized some of the tyrannical practices of the "Old" World system of governance. Living in the "New" World brought novel opportunities, and the European models had to be modified to fit the needs of frontier life. After all, did not the existence of Republican militias in the colonies obviate the need for the billeting of troops or the funding of standing armies?[6] This new idyllic land, with its bountiful forests and endless tracts of land, seemed to be the ideal place for the renegotiation of the lines that existed between "liberty" and "necessity."

As I argue below, the colonial debates about the relative merits of George Washington's military court of inquiry became a part of some complex national and international discussions, and I share Jonathan Turley's belief that we sometimes forget that "military tribunals have had a long and troubled history in this country."[7] Gerard Clark recently noted that military "tribunals have a history that runs back to the Revolutionary War,"[8] but that fact should not automatically mean we treat the very existence of these organizations as "direct and unassailable" precedents "for the Bush military tribunals."[9]

When modern commentators mention the precedential value of Washington's court of inquiry (Board of General Officers), they selectively leave behind many of the social and legal questions that preoccupied this generation. During the last quarter of the eighteenth century, many citizens and soldiers understood the importance of having a strong and well-regulated military, but they also worried about the discretionary power given to America's military leaders. For example, James Madison warned that the "claim to inherent Executive power is usually based on the President's own judgment of a crisis or emergency . . . this may cause problems in constitutional balance."[10] The nation needed strong leaders, but it did not need Cromwellian leaders.

One of the key legal narratives that has often resurfaced in the modern debates over the legitimacy of George W. Bush's 2001 Military Order involves the retelling of the story of George Washington's reluctant trial of Major André.[11] Timothy MacDonnell has characterized this proceeding as one "of the first" and one of the "most famous" of the American "military commissions."[12] The tales that were told about the trial[13] were turned into commemorative forms of "monumental didactics,"[14] where various historical audiences read about the treachery of Benedict Arnold,[15] or the justness of George Washington's military system. Larry Reynolds once observed that the story of Major André's misfortunes became "one of the most popular incidents represented in nineteenth-century art about the American Revolution."[16] Even today, some contemporary military experts believe that Washington's use of his Board of General Officers stands for the proposition that the "jurisdiction to try enemy soldiers for war crimes at a military commission" was established as early as 1780.[17]

Our own acts of cultural amnesia have erased the memories of how these incidents also served as major backdrops for national and international commentaries about military law, civic virtue, and American independence. We have forgotten that there were many domestic and international critics of Washington's Board of General Officers, and that some of his contemporaries worried about the legality of the trial. In the same ways that modernists debate the legal status of "enemy combatants," prisoners of war, terrorists, and American citizens, Washington's contemporaries worried about the wartime status of uniformed officers, "spies," and the irregular militia. American officers held different views on the meanings of particular "laws of war," and their subalterns may have had their own ideas about military justice. James Martin and Mark Lender noted that "the majority of recruits who fought with Washington after 1776 represented the very poorest and most desperate persons in society, including ne'er-do-wells, drifters, unemployed laborers, captured British soldiers and Hessians, indentured servants, and slaves."[18] American leaders had to make sure these necessitous fighters understood the importance of discipline and regimentation.

When many of André's contemporaries and chroniclers commented on his case, they were doing more than simply retrieving an unalloyed sliver of the historical past—they were also leaving us fragments that give us clues about their own interests, identities, and political viewpoints. The topoi and arguments that appear in their performative poems, memos, books, pension letters,[19] monuments, and other symbolic markers tell us a great deal about how these communities thought about liberties and necessities.

In this chapter, I begin by providing a brief contextual overview of

Major André's capture, and then I focus in on the formation of Washington's Board of General Officers. This is followed by a section that synchronically compares how some of his contemporaries viewed this proceeding, and it is in this portion of the chapter that I underscore the polysemic nature of the arguments used in debates about war crimes and the "laws of war." In the concluding portions of the chapter, I shift our gaze and provide a diachronic analysis that shows how various generations selectively remembered some of these earlier debates about Washington's board of inquiry.

The Capture of Major André
and the Treachery of Benedict Arnold

During the late 1770s, Major John André met Benedict Arnold and many of the royalists who lived in the Lower Salem and New York areas.[20] André was viewed as one of the rising stars within the British army and was considered to be a clever soldier, talented artist, and loyal subject. On one of his many assigned missions, Major André ended up missing the ship he was supposed to board, and he had to borrow a blue coat and a spare horse as he tried to make his way back to the British lines. A pass from Arnold indicated that André would travel under the alias of "John Anderson."[21] After leaving behind a companion [Joshua Smith],[22] André managed to travel some fifteen miles through "no man's land." At this point in our reconstructed narrative, "John Anderson" accidentally ran into three American "volunteers"—John Paulding, Isaac Van Wart, and David Williams[23]—who were said to have been "concealed in the bushes, watching the road to intercept any suspicious stragglers . . . "[24] A surprised "André avowed himself to be a British officer; upon which, disregarding his pass, and then proceeding to search his person, they found the secret papers concealed within his boots."[25] In a very polemic account of this encounter, James Thomas Flexner writes about what he thought happened next:

> Andre was led to a gate. . . . When they were all deep in a thicket, he was ordered to undress. Each garment was snatched from him as it came off and thoroughly searched. By the time he was nude, ex-

cept for his boots and the stockings that contained the incriminating papers, his tormentors had found the gold watch and chain and the Continental dollars he had borrowed from Smith. For the moment it looked as if they were satisfied, but then, so Williams remembered, "We told him to pull off his boots, which he seemed indifferent about, but we got one boot off, and searched into that boot, but could find nothing; and we found that there were some papers in the bottom of his stocking, next to his foot. . . . Of his captors, only Paulding could read. As the naked royal officer watched anxiously, the gigantic yokel labored through the documents.[26]

The three captors then decided they needed to take their prisoner to Colonel Jameson at the North Castle Outpost.[27] Jameson, who read the captured papers and sensed the importance of the capture, made the mistake of sending Benedict Arnold a message informing him of André's capture, and Arnold made good his escape.

Many of the laypersons, militia members, regular soldiers, and Continental officers who learned of André's capture viewed this as a truly providential event that showed the righteousness of the American cause. How else could one explain the myriad coincidences that led to his arrest, and the foiling of Arnold's plans? While many American soldiers and civilians would later admit that they had ambivalent feelings about Major André's capture, this would not be the case when they heard about the defection and treachery of Benedict Arnold. In an ideological universe filled with fears of degeneration and moral decay, the former war hero became the emblematic reminder of what could happen when a person lacked character and independence. "Americans, then and now," noted Robert Ferguson, were "obsessed with the notion of treason because they come to their own original identity through the concept."[28]

Many Americans also worried about Arnold's treachery because they understood the strategic importance of West Point, which was considered to be the "key to the control of the Hudson highlands,"[29] and American control of this key military fortress prolonged the conflict.[30] 1780 was an especially important year for Washington and his political supporters because his armies were disintegrating. André's superior, Henry Clinton, knew the American loss of West Point would be a devastating blow to the rebels who were already dealing with an intransigent Congress, the vacillation of French allies, and military setbacks on the battlefield.[31] For example, a disillusioned Benedict Arnold lamented the fact that Washington's army was "permitted to starve in a land of plenty."[32]

In spite of these complaints, Arnold was often viewed as one of the stalwarts of the rebel cause, and his turncoat behavior brought puzzlement and bewilderment. Benedict Arnold the man was soon transmogrified into Benedict Arnold the traitor, and he was vilified for endangering the lives of those who lived in the fragile Republic. Lieutenant Colonel John Laurens told George Washington that he believed "Arnold must undergo a punishment comparatively more severe in the permanent, increasing torment of a living hell."[33] Nathaniel Greene echoed these sentiments when he would send this letter to Colonial Jeremiah Wadsworth:

I think I have not written you since the late desertion of Arnold. Was [*sic*] you ever more astonished in your life? A man high in reputation, and with the fairest prospects of domestic happiness. The love of parade and the thirst for gold has proved his ruin. How black, how despised, loved by none, and hated by all. Once his Country's Idol now her horror. Curse on his folly.[34]

The "former apothecary-merchant from Connecticut," averred James Martin, "became the personification of what" the American "Revolution was not."[35] His treacherous behavior was often linked to his necessitous behavior—his dependence on British money, his love of extravagance, and his insatiable need for glory. Alexander Hamilton predicted that Arnold's memory would be "handed down, with execration," while "posterity will repeat with reverence the names of Van Wert, Paulding, and Williams."[36] A popular Hudson River ballad contained these lines:

Now Arnold to New York has gone,
A-fighting for his King,
And left poor Major André
On the gallows for to swing.[37]

Years later, Carroll Judson could characterize anyone who tried to defend Arnold as a sophist who knew nothing of the value of truth and heroism.[38] This was because he was sure the traitor had "laid violent hands upon property belonging to those who did not enter fully into the cause of patriots."[39] While Arnold had escaped the wrath of his former colleagues, Major André was not so fortunate. In the cyclical worldview of the children of the Enlightenment, some luckless soul had to pay for this treachery.

One key thread within these complex tapestries of nationalist rhetorics involved the issue of how the American colonialists were going to be dispensing justice in treasonous situations. Were they going to formulate their own rules, follow some international norms, adopt the British common law, or create novel hybrids? If the signing of the Declaration of Independence and the performance of other revolutionary acts brought liberty, did not these same social agents need to be thinking about military governance and the maintenance of law and order? Moreover, if these colonialists were going to show their maturity and restraint, did not the Americans need proof that Arnold and André had violated some of the "laws of war"? Given the fact that Major André had been wearing civilian clothes at the time of his capture, perhaps General George Washington could justifiably ask for a board of inquiry.[40] During this period of time, this trial was considered to be a quasi-judicial proceeding that could be viewed as an extension "of the standard military court-martial."[41]

Ironically, many of the military rules that Arnold and André allegedly violated came from the American adaptations of British rules of warfare.[42] This was a time when many a soldier or sailor learned that "Justice" was "found in the 'Cat o' Nine Tails or the hangman's noose,'" and discipline came from following "a code derived from British law and custom."[43] Whigs and Tories alike thought that a certain number of lashes had to be administered to keep an army together.[44] In theory, civilian authorities needed to understand the prudential concerns of those who fought on the battlefield. "Military necessity," noted Maurer Maurer, "was justification for military law."[45] William Tudor, Washington's Judge Advocate, was convinced that "when a man [*sic*] assumes the soldier he lays aside the citizen, and must be content to a temporary relinquishment of some of his civil rights."[46] Maurer explains:

The articles of war in effect at Cambridge when Washington took command had been enacted by the Provincial Congress of Massachusetts two weeks before Minutemen and Redcoats met at Lexington. . . . Congress amended this code on November 7, 1775, and revised it completely on September 20, 1776, bringing it more in line with British law. Military law, one of the most powerful instruments available to Washington for establishing and maintaining discipline, extended over both enlisted men and officers, as well as over civilians who served with or accompanied the army in the field. Americans, however, cherished the privileged of the common law and objected to a legal system in which indictment by grand jury and other fundamental rights were unknown. They were familiar with the long struggle of the English people against military law, and the war they were fighting was itself a protest against arbitrary government.[47]

These competing principles had be reconciled and evaluated by some of the colonists who found themselves fighting a necessitous war in the name of independence. We should not automatically assume they spoke in unison or bequeathed the same precedents as they debated the parameters of these military laws. In the abstract, one might talk about the importance of cherished liberties and individual safeguards, but cold winters and lost engagements brought desertions, complaints, and treachery. During the American Revolution, soldiers and citizens had to deal with a welter of contested laws that came from both civilian and military traditions.

A rhetorical analysis of some of the published materials that circulated during this period reveals how many commentators believed that any enlisted personnel who were accused of violating the military law could be taken into custody by a provost, and then "courts of inquiry" could be formed that would look into the sufficiency of the material presented in each case. A lack of evidence often meant that the charges were dropped, and that the jailed prisoner was "honorably acquitted." If the court of inquiry did find sufficient evidence of a violation, then the officer or soldier who was accused of the violation was usually tried within a matter of days or weeks.[48] Minor offenses brought a trial by a "regimental" or "garrison" court—perhaps five officers—while more serious allegations brought trials by a general court-martial, involving thirteen officers.[49]

How would the Americans characterize Arnold and André? Would they be treated as military prisoners of war, or civilians who stumbled across enemy lines? Would they be labeled as spies under the traditional rules of military justice? Would these villains be tried by a larger board of inquiry?

The Creation of Washington's Board of Inquiry and the Trial of Major André

In André's case, General Washington decided he needed a larger type of board of inquiry, and he determined that Major General Nathaniel Greene would preside. Some of the fourteen officers on the board included Clinton, Glover, Knox, Lafayette, Steuben, and Sterling.[50] This military body would be given the responsibility of deciding whether their famous prisoner would be treated as a fellow soldier or as a common spy.

For several days, it appears that this nascent type of military tribunal had members who reviewed many of the claims being advanced by those who sent letters to Washington, and these became a part of the official "Proceedings" that would be published throughout the colonies.[51] Some of Washington's soldiers had ambivalent feelings about the trial, but they understood the "necessities" that motivated their leaders. Alexander Hamilton, for example, argued that,

> the officers generally declared that if they were not to be protected against such traitorous Conduct, it was time to leave the Army. That if they were to be exposed to external Spys and internal machinations, & no punishment inflicted on them, who were taken & proved guilty, there would be no safety in the Camp & resignation was the only protection.[52]

This passage is notable for several rhetorical reasons. It reminds us that the trial was viewed as another test of American support for the rebel cause, and it shows us the extent of the disillusionment of the Continental officers. At the same time, it illustrates how these proceedings were tied to issues of "safety," thus magnifying the symbolic significance of these quasi-judicial proceedings. Many colonials apparently believed these deceptive acts needed to be punished because they threatened the survival of the officers.

These arguments may have persuaded some Continentals that the formation of this "Board of General Officers" was an exercise of legitimate power, but for some contemporary onlookers the rebels had predetermined Major André's guilt. Even worse, they were trying to adopt a system of military justice that was better left in the hands of more mature nations.

Long before President Bush found himself accused of American unilateralism, some of the early American colonists discovered that they had to explain to the world some of the reasons why Washington's board of inquiry was justified under international law. For example, a few British writers began treating André's military captors as perpetrators of crimes. Benedict Arnold sent out this threat to his former allies in early October 1780:

> [I]f, after this just and candid representation of Major André's case, the Board of General Officers adhere to their former opinion, I shall suppose it dictated by passion and resentment; and if that Gentleman should suffer the severity of their sentence, I shall think myself bound by every tie of duty and honour, to retaliate on such unhappy persons of your army, as may fall within my power, that the respect due to flags, and to the laws of nations, may be better understood and observed.[53]

These types of remarks did not help Major André's cause, because they inflamed American opinion, and they magnified the threats associated with British spying activities. At the same time, mass circulation of these commentaries on both sides of the Atlantic indicated that these military discussions were going to become fragments in diplomatic debates, as various nations commented on the activities of this American tribunal. Washington's own troops, the citizens of New York and New Jersey, the other colonists, and readers in Europe were all going to be potential audiences.

André's proceedings thus served as a barometer for how the Americans were going to interpret their own military laws, and they provided some symbolic indications of how these patriots were going to balance the interests of individual justice and military necessities. The British attacks on Washington's board of inquiry showed that these legal debates were also matters of national pride. Many former colonists worried that if the captured prisoner was freed, it would look like the Americans were still dependent on British legal interpretations, or that the revolutionaries feared British retaliatory power. Francis Vivian once surmised that the British might have been in a stronger position if they had made "an appeal to mercy," because there had been times when nations that had acted under "international law" had spared the lives of defendants. Many years later, MacDonnell surmised that it "would be difficult for the British to claim that the trial ordered by General Washington lacked jurisdiction, given Britain's use of a less formal proceeding to find Nathan Hale guilty and execute him four years earlier for the same offense."[54]

These modern critiques of the older British commentaries may tell us a little bit about some of the formalistic arguments that could have been used during these Enlightenment years, but we need to remember some of the "extra"-judicial factors that also influenced the trajectory of these proceedings. Many British audiences may indeed have believed that Washington's generals were members of an "ignorant crew," "incapable of making decisions where the niceties of military and international law were concerned." In his own reconstruction of these events, Vivian was sure that what exacerbated the situation was the fact that the British were trying "to stand on nonexistent legal rights."[55]

There were of course some Americans and their allies who could appreciate the major's plight, and who may not have shared Vivian's assessment of the jurisprudential situation. For example, General Lafayette has left us with the notion that the "feelings of the whole army" were "most liberal in behalf of André."[56] Frederick William Von Steuben, another member of the Board of General Officers, wished to "God the wretch who drew him to death could have suffered in his place."[57] Both Lafayette and Alexander Hamilton sent their leader petitions that asked for the commutation of the Major's sentence, but these were refused.

These partial and divisive memories of the André commission were clearly tied to issues of class and rank, and there is little question that notions of military decorum were perhaps connected to conflicting no-

tions of heroism and sacrifice. As noted above, many of Washington's officers understood the strategic importance of West Point and the needs
associated with military discipline, but they were bothered by the fact that
their prisoner had been captured on "neutral grounds" by some unsavory
characters.[58] Unlike many of the early-nineteenth-century pundits who
uncritically celebrated the deeds of John Paulding, Isaac Van Wart, and
David Williams, some members of Washington's staff began asking pointed
legal questions about both the capture of the major and the some of the
procedural aspects of the trial—what was the military status of these "volunteers," and what were his captors doing in that section of the country
in the first place?[59] General Washington was already dealing with delin-
quents and a "Commissioned Mob,"[60] and the forces in that particular region of the East were known for shifting alliances

Moreover, the Federalists in the Continental army felt that a special
bond existed between officers of warring armies, because they supposedly
shared a host of common values and martial faiths. The maintenance of
these symbolic bonds depended on mutual admiration and respect, and
the British clearly expected that their former colonials would show the
proper deference. However, when the British kept insisting that Washington was ignoring the rules of international law, they were creating a situation where the American officers had to defend the actions of André's
captors and Washington's Court of Inquiry. Nationalist passions trumped
some potentially problematic issues. Alexander Hamilton, in a letter to
Count de Rochambeau, lamented the fact that the Americans had "yielded
to the necessity of rigor."[61]

There is some textual evidence that even Washington had some mixed
feelings about these conflicting representations of Major André's actions.
After all, the American general had defended Arnold in the face of earlier
congressional disapproval, and he was the person who had signed off on
the idea of Arnold's possible command of West Point. Yet when Rochambeau wanted to know just why this justified hanging, Washington fell back
on a very ancient and well-tested argument—this "disagreeable action"
was "necessary for the preservation of America."[62] One of Washington's
admirers would later proclaim that this was an issue of "sovereignty," and
that the "Americans were determined to assert the dignity of their government."[63]

When all was said and done, General Washington stood behind the decision of his Board of General Officers. On September 29, 1780, his committee announced that Major André would be treated as a spy, and that he deserved the harshest of punishments. They were convinced that,

> he [André] came on shore from the *Vulture,* sloop of war, in the night of the 21st of September, on an interview with General Arnold, in a private and secret manner. That he changed his dress within our lines, and under a feigned name [John Anderson] and in a disguised habit passed our works . . . and when taken he had in his possession several papers which contained intelligence for the enemy.[64]

Given this statement of the facts, Washington's military commission concluded that "Major André, Adjutant General to the British army, ought to be considered as a spy from the enemy, and that agreeable to the law and usages of nations, it is their opinion, he ought to suffer death."[65] On October 2, 1780, André would be hanged. One witness remembered that he "put the rope round his neck himself."[66] The Americans may have believed they did this deed in the name of "necessity," but these interpretations of the "laws of war" would not go uncontested.

British Commentaries on André's Capture and Trial

In many of the contemporaneous and popular British accounts of André's capture and subsequent ordeal, it is the Americans who violated the supposedly well-established international protocols of martial conflict. Many modern commentators have casually mentioned a few of these arguments, but they are usually dismissed as political commentaries or misrepresentations of the extant rules of war. I do not dispute the ideological nature of these remarks—I just think we need to at least look at some of these British claims before we jump on the bandwagon that automatically assumes the legitimacy or desirability of Washington's board of inquiry.

Within these British counternarratives, George Washington and his board members were vilified for having ignored the circumstances of this peculiar case, and for misunderstanding the applicable military codes that governed international law at the time. I should note from the outset that some of these European commentaries about the formalistic nuances of British military law were inextricably tied up with their own imperial biases and prejudices. In the process of showing what they considered to be clear violations of the "laws of war," they also commented on the inherent flaws in the physical and moral make-up of the American rustics who pretended to be civilized soldiers.

Any analysis of the British interrogation of the taken-for-granteds of the American tales needs to begin with the commentary on the unfortunate Major André, who seemed initially to have had high hopes that his eloquence might stir the hearts and minds of his captors. On September 24, 1780, he wrote to General Washington and claimed he should be treated as "adversary" and not a spy.[67] Since his search for intelligence had not taken him behind enemy lines, he opined that he should be viewed as a common soldier. In André's own narration of events, circumstance had forced him to be taken to the area that got him into trouble:

> Your Excellency may conceive my sensation on this occasion, and will imagine how much more I must have been affected by a refusal to reconduct [sic] me back. . . . I quitted my uniform and was passed another way in the night without the American posts to neutral ground, and informed [sic] I was beyond all armed parties, and left to press for New York. I was taken at Tarrytown by some volunteers. Thus, as I have had the honor to relate, was I betrayed, being Adjutant General of the British army, into the vile condition of an enemy in disguise without your posts.[68]

This chronology of events created the impression that André had never been interested in spying, and that if he had had his way, he would have been satisfied with the information that he could have collected "on neutral ground." Chance and misfortune had turned this "gentlemen" into an "involuntary imposter," and he asked Washington to look into the possibility that he might be exchanged for an American prisoner being held in Charleston.[69]

When news of André's capture reached the city of New York, many British officers and their loyalist allies were convinced that the major's power of moral suasion—and the fear of possible retaliation—would save their hero's life.[70] On September 25, 1780, a colonel aboard a British ship, the *Vulture,* sent this letter to General Washington:

> It is . . . incumbent on me to inform you of the manner of his falling into your hands: He went up with a flag at the request of General Arnold, on public business with him, and had his permit to return by land to New-York [*sic*]: Under these circumstances Major André cannot be detained by you, without the greatest violations of flags, and contrary to the custom and usages of all nations; and as I imagine you will see this matter in the same point of view as I do, I must desire that you will order him to be set at liberty and allowed to return immediately.[71]

Some New York residents were convinced that the "colonial rabble would not dare to execute the British Adjutant General."[72] Lieutenant General James Robertson asked the Americans to remember that the captured major was simply "visiting an officer commanding in a district at his own desire," and that he was therefore protected by the "rules of war" that existed "between civilized nations."[73] Many Europeans implied that the treatment of Major André would serve as some type of moral and legal yardstick that would measure America's maturity.

The death of Major André would not be forgotten by the British publicists, and several generations of commentators used the debates about the trial as the starting points for their analyses of America's frontier culture. Some of the argumentative templates that framed this discussion tried to recontextualize the tales told about André's capture,[74] and the mutual hatreds of the warring parties could not help but impact the form of arguments that circulated within this cultural milieu. Benedict Arnold, who reveled in his escape, now explained to his former colleagues just why the rebels were living in a veritable wasteland:

> Your country was once happy, and had the profered [*sic*] peace been embraced, your last two years of misery had been spend in peace and plenty, and repairing the desolations of a quarrel that would have set the interest of Great Britain and America in a true light, and cemented their friendship; whereas you are now the prey of avarice,

the scorn of your enemies, and the pity of your friends. You were promised liberty by the leaders of your affairs; but is there an individual in the enjoyment of it, saving your oppressors? . . . You are flattered with independency as preferable to a redress of grievances, and for that shadow, instead of real felicity, are sunk into all the wretchedness of poverty by the rapacity of your own rulers.[75]

Arnold may have hoped these messages might help some Americans escape their necessitous circumstances, but some members of the British public were not that charitable. An essayist for the *London Evening Post* warned readers that the death of Major André would "be followed by massacres of every kind."[76] Lieutenant General Robertson wondered just why a man like Washington could condone such a decision, when the American leader knew that "Sir Henry [Clinton] had never executed a spy."[77]

The passage of time may have solidified the American faith in the rectitude of their ancestors, but for decades British writers did not hesitate to point out some of the legal and moral problematics associated with Washington's board of inquiry. Lord Mahon—who thought there was a difference between military prowess and judicial ability—had this to say about the individual members of the Board of General Officers:

First, then, had Washington any good ground for relying on the judgment of the Court of Inquiry? Of whom did that Court consist? As we have already seen, of twelve American and of two European field officers. Now, it must be borne in mind that the American Generals, at that time, were, for the most part, wholly destitute of the advantage of a liberal education. They were men drawn from the ploughhandle, or from the shop-board, at their country's call. Greene himself, the President of the tribunal, had been a blacksmith by trade. These humble advocations afford no reason why such men might not always do their duty as become them in the field. . . . But . . . the verdict of such a tribunal ought to have no weight in such a case.[78]

These arguments made sense to many elite Europeans, but something else needed to be done to show the Americans that the British did not forget the martyrs who had died for the Empire. During the fall of 1821, arrangements were made to disinter André's body and bring it back home.[79] One writer was convinced that it "was not fit" that this hero "should rest in American ground."[80] The major's remains would be moved to Westminster Abbey, where the British public could honor "his zeal for his king and country."[81] André's remains were put into a coffin draped with velvet, and a peach tree was replanted in George IV's gardens in London.[82]

These various contextualizations of the activities of Washington's board would be reconfigured in a host of nineteenth- and twentieth-century commentaries on the treatment of spies, the applicable laws regarding treason, the inherent power of military officers, and the need for courts-martial and military commissions. Some of these discussions focused on the quality of the military leadership that had to make such momentous decisions, while others highlighted the jurisdictional issues involved in the case. Not surprisingly, one's nationalist ideals and political views influenced the rhetorical framing of the historical remembrances of Washington's board of inquiry and André's capture.

For example, not everyone believed in the sterling character of those who hid under bridges in neutral territories, and various biographers, historians, and other interdisciplinary scholars chose up sides in the generational recollections of these contested affairs. Flexner, for example, once characterized the British officer's three captors as "Loyalist Cowboys and Rebel Skinners—lawless ruffians of uncertain allegiance who often cooperated for their own basic purposes of loot."[83] However, most American accounts of the Revolutionary War treated these same captors as heroes who had saved West Point and the nation.

The Maintenance of the American "Character"

On first impression, one might argue that when Washington and his staff decided to convict André, they were dealing with a relatively straightforward formalistic interpretation of the European military traditions regarding spies. Look up the rules of war that appeared in British treatises or cases, or pay attention to the customs of war, and then you can evaluate the legitimacy or the desirability of military tribunals. This is the type of formalistic framework I have critiqued in much more detail in the previous chapter of this book.

The problem with this approach is that it treats the "laws of war" as some apolitical body of convergent information that can somehow deductively resolve our legal conundrums. Taking this type of stance might help us if we want to automatically dismiss the British claims and focus on the correctness of Washington's decisions, but it does not help us understand the range of opinions about the "laws of war" that circulated in many different legal and public cultures.

Like many other legal issues, the judgments made about the legitimacy of Washington's board of inquiry were impacted by the select ideographs, narratives, myths, and other units of analysis that resonated with Enlightenment audiences. In the popular legal imaginations of both American elites and members of the public, the story of the capture of Major André was a tale of colonial justice, a sacred allegory that explained how poor militia members had withstood the temptations of European materialism.

In many of the nineteenth-century renditions of this affair, André had tried to bribe the "volunteers" so they would let him go free, but one of the captors was quoted as having said: "[N]o, by God, if you would give us then a thousand guineas, you should not stir a step."[84] While elitist tracts focused on the stories of George Washington's difficult decisions and his formation of the Board of General Officers,[85] more mundane and populist narratives highlighted the social agency of the militia members who had helped the Continentals during the Revolutionary War. For example, James Fenimore Cooper recalled that "Providence had ordained" that these "young yeomen [*sic*]" would be "true to the sacred cause of their country."[86]

Cooper went on to explain:

> The fate of André became an object of the keenest solicitude to both armies. From the commencement of the struggle, to the last hour of its continuance, the American authorities had acted with a moderation and dignity that gave it a character far more noble than that of a rebellion. In no one instance had the war been permitted, on their part, to assume the appearance of a struggle for personal aggrandizement. It was men [*sic*] battling for the known rights of human nature.[87]

In theory, the Founders had discovered the military principles that needed to be observed; now the other generations that followed them needed to stay the course. After the end of the Revolutionary War, André's three captors each received $200 pensions, and General George Washington provided them with silver medals inscribed with the motto "Vincit Amor Patriae."[88]

By the third quarter of the nineteenth century, very few American observers questioned the legality of André's proceedings. His ordeal was now being remembered as just one of a long line of cases that showed the desirability and efficacy of military tribunals. For example, in an essay on Major André's trial that appeared in the *North American Review* in 1861, one writer opined that by "all the rules of war his life was justly forfeited." This author also reminded readers that Washington and his officers had deplored the fact that they had to "pass sentence on him."[89] Not coincidentally, the defense of Washington's board of inquiry could be used as "precedent" for Lincoln's suspension of habeas corpus, or the imposition of martial law.

In the nineteenth-century recirculation of these tales, the ambivalence of the American officers simply underscored their compassion and their resolve. The former colonists had created state and federal governments that had their own forums, and these governmental bodies had no trouble handling either foreign or domestic laws. The American military leaders and treatise writers who retold the story of Major André's capture and trial could use this tale in their categorizations of the respective rights of civilians, soldiers, and spies. During the 1880s, J. Dykman was sure that

> A few words respecting the justice of the execution of André may not be out of place. Spies are those who introduce themselves to the enemy to discover the conditions of affairs, penetrate his designs and communicate them back to their employers. Such is the well-sustained definition of a spy given by an eminent writer upon the law of nations, and it seems plainly to comprehend the case of Major André within its scope and terms.[90]

Notice here both the presence and absence of certain argumentative lines. Here it is taken for granted that André was indeed a spy, or that there was a "well-sustained definition" of a spy that was used by Washington's board of inquiry. Here we have no detailed discussion of the laws regarding "neutral" grounds, the procedures that were used during the trial, the status of the captors, or British treatment of spies. It is automatically assumed that we can "plainly" comprehend the justice of his execution. Moreover, American audiences were now being invited to reframe the major's case as one that contributed to the "law of nations." The British interpretation of these affairs was sometimes mentioned in passing, but the anxieties of an early age were forgotten in the defense of Washington's board or the valorization of André's captors.

Throughout the twentieth century, various scholars could not avoid taking sides in the controversies that surrounded the capture of Major André. The passage of time had not dulled the patriotic sensibilities of those who were convinced his captors were still being treated rather shabbily. For example, Charles Harvey Roe, writing in 1966, wanted his readers to realize that

> the three young Americans, who recognized clearly the simple elements of the case and did exactly what any loyal soldier would have done under the circumstances, have been maligned and denigrated, sneered at, snubbed and ignored, while the glamorous André has been praised for his manly virtues, admired for his many gifts and abilities, and mourned for his tragic and untimely death.[91]

The Americans living through the Cold War era were thus encouraged to remember that there had been other "loyal" soldiers ready to defend their country. Years later, other evaluators of twenty-first-century tribunals were still writing about how "Washington scrupulously complied with the limits imposed by the laws of war, including when he ordered a trial, by military commission, of Major John André."[92] Modernists remembered that Washington might have used some type of military "commission," that this was the trial that involved spying, or that the generals stayed within the "limits" of the laws of war, but we get very little sense of the contested nature of these competing rhetorics.

Conclusion

The commentators who wrote about Washington's Board of General Officers would be some of the first defenders of America's use of military tribunals, and their arguments formed some of the rhetorical templates that would be handed down from generation to generation. The inevitable reductionism of formalistic legal historicizing, and the corrosive power of nationalistic memories and cultural amnesias, contributed to situations where American generations conveniently forgot about some of the complexities of Major John André's situation.

In my critical rhetorical revisitation of this affair, I hope that I have complicated the situation so that we can see some of the types of issues that will confront the modernists who use this case as precedent. For example, let us assume for the moment that David Hicks, an Australian detainee at the U.S. Navy prison in Guantánamo Bay, may be one of the first individuals tried before a military tribunal. News sources indicate that Hicks was arrested while "allegedly fighting with the Taliban in Afghanistan in late 2001."[93] Michael Mori, the military defense lawyer assigned to the *Hicks* case, contends that the "commission process has been created and controlled by those with a vested interest only in convictions."[94] As I read these words, I wonder whether Major John André—who walked into another contested zone—might have thought the same thing about his conviction.

Will our civil courts be allowed to review the decisions of those who participate in modern military tribunals, where audiences will likely hear about Taliban involvement in the affairs of al-Qaeda, the status of prisoners of war, the characterization of enemy "belligerents," the wearing of irregular clothing, the extent of war zones, the jurisdiction of the tribunals, and so forth? Can field commanders use the John André case as precedent if they find "spies" in the field, and will they put together forums that "resemble political trials in authoritarian Third World countries"?[95]

Americans may indeed decide they want military tribunals, but before we make our final decisions about composition of those tribunals and the rules that will regulate these proceedings, we need to rethink the ways we decontextualize some of these historical precedents in our search for justificatory materials. We need to remember the contested rhetorics that surrounded Washington's board of inquiry, the legal ambiguities associated with capture in "neutral" grounds, the clash of nationalist narratives, and the vagueness of the "laws of war."

Those who decontextualize this decision and consider this to be an example of the inherent power of generals like Washington, or automatically assume that the board had jurisdiction, end up ignoring many of the controversies that surrounded the use of this commission. Whether we like it or not, the unfortunate Major André was tried by officers who had their own vested interests, and they were dealing with more than the search for the correct interpretation of the American adaptation of British military law. Their superiors wanted a quick decision in order to maintain discipline, and nationalist ideological pressures turned this into a contest that tested America's resolve.

Was André's hanging really necessary? If so, did he have to be tried in a military tribunal? This type of tribunal? By Washington's generals, with no avenues for appeal? We had better revisit this case before we abstract out the idea that our president has authority to form tribunals because an earlier commander in chief was given that same power.

3

Cultural Amnesias and Legal Recollections

Forgetting and Remembering
the 1862 U.S.-Dakota War Tribunals

Attend to the Indians. If the draft cannot proceed, of course it will not
proceed. Necessity knows no law.
—Abraham Lincoln, wire to Minnesota governor Alexander Ramsey

As I noted in chapter one,[1] President Bush startled some observers when
he publicly announced the promulgation of an executive order for military
tribunals,[2] but a few months later the Department of Defense (DOD)
made it clear that it was going to modify some of these rules so it could
provide "full and fair" trials for some of these defendants.[3] Eventually the
president and other members of the executive branch decided that Taliban
prisoners were not all al-Qaeda operatives or supporters, and some of
these modified rules stipulated that any "accused" prisoners who appeared
before potential tribunals would have the right to choose their own counsel, would have copies of these charges provided them in their "native
language," and would have the right to obtain witnesses and documents
that were needed for their defense.[4] Bush administrators made it clear
they felt that these guidelines ensured that detainees would receive the
same type of legal protections that would be given to any U.S. soldier who
might appear before parallel courts-martial proceedings.[5]

When interdisciplinary scholars and legal experts have looked back
through the annals of American history to see how other generations dealt
with the legality of military tribunals, they have often cited material from

Ex parte Milligan[6] (chapter four) or *Ex parte Quirin*[7] (chapter six), but they often forget that American authorities had to deal with many other national "threats." For example, there have been times when the American Indian "other" was considered to be an enemy of the U.S. military.[8] Heather Maddox explains the relevance of these various rhetorical constructs when she notes:

> Just as the current administration characterizes al Qaeda, Taliban, and other extremist groups or sympathizers, early American leaders also characterized slaves and Native Americans, through simplification and distortion. If groups or individuals are systematically denied their humanity, then they can be denied their natural rights. . . . Before there were "war criminals" there were "barbarians," "heathens," and "savages" who did not qualify as equals in the arena of "civilized warfare."[9]

Carol Winkler goes even further and documents how "Bush officials" appear to be borrowing "heavily from the rhetorical history of the United States' experience with American Indians" when they "construct the public rationale for the government's response" to al-Qaeda and the Taliban.[10]

In this chapter I look at some of the cultural amnesia and legal forgetting that impact our memories of the U.S.-Dakota war tribunals. On December 26, 1862, thirty-eight "Sioux" fighters were executed in the town of Mankato, Minnesota. Although many scholars consider this to be the largest mass execution of individuals in United States history,[11] the stories behind this incident rarely get mentioned in our modern critiques of military tribunals. A host of possible reasons exists for this glaring omission: this was an older case that did not involve twentieth-century warfare; there were not a lot of discussions of habeas corpus or due process right; and there were few people living at the time who viewed these "savages" as the owners of "Anglo-Saxon" rights. For example, Charles Bryant and Abel Murch, writing in 1864, claimed that the Christian ministers who sympathized with the condemned Sioux simply did not understand that these "dusky natives" have violated both "human and divine law."[12] If these Indians had "engaged in open war, such as the law of races of nations [*sic*]," Bryant and Murch would have conceded that "their advocates might have claimed for them the rights extended to prisoners of war."[13]

Today we have no shortage of liberals, moderates, or conservatives who complain about Bush's Military Order or the DOD modifications,[14] and there are some skeptics who critique many of the rationalizations associated with these proceedings. Yet in my study of the politics of the Mankato hangings, I have reluctantly concluded that one cannot be totally dismissive of all expeditious usages of executive power—we have to remember that sometimes *civilian* forums become the repositories of local prejudices. As William Lee Miller recently wrote in *Lincoln's Virtues,* the president's intervention in the winter of 1862 may have saved the lives of more than 260 Dakota Indians.[15] While many local Minnesota residents wanted the summary execution of hundreds of these "savages," the military chain of command provided for executive review of the Dakota trials. Scholars therefore need to be wary of automatically assuming that local civilian courts are always more generous in their dispensation of justice.

Both contemporaries and modernists have debated the desirability and the legality of these Dakota military tribunals, but what is rarely at issue is the fact that these decisions were just a small part of the much larger discussions associated with the "Indian problem."[16] In theory, the legal and military actions taken in December of 1862 brought an "end" to what some called the Dakota "war,"[17] "conflict,"[18] "uprising,"[19] or "massacre,"[20] and within a matter of a few years, tens of thousands of white Minnesotans traveled home. Yet the Santee Sioux and some of their Indian allies received the lion's share of the blame for instigating the Dakota War, and they would be "removed" to other territories—all in the name of "necessity." Thousands of "friendly" and "hostile" Dakota Indians would be "deported," and their treaties would be abrogated. Moreover, they would lose what little land that they had left in the region.

For almost a century and a half, the Civil War battles taking place during these same months have often overshadowed what many considered to be the beginnings of the Plains wars with the Indians.[21] This has incrementally changed as an increasing number of interdisciplinary scholars and public servants have invited us to reconsider the role that the U.S.-Dakota War played in the way observers think about "manifest destiny," ethnic histories, and apologies for past misdeeds. For example, in 1987, then Governor Rudy Perpich of Minnesota announced that a "Year of Reconciliation" would allow for the healing of some traumatic wounds.[22] Several years later, in one of the few articles that has focused attention on the denial of due process in these tribunal cases, Carol Chomsky argued:

> The evidence demonstrates that the trials of the Dakota prisoners were objectionable in a number of respects. The speed of the proceedings, the nature of the evidence, and the identity of the judges all combined to preclude judicious decisionmaking [*sic*] and to guarantee an unjust outcome. The commander who ordered the commission trials did not have the authority under the prevailing statutes to convene the tribunal, and it is questionable whether a military commission had any lawful authority to try the Dakota.[23]

Ellen Farrell similarly lamented the fact that some critics assume the "Dakota were uniformly and without exception guilty of unprovoked atrocities."[24]

At the very center of these discursive debates over our histories and memories of the U.S.-Dakota War is the question of the legality of the military "commissions" established by President Lincoln and his subalterns in the fall of 1862. Both General John Pope and Minnesota's Colonel Henry Hastings Sibley defended these tribunals on the basis of "necessity," but interestingly enough, many Northerners questioned the wisdom of having mass hangings in the aftermath of this tragic period. The sadness of these times is only magnified when we realize that this Western frontier violence would only "end" with the final surrender of some of the Sioux at Wounded Knee, South Dakota, in 1890.[25] The myriad problematics associated with the U.S.-Dakota War were considered to be emblematic of what could happen when anxious settlers and their military defenders patrolled thousands of square miles of territory.[26]

The Americans who sympathized with the plight of the Dakotas and the other Indian tribes rarely questioned the expansionist policies of whites, and most of the commentaries on topics such as "removal" or the desirability of the reservation system muted some of the criticism by magnifying the social agency of individual traders or treaty violators. An infinite number of biological, cultural, or environmental explanations could be used to justify the administrative oversight of the Indians. Nelson Miles, in a typical social Darwinian commentary, had this to say about the "terrible wars of race":

> The real issue . . . which is now before the American people is, whether we shall continue the vacillating and expensive policy that has marred our fair name as a nation and a Christian people, or devise some practical and judicious system by which we can govern one quarter of a million of our population, securing and maintaining their loyalty, raising them from the darkness of barbarism to the light of civilization, and put an end to these interminable and expensive Indian Wars. . . . Could we but perceive the true character of the Indians, and learn their dispositions, not covered by the cloak of necessity, policy, and interest, we should find that they regard us a body of false and cruel invaders of their country, while we are too apt to consider them as a treacherous and bloodthirsty race, that should be destroyed by any and all means.[27]

Miles, unlike many of his contemporaries, at least was willing to look at some of the historical roots of these public perceptions. Charles Flandrau, who had been one of the participants in the New Ulm battles during the war, provided a very different recollection in 1890 when he wrote about how the mollycoddling of some of the condemned "savages" had actually perpetuated the Western Plains wars.[28] He told readers that the "only proper course to have pursued with them, when it was decided not to hang them," was to have "exiled them to some remote post—say the Dry Tortugas [*sic*]—where communication with their people would have been impossible." This purportedly benevolent and prudential policy would have the advantage of setting "them to work on fortifications or some other public works," and it would "have allowed them to pass out by life limitation."[29]

Clearly the circulation of these types of opinions influenced the dispensation of territorial justice, and these stories need to be recontextualized. With that in mind, this chapter is divided into five major sections. The first supplies a short contextual look at how contemporaries and modernists have written about some of the early Minnesota treaties and land disputes. This is followed by a second segment that provides an explication of some of the material and symbolic forces that helped create these volatile situations. The third part of the chapter then looks into the formation of what would be known as the "Sibley" commissions, while the fourth section examines how various publics interpreted these trials. Finally, in the conclusion, I discuss the heuristic importance of these Dakota trials for our modern-day critiques of executive authority and military commissions.

Conflicting Remembrances of the Sioux before the U.S.-Dakota War Years

In the vast majority of the contemporary and historical accounts of Indian life before 1850, the Dakota tribal members who lived in Iowa, Dakota, and Minnesota were portrayed as the temporary denizens of vast tracts of underdeveloped and underutilized land. Some of the leaders of these Indian tribes—the ones who were not willing to go to war to stop white expansion—were viewed as realists who voluntarily gave up their rights in fair commercial exchanges. For example, with the signing of the 1851 treaties, some 24 million acres of land were supposedly ceded by the Sioux to the United States government and the whites who wanted to occupy the region.[30] This meant the Dakota tribes were relinquishing their rights to much of the land in Iowa, Dakota, and Minnesota, "except for a tract along the Upper Minnesota, which they reserved for their future occupancy and home."[31] One seemingly innocuous provision of these treaties, which would be approved by the Senate, indicated that it would be the president of the United States who would be responsible for the selection of the location of the reservation lands.[32]

Seven years later, some of the Dakota tribes ended up ceding another half of the reservation land that they had been given in 1851. Gerald Henig notes that what they were left with was a "ten-mile-wide reservation on the side of the Minnesota River from west of New Ulm to Big Stone Lake," and the lack of hunting grounds meant that the "nomadic and proud" Sioux "found themselves largely dependent for food and money on the form of annuities provided by the government under the terms of the various treaties."[33] Many whites now hoped the "farmer" Indians—with their "plows, hoes, scythes, cradles, ox-gearing, harness, carts, wagons," coats, pants, "shirts, coffee, tea," and such, would become productive neighbors and adapt to the new frontier life.[34] Protestant and Catholic missionaries were busy converting their new wards, and Indian agents sent their superiors monthly records of the needs and requirements of the communities living on the reservation.

Most contemporary accounts of these pre–U.S.-Dakota War years gave the impression that the Indians had eagerly ceded their land, and that the vast majority of the Dakota tribes profited from the existence of white settlements and agencies. Isaac Heard, one of the first chroniclers of what he called "the Sioux War," explained that just before the outbreak, agents could congratulate themselves "on the thriving appearance of affairs."[35] If Little Crow and the other leaders were displeased with the recent turn of events, they reportedly did not appear to have given the whites any notice of their disaffection. Heard was convinced that before the "war," it seemed as though the Indians and the "half-breeds" had learned the lessons of the universe and the order of things:

> Over the soil which [the] Indians had sold[,] civilization had made rapid strides. From Ireland, Germany, Norway, and Sweden, and many another country of the Old World, and from every part of the New, had come a quarter of a million people, and made the land their home. . . . Almost within stone's-throw of the reservation was the prosperous town of New Ulm, and emigrants even crowded upon the land invacated [*sic*] by the treaty of 1858. Every where appeared those works by which the great Caucasian mind asserts itself supreme.[36]

In this eulogistic tale of benign and benevolent progress, nothing could prevent the "certainty of" the "not very distant extinction" of the Dakotas, and it would be the European immigrants who were the primary social agents of productive change. Neither the Dakota memories of their rivers, lakes, and hills nor the "weird religion of the savage" could prevent the development of cities and states.[37] When the Dakota Sioux refused to die on their reservations, their survival and their apparent violation of nature's laws contributed to an atmosphere of mutual deception, distrust, and mis-understanding.

The Events That Contributed to
the Sioux-Dakota "Uprising," 1861–62

Scholars now believe there were a number of symbolic and material causes that contributed to the advent of the U.S.-Dakota War of 1862. Life on the reservation bore little resemblance to life in New Ulm, and many of Dakota Indians had to deal with a number of contradictory white positions on such issues as the payment of annuities, the placement of the camps, the degree of assimilation that was expected, and the uncertainty that accompanied the abandonment of the "nomadic" way of life. The Dakota who depended on the annuities that came from the 1850s treaties learned that Indian agents could often withhold payments if "outlaw" bands of Dakotas caused any trouble in the region.[38]

At the same time, there were interpretative disputes about the letter and the spirit of both tribal and treaty agreements. Many of the Dakota believed they had retained some rights to occupy, fish, and trap on the very lands that settlers now considered to be theirs. The schisms that existed both within and between the M'dewakanton, Wahpekuta, Wahpeton, and Sisseton tribes simply exacerbated an already volatile situation.

By 1862, the payment of annuities to the Dakotas had become a cumbersome process. The "annuity Indians" first had to wait until Congress approved the coinage being used, and then hundreds of small steps had to be taken before the money actually reached Minnesota. One commentator has noted that even the depth of a river could influence just when starving Indians got their money.[39] Many traders took advantage of the situation by giving the Dakotas credit in anticipation of the federal payments, which in turn meant the government now had to get involved in the policing of the funds. By this time there were some 1,000 regular troops stationed in the region, and they were supposed to be protecting the "white Minnesota population of 175,000."[40] Thomas Blegen once argued that the combination of the "pauperizing effects of the annuities," the "political appointment of the Indian Agents," the compression "of the natives into narrow reservations," and the dissipation of traditional hunting grounds helped to create situations where conflicts between the whites and the Sioux seemed to be inevitable.[41] Things got so bad that when some of the M'dewakanton Sioux sought more credit from one Indian agent and trader, Andrew Myrick, he dismissed their complaints by telling them "they could eat grass."[42] Legend has it that during the U.S.-Dakota conflict, Myrick would be one of the first casualties. When his body was found, it was said that his mouth was stuffed with grass.[43]

Many of the scholars who have studied the origins of the Minnesota-Dakota Wars contend the metaphorical event that constituted the "lighted match" that was "flung on a trail of powder" came when four "young devil-may-care Wahpetons" stopped at the farm of an Acton farmer on August 17, 1862.[44] On that particular day, Killing Ghost, Breaking Up, Runs Against Something When Crawling, and Brown Wing all got into a heated exchange with Robinson Jones, and a game of target practice ended with the murder of five whites. When the four Wahpeton youths reported back to Red Middle Voice, there was a great deal of discussion about how the whites would react to the murders, and whether these actions would lead to an end of the annuity payments. Little Crow warned his followers about the power of the whites, but he nevertheless agreed to lead into battle those Indians who favored war. The next day, hundreds of Sioux warriors launched a surprise raid on the Lower Agency, where both the traders and the "short hairs" (assimilated Indians) became the targets.[45]

In many of the stories that are told about the "Dakota Conflicts" or the "Sioux Wars," the focus of attention is on the settler-Indian conflict, when in fact many of the Dakota tribes had members who were divided on the question of whether they should go to war because of their grievances. The majority of the two Northern Dakota tribes, the Sissetons and the Wahpetons, were opposed to the fighting for a variety of reasons, including intermarriage, conversion to Christianity, and the recognition that they would be fighting overwhelming odds. Unlike some of the other Dakota communities, their subsistence farming allowed them to survive in a hostile environment. Their neighbors to the South, the M'dewakantons and the Wahpekutas, supplied most of the warriors who fought in the U.S.-Dakota conflicts.

Although some chroniclers of these events like to give the impression that all of the Minnesotans or Northerners were united in their struggle against the alleged barbarism of the Indians, many whites in various regions also disagreed about the exact causes of the U.S.-Dakota conflicts. One of the most popular narratives circulating during the early 1860s was an idea that the Indian troubles were just one small part of the much larger Civil War. Many of the newspaper editors in the North believed the Dakota conflicts had been encouraged by "rebel emissaries" in search of allies and traitors. For example, in August of 1862, one of the editors for the *New York Daily Tribune* wrote about some of the causal similarities that brought on the Dakota and Civil Wars:

> The Southern Rebels and their Indian allies are alike slave holders—a "brotherhood of thieves." The White [*sic*] traitors are fighting for Slavery; and the Indians are impelled by a common interest, a common crime, to go in with them. . . . The Sioux have doubtlessly been stimulated if not bribed to plunder and slaughter their White neighbors by White and Red villains sent among them for this purpose by the Secessionists. These [*sic*] perfectly understood that the Indians will be speedily crushed and probably destroyed as tribes; but what care their seducers for that? They will have effected a temporary diversion in favor of the Confederacy, and that is all *their* concern. But a day of reckoning for all these inequities is at hand[46] [emphasis in original].

After several weeks of conflict, Governor Ramsey sent a message to Abraham Lincoln, asking for federal assistance.[47] The president responded by appointing Major General Pope to be the commander of the newly created Department of the Northwest.[48] Pope, who had been embarrassed by Confederate victories at the Second Battle of Bull Run, was now in charge of a department that "encompassed the states of Minnesota, Iowa and Wisconsin and the territories of Dakota and Nebraska."[49] Harry Williams once sarcastically remarked that if "Pope had possessed a coat of arms, it would have been bombast rampant upon an expansive field of incompetence."[50]

The new leader of the Department of the Northwest let it be known that the American Civil War was not the only conflict that would involve "total" warfare. Pope informed Sibley that he wanted to put "a final stop to Indian troubles by exterminating or ruining all the Indians engaged in the late outbreak."[51] For several months, many newspapers in the region carried daily stories of how the Sioux were raping, scalping, disemboweling, and beheading their victims. In the white imagination, if would be the Indian who "was merciless, brutal," and "treacherous."[52]

After six weeks of bloody fighting in the fall of 1862, some five hundred whites and an "unknown but substantial number of Indians" had lost their lives.[53] During some of the initial engagements, the "belligerent" Dakota warriors did stage some successful ambushes, and they managed to destroy entire towns, but the Fort Ridgely and New Ulm defeats[54] created schisms within the ranks of the Indian forces. Many of the Sisseton and Wahpeton camp members wanted to end the conflict and return to the reservation.[55] After the battle of Wood Lake, most of the remaining combatants fled to Canada.[56] Some of the "peace" chiefs convinced Little Crow[57] that he needed to let them save some of the hundreds of captives.

Before surrendering, Dakota tribal leaders wanted assurances from Colonel Henry Sibley that they would receive fair treatment. He responded by telling them he was interested only in punishing those who had committed "murder and outrages upon the white settlers."[58] Sibley then received word from the Dakotas that his military companies could safely march into what were then called "peace" camps.

Those who surrendered may have believed that the Indians who continued to fight and those who had given up were going to receive differential treatment, but many of the whites who fought in the conflict or who had suffered through the burning of towns had other ideas.[59] Sibley sent word to General Pope that he was planning to appoint a three-member military board of inquiry to look into the matter of Indian culpability. Many of the Dakotas naively believed they would be treated as prisoners of war in a conflict among warring nations, and not as common criminals.

The End of the Dakota Conflict

When Sibley marched into the Dakota camps, some "107 white" and "162 half-breed" captives rejoiced as they witnessed the arrival of their liberators.[60] White flags were hanging from tepees, wagons, and trees, and Sibley decided this new bivouac site should be christened with the name of

"Camp Release." Within a matter of days, some 2,000 Sioux Indians had formally surrendered to the victors.[61]

The losers of this U.S.-Dakota war were now being tried by some of these victors, and a rhetorical analysis of some of the contemporary military correspondence provides us with some evidence of the mindset of those who were put in charge of these proceedings. In a letter that was sent from Pope to Sibley (September 28, 1862), the leading military authority in the Northwest gave his subordinate some very clear directions:

> The horrible massacres of women and children and the outrageous abuse of female prisoners, still alive, call for punishment beyond human power to inflict. There will be no peace in this region by virtue of treaties and Indian faith. It is my purpose utterly to exterminate the Sioux if I have the power to do so and even if it requires a campaign lasting the whole of the next year. Destroy everything belonging to them and force them out to the plains[,] unless, as I suggest, you can capture them. They are to be treated as maniacs or wild beasts, and by no means as people with whom treaties or compromises can be made.[62]

This was not an unusual sentiment. The St. Paul *Pioneer and Democrat* in December of 1862 proclaimed the "law of retaliatory war is the common law, and the law of the savage, which takes life for life," demands "that these prisoners should die."[63]

Sibley now had the unenviable task of carrying out these orders, and he expanded his court of inquiry and turned it into a five-person commission. His "Order 55" charged his own subordinates with the responsibility of finding those who had committed murder and other outrages "during the present State of hostilities."[64] The panel of military leaders that tried the more than 390 prisoners included Colonial William Crook, Colonel William Marshall, George Bailey, Captain Hiram P. Grant, and Captain Hiram S. Bailey. Interestingly enough, it would be twenty-two-year-old Lieutenant Rollin C. Olin who would be given the task of serving as judge advocate, and he was going to be assisted by Lieutenant Isaac Heard.[65]

What made this situation even more complicated was the fact that this was a period of time when many of Abraham Lincoln's officers were busy formulating and codifying some of the rules and regulations that would govern modern warfare.[66] Karin Thiem has argued that one "may assume that martial law, declared or undeclared, ruled the Minnesota frontier," because of the absence of "civil law" in the fall of 1862.[67] The Dakota defendants were certainly not going to be treated as U.S. citizens, which meant they had to be treated as members of "foreign nations under presidential treaty making powers."[68] Yet this did not mean that Indians were going to be treated as traditional prisoners of war. William Winthrop, one of the leading authorities on American martial law, later reviewed many of the opinions of the judge advocates written between September of 1862 and July of 1867, and it was his contention that

> Active hostilities with Indians do not constitute a state of foreign war. . . . Warfare inaugurated by Indians is thus a species of domestic rebellion, but it is so far assimilated to foreign war that during its pendency and on its theatre the laws and usages which govern and apply to persons during the existence of a foreign war are to be recognized as in general prevailing and operative.[69]

Sibley's military tribunals could therefore be categorized as specific types of military proceedings that still needed to follow unwritten customs and usages, military precedents and traditions, statutory codes of the Articles of War, specific army regulations, and special orders.[70] This meant the members of the commission were supposed to act as judge and jury, where they made decisions about the competency of witnesses, the admissibility and sufficiency of evidence, and legal burdens of proof. Since the Dakota Indians did not have any adversarial representation, the judge advocate served as their counsel and their protector. Some prisoners were allowed to become witnesses who could testify against other defendants, and the Sibley commission established the guilt of prisoners through the use of "hearsay confession of crimes committed against non-combatants in time of war."[71]

Many of the military leaders who dealt with these cases knew about the magnitude of their decisions. Flandrau later remarked that the "eyes of the world were upon us."[72] Sibley, General Pope, General-in-Chief Henry Halleck, and President Lincoln deliberated about the nature and scope of their authority in this situation.[73] Sibley, for example, thought he could judiciously separate out the guilty from the innocent, but he left us with fragments that show he also thought most of the defendants were "deeply implicated in the late outrages."[74] In a letter to Charles Flandrau he made these remarks: "If found guilty, they will be forthwith executed, although perhaps it will be a stretch of my authority. If so, necessity must be my justification."[75] Given the rhetorical history of the successful usages of this term, this was not a bad argument to have at one's disposal.

Sibley's military commission first convened at Camp Release in late September, and on the first day of the proceedings the commission tried sixteen men[76]—ten were convicted and six were acquitted.[77] A rhetorical analysis of the structural trajectory of these trial transcripts shows that after the first few cases, the commissioners seemed to have taken the attitude that the same witnesses did not need to repeat their entire testimony in order to gain the conviction of that particular defendant. In theory, each of the suspects was questioned about his participation in the war, and witnesses were then called who could testify about the facts in each case. In some situations, shooting at the soldiers or militia members was considered to be a lesser offense than firing on civilians, and Isaac Heard remarked that the brevity of these cases did not matter that much because "ninety-nine hundreds of these devils are guilty."[78]

When the trials actually got underway, it would be the former captives and "friendly" Indians who took center stage. Many of the first prisoners tried were convicted on the basis of the testimony of Joseph Godfrey (Otakle), a "mulatto" who was "born of a Black mother and a French-Canadian father."[79] Godfrey was the first prisoner to be tried, and he was sentenced to be "hung by the neck" until he was dead. After he turned state's evidence, the commission decided to commute his sentence to ten years in prison. His name appears in the records of dozens of other defendants, and many of the critics of these proceedings treated him as one of the major villains in this morality play.

After the first trial of Godfrey, the order of the tribunals seemed to have been organized around the alleged severity of the crimes committed during the "revolt." For example, during the second trial of Te-he-hdo-ne-cha [One Who Forbids His House], the trial recorder noted that this was a "Sioux Indian" who went on a "war party against the white citizens of

the United States."[80] The specifications alleged that he had "forcibly" rav-
ished Margaret Cardinal and killed several others in August and September
of 1862. Te-he-hdo-ne-cha supposedly stated that he did not "remember"
killing "any white persons, or committing any depredations."[81] Yet he also
admitted he had "slept with this woman once," and that "another Indian
may have slept with her."[82] Te-he-hdo-ne-cha would later be convicted and
he would be one of the thirty-eight prisoners who lost their appeals.[83]
This type of case helped create the template used in framing the trajectory
of many other trials.

After the first half dozen trials, the records of the proceedings get
shorter and shorter, and we do not read about the voicing of any evidentiary objections on the part of the judge advocate. Heard later asserted
that these trials "were elaborately conducted until the commission became
acquainted with the details of the different outrages and battles, and then,
the only point being the connection of the prisoner with them, five minutes would dispose of a case."[84] Such a position reflected a very truncated
view of the contemporary and modern rules and regulations of American
martial law, even in times of emergency.

What Heard and many of the other defenders of these trials conveniently forgot was the fact that in many of these cases, "no witness testimony was recorded" and "presumptive evidence was sufficient proof for
the military commission."[85] Nancy McClure [Faribault Huggan] was one
of the few witnesses who later admitted "she couldn't recognize any of the
prisoners as those I saw taking part in the murders of whites."[86] Several of
the "friendly Sioux," including Wakinyan Washtay [Good Thunder], were
allowed to testify against the defendants, and during one trial (#281), he
claimed he "heard other indians [sic] say he went down to the Fort with
the others."[87] The act of testifying against the other defendants often
brought exoneration, clemency, or lighter sentencing.

Some witnesses, like David Faribault, were allowed to testify in multiple proceedings, and his name appears in the brief records of more than
sixty trials. Most of the recorded material we have on these proceedings
indicates that many testimonials focused on the identification of particular
individuals or specific acts of violence against civilians. For example, in the
trial of Amdacha (trial #69), Faribault claimed that the "Deft. took us
prisoners" and "shot two at my house," and on the basis of this testimony

the defendant was convicted and hanged.[88] The defense protestations that contradicted these claims could easily be dismissed as self-serving and untruthful commentaries on these "massacres."

When some of the Dakota defendants tried to explain their positions on the origins of the conflict or rules of engagement, these commentaries could be characterized as "confessions" that obviated the need for further inquiry. These confessions could have been overheard by other witnesses, and this end around the hearsay rule helped speed up the process. As soon as the military court "got the knack of it," argues Ralph Andrist, they began grinding out "convictions at a fast clip."[89] This "knack" could help or hurt the cause of the Dakotas who suffered through the trial, depending on the preconceptions of the participants in the makeshift courtroom. If some of the commissioners or witnesses had evidence of an accused's "character" and affability prior to the "massacre," he had a better chance of being catalogued as a "friendly" rather than "savage" Indian.

Even though none of the whites in the region had to suffer through these trials, many of the local settlers were convinced that Sibley's commission was being too lenient in the handling of the Dakotas. Some argued that too many Indians had escaped justice, and that having these trials was a waste of time and energy. Critics complained that the military authorities needed to track down other war criminals. For example, one tribunal witness, Nancy McClure Faribault Huggan, remarked that she "was sorry that the guilty wretches" she had seen "were not brought up."[90]

Many of the missionaries and settlers who lived in this region were invited to become active participants in the legal procedures of Sibley's commissions, and they were given an incredible amount of discretion. Several of these local residents were considered to be familiar with the Dakota language and Indian habits, and they were supposed to help pick out those persons who would have to stand trial for the "murder or other outrages on whites."[91] Some of our surviving fragmentary shards of memory about this trial have been filtered through the interpretative work of Antoine D. Freniére and Reverend Riggs. Riggs appears to have been the individual who was given the primary responsibility for identifying and arraigning the prisoners, and this awesome discretion meant Riggs "served in a sense as a grand jury of one."[92]

By mid-October 1862, the Dakota appeared in more than a hundred trials. The newly promoted Brigadier General Sibley moved the proceedings to Fort Snelling. A log house now served as the courtroom, and the commission decided to try hundreds of other cases in less than two weeks. Even if we assume the first cases I discussed were handled in a careful manner, there is little question that these second series of trials were rushed affairs. Reverend Riggs had these words reprinted in the St. Paul *Pioneer and Democrat:*

> Many of those that [*sic*] are tried and condemned are doubtless guilty of participating in the murders and outrages committed on the Minnesota frontier—some of them guilty as Satan himself, and richly deserving the punishment of death. Others were guilty only to the extent of taking property. A military commission, where the cases of forty men are passed upon in six or seven hours, is not the place for the clear bringing out of evidence and securing a fair trial to everyone.[93]

By the end of the proceedings it became clear that most of the defendants were "charged" with murder, and that the "specifications" often included a few details about the alleged activities of the particular defendant. Unfortunately, "the general statement of participating in the fighting was the only specification to the charge."[94]

By November 5, 1862, Sibley's commission had tried 392 prisoners, and more than three hundred had been sentenced to death.[95] Pope sent these names to Lincoln, and the general also sent the president the full records of all of the trials.[96] Governor Ramsey urged the president to approve the execution of *all* of those who had been convicted by the tribunal, and one Mankato newspaper warned that if Lincoln hesitated, the Indians would be executed by "the will of the people, who make Presidents."[97] Contemporaries who shared these sentiments authored many other editorials, letters to the editor, and press commentaries.[98] If any of the Easterners were going to try and modify the findings of this commission, this was considered to be a violation of Minnesota's state "sovereignty" and a rationale for vigilante justice.

As noted above, many of the Sioux had expected they would be tried as prisoners of war, and they felt the leaders who had talked them into surrendering had betrayed them. After watching the first few convictions, the accused Dakota fighters quickly realized that one's participation in the battles at New Ulm or Birch Coulee could bring death. At this point in the proceedings, some of the prisoners began testifying about their poor aim, or their sore eyes. Some even tried to talk about how they had suffered from bellyaches that prevented them from fighting. A few were so desperate they argued that they were cowards who refused to join the fray.[99]

Many chroniclers of the activities of the Sibley commissions were not overly sympathetic to the plight of the Dakotas. Heard, for example, in the opening chapter of his *History of the Sioux War* (1863), averred that the "Indians were predisposed to hostility toward the whites. They regard them with that repugnance which God has planted as an instinct in different races."[100] These disputes about property, land, and the rules of engagement could therefore be framed as evolutionary matters that involved the survival of the fittest.

Not all of President Lincoln's advisers, officers, administrators, and agents shared Heard's views on the biological limitations that stood in the way of Indian and white cohabitation. Bishop Whipple, who sent the president a letter on the subject in the spring of 1862, wanted honest Indian agents, better treaties, workable plans for representing the legal positions of the Sioux, control of the supply of liquor, and a "paternal relationship under which the Indians would be fairly treated as wards." As far as Whipple was concerned, it had been the corrupt Indian trading that had created a "nursery of fraud."[101] William Dole, the president's Commissioner of Indian Affairs, wrote in November of 1862 that many of the Indians' problems stemmed from their environmental and cultural challenges:

> [T]he Indians, small and insignificant as they are when compared with the broad domain of which they were once the undisputed masters, are the objects of the cupidity of their white neighbors. . . .
> They find themselves in the pathway of a race they are wholly unable to stay. . . . Surrounded by this race, compelled by inevitable necessity to abandon all their former modes of gaining a livelihood . . .
> they are brought in active competition with their superiors in intel-

ligence and those acquirements which we consider so essential to success. . . . If a white man does them an injury, redress is often beyond their reach. . . . If one of their number commits a crime, punishment is sure and swift, and oftentimes is visited upon the whole tribe.[102]

Many Minnesota settlers and newspaper editors dismissed these commentaries as the rants of sentimentalists who had little understanding of life on the frontier.

In the aftermath of the Mankato trials, the U.S. Congress passed legislation that voided all of the treaties that had been signed by the Dakota tribes. They no longer had any reservation land in Minnesota, and the federal government no longer had to pay annuities to the survivors of the Dakota conflict. The millions of acres of land that had formerly belonged to the Minnesota Dakota tribes were now sold to emigrating whites.[103]

Given these conflicting biological and cultural explanations for Indian behaviors, how would various publics react when they heard about the Dakota "rebellion" and Sibley's military commissions? What would posterity think about the expeditious nature of these proceedings?

Assessments of Sibley's Military Tribunals

Before the 1960s, few national or international scholars paid much attention to the activities of the military commission formed by Sibley in the aftermath of the surrender of the Dakota Indians, but we do have some local commentaries on these incidents. It should come as no surprise that many of these accounts upheld the legitimacy of the proceedings and focused on the rights of the Minnesota settlers. For example, when some New Englanders showed some sympathy for these "savage captives," Bryant and Murch wrote in 1864 that these interlopers had forgotten about the "revenge" that had been carried out during King Philip's War.[104] These authors told their readers the "descendants of the primitive stock" seemed to have abandoned the "Puritan ideas" of these earlier pioneers.[105] The "whiggish" views of the reformers carried little weight out on the plains.

Thirty years later, American authors who were interested in these commissions were still defending the actions of Sibley, Pope, or Lincoln, and criticisms of these proceedings were contextualized as regional squabbles or cultural misunderstandings. J. Fletcher Williams, the Secretary of the Minnesota Historical Association, wrote an 1894 essay that vilified the "pseudo humanitarians in the East" who had encouraged President Lincoln's intervention in the trial of the "condemned for murder and massacre."[106] General Sibley was praised for having established a cordon of posts and garrisons in the winter of 1863, and for "securing protection to the people in the western part of the state."[107]

Some of the early researchers who looked into these incidents also tried to document how some of the Dakota tribal members remembered these contested histories. Stephen Riggs, Samuel Bond, and Thomas Williamson tried to preserve some of the arguments that appeared in the narratives supplied by Big Eagle, Robert Hakewaste, Little Crow, and White Spider.[108] George Quinn, for example, recalled that at the time of the uprising he had been a nineteen-year-old who had fought with his "people against the whites," because he had "never learned to speak English" and had been "raised among the Indians." Although he admitted fighting the white soldiers, he did not wage war against "the unarmed white settlers."[109]

An analysis of these extant records illustrates how some Dakota tribal members—especially the assimilated or "half-breed" Indians—may have shared some of dominant culture's views about the fairness and legitimacy of these military commissions. For example, Snana, one of the captive Indian women who came to Fort Release, recalled the problems she faced when "bad Indians" threatened her. She remembered how she and her own two children had been rescued by Sibley, and the kindness of the troops who gave them food.[110] Samuel Brown, seventeen years of age in 1862, later commended members of Sibley's tribunal for adjudging that Charles Crawfold (Brown's uncle) was not guilty of the charges brought against him. One member of the commission, Lieutenant Colonel Marshall, had apparently known that Crawford was one of the "friendlies" who did not belong with the "worst kind."[111] During Crawford's trial, a soldier by the name of John Magner accused Crawford of participating in the battle of Wood Lake, but it appears the soldier made the mistake of confusing two sides of a battlefield.[112]

Modern-day collectors of these narratives encourage us to be circum-spect in the weight that we give some of these tales. Gary Anderson and Alan Woolworth, writing in 1988, contend:

> In 1897, the year his [Brown's] narrative was published, strong preju-dice against people of color openly existed in America. It was the era when Herbert Spencer's doctrine of Social Darwinism and the sur-vival of the fittest reigned supreme and when newspaper editors wrote of the "White Man's Burden." Brown's condemning prose fit into the context of the times, when all nonwhites who resisted the so-called benefits of western cultures, whatever their justification, were quickly marked as uncivilized savages.[113]

I would argue that this does not mean scholars and laypersons need to be totally dismissive of these accounts, but rather that observers need to re-member the inherent rhetoricity of all documents and historical records.

After the deportations of thousands of the Dakota Indians, few white settlers were interested in reading the accounts of the Indian participants, but a wave of nostalgic feelings, the need for archival records for court claims, and the belief that Minnesota needed to remember the deeds of the "good" Indians helped with the preservation of some of these frag-ments. Mary Crook, for example, would be remembered as one of the Dakota tribal members who protected two white captives, Urania White and her baby, and a monument would be erected by the Minnesota Valley Historical Society to "commemorate the brave, faithful, and humane con-duct of the loyal Indians."[114]

For many decades, American military experts and politicians assidu-ously avoided writing or talking about the Sibley commission's activities. When researchers wrote about the formation of martial regulations or military commissions, they focused on the East and on Lincoln's generals in the East during the American Civil War (see chapters four and five).[115] Military theorists and other researchers averted their gazes, and only a few individuals looked at the trial transcripts preserved in some dusty and unused archives.[116]

In the 1960s, 1970s, and 1980s, a number of interdisciplinary research-ers reassessed the role that the Sibley military commissions played in the traditional histories and memories of the 1862 U.S.-Dakota conflict. Had the five-member commission that sentenced 303 Sioux Indians to death been the type of judicial body that provided military justice? How many of those who were hanged were really innocent, and why was the swiftness of this punishment considered a military "necessity"? Kenneth Carley, in *The Sioux Uprising,* claimed that reading "the records today buttresses the impression that the trials were a travesty of justice."[117] Michael Clodfelter was convinced that

> The real work at Camp Release was vengeance. With Pope's blessing, Sibley set up a five-man kangaroo court to judge the Santees. The accused were provided with no legal representation and hardly given a chance to defend themselves. Simply placing an accused miscreant at the scene of the crime was sufficient to condemn him. Because so many Indian names in their vernacular were similar and because the white man had trouble pronouncing those names, the wrong man was often accused of mistaken identity.[118]

Just how many individuals lost their procedural and substantive due process rights when they had to appear before these military commissions has been—and will continue to be—a contentious issue. For example, some researchers remind us that Sarah Wakefield, one of the former prisoners of the Dakotas, wrote in 1864 that a man by the name of "Chaska" [#20][119] had saved and protected her from death or harm during her captivity.[120] Wakefield was allowed to plead for his life in front of Sibley's military commission, but several days later she found his name on the list of those who had been executed. Many now believe the tribunal confused Chaska's name with that of Chaskadon, a man who had been accused of killing a pregnant woman.[121]

With the passage of time, we now know that the mass executions of the Dakota Indians at Mankato were probably considered by many whites to be necessary deterrents that would help bring peace to the Minnesota communities. Given local prejudices, Lincoln's intervention could be viewed as having saved some lives, but there still had to be some hangings, some symbolic public spectacles that would show that justice had been served. The military tribunals that meted out these sentences were therefore "social dramas" that were "used to manage emotional responses to troubled situations."[122] The guilty were being punished, and the federal officials who dispensed this punishment could now say that President Lincoln cared about the lives of the American citizens who lived in the Northwest. At the same time, many Minnesotans viewed the public hangings as an essential step in the process of taking back the American states and territories.

The public nature of these executions meant that both immediate and distant audiences could vicariously participate in these social dramas. Tens of thousands of settlers had lost their homes, and they were in no mood for cultural sentimentality or racial tolerance.[123] For example, the executioner of the thirty-eight condemned Sioux, William Duley, had lost three of his children in the raids around Lake Shetek, and after three drum taps he was the one who had the honor of springing the trap doors. At first the bodies of the dead Dakota warriors were buried in a mass grave, but later on, local physicians were allowed to use their skeletons for purposes of research and medical education.[124]

As we contemplate the use of military tribunals, how will we remember these Dakota trials? What will we do with these conflicting accounts of an incident that is now a part of what Donald Bloxham calls our "judicial" memory?[125] Are there any didactic lessons we can learn from visiting these earlier military situations?

Conclusion

This chapter's analysis of the U.S.-Dakota Minnesota war and the Sibley commissions may leave some critics with very ambivalent feelings about the uses of the military commissions in this particular situation. It would be easy to take the categorical stance that all military tribunals are inherently unfair, and that they are problematic in all situations. I must admit that I am leaning in that direction. As I noted at the outset, I have yet to see any historical example of a defensible military trial that could not have been handled by civilian authorities. One could argue that Lincoln and his generals were given too much power, that wars have a way of eroding the civilianization trends in American history, and that tribunals during this period did not have any of the protections that would later appear in the

Uniform Code of Military Justice.[126] If that is the case, Bush's tribunals had better adopt many of these UCMJ protections.

Perhaps one of the key lessons we should take away from the study of the U.S.-Dakota war and Sibley's commission is that all judicial proceedings—military or civilian—are rhetorical forums involving a host of legal and political negotiations. The Minnesota authorities who fought against some of these Dakota tribes sometimes described this as a "war," and yet they refused to treat their enemies as prisoners of war, who were entitled to at least a modicum of legal protection. Even those who viewed this as a "rebellion" refused to talk about the possibility of restitution or reconciliation. The liminal status of these defendants meant that they be characterized as "murderers" who could not claim noncitizen combatant status.

As modern researchers and laypersons grapple with the complexities of modified forums, rhetorics of "necessity," and the "war" on terrorism, they may want to remember some of the historical arguments used in earlier struggles, where the "other" was also treated as an implacable, uncivilized foe. Peter Maguire, who was one of the few writers in the fall of 2001 who remembered the U.S.-Dakota wars and the Sibley commission precedent, had this to say about the announcement of the U.S. president's Military Order:

> President George W. Bush's executive order establishing military tribunals came as a shock to many human rights advocates who had hoped to see Osama bin Laden wearing headphones in a United Nations courtroom. This move is a direct challenge to those who believe individual rights take precedence over national sovereignty[,] and that is a part of Bush's broader attempt to roll back the human-rights advances of Bill Clinton's administration. . . . Although military commissions have been used throughout American history, given their uncertain historical legacy the President's decision raises as many questions as it answers. . . . Many of these trials were primitive forms of political justice such as the 1862 Dakota War trials. . . . Primitive political justice had no presumption of impartiality, over a very public spectacle of vengeance usually followed by an amnesty of wartime acts.[127]

Are nationalist forums the best options we have in wartime situations? Can military tribunals provide that precarious balancing of civil liberties and state necessities? Will the Iraqi prisoners or the Guantánamo detainees be the beneficiaries of these martial histories as modernists learn from the lessons of the past? Only time will tell as our contemporary societies deal with new characterizations of defendants who have to face different enraged citizenries.

4

Abraham Lincoln and
Ex Parte Milligan

No doctrine, involving more pernicious consequences, was ever invented
by the wit of man than that any of its provisions can be suspended during any of the great exigencies of government. Such a doctrine leads
directly to anarchy or despotism, but the theory of necessity on which
it is based is false.

—David Davis, *Ex parte Milligan,* 1866

With the passage of time and the benefit of hindsight, one can readily
understand why some laypersons and scholars valorize the heroes in their
rhetorical histories or vilify the villains who threaten their belief systems.[1]
Consciously or unconsciously, we may align ourselves with various generational members who interpret ideographs and other discursive forma-
tions in ways that appear to be encapsulating our ideas regarding common
sense, prudential politics, or immutable standards of justice. Our commentaries on "whig" or "tory" interpretations of civil liberties help to define what we consider to be transcendent principles or feasible policy alternatives.

This is especially important to remember when we talk about legal
rights and duties because we often forget that elites and publics are influenced by propositional logics and persuasive narratives. As Robert Cover
eloquently noted in 1983:

We inhabit a *nomos*—a normative universe. We constantly create and
maintain a world of right and wrong, of lawful and unlawful, of valid
and void. The student of law may come to identify the normative
world with the professional paraphernalia of social control. The

rules and principles of justice, the formal institutions of the law, and the conventions of a social order are, indeed, important to that world; they are, however, but a small part of the normative universe that ought to claim our attention. No set of legal institutions or pre-scriptions exists apart from the narratives that locate it and give it meaning.[2]

Clearly, I believe that in the first years of the twenty-first century we are living in a necessitous world that has made us question many of our libertarian, Enlightenment assumptions.

In this chapter I extend some of the insights I provided in the previous chapter on the Dakota tribunals by focusing on some other key stories that sometimes get truncated in our post-9/11 world—the tales that were once told about the post–Civil War cases revolving around *Ex parte Milligan*. In many of the "whig" narratives that underscore the importance of civil liberties, this case stands for the proposition that "there is no traditional or constitutional authority legitimating trial by a military tribunal when the crime is subject to prosecution under American law and the appropriate American courts are open and functioning."[3] Jonathan Turley contends that the Court in this case "stood against the concept of a constitutional necessity defense," and "was a direct rebuke to the positions of leaders like Andrew Jackson and Abraham Lincoln, who espoused such necessity claims."[4]

This *Milligan* case came to the courts because of the activities of an Indiana "Copperhead"—Lambdin Milligan—who allegedly helping organize pro-Southern groups. Milligan was convicted and sentenced to death by one of Abraham Lincoln's military tribunals, and he petitioned the federal circuit court in Indiana for a writ of habeas corpus.[5] Union officials responded by noting that the president's declaration of martial law extended the military's jurisdiction. More specifically, Lincoln's procla-mations had declared that "rebels," "insurgents," and "aiders and abettors" who interfered with the draft were "guilty of disloyal practice." Violators were subject to "martial law, and liable to trial and punishment by courts-martial or military commission."[6]

In *Ex parte Milligan*—decided during the early post–Civil War years—

several judges and jurists were interesting in debating questions regarding the relative power of state and federal governments during wartime. These cases were ostensibly decisions that dealt with federal habeas corpus writs, but they became fragments in some larger ideological debates about the power of various social agents and governmental institutions. Eventually, the majority of the United States Supreme Court justices had to make some key decisions regarding the nature and scope of what would later be called "civilianization" of the military, and Justice Davis and some of his colleagues seemed to be openly skeptical when they heard the government prosecutors talking about military necessities and military commissions. In the end, these jurists determined that the military did not have any authority over a civilian who was not in the "theatre of active military operations."[7]

For more than a hundred years, the *Ex parte Milligan* case stood for the whiggish principle that "there could be no criminal trials of U.S. citizens by military tribunals while the courts remained open."[8] In many ways, several members of the Supreme Court in the *Milligan* case were trying to reign in some of the executive power that had been given to President Abraham Lincoln during the Civil War. Ann French explains:

> On April 27, 1861, President Lincoln simultaneously declared martial law and authorized Commanding General Winfield Scott to suspend the writ of habeas corpus in Union territories. . . . Lincoln proclaimed that all persons who discouraged enlistments or engaged in disloyal practices would be subject to trial in a military commission, regardless of whether they were citizens or military. Lincoln thought that military commissions were necessary because, according to him, state courts did not have the authority to convict war protesters.[9]

In many ways, one's adaptation or rejection of the *Milligan* rationale tells us a great deal about one's willingness to give up or retain some key civil liberties, or one's views on the expansiveness of the powers of America's commander in chief. As Donald Downs and Erik Kinnunen astutely observe, many believe that

Milligan stands as a paragon of the commitment to the rule of law at all times, including law. . . . [However] the Court waited until the Civil War was over to render its decision, thereby strategically avoiding a conflict with the Executive Branch during time of actual war. . . . Milligan was not tried as an enemy combatant, but rather he was tried as a civilian. . . . In the end, *Quirin* is still the primary constitutional precedent dealing with military commissions and has been relied upon by federal courts dealing with the Bush administration's detainment of enemy combatants. The case [*Quirin*] has to be dealt with by anyone who argues that military tribunals violate the letter or spirit of *Milligan* per se.[10]

I will analyze the *Quirin* cases in another chapter (six), but for now I would like to note the strategic use of temporal space and historical distance as commentators pick and choose how to punctuate time, or where to begin when considering the "origins" or the legality of military tribunals.

In today's normative world, we rarely study the lawyers' arguments or the public commentary that surrounded the *Ex parte Milligan* debates, and this decision is often brushed aside as some ancient, metaphysical relic.[11] Yet during the nineteenth century, the cases that led up to this seminal Supreme Court decision were viewed as bulwarks that protected individual liberties.

As I will argue in chapters eight and nine, these "whig" interpretations of civil-military relations are losing their rhetorical power as our nation tries "to avert more catastrophic terrorism."[12] Minimizing the precedential value of *Ex parte Milligan* simply means that governmental officials can now maximize the significance of Lincoln's words and deeds. Jill Hasday explains that

the Civil War . . . fostered a pervasive sense of crises centered on the premise that resort to undemocratic measures was necessary to save the nation. Spurred by the felt necessities of wartime, this way of thinking prioritized action over contemplation, and effectiveness over consultation. Proponents argued that war sped up time and shrank space. Responding as quickly as possible to national crises was both necessary and desirable, even at the expense of compro-

mise and deliberation. Wartime emergency measures could appropriately apply to people far from actual fighting. This mentality drove
fundamental restructuring of the national government.[13]

Turley has characterized this as a "consequentialist view" that allowed
for the "unilateral assertion of authority to try civilians."[14] The expansiveness of the Civil War altered the ways that Americans thought about the
geographic locations of battlefields, the desirability of military trials of
civilians, and the scope of federal power. In the same ways that our federal
circuit courts talk about the U.S. "zone of active combat,"[15] the Union
judges worried about behind-the-lines Confederate sympathizers.

One of the key characters who entered many of these Civil War dramas
was Abraham Lincoln, and in the same year that he was hearing about the
Dakota troubles in the Northwest he was mulling over the necessities of
slave emancipation and the imposition of martial law in cities like New
Orleans.[16] Contemporaries often disputed many of the arguments he advanced about centralized power and wartime necessities, but his assassination brought adulation, veneration, and hagiographic memories. G. R.
Tredway complained:

> Writing on the subject of opposition to the Lincoln administration
> is naturally affected by the attitude of the author towards Abraham
> Lincoln and his policies. The popular thesis [is] that the martyred
> President was above reproach. . . . It is not an exaggeration to say
> that most seem to regard Lincoln as somewhat of a saint and his
> program as something on the order of the Ten Commandments. . . .
> The Civil War President has been rather consistently exempted from
> the critical review visited upon his contemporaries, particularly
> those on the other side of the political fence. This creates a frame of
> reference which greatly distorts the view of Lincoln's opposition.[17]

Yet almost two decades later, Mark Neely wrote that now scholars have
"been more or less embarrassed by Lincoln's record on the Constitution"
and in the process they have "shied away from the subject."[18]

In the post-Reagan era, many elite and public commentators are no
longer embarrassed by Lincoln's defense of a strong executive branch, or

his stance regarding the need for military commissions. Chief Justice William Rehnquist, for example, in *All the Laws but One* (1998), averred:

> There is no reason to think that future wartime presidents will act differently from Lincoln, Wilson, or Roosevelt, or that future Justices of the Supreme Court will decide questions differently from their predecessors. But even though this be so, there is every reason to think that the historical trend against the least justified of the curtailments of civil liberty in wartime will continue in the future. It is neither desirable nor is it remotely likely that civil liberty will occupy as favored a position in wartime as it does in peacetime. But it is both desirable and likely that more careful attention will be paid by the courts to the basis for the government's claims of necessity as a basis for curtailing civil liberty.[19]

These arguments, which were presented several years before the terrorist attacks of 2001, remind us that we cannot automatically assume that one generation's balancing of these rights and necessities will become the eternal yardsticks for decisions that have to be made during times of war and peace.

How can researchers explain these vacillating views on Lincoln, civil liberties, and martial necessities? While many scholars might argue for an "objectivist" position that sees through the "rhetoric" to get to the "reality" existing beneath the politics of the mundane world, one soon finds that the peeling away of some of these sedimented layers will only reveal the existence of other foundations that are based on earlier rhetorics. Instead of looking for the "real" Lincoln or "the" rule of law governing Civil War policies, we need to be more modest in our aspirations and look for the range of oppositional arguments that appeared in these Civil War rhetorical cultures.

From a rhetorical perspective, what makes many of these debates even more intriguing are the ways that scholars and laypersons who talk about the Civil War often assume the *perceptions* of exigencies and necessities were themselves naturalized markers that showed that drastic measures needed to be taken during wartime. Given temporal and spatial distance, there has been a general reluctance on the part of critics to evaluate the extent of alleged military dangers, the actual numbers of members who belonged to secret organizations, the records of the thousands arrested between 1862 and 1865, or the alleged connections that existed between Southern soldiers and their Northern supporters or sympathizers. Often it is assumed that if Lincoln or one of his military generals said there was a "conspiracy" or some other act of "treason," this automatically meant we needed to give them a great deal of deference in dealing with these alleged exigencies. Conversely, those who denigrated the importance of the Reconstruction, or who want to remember the opposition's stance on state rights, individual liberties, the right to rebellion, and such, underestimate the power of those perceptions in the shaping of official policies and public rhetorics. Simply arguing that the other side's forces were the "real" conspirators did not help matters. If we are going to understand the contested nature of these characterizations and emergency narratives, we need to recontextualize these debates in ways that allow readers to see the ambivalences, contradictions, and difficult choices that confronted both Lincoln's supporters and his detractors in these martial debates.

In order to help with this contextualization, I have decided to focus attention in this chapter on the political debates that took place in Indiana during the Civil War, and I want to spotlight some of the arguments advanced by members of Lincoln's administration, the defenders of Milligan, and the judicial arbiters who heard his case. I conclude by commenting on some of our rhetorical histories of this decision and the impact these choices have had on our views of "necessity" or military tribunals.

Lambdin Milligan and Indiana's Political Culture during the Civil War

The wartime activities that took place in Indiana were rhetorically significant for a number of reasons. This state was a microcosm of the larger material and symbolic forces that operated in this "war of rebellion"—the families who sent their sons off to fight for the North contributed a higher proportion of soldiers for the population than any other state besides Delaware, and yet at the same time this border state was believed to be filled with peace advocates or Southern sympathizers. Milligan, a member of Indiana's Democratic Party and one of the president's harshest critics, would be remembered in hundreds of newspaper articles, journals, and books as the person who helped delineate the mythic line that prevented "martial autocracy," where the "Supreme Court established the rule [in 1866] that, no matter how grave the emergency, and no matter how high the public excitement, the civil authority is supreme over military authority."[20]

States like Indiana—and people like Milligan—drove Lincoln crazy. He could not treat the residents of Indiana in the same way that Ben Butler treated folks in Louisiana, and his subordinates could not prove that Milligan was actually a rebel spy. They felt certain, however, that his words and deeds were aiding and abetting the enemy. Lincoln and some of his military administrators apparently believed that without their Union bayonets, the civil courts would close down, and that the Democrats in the state would hand Indiana over to the Southern forces.

During one public address in front of an audience in Fort Wayne, Indiana, Milligan claimed "the crimes and all of the horrible sins that are attendant upon the prosecution of an unjust and necessary war" could be tied to Lincoln's practices.[21] In early October 1864, soldiers under the command of General Alvin Hovey arrested Milligan, and he was said to be "inciting" insurrection and giving aid to the enemies of the United States. Hovey would bring him before an Indianapolis military commission several weeks later, and Milligan would be sentenced to be hanged on May 19, 1865.[22] Milligan petitioned for habeas corpus relief so that he could be discharged from what he considered to be unlawful imprisonment. By the winter of 1866, the case of *Ex parte Milligan* reached the United States Supreme Court, where several justices decided that in some situations, a declaration of "military necessity" did not justify the establishment of "military commissions in areas where civil courts were open and functioning."[23]

While the jurists who heard the case had disagreements about the scope of executive power in cases of national emergency, they realized that hanging Milligan for his words and deeds might be problematic. Members of the Court reasoned:

> Citizens of States where the courts are open, if charged with crime,
> are guaranteed the inestimable privilege of trial by jury. This privi-

lege is a vital principle, underlying the whole administration of criminal justice; it is not held by sufferance, and cannot be frittered away on any plea of state or political necessity. . . . [military commissions and laws and usages of war] can never be applied to citizens in states which have upheld the authority of the government, and where the courts are open and their process unobstructed.[24]

As a pragmatic matter, Lincoln's military tribunal did not have jurisdiction over Mr. Milligan, and he was released from custody.[25]

Outraged radical Republicans and other Northern audiences often claimed that *Ex parte Milligan* was a rash and unrealistic peacetime decision. After all, did not these jurists know that Lincoln and his generals were dealing with real life crises, where the scope of the "rebellion" meant that some liberties had to give way to "military necessity"? If keeping the Union together meant executives had to be given extra-ordinary powers, then so be it. During many of the Civil War years, Lincoln had to make decisions regarding the arrest of those who disrupted the railway travel of Federal troops, the drawing of the line between loyal opposition and seditious speech, the limits of public activism, the suspension of habeas corpus, and the relative power of the executive in confrontations with either Congress or the federal judiciary.[26] Many of the commander in chief's supporters claimed the constitutional provisions that touched on public safety and national survival needed to be given priority over the lesser individual rights embodied in other parts of that sacred parchment. Antiquated idealism had to give way to pragmatic realism.

Was the *Milligan* court fair in its recontextualization of the Lincoln's tribunals and the openness of the civil courts? In order to help answer that question, I take a look at how various audiences perceived the emergency situations during the early years of the Civil War.

Secession, the Election of Abraham Lincoln, and American Civil Liberties

Existing archival and press materials provide us with some evidence that during Abraham Lincoln's tenure as president, at least 14,000 individuals were imprisoned by Union military authorities during the Civil War, although the "exact figure will never be known because of unreliable nineteenth-century record keeping."[27] Some of these arrests involved questions of fraud, desertion, selling contraband, and engaging in guerilla warfare,[28] but other detentions were based on seditious libel charges or allegations of treason. President Lincoln determined that he had to suspend habeas corpus, and during a special address to Congress he explained that "The Constitution itself, is silent as to which, or who, is to exercise the power [to suspend habeas corpus]; and as the provision was plainly made for a dangerous emergency, it cannot be believed the framers of the instrument intended that in every case, the danger should run its course, until Congress could be called together."[29] More than a year and a half later, Congress passed the Habeas Corpus Act, which provided the American president with the power to suspend habeas corpus whenever he decided that public safety required suspension.[30]

During these early years, when Lincoln and his supporters used the concept of "necessity" to justify their wartime restrictions on various civil liberties, they were simply knowingly or unknowingly tapping into a permutation of the ancient "tory" argumentative structure (see chapter one). They prioritized the power of the commander in chief during wartime, they underscored the importance of hasty decision-making on the battlefield, and they reminded readers that the "will" of the sovereign or subordinate was of paramount importance in exigent situations. Executive discretion was needed, and protracted legislative or judicial debates only got in the way. As Justice Rehnquist once noted in a commentary on Lincoln's authority, peacetime "offers an opportunity for detached reflection on these important questions which are not so calmly discussed in the midst of a war."[31] James Speed, the president's attorney general, provided this typical commentary on how the nation needed to view the civilian-military relations during these hectic periods:

As war is required by the framework of our Government to be prosecuted according to the known usages of war among the civilized nations of the earth, it is important to understand the obligations, duties, and responsibilities imposed by war on the military. Congress, not having defined, as under the Constitution it might have done, the laws of war, we must look to the usages of nations to ascertain the powers conferred in war, on whom the exercise of such powers devolve, over whom, and to what extent do those powers reach, and in how far the citizen and the soldier are bound by the legitimate use thereof. . . . The legitimate use of the great power of war, or rather the prohibitions upon the use of that power, increase or diminish as the necessity of the case demands. When a city is besieged and hard pressed, the commander may exert an authority over the non-combatants which he may not when no enemy is near.[32]

Speed, who in a few short months would play a leading role in *Ex parte Milligan,* is one of those forgotten figures who helped popularize the arguments picked up by those who wanted a separate and empowered system of military justice. His story about congressional silence would not go unchallenged, but in many ways he was simply bringing together those fragmentary ideographs, topoi, and narratives that had been circulating within Anglo-American rhetorical cultures for centuries. Many generations of Americans since the time of Washington had been turning to these protean "laws of war," in part because of the wealth of extra-judicial discourse that surrounded these ancient and well-tried uses of "necessity." The beauty of these types of arguments is that the *absence* of textual material constraining the commander in chief could be used as an illustration for why certain authority needed to be granted.

Speed, who was once characterized by Rehnquist as "one of the least competent Attorney Generals in the history of that office,"[33] was nevertheless an important purveyor of the "tory" narratives popular at this time. Lincoln's supporters built on, and helped legitimize, many of these previous "pleas" of necessity, by leaving us with mounds of documentary evidence and arguments that focused on three key aspects of this multilayered discourse:

1. It should be the president, or his delegates, who should have the discretion to decide whether a nation was in a state of "necessity";
2. Given that the entire North and South were impacted by this "rebellion," the constitutional provisions that provided for the president's war powers should be liberally construed;

3. This in turn meant that entire regions were in a state of war or preparation for war, and this included places that were far from the battlefield. If thousands of troops had to be stationed in order to keep the courts open, then this provided ample proof that these were not ordinary times. Permutations of these types of arguments would resurface in the *Ex parte Quirin* case, and they would be re-appropriated by many of President Bush's supporters.

In the minds of many Unionists, the exigencies of war demanded that the various political parties set aside their differences and realize the nation was fighting for its very survival. Both military leaders and public observers often deliberated about the concept of *inter arma silent leges* [in times of war the laws are silent].[34] Judge Advocate Major H. L. Burnett, for example, explained that the various colonels who served on many of the Indiana military commissions understood that the "civil liberties of the citizen become dead for the time being, if necessary to preserve the life of the nation."[35]

In the early years of the Civil War, Lincoln tried to maintain a fragile alliance of War Democrats,[36] moderate Republicans, and abolitionist supporters, and his early discourse avoided any extreme commentaries that would alienate potential supporters. This is one of the reasons he did not immediately come forward with the Emancipation Proclamation. At the same time, the president claimed the preservation of the Union demanded that he occasionally take drastic measures in a time of emergency, and he opined that military "necessity" superseded the traditional protections provided by civil courts. One of his first proclamations announced that any persons who were accused of disloyalty could be arrested, tried, convicted, and confined by the North's military authorities.[37] Just how one causally determined the existence of "disloyalty," or the impact of this alleged disloyalty, became a subjective matter. Later commentaries indicated that even in the absence of any overt acts on the part of defendants, the mere threat or tendency of particular words or activities could be construed as libelous or treasonous acts. This complemented the idea that the mere perception of a danger warranted the use of discretionary powers.

Opposition to Lincoln's policies came from all parts of the political spectrum—abolitionists demanded immediate emancipation for all ex-slaves, while "ultra" Democrats were convinced that Civil War was based on false claims of "necessity." The very idea that troops had to be stationed in the border states became evidence that "coercion" rather than "concilia-tion" was in the air. A complex mosaic of arguments based on states' rights, regional comity, and principles of secession were used in a plethora of speeches that criticized the new president's compromising policies. Horace Greeley, an influential Republican who served as the editor of the *New York Tribune,* spoke for many anxious Northerners when he wrote in 1860:

> If the Cotton States shall decide that they can do better out of the Union than in it, we insist on letting them go in peace. The right to secede may be a revolutionary one, but it exists nevertheless. . . . Whenever a considerable section of our Union shall deliberately re-solve to go out, we shall resist all coercive measures designed to keep in it. We hope never to live in republic [*sic*], whereof one section is pinned to the residue by bayonets. [38]

In spite of such sentiments, Lincoln weathered these early political storms.

This was no easy task. In May of 1861 the case of John Merryman be-came the first major challenge to the president's authority. [39] Dissidents in the state of Maryland had seriously disrupted railroad transportation and telegraph lines around the nation's capital, and Merryman was arrested for treason by some Union officers. Merryman responded by petitioning for a writ of habeas corpus, and he had the good fortune of applying for this remedial help at a time when Chief Justice Roger Taney was riding circuit in the area. [40] In *Ex parte Merryman,* Taney asserted that if there was any "necessity" involved, it involved the "personal liberty" of rights like habeas corpus that had been defended since colonial times. [41] The Chief Justice argued that Merryman should have been brought before Mary-land's civil authorities, and he accused the military authorities of having gone "far beyond the mere suspension of the privilege of the writ of habeas corpus." [42] Force of arms had been used to "thrust aside the judicial authorities and officers to whom the constitution [*sic*] has confined the power of duty of interpreting and administering the laws," and "there was no reason whatever for the interposition of the military."[43] For this eighty-three-year-old jurist, this usurpation of authority meant that the "people of the United States are no longer living under a government of laws, but every citizen holds life, liberty and property at the will and pleasure of an army officer in whose military district he [*sic*] may happen to be found."[44] In a move that infuriated Lincoln and many of his supporters, Taney granted Merryman's habeas corpus writ.

The Chief Justice's comments brought responses from a number of Lincoln's supporters, including Horace Binney of Philadelphia,[45] Joel Parker of the Harvard law faculty,[46] and Francis Lieber of Columbia University.[47] These intellectual leaders, along with Attorney General Edward Bates, put together a number of essays, articles, and treatises that argued that the national emergency justified Lincoln's use of extraordinary military powers. Almost all of them discussed the importance of "military necessity" in times of national emergency. For example, in October of 1861, Parker wrote in the *North American Review* about the attacks on troops from Pennsylvania, the mobs who destroyed railways and bridges, and need for liberal interpretations of executive authority:

> martial law includes military law, and it exists only in time of war. . . . It has been said that it is "founded upon a paramount necessity." Of course, then, it extends as far as the necessity extends, and no further. It may be that in certain cases the military authority must judge the military exigency, so that its determination whether the military necessity exists will be conclusive; but . . . if an arbitrary force is used, having no connection with the exigency, or not within the possible scope of the necessity, the party guilty of it will be civilly responsible for his [*sic*] acts.[48]

Like Speed, Parker believed that time was of the essence, and that restrictions could be placed on those who acted illegally—any abuse of discretion could be dealt with later on. Parker was convinced that Taney's opinion in the *Merryman* case was wrong, and that only the quick actions of General Butler and his troops had prevented the city of Washington from falling into the hands of "secessionists" in Maryland and Virginia, thus preventing the "dismemberment of the Union."[49]

Throughout 1862, the Union forces suffered a number of setbacks in the Eastern theater of war.[50] In February and March of that year, the Lincoln administration barred from the mails such newspapers as the *Albany Democrat,* the *Eugene Democratic Register,* the *Los Angeles Star,* and the *San Jose Tribune.* Editors of Democratic newspapers were hit by "a sweeping order that barred their publications from the mails on April 30, 1862."[51] In the first two years of the war, there were a number of United States marshals and local jurists authorized to imprison individuals who supposedly discouraged enlistments or engaged in treasonous practices.[52] The vagueness and open-ended nature of many of the military documents used at the time meant that a person could be arrested for talking about the right of secession, commenting on the problems with conscription, or advocating that citizens vote for peace parties. The status of the person, the tone of the writings, and the tolerance of local commanders were all factors in determining whether a particular civilian had to appear before one of Lincoln's military tribunals.

As casualties mounted, some of the radical Republicans became more vocal in their demands that Lincoln issue some type of proclamation of emancipation. On April 4, 1862, the *Cincinnati Commercial* predicted that before "the first day of January, 1863, the President will declare general emancipation of the slaves of rebels a military necessity."[53] As late as September of that year the president held his ground and refused to openly advocate such policies, and he remarked that issuing such a document at that time was as "inoperative" as the "Pope's Bull against the Comet."[54] What good could come from such edicts, if he could not enforce the Constitution in the Southern states?

When Lincoln finally relented and issued the Emancipation Proclamation, this was considered to be a reversal of policy by many of his opponents. A necessitous war, fought for the purposes of maintaining the Union, was very different from one that was now going to be about the morality of slavery, the migration of former Southern laborers, or the compensation of property owners. In January of 1863, he was excoriated for engaging in tyrannical practices, and accused of usurping his executive powers. His Democratic critics in the North and East were now joined by secessionists in the South, and moderates in the West. The determined president was stung by this criticism. One contributor to a Massachusetts newspaper, the *Springfield Republican,* remarked:

> Some one sent Mr. Lincoln a batch of newspaper criticisms upon [*sic*] him and his conduct of the war last week. In speaking about it to a friend, Mr. Lincoln said, "having an hour to spare on Sunday I read this batch of editorials and when I was through reading I asked my-self, 'Abraham Lincoln, are you a man or a dog.'" . . . The editorials in question were very able, and as bitter in their criticisms upon him as they are able; yet Mr. Lincoln smiled very pleasantly as he spoke of them, though it was evident that they made a decided impression upon his mind.[55]

This was obviously not the first time the president had to deal with criticism, but now newspapers writers across the country began drafting even more inflammatory essays that came to the attention of many of the Union generals responsible for maintaining order within their jurisdictions. In the name of "necessity," any speech or newspaper that might have any bad "tendencies" could be shut down or regulated by local commanders or their soldiers. Partisan Democratic judges were able to protect some newspapers, but others were shut down, and the editors fined or imprisoned.

The battlefield stalemates and the loss of hundreds of thousands of lives led to many soap boxes across the country being used to discuss the relative merits of ending the war peacefully and allowing the South to have its independence. From an ideographic perspective, the words "liberty," "freedom," and "conciliation" were merged in narratives that talked about the rebels' rights of "independence."

The president responded by circulating his own messages. In March of 1863, Lincoln got much needed legislative help from Congress when that deliberative body decided to pass the Habeas Corpus Act, which legitimized the president's suspension of the writ "anywhere in the United States whenever, in his judgment, the public safety required it."[56] This blurred the line between martial law and military law,[57] and now defendants had to deal with two systems of law, the civil and the military.

Lincoln construed these congressional actions as symbolic acts that ratified his earlier efforts and legitimated his interpretations of his executive power in his running battle with the judiciary. Lincoln's supporters began to argue that their chief executive was judicious in his use of these powers in that he could now check the abuses of his generals as well as the enemies of the Union. Relatively few jurists followed Taney's example in *Merryman,* and Northern victories on the battlefield seemed to provide providential proof of the righteousness of the president's stand. One of Lincoln's admirers, Charles Stille, remarked that even if some minor violations of civil rights during wartime occurred, these needed to be tolerated "if we are saved from" dangers "ten-fold more fearful in the future."[58]

The president's critics responded by pointing out that Lincoln was now allowing the military to exercise control over too many regions and too many activities. The use of courts-martial tribunals for soldiers was one thing; claiming that military commissions had jurisdiction over civilians in areas that were not in immediate danger was another. The editors of the *New York World* painted this vivid scenario of the problem:

> He [the president] can send one of his countless provost-marshals into the house of the governor of a state or any other citizen, in the dead of the night, drag him [*sic*] from his bed, hustle him away under the cover of darkness, plunge him in a distant and unknown dungeon, and allow his friends to know no more of the whereabouts of his body than they would of the habitation of his soul, if, instead of imprisoning, the provost-marshal had murdered him. . . . The President is as absolute a despot as the Sultan of Turkey.[59]

As the war dragged on, these complaints were echoed in countless newspapers and journals. Writers in the border states and other regions had to avoid giving the impression that they condoned the dissemination of "opinions and sentiments" used to give "aid, comfort, and encourage those in arms against the Government." They avoiding writing about topics that might induce in "hearers a distrust of their own Government, sympathy for those in arms against it, and a disposition to resist the laws of the land."[60] At one military hearing, Captain H. R. Hill testified that he stood not more than six feet away from a defendant [Vallandigham] and heard him say that General Order No. 38 "was a base usurpation of arbitrary authority," that he despised it, and spit on it.[61]

Some of the most famous fragments we have about Lincoln's own views on the limits of freedom of expression can be found in his open letter to Erastus Corning that was written in June of 1863. In that document, the president explained that he thought there was a major difference between constitutional rights before and during wars of rebellion.[62] Lincoln argued that civilian courts had jurisdictions in cases of individual wrongdoing, but that when a large-scale rebellion was being planned by many "insurgents," the chief executive had to take drastic steps in the name of public safety. The president made the astonishing claim that rebels had been preparing the civil war for "more than thirty years," and that they had been trying to destroy the "Union, Constitution, and law."[63] Furthermore, Lincoln was sure that

> Their sympathizers pervaded all departments of the Government and nearly all communities of the people. From this material, under cover of "liberty of speech," "liberty of the press," and "habeas corpus," they hoped to keep on foot among us a most efficient corps of spies, informers, suppliers, and aiders and abettors of their cause in a thousand ways. They knew that in times such as they were inaugurating, by the Constitution itself, the [sic] "habeas corpus" might be suspended; but they also knew they had friends who would make a question as to *who* was to suspend it[64] [emphasis in original].

Feigned liberties were now being advocated at a time of real necessities.

Those who magnified the military exigencies also minimized the effectiveness of the traditional avenues of legal redress and civil appeals. In another section of the Corning letter, Lincoln argued that "[E]ven in times of peace, bands of horse-thieves and robbers frequently grow too numerous and powerful for the ordinary courts of justice."[65] The president conjured up pictures of "insurgent sympathizers" getting on juries in order to stall the prosecution of traitors, or speakers who were using "dissuasion or inducement" to encourage desertions.[66] In one popular fragment, the president opined:

Long experience has shown that armies cannot be maintained unless desertions shall be punished by the severe penalty of death. The case requires, and the law and the Constitution sanction, this punishment. Must I shoot a simple-minded soldier boy who deserts, while I must not touch a hair of a wily agitator who induces him to desert? This is none the less injurious when effected by getting a father, or brother, or friend, into a public meeting, and there working upon his feelings till he is persuaded to write the soldier boy that he is fighting in a bad cause, for a wicked Administration of a contemptible Government, too weak to arrest and punish him if he shall desert. I think that in such a case to silence the agitator, and save the boy, is not only constitutional, but withal a great mercy.[67]

The troops and leaders who jailed the thousands who disagreed perhaps shared such righteous indignation.

How could Milligan's defense team respond to these necessitous pleas? In this next segment of the chapter I provide a rhetorical analysis that looks at some of the "whiggish" fragments deployed by critics of Lincoln's policies.

Milligan, Lincoln's Critics, and the Defense Team

By 1864, the tide of battle had turned, and many commentators in various regions of the country were convinced that the Union forces would ultimately prevail. This confidence, however, did not bring an end to the alleged infractions of the military law. Critics later claimed that Lincoln and his generals were using these military regulations as a way of circumventing the principles embodied in the written Constitution, but there is some evidence that even the civil courts of the period were involved in the politics of the times. Take the case of E. N. Fuller, the editor of the *Newark Evening Journal,* who was arrested in 1864 and fined for inciting insurrection and discouraging enlistments in the Union army.[68] The following editorial is what got Fuller into trouble with the civil authorities:

It will be seen that Lincoln has called for another half million of men. Those who wish to be butchered will please step forward. All others will please stay home and defy old Abe and his minions to drag them from their families. We hope that the people of New Jersey will at once put their feet down and insist that not a man shall be forced out of the state to engage in the Abolition butchery, and swear to die at their own doors rather than march one step to fulfill the dictates of the mad, revolutionary fanaticism which has destroyed the best government the world ever saw.[69]

Moderates during this period were caught in a major ideological bind— they wanted to show their loyalty to the Northern cause and the troops who were fighting on the battlefield, but they also wanted to be able to write about conscription or a peaceful resolution to this war of rebellion. At the beginning of the conflict, President Lincoln seemed to be one the representatives of this moderate position, but eventually the radicals and the abolitionists may have influenced his positions. Abe the compromiser became Abe the promoter of total war.

With the passage of the Civil Rights Amendments many of these attacks on abolitionism and the emancipation would be forgotten—everyone's family seemed to be mythically supportive of Union policies. Yet these same arguments used by Lincoln's opponents would ironically become a part of the dissenting tradition in American politics, and the famous (or infamous, depending on one's perspective) case of *Ex parte Milligan* became a key incident in these sedimented counternarratives.

Milligan and several other defendants had to listen as governmental officials talked about their participation in a "secret society known as the Order of American Knights or Sons of Liberty" that operated in Indiana in 1863 and 1864. The Unionist prosecutors assumed the avowed goal of this organization involved the "overthrowing" of the U.S. government.[70] During this period, Milligan and his colleagues were said to be "holding communication with the enemy," "conspiring to seize munitions of war stored in the arsenals," trying to "liberate prisoners of war," "resisting the draft," "&c." All of this was taking place in a Northern state that was now being spatially described as an area "within the military lines of the army of the United States, and the theatre of military operations." Furthermore, all of this region "had been and was constantly threatened to be invaded by the enemy."[71] Given this geographical description of the war zones, it would be difficult to find any place on the North American continent that did not fall under the jurisdiction of the Union military authorities.

By the time the *Ex parte Milligan* case reached the Supreme Court, the war on the battlefield was over, but the discursive wars over the meaning of military "necessity" were just beginning. The Circuit Court that initially heard the defendants' appeals was hopelessly divided. This certified the questions that had been raised and ensured that the members of the highest court in the land would enter the fray. The U.S. Supreme Court would now have to decide if habeas corpus relief had been warranted, and they contemplated whether military commissions had jurisdiction over civilians in these cases. Furthermore, these jurists had to comment on whether the defendants had been denied any of their constitutional rights, like the right to a jury trial.[72] Rehnquist contends that the "basic argument of the petitioners was that, even in times of war, civilians could not be tried before a military commission so long as the civil courts were open for business."[73] This, however, was just one shard in a complex mosaic of conflicting legal visions.

For many of Milligan's contemporaries, this was clearly an epic battle between various branches of government, and its significance can be gauged by the legal names associated with both sides in this legal confrontation. The government would be represented before the Supreme Court by Henry Stanberry, Benjamin Butler, and Attorney General James Speed, while the prisoners would be defended by Joseph McDonald, David Field, James A. Garfield, and Jeremiah Black.[74] Both sides provided legal briefs and judicial arguments based on many of the claims that had been circulating in the public sphere for almost a decade.

The government took the position that it should be the chief executive who had the right to make many of the key decisions regarding the establishment of military commissions, the enlargement of martial law, and the application of military law. In their written brief, Speed and Butler opined that the correct definitions of these concepts, along with an understanding of the "laws of war," were supposed to be defined by those who were in the heat of battle:

Offences against military laws are determined by tribunals established in the acts of the legislature which create these laws—such as courts-martial and courts of inquiry. The officer executing martial law is at the same time supreme legislator, supreme judge, and supreme executive. As necessity makes his will the law, he only can define and declare it; and whether or not it is infringed, and of the extent of the infraction, he alone can judge. . . . It would be impossible for the commanding general of an army to investigate each fact which might be supposed to interfere with his movements, endanger his safety, aid his enemy, or bring disorder and crime into the community under his charge.[75]

Given this type of argument, where would one look for historical precedents and stories that support such claims? Why would the Attorney General and his colleagues need to be able to point to those domestic and colonial positions that were taken by those who needed a lot of discretionary power? No wonder that in these "tory" stories of military necessity, the representatives of the government's position quoted the now familiar claim of Wellington's (see chapter one) that it was the will of the commander that was key.[76] Major André's trial before Washington's board of inquiry (chapter two) was also used as one of the examples that showed how Americans had accepted the fact that some offenses could be tried in front of military commissions.

From an ideographic perspective, it was supposed to be the "sovereignty" of the American commander in chief that was key. The defendants had violated the "the laws of war,"[77] and the president and his generals thus needed to delegate authority to military tribunals so they could maintain order and control all "warlike activities." Legally, they felt there were a vast number of domestic and international precedents that could be used to legitimate their use of coercive force in exigent situations. For example, did not some of the constitutional amendments mention that "well-regulated militia" were "necessary to the security of a free state"?[78] Ben Butler—certainly no stranger to controversy—vividly outlined the government's position:

We do not desire to exalt the martial above the civil law. . . . We demand only that when the law is silent; when justice is overthrown; when the life of the Nation is threatened by foreign foes that league and wait and watch without, to unite with domestic foes within, who had seized almost half the territory; and more than half the resources, of the Government . . . when the traitor within plots to bring into its peaceful communities the braver rebel who fights without; when the judge is deposed; when the juries are dispersed; when the sheriff, the executive officer of the law, is powerless; when the bayonet is called in as final arbiter . . . then we ask that martial law may so prevail.[79]

It would be difficult to find any more eloquent summary of the "tory" position on civilian and military relations.

When interdisciplinary scholars study the *Ex parte Milligan* case, they usually spotlight the traditional positions that were taken by Justices Davis and Chase, but it is a shame that the available arguments of the lawyers have not been scrutinized, because they show us how these "extra-judicial" commentaries can add some much needed insight into some of the rhetorical factors that may have influenced the judges' decisions.

In this particular situation, it is clear that the three major appellate lawyers for *Milligan*—Field, Garfield, and Black—had done an incredible job of researching the extant Anglo-American literatures on military necessity, the use of martial law, and military commissions. The narratives they presented mixed together idealistic with pragmatic arguments, and between them they covered just about every case that could possibly be raised by those who supported the "whig" position on civilianization of the military.

David Dudley Field started things off for the petitioner by noting that this was a case that involved discipline in the camps of the "power of a conqueror." Since the lower Circuit had acted under the fourteenth section of the Judiciary Act of 1789 and the Habeas Corpus Act of 1863, Milligan was well within his rights, and the Supreme Court had jurisdiction to hear the case.[80] Not surprisingly, Field's whiggish arguments focused attention on the Anglo-American cases that showcased the power of Parliaments and Congresses during times of peace and war. "Let it also be remembered," he noted "that Indiana, at the time of this trial, was a peaceful State; the courts were all open; their processes had not been interrupted; the laws had their full sway."[81] Military officials might have jurisdiction over members of the army or navy, but these were "simple citizens." Field claimed that if a person looked at the history of the founder's discussions of military commissions, they would find that these were initially only advisory "boards" made up of military officers. The first mention of the phrase "military commission" that could be tied to an act came with the "act of July 22, 1861, where the general commanding a separate department, or a detached army, was authorized to appoint a military board, or commission, of not less than three, or more than five officers, to examine the qualifications and conduct of commissioned officers or volunteers."[82] Field averred that if the Supreme Court justices looked at the four acts of Congress that mentioned military commissions, they would find that most of these talked about spies and members of the military service, and they were not talking about the "organization, regulation, or jurisdiction" of the commissions.[83] The Court needed to look at some of the other constitutional documents that were in existence, and the jurists needed to hear about the British history of some of these commissions.

This was a brilliant legal maneuver, because it moved the debates away from the powers of Lincoln and the perceived exigencies of the Civil War, and toward the study of narratives that showed the historical *abuse* of military authority. Field could now use language that talked about "usurpation," the limits that had historically been placed on the "will" of Kings and Queens, of how nations needed to respect the constitutional rights that must have existed even in times of war. Moreover, he could talk about how the Founders were so worried about executive power they put the control of domestic violence primarily in the hands of the states. If one looked "upon the text of the original Constitution, as it stood when it was ratified, there is no color for the assumption that the President, without act of Congress, could create military commissions for the trial of persons not military, for any cause or under any circumstances whatever."[84]

After arguing that the Bill of Rights was filled with restrictions on executive power, Field claimed that the Attorney General and his colleagues were trying to defend military necessities based on "martial law," which he considered to be "the will of the commanding officer . . . nothing more, nothing less."[85] At this point in his presentation, he is taking one of his adversary's positions on this topic and twisting it to his advantage. If Speed and Butler were going to talk about martial law, they needed to consider some of the limits that had been placed on the "usages of war, or the *jus belli,* accepted as part of the law of nations, and extended from national to all belligerents."[86] Field elaborated by noting:

> What is ordinarily called martial law is no law at all. Wellington, in one of his despatches from Portugal, in 1810, in his speech on the Ceylon affair, so describes it. Let us call the thing by its right name; it is not martial law, but martial rule. And when we speak of it, let us speak of it as abolishing all law, and substituting the will of the military commander, and we shall give a true idea of the thing, and be able to reason about it with a clear sense of what we are doing. Another expression, much used in relation to the same subject, has led also to misapprehension; that is, the declaration, or proclamation, of martial rule; as if a formal promulgation made any difference. It makes no difference whatever.[87]

This is the type of whiggish position that revived the fears of civilians who worried about "feigned" necessities (chapter one). Field, like many defenders of civil liberties, admitted there were times when pressures "of necessity, real or supposed," existed, but he was convinced it was courts and juries who had the right to judge "the correctness" of such conclusions: "The creation of a commission or board to decide or advise upon the subject gives no increased sanction to the act. As necessity compels, so that necessity alone can justify it."[88]

Field, perhaps sensing that he needed to include the Americans in his narratives about military necessity, asked that the Court look at what the Founders said about "military usurpation." In some very moving passages, he talks of how the Declaration of Independence had included grievances against the King of Great Britain's attempt "to render the military independent of and superior to the civil power." The freedom-loving colonialists were said to be living at a time when they saw how General Gage in Boston and Lord Dunmore in Virginia were using arguments about necessity in their imposition of martial law. Many of the state constitutions were therefore written in ways that tried to control any future abuses of executive power.[89] As far as Field was concerned, all of this evidence tended to show that "from the day when the answer of the sovereign was given in assent to the petition of right, courts-martial for the trial of civilians, upon the authority of the crown alone, have always been held illegal."[90]

Standing by itself, Field's presentation must have been an incredibly powerful oration, but when you add the arguments presented by James Garfield, you get some sense of just why Davis and the other justices wrote what they did in *Ex parte Milligan*. Garfield reiterated many of the points made by Field about the Founders, and he supplemented these arguments with tales of military abuse in colonial situations. He lamented the fact that when "personal rights are merged in the will of the commander in chief," what you have is "organized despotism." After all, did not the "first law of the Revolutionary Congress," which was "passed September 20th, 1776," say that "no officer or soldier should be kept in arrest more than eight days without being furnished with the written charges and specifications against" him?[91] Garfield was sure that

> To maintain the legality of the sentence here, opposite counsel are compelled not only to ignore the Constitution, but to declare it suspended—its voice lost in war—to hold that from the 5th of October, 1864, to the 9th of May, 1865, martial law alone existed in Indiana; that it silenced not only the civil courts, but all the laws of the land, and even the Constitution itself; and that during this silence the executor of martial law could lay his hand upon every citizen; could not only suspend the writ of habeas corpus, but could create a court which should have the exclusive jurisdiction over the citizen to try him, sentence him, and put him [sic] to death.[92]

Within this defense narrative, for five hundred years, various "Anglo-Saxons" had carefully drawn a line between civil and martial law.

In their own ways both Field and Garfield had provided some interesting commentaries on the problems with martial law and military commissions, but it seems as though their colleague Jeremiah Black was the most eloquent of the three. It would be his peroration in *Ex parte Milligan* that would be republished in miscellaneous works and collections of great speeches. His 1866 arguments would be regarded as some of the classic defenses of Anglo-American civil liberties.

During his argument before the Supreme Court, Black complemented the work of his colleagues by developing a narrative that put the spotlight on Milligan and his trials and tribulations. This lawyer characterized the individuals who sat on the Union military tribunals as interlopers who were "connected in no way whatever with the Army or Navy." These supposed busybodies "dragged" his client in court, at a time when Indiana had "social and legal" organizations that "had never been disturbed by any war or insurrection." Black admitted that the commissioners themselves were not on trial in this case (implying that they could or should be!), so he was willing to be charitable and focus his attention on the issue of "jurisdiction" in the *Milligan* case.[93]

Black then shifted gears and recontextualized the case as one that pitted the judicial forces of the Enlightenment against the allegedly dark forces of the military. He asserted that the parties who formed these tribunals were trying to take on the type of powers that resembled the old "ecclesiastical tribunal." Within this narrative, some of Lincoln's former department secretaries were acting like "clergymen" who wanted to convict anyone who prayed in a "fashion inconsistent with the supposed safety of the State."[94] This deflected attention away from the mythic "Order of American Knights," and put the government officials on the defensive. Black vilified those who were willing to treat "political errors" as crimes that were punishable by military commissions, and he read from a recent Attorney General report that claimed the military could "take and kill, try and execute" persons who "had no sort of connection with the Army or Navy."[95] Moreover, Black was adamant that these types of military arguments had been around since at least the time of Charles I and the revolution of 1688:

> All history proves that public officers of any Government, when they are engaged in a severe struggle to retain their places, become bitter and ferocious, and hate those who oppose them, even in the most legitimate way, with a rancor which they never exhibit toward actual crime. This kind of malignity vents itself in prosecutions for political offenses, sedition, conspiracy, libel, and treason, and the charges are generally founded upon the information of hireling spies and common delators [*sic*], who made merchandise of their oaths and trade in the blood of their fellow men.[96]

This last point must have really struck a nerve, because the jurists who were hearing this case knew that some of the evidence that had been presented in the *Milligan* case—and that would survive as a part of the court records—came from spies who had been richly paid by their Union employers.

Many generations of American scholars and jurists have indicated that they felt puzzled when they read the decision, but this case looks very transparent when we compare the arguments of the defense lawyers with the rhetoric that appears in the *Milligan* decision itself. Many of us may have underestimated the social agency of Jeremiah Black and the defense attorneys, and the suasory impact of the narratives that were presented in front of the U.S. Supreme Court. The lawyers for the petitioner were not just quoting passages from Hale or Blackstone that contained propositional phrases; they were also infusing these passages with highly evocative rhetorical figurations that aligned the Founders—and these jurists—with the whiggish tradition that protected the civilianization of the military.

Milligan's attorneys did not make the same mistake that had been made by the Indiana Democrats who had been talking about states' rights, the right to secede, and so forth. These types of arguments carried little weight in the aftermath of the Civil War. What Milligan's lawyers realized is that they had to find a way of allowing the members of the Supreme Court to be performative defenders of more generalized rights. At the same time, they had to come up with counternarratives that could withstand the necessitarian tales that were going to be told about the Anglo-Saxon traditions that prioritized inherent rights and executive power during times of war and rebellion. All of these documents needed to be interpreted by jurists who understood that unpopular petitioners faced ex post facto laws, arrests without warrants, compulsion in testifying, indefinite imprisonment, irregular courts, partial juries, and secret trials.[97]

Black's reminiscing also allowed the defendants to be cast as victims rather than criminals who resembled the Saxons fighting the Normans, the critics of James II, or the stalwarts who stood in the path of "court sycophants and party hacks."[98] Such arguments may seem trivial or silly in today's modern legalistic world, but in the rhetorical culture of the post-emancipation years, these figurations tied together a number of key cultural and legal tropes and principles. Black was able to tell his listeners that he knew of no book that could be "found in any library to justify the assertion that military tribunals may try a citizen at a place where the courts were open." Furthermore, he knew he was fighting an ancient and well-entrenched foe:

> There you have a rule of conduct denounced by all law, human and divine as pernicious in policy and false in morals. See how it applies to this case. Here we have three men whom it was desirable to remove out of this world, but there was no proof on which any court would take their lives; therefore it was necessary, and being necessary it was right and proper, to create an illegal tribunal which would put them to death without proof. . . . Nothing that the worst men ever propounded has produced such oppression, misgovernment, and suffering as this pretense of State necessity. A great authority calls it "The tyrant's devilish plea," and the common honesty of all mankind has branded it with everlasting infamy.[99]

Black did not need to provide any citations for this famous phrase. By then it was an old canard, hundreds of years old, and many governmental officials had used it.

The Supreme Court's Decision-Making in *Milligan*

Legal commentators today think the *Milligan* case sets the standards for several key legal principles: the importance of open civil courts, the need for federal court review of military commissions, and the differences between members of the military and civilians.[100] But these propositions capture only a part of the letter and spirit of the decision. When Justice David Davis began writing the majority opinion in *Ex parte Milligan*,[101] he knew this was a case that went to the "very framework of government and the fundamental principles of American liberty."[102] Since at least as far back as the Judiciary Act of 1789, petitioners were granted the right to ask for a writ of habeas corpus, and the "certificate" division of opinion at the Circuit Court provided the Supreme Court with jurisdiction to hear the case.[103] Moreover, Justice Davis believed the entire nation needed to know if the "exigence of the times" justified the president's "suspension" of the great writ of habeas corpus.[104] They were therefore relying on a definition of judicial power that came from "Article III of the Constitution, and on the Sixth Amendment guarantee of the right to a jury trial."[105]

In Milligan's application for release from imprisonment, he had alleged that he was a citizen of Indiana, and that he had never been in the military or naval service. Davis underscored the fact that Milligan had been a citizen of Indiana for twenty years, and he explained how the defendant found himself arrested, imprisoned, tried, convicted, and sentenced to be hanged by a military commission organized under the direction of the leading military commander of the district of Indiana.[106]

In this interesting interpretation of Anglo-Saxon legal history, the written Constitution supposedly outlines the nature, scope, and limits of the power of "necessity"—an interpretation that directly counters the claims of those who treat it as an extra-judicial power. Davis was not denying that real emergencies existed or that the government did not need a great deal of power—what he was arguing was that the use of the plea of necessity did not automatically mean that governments could suspend key constitutional guarantees. Simply arguing that the chief executive had some power under "unwritten criminal codes" or the "laws and usages of war" was not going to nullify the written words of the Founders.[107] Since the facts showed that in Indiana the "Federal authority was always unopposed," this implied that the criminal courts in that state were always open. This included the Circuit Court, which needed no bayonets to protect it.[108]

From an ideographic perspective, Davis was arguing that "liberty" could not "be frittered away on any plea of state or political necessity."[109] If the entire country could be divided up into military districts at the "will" of the generals or the president, then the person in authority could use the "plea of necessity" and "substitute military force for and to the exclusion of the laws."[110] For Davis, an unfettered "martial law" and "civil liberties" were mutually exclusive ideals. During wartime there may be situations that allowed for the imposition of martial law, but as soon as the war was over, talk of emergencies needed to give way to discussions of civil matters. "The necessity," argued Davis, "must be actual and present; the invasion real," and of the type that "effectually closes the courts and deposes the civil administration."[111]

It is at this point in the opinion where the whiggish narratives told by Field, Garfield, and Black provided some of the fragments that went into the majority opinion in *Ex parte Milligan*. Davis talks of how the "Revolution Fathers" objected to General Gage's declaration of martial law in Boston, and the Virginia Assembly's attack on the assumed powers of Governor Dunmore of Virginia.[112] Scholars in search in propositional "rules of law" may dismiss these narratives as "mere rhetoric," but they formed a substantive part of the entire *Ex parte Milligan* atmosphere.

Interestingly enough, it seems Davis did share many Northerners' views on the existence of dangerous conspiracies in the border states. He implied that an impartial jury might have convicted Milligan, and that the petitioner might have deserved some severe punishment:

> Conspiracies like these, at such a juncture, are extremely perilous; and those concerned in them are dangerous enemies to their country, and should receive the heaviest penalties of the law, as an example to deter others from similar criminal conduct. It is said the severity of the laws caused them; but Congress was obliged to enact severe laws to meet the crisis; and as our highest civil duty is to serve our country when in danger, the late war has proved that rigorous laws, when necessary, will be cheerfully obeyed by a patriotic people, struggling to preserve the rich blessings of a free government.[113]

Given these positions, it is conceivable that Davis might have upheld a similar sentence if it had come from a civil system of justice.

Conclusion

Even though the primary, propositional focus of the *Ex parte Milligan* case centered on issues involving habeas corpus relief, this was a much more complex affair where both elites and citizens were writing about the existence of conspiracies, the need for loyalty in turbulent times, or the validity of necessitarian pleas. Today we have legal scholars talking about the importance of "open" courts and importance of habeas corpus relief, but we have occasionally forgotten some of the other parts of these complex "whig" tales.

For example, near the end of his book on civil liberties during wartime, Justice Rehnquist implies that we are living at a time when we need to pay as much attention to the pleas of necessity as we do the pleas that are made in the name of protecting civil liberties. He is more optimistic than I am in his discussion of how President Lincoln was able to maintain a nice balance between civil liberties and military duties. Rehnquist admires the way this wartime president made difficult decisions that showed that he was unwilling to "risk losing the Union that gave life to the Constitution."[114] Unless I am mistaken, the Chief Justice treats Lincoln's *perceptions* of an emergency as if they were accurate reflections of the conditions of the times. He also accepts as fact that the suspension of the writ of habeas corpus was "necessary to guard against further destruction of the railroad route" that was "used to transport those troops" through Baltimore.[115] Such a position begs the question of whether an actual emergency existed in the first place. It also ignores the ways that press restrictions may have helped exacerbate the tensions that existed between 1862 and 1865. As one critic has remarked, "Military necessity does not explain itself."[116]

Other defenders of Lincoln's decisions regarding civil rights take a slightly different approach, and claim that this was one president who understood the primacy of individual liberties. Nat Hentoff, for example, espoused the belief that Lincoln was "mindful of the First Amendment" and that he was hesitant to act against that part of the press he thought was aiding the Confederate rebellion. He therefore reluctantly ordered that some newspapers be closed.[117] More recently, Mark Neely Jr. has tried to rehabilitate the sixteenth president's tarnished reputation by arguing that "a majority of the arrests would have occurred whether the writ was suspended or not."[118] Unfortunately, Neely sidesteps the question of the legitimacy of these speech and press restrictions.

The *Ex parte Milligan* opinions were written by jurists who shared Lincoln's Unionist visions—five of them had been his appointees.[119] When these commentaries are juxtaposed to more radical "tory" notions of martial law, they appear to be liberal and respectful of civil liberties, but they were written in ways that made it clear that during wartime both executives and legislatures were going to be given a lot of deference by the judiciary.

On balance, I have to say that I join those critics who believe the Lincoln administration did a poor job of handling the constitutional issues raised during the Civil War. As Craig Smith and Stephanie Makela noted in 1996,

Lincoln's discourse "supplies examples of rhetoric bordering on a clear and present danger in wartime."[120] At times, the president did allow the imposition of martial law in some regions of the country, even when the civil courts were still functioning. Many generals simply asserted that an emergency existed, and then they proceeded to make auxiliary arguments about the need for confiscation of property or massive detentions. Thousands of citizens were arrested and fined in situations where even the *perception* of the threat could not be questioned.

Moreover, an examination of the president's discourse—and that of many of his followers—illustrates how many of these necessitous arguments were tied to outlandish ideas of decade-long conspiracies. Where do you see Davis or Milligan's lawyers defending even the remotest of possibilities that the nation needed to hear about peace or reconciliation? Their complaint was that he was not tried in civil court, or that Congress had not exercised certain types of authority. There was little interrogation of the linkages being made between open criticism and overt acts. Lorraine Williams once remarked:

> During the Civil War the government under Lincoln carried its authority far beyond the normal restraint of civil justice. As a result of constitutional interpretations by the President and his Attorney General, Lincoln's war power included the following: the determination of the existence of rebellion, calling forth the militia to suppress it, exercising the right to increase the regular army, suspension of the habeas corpus privilege, proclamation of martial law, the right to place persons under arrest without warrant, the right to seize the property of citizens, the right to spend money from the United States Treasury without Congressional appropriation, the right to suppress the newspapers, and the control of the telegraph lines radiating from Washington.[121]

Were all of these actions really justified on the basis of "necessity"?

I believe we need a dose of healthy skepticism when the tyrant's plea comes our way. Perhaps some of the best advice on how to handle the plea of military necessity comes from J. G. Randall, who admitted that there were times where the public "safety, perhaps the life of the nation, may require the exertion of force against civilians."[122] Yet Randall also admitted that these would be rare occasions, and that scholars needed to be aware that there were times when this plea would be "abused or wrongfully interpreted."[123]

As I will argue throughout this book, perhaps we need to remember both the letter and spirit of the *Ex parte Milligan* decision. We too need to think about the linkages that are made between the necessity of war and the need for tribunals, the openness and ability of civil courts, the legitimacy of certain actions that are taken in the name of the tyrant's plea of necessity. In our rush to embrace the lessons of *Ex parte Quirin,* we have forgotten the eloquence—and pragmatism—of those who defended Milligan.

5

The Military Trial
of Major Henry Wirz

there has been no time . . . since this trial was held when I felt that I
owed an apology to anyone, not even to the Almighty, for having voted
to hang Henry Wirz by the neck until he was dead.

—John H. Stibbs, 1911

Reading of the death warrant prior to execution of Captain Henry Wirz, November
1865. Courtesy of the Library of Congress.

Michael Griffin once argued that many of the photographic images taken during the Civil War[1] provide us with some "discernable narrative allusions" filled with "symbolic moments of death, sacrifice, and patriotism,"[2] and Robert Hariman and John Lucaites are certainly on to something when they remind us that select iconic photos can coordinate "multiple transcriptions" of key historical events that are tied to some of the "contradictions in public life."[3] This particular visual representation of the hanging of a former Confederate officer, taken by Mathew Brady or one of his assistants, may no longer resonate with modern audiences, but during the nineteenth century it was viewed by many Americans as a realistic portrayal of some of the sacrifices that had to be made before the nation could heal its wounds and go on with the business of enacting the Radical Reconstruction.

In many different ways, this iconic martial image was more than just a visual register that provided posterity with an accurate depiction of some historical fact; it was also a fragmentary part of the "culture and constituents of a collective memory."[4] It supplied nonverbal evidence that some military necessities demand drastic actions, where violations of the "laws of war" bring swift retribution. This particular photograph was taken in the Old Capital Prison Yard in Washington, DC, on a cool November day in 1865, and the phalanx of soldiers who watched these proceedings were some of the social actors who would be involved in the performative rituals associated with a complex legal affair. The solitary figure standing at the top of the scaffold is Henry Wirz, and he would be remembered as one of the worst American war criminals.[5] The Union forces who won the bloody Civil War on the battlefields now wanted to make sure their monumental achievements would be etched in the minds of future generations. The prison yard and a nearby courtroom would become key forums for symbolic memorializing, where Wirz—and his beloved South—paid the ultimate price for legal and moral transgressions.

In the wake of any mass atrocity of traumatic war, all societies have to make decisions and walk the "path between vengeance and forgiveness,"[6] and during the post–Civil War years diverse communities had to make agonizing choices about the shape of the nation's scholarly histories and public memories.[7] David Blight contends that with the passage of time, some Americans would forget that the Civil War involved moral crusades,[8] but during the fall of 1865 many audiences remembered quite vividly the righteousness of the Union cause. They wanted revenge, and in the aftermath of war the courtroom served as an outlet for many forms of witnessing—those who were physically and mentally scarred could face their tormentors, those who fought the bloody battles could explain their martial decisions, and the citizens who survived the war could remember the sacrifices of dead loved ones. In the process, these "pedagogical spectacles" served as judicial forums for commenting on individual guilt and collective responsibility.[9]

Wirz eventually was found guilty of conspiracy and murder, but it is interesting to note that his contemporaries did not always agree on the legality or desirability of these proceedings. A trial that was supposed to focus exclusive attention on the transgressions of the South was turned into a public space where various communities could voice their opinions about the causes of the war, the end of prisoner exchanges, the move toward total warfare, and the granting of blanket amnesties. Wirz and his lawyers tried to save this commandant's life by arguing that he was simply obeying Confederate orders, and that natural "necessities" prevented him from providing adequate care; these types of defenses ended up raising a host of questions about both Union and Confederate wartime activities.

Many Unionists tried to end some of this questioning by ignoring the defense pleas and underscoring the horrors of Fort Sumter. For the victors, the *Wirz* trial was turned into a ritualistic proceeding that preserved the memories of some fifteen thousand soldiers who died at a place that would forever be remembered as "Andersonville."[10] Wirz endured several months of military proceedings,[11] and as he walked to the gallows he allegedly told the commanding Federal officer: "I know what orders are, Major. And I am being hanged for obeying them."[12]

This was certainly not the view of the hundreds of Washingtonians who held spectator's tickets, or who sat perched on the nearby elm trees or rooftops near the prison yard. Fighting troops in open battle for a misguided "lost" cause was one thing, but cursing, slapping, starving, and shooting prisoners were considered to be martial offenses. It was rumored that perhaps the Confederate commandant could save his own neck if he implicated Jefferson Davis in these Andersonville atrocities.[13] Wirz, however, refused to compromise, and he allegedly viewed this as a treasonous offer. He paid the ultimate price for his intransigence, and after his death the Unionists added insult to injury when they buried him alongside George Atzerodt, one of the executed Lincoln conspirators.[14]

For more than a century and a half, the afterimages of the hanging of Captain Wirz and the horrors of Andersonville have become a part of a plethora of new narratives about military justice and judicial fairness.[15] When some Northerners defended these proceedings as forums that helped provide closure for the traumas associated with the Civil War, Southern critics responded by arguing that this was a "political" trial— detractors now had concrete evidence that the Radical Republicans and their allies were not really interested in justice, forgiveness, or recon- struction.

As various generations pass down their memories and histories of the *Wirz* trial, they inevitably refashion both the factual and legal frameworks that describe and explain these proceedings. These retrospective recollec- tions, notes one scholar, provide us with illustrations of how some of these "enduring historical myths" can "help win battles in the present."[16] Over time, Andersonville remembrances have been used for numerous nineteenth- and twentieth-century needs—they helped explain Northern war aims, they exonerated Southern leaders, they supplied the rationale for memorial plaques and monuments, and they were even used to justify governmental payment of pensions for veterans. Between 1862 and 1921, more than two hundred books, pamphlets, and magazine articles were written by former soldiers about Andersonville and Wirz,[17] and these have been supplemented by a growing number of photographic collections,[18] fictional novels,[19] plays,[20] books, and movies.[21] Governmental agencies be- gan collecting and recategorizing material on the trial,[22] and for a time, one's perceptions of the *Wirz* trial served as a barometer that gauged one's views of the morality of the Civil War or Southern Reconstruction.

As with several of the cases I have selected for analysis in this book, some of these altered shards of legal histories and cultural memories are receiving renewed attention during our own twenty-first-century "war" on terrorism. This particular case is quoted more than the U.S.-Dakota war trials, and less than the *Quirin* and *Yamashita* cases. The *Wirz* case is another one of those linear precedents often quoted when officials need a formalistic rationale that will help them legitimate the use of executive military commissions. Griffin Bell, who appeared as a witness before Congress in November of 2001, had this to say about the relevance of the earlier proceedings:

> Did the president [Bush] have the power to issue this order setting up military tribunals? I don't think there's any doubt that he had the power. I don't think there's anything irregular about it. I don't think there's anything illegitimate about it. I picked out three cases. First there's the revolution. Major John André was tried by a military tribunal. He was a negotiator with the traitor Benedict Arnold. After the Civil War, the commander of the Andersonville prison camp, Captain Wirz, was tried by a military tribunal in Washington although he lived in Georgia, and was executed. . . . So, military tribunals are not uncommon in a time of war.[23]

Again, we are not provided with any details about the trial, and we get very little context that helps us understand why civil courts could not try this person. The fact that earlier generations simply used "military tribunals" made them "uncommon," and ergo, legitimate.

Given the rhetorical importance of this case, we can readily see why modern audiences recall different aspects of the proceedings. In some contemporary press accounts of this military affair, the former commandant of Andersonville is remembered as the person who abused "POWs" and violated the laws of war.[24] At other times, the *Wirz* case is used as a judicial container for the legal principle that qualifications can be placed on the "superior orders" defense.[25]

While the question of Wirz's guilt or innocence may be part of any critical inquiry, my primary focus in this chapter will be on the generational, communicative usages of these proceedings. In order to help accomplish these related tasks, this chapter has been divided into six major sections. In the first segment I extend some of David Blight's theoretical work by noting how the debates surrounding the *Wirz* trial were connected to a series of competing Civil War memories.[26] The second portion extends this analysis by illustrating how emancipationist visions impacted the framing of the narratives told about Andersonville before the *Wirz* trial. The third part spotlights the discourses that circulated during the trial itself, while the fourth part focuses attention on the Northern defenses of this military tribunal. In the fifth section of the chapter, I illustrate how many Southerners deployed competing reconciliationist visions in their attempted recharacterizations of Wirz, who was now portrayed as a Union scapegoat and martyr for the Lost Cause. I then discuss the heuristic importance of this case for our theoretical debates about legal memories, and our modern discussions of military necessity and military tribunals.

Critical Legal Analyses, Civil War Rhetorical Histories, and the Power of Collective Memories

By now, readers may have sensed that I am firmly convinced that *both* academic legal histories and public memories are rhetorical in nature, meaning that they gain their material significance when audiences accept them as truthful facts or objective realities. As motivated human beings we have to make decisions about morality, legality, and truthfulness, but we do not make these decisions in a vacuum. We all have to make selective decisions that depend on the persuasiveness of particular "socially framed"[27] belief systems, and even our histories are inextricably tied to our social memories.[28]

Clearly there are material realities that exist independent of language, and there are actual events that have transpired, but the symbolic meanings we attach to those objective realities are rhetorical in nature. The past does not speak for itself. E. Culpepper Clark and Raymie McKerrow, for example, remind us that "history" involves public deliberation and argumentation in that the claims that suture together the past and present are based on "selective" remembrances that validate certain thoughts and actions.[29] Kathleen Turner similarly remarks that the critic who studies "rhetorical history" as "social construction" needs to pay attention to the ways that "rhetorical processes have constructed social reality at particular times and particular contexts," while simultaneously acknowledging that the very "nature of the study of history" is itself a "rhetorical process."[30]

As I have argued in earlier chapters, critical scholars who adopt this type of stance now have to pay attention to the contested nature of both academic histories and public memories, and they join the ranks of the interdisciplinary researchers who are studying the "return of 'repressed memories' of the abused individual," the "black holes" in a nation's recollection of its past, and the "identity politics" associated with vexing collective memories.[31] For example, they might keep track of both legal and extra-legal interests as they chart the "didactic moralism" and "strategies of remembrance"[32] that appear in legal sites of memory, where "historical" narratives of "truth" are "aimed at securing reconciliation and social solidarity in the aftermath of genocide."[33]

These insights are especially important when we review the *Wirz* proceedings, because the "drive to build the nation after the Civil War" involved the paradoxical processes of unifying and dividing, consolidating and fracturing, remembrance and amnesia."[34] While Union soldiers and politicians wanted to turn the *Wirz* proceedings into a *lieu de mémoire* (a part of our collective memory), their former adversaries wanted more organized forgetting, ensconced in *lieux d'oubli*—sites that are "expressly avoided because of the disturbing affect" of their invocation.[35] With the passage of time, the traumas experienced on the battlefield or behind the lines helped frame parts of key scripts that influenced the trajectories of generational memories. Both defenders and detractors of the *Wirz* proceedings provided some of the rhetorical materials used in future debates about civil rights, the protection of personal property, the duties of combatants, and the limits of total warfare. "The shift from slavery to freedom precipitated by the Civil War," argues Kirk Savage, "was the cataclysmic event and central dilemma of the century," one that "reverberated throughout public space in countless ways."[36]

In this chapter I will continue to provide an interrogation of some of the usages of the ideographs "necessity" and "military necessity," but I would like to tie these units of analysis to some of the larger social frames that may have influenced the interpretations and valences associated with those terms during this period. While there are a number of heuristic approaches that could be taken in the study of these Civil War memories and courtroom rhetorics, one of the most intriguing possibilities involves the decoding of the overarching narratives that resonated with postwar audiences. As Eric Foner explains:

Two understandings of how the Civil War should be remembered collided in post-bellum America. One was the "emancipationist" vision hinted at by Lincoln in the Gettysburg Address when he spoke of the war as bringing a rebirth of the Republic in the name of freedom and equality. The other was a "reconciliationist" memory that emphasized what the two sides shared in common, particularly the valor of individual soldiers, and suppressed thoughts of the war's causes and the unfinished legacy of Emancipation. . . . Another way of putting it is that the Confederacy lost on the battlefield but won the war over memory.[37]

Foner's assessment may provide us with an accurate overview of the rhetorical power of the "reconciliationist" script during the last quarter of the nineteenth century, but if we go back a little further we find that the "South was remade in the North's image and harshly punished, the freedpeople [*sic*] enfranchised as citizens, and the Constitution rewritten."[38]

For more than a dozen years, Northern generals and thousands of their troops carried out the reconstruction of the nation, and many of the victors saw this work as a fulfillment of the promises that had been made when the president announced the Emancipation Proclamation. As Barry Schwartz once noted in his study of Lincoln's memory, the "South's vices" dominated the rhetoric of the times, and the Union president's assassination "was a piece with other Confederate atrocities: deliberately starving prisoners, shooting wounded men, mutilating corpses . . . spreading pestilence, burning towns and villages." "Denunciations of the South," Schwartz explains, were tied to commentaries on "retaliation" and "justice."[39]

What began as a legal proceeding that looked into the culpability of a single commandant turned into a protracted debate about the motivations of the Southern leaders, the inhumane activities of Southern prison wardens, and the degenerate nature of the Southern methods of waging war. Donald Bloxham once noted that various "war crimes trials" provide "didactic" lessons that are supposed to illustrate to "conquered peoples the benefits" of legal process,[40] but in this case many of these audiences refused to accept the legitimacy of this particular "judicial memory."[41] Wirz and his supporters soon found that during these traumatic periods they

would be caught between ideologies that focused on forgiveness and reconciliation, and those that were framed around notions of retribution and
revenge.

Emancipationist Prefigurations and
the Circulation of Andersonville Tales, 1864–65

Long before the capture of Wirz and his fateful trip to Washington, DC,
reporters throughout the country spread many rumors that alerted readers to the horrible conditions in both the Union and the Confederate
prison camps. Sometimes reporters lumped together statistics from all of
the Southern camps, and at other times they singled out particular places
for special attention. A variety of newspapers and popular magazines carried stories about the overcrowding, the starvation, and the atrocities that
were committed at places like Belle Isle, Libby Prison, and Salisbury. Some
of these same publications also recycled some of the gruesome photographs taken by Alexander Gardner, Timothy O'Sullivan, George Bar-
nard, and Mathew Brady.[42] Susan Sontag opined that these "photographs
of skeletal prisoners held at Andersonville inflamed public opinion," and
that these visual images reinforced the textual arguments that appeared in
the press.[43]

Returning escapees, or the lucky participants in prisoner exchanges,
provided some the most graphic reminders of the horrors of the Southern
prison camps. They appeared to be providing iconic proof of the malevo-
lent intentions of their captors and the injustice of the Confederate cause.
Walt Whitman, who always characterized this as a "Secession War," took
pen in hand to explain to his readers that

> I have seen a number of them. The sight is worse than any sight of
> battle-fields, or any collection of wounded, even the bloodiest. . . .
> Can those be *men*—those little livid brown, ash-streaked, monkey-
> looking dwarfs"—are they really not mummied, dwindled corpses?
> They lay there, most of them, quite still, but with a horrible look in
> their eyes and skinny lips (often with not enough flesh on the lips to
> cover their teeth.) Probably no more appalling sight was ever seen
> on this earth[44] [emphasis in original].

Audiences who once talked about the importance of preserving the Union or the evils of slavery could now sprinkle their discussions with commentaries on Southern violations of the laws of war.

During the first few years of the Civil War, both sides had captured tens of thousands of troops, but prisoner exchanges (cartels) reduced the number of prisoners that had to be taken care of in stockades and camps.[45] This all changed after the passage of the Emancipation Proclamation and the battle of Vicksburg. As the Northern forces gained the upper hand in 1963 and 1964, there were fewer and fewer prisoner exchanges as the warring parties disagreed on such issues as the exact numbers that should be involved in these exchanges, or whether captured African Americans would be regarded as wartime prisoners.

The rhetorical framing of any particular policy as a "military necessity" obviously impacted the continuance or termination of these various prisoner exchanges. In a famous letter sent from General Ulysses S. Grant to General Butler (dated August 18, 1864) the Union commander remarked that "If we commence a system of exchange which liberates all prisoners taken, we will have to fight on until the whole South is exterminated. If we hold those caught, they amount to no more than dead men."[46] Within this permutation of the emancipationist vision, the temporary loss of prisoner freedoms was a harsh but necessary sacrifice.

Many Federal officers and soldiers may have believed that this move toward total war would hasten the emancipatory process, but the leaders of the Confederacy were now faced with some complex logistical and moral dilemmas. If they could not exchange any more prisoners they needed to find other ways of caring for their wards, and they had to alleviate the overcrowding that existed in some of the Richmond prison camps. In February of 1864, Confederate authorities thought they would be acting humanely when they created Camp Sumter, a military outpost that would stand next to the infamous "Andersonville" prison. The location was supposed to be a nice spot for a Confederate prison—it would be far behind enemy lines, it offered a "salubrious climate,"[47] and it could be built by locals who could profit from sale of the timber. Henry Wirz, who had worked at Libby Prison in Richmond and at another facility in Tuscaloosa, assumed command of the new military prison in April of 1864.[48]

The length of the war, the Northern blockade of ports, the loss of Southern resources, and a host of other factors turned this model prison into a hellish nightmare, and Andersonville eventually housed three and four times the number of prisoners it was designed to hold. Within a matter of months, thousands were dying as Wirz and other commanders pleaded with their superiors for needed food and other supplies. John Ransom, a First Sergeant in the 9th Michigan Cavalry, recalled how he survived that 1864 summer because he "formed the habit of going to sleep as soon as the air got cooled off. . . . I wake [*sic*] up at two or three o'clock and stay awake. I then take in all of the horrors of the situation. Thousands are groaning, moaning, and crying, with no bustle of the daytime to drown it. Guards every half hour call out the time and post, and there is often a shot to make one shiver as if with the ague. . . . Have taken to building air castles of late, on being exchanged. Getting loony, I guess, same as all the rest."[49] Some fifteen thousand Union soldiers never made it home, and the vast majority were buried in graves surrounding Fort Sumter. This was out of a total of 45,613 men who were imprisoned there at one time or another.[50]

While relatively few Southern newspapers wrote about these horrid conditions, the Northern presses were filled with lurid tales of victims of dysentery, scurvy, and gangrene. Some of the lucky emissaries involved in the last prison exchanges published vignettes depicting incredible acts of personal cruelty, and city newspapers kept running lists of some of the worst death registers.[51] Many editors and readers understood the trials and tribulations of wartime life, but they were convinced that Southern leaders had shirked their moral and legal duties.

By the spring of 1865, many believed the Union was simply trying to finish up the war and move toward Reconstruction, but peace had not been formally declared. The last months of the war ruined the South, and the Confederate economy was sinking in "a sea of worthless banknotes."[52] Southern civilian and military leaders had hoped that a reconciliationist vision would guide Union policies, but the death of Lincoln and the rising power of the Radical Republicans dashed those hopes. On May 7, 1865, an anxious Wirz sent this letter to Major General J. H. Wilson, the commanding officer at Macon, Georgia:

I am a native of Switzerland, and was before the war a citizen of Louisiana; by profession a physician; like hundreds and thousands of others, I was carried away by the made storm of excitement and joined the Southern army. . . . the Commandant of the military prison at Andersonville, Ga., . . . assigned me to the command of the interior of the prison. The duties I had to perform were arduous and unpleasant. I am satisfied that no man can or will unjustly blame me for the things that happened here, and which were beyond my power to control. I do not think I ought to be held responsible for the shortness of rations; for the overcrowded state of the prison which was in itself a source of the feared mortality: for the inadequate supplies of clothing, want of shelter, & c., & c.[53]

An analysis of the trial records shows that Wirz tried to ask General Wilson for a safe conduct pass,[54] but that he would be arrested by Wilson's aide-de-camp, Captain Henry Noyes. The former Andersonville commander now had to take to a dangerous trip from Macon, Georgia, to Washington, DC, and he would eventually stand trial for a number of serious martial charges.

Blight contends that near the end of the war there were many audiences who believed in their own brand of "mystical unionism,"[55] and during the last of May of 1865, there had been several grand parades on Pennsylvania Avenue. While many of the weary soldiers finally left for their farms or homes, a few members of the Union officer corps stayed behind to help with postwar planning.[56] This was all taking place at a time when magazines and newspapers like *Harpers Weekly* still displayed engravings that provided even more evidence of wartime prisoner neglect.[57]

Lincoln's assassination simply added fuel to the fire as controversies raged over the amount of magnanimity that would be shown the vanquished.[58] The voices of those who called for moderation, forgiveness, and forgetting were now being drowned out by those who argued that Southern leaders had to be taught some harsh lessons. Judge Advocate General Joseph Holt, who believed the "common law of war" applied in "times of insurrection or rebellion," wanted to make sure all rebel conspirators, traitors, and spies would be "prosecuted to the fullest extent by military courts."[59] The "leaders of the radical" Republicans, argues Glen LaForce, "saw Henry Wirz as an ideal scapegoat, since they had been frustrated in their attempts to link Jefferson Davis with the Lincoln assassination."[60] Some of the arguments used in the *Wirz* trial would therefore serve as answers to those critics who questioned the legitimacy of the earlier proceedings.[61]

In this next section, I explain how both the prosecutorial and defense teams in the *Wirz* trial reacted to these emancipationist visions, and how some social agents talked about "military necessity," Andersonville, and Wirz during the post–Civil War period.

The *Wirz* Trial and Post–Civil War Memories of Andersonville

The *Wirz* trial began on August 23, 1865, and ended on October 24, 1865, and during that time the nine officers of the commission who served as judges heard testimony from more than 150 witnesses. An analysis of the first sections of the official transcripts shows how they were obsessed with finding evidence that would tie Andersonville to some larger Southern conspiracy. The newly formed Bureau of Military Justice had the responsibility of overseeing these proceedings, and Major General Lew Wallace was asked to head the commission. Norton Chipman became the judge advocate who represented the government's position.[62] Some of the members of this commission later became influential civil[63] and military leaders, and most were "battle-hardened veterans" who shared "Unionist" sentiments.[64] What often gets glossed over in the defenses of this tribunal is the fact that only some of them were familiar with either the U.S. military regulations or the international "laws of war."[65]

From the very beginning this seemed to be an unusual trial in that Wirz's civilian lawyers had to deal with arguments that focused on both the activities of their client and those of the Confederate leadership. The captain's first defense team, which included James Hughes, James Denver, and Charles Peck, came from a local Washington, DC, law firm, and they withdrew from the case when they received a copy of the charges on the day before the beginning of the proceedings.[66] The next team of defense lawyers, Louis Schade and Otis S. Baker, stayed on, but they too were frustrated when they confronted the challenges of legal argumentation before a military tribunal. The judge advocate had the discretionary power to decide just who could be summoned as witnesses, and he was the person who decided what defense positions would be considered relevant. The ex-confederates who tried to talk about Union conditions, the lack of prisoner exchanges, or the multiple causes of the Andersonville troubles could be characterized as biased witnesses who did not understand the dictates of American justice.

The Wirz defense team tried to employ strategies that appropriated some of the variants of the post–Civil War "reconciliationist" memories. For example, during the first few days of the trial, Baker and Schade used a defense strategy known as a dilatory plea, so they could question the jurisdiction of the commission, the wording of the charges of conspiracy, and the severity of the charges against the accused. They began by arguing that this commission had no legal grounds to try Captain Wirz, because he should have received some protection under the surrender agreement issued by Generals William Sherman and Joseph Johnston. In theory, the end of the war would also end the need for military tribunals. At the same time, the defense team tried to talk about the traditional problems associated with double jeopardy and the vagueness of the specifications.[67]

Wirz became a cipher for the barbarism of the Confederacy, and at one point in these military proceedings the prosecutors tried to draft an indictment that included the names of Jefferson Davis and other ranking Confederates. These other names were later dropped from the charges, and the judge advocate now argued that Wirz had been personally involved in conspiracies that destroyed Union prisoners' lives.[68] One chronicler of the events contended that "Wirz was a dead man from the start."[69]

The prosecutors had months to prepare for the trial, and they could supplement this oral testimony with bureau evidence that came in the form of hundreds of written documents. While the defense had to constantly spend time and money searching for any shred of helpful material, the judge advocate and his subalterns could quickly find the specific surrender terms offered by Northern generals. From the very outset, they made it abundantly clear that they were not going to accept any defense positions that focused on Confederate necessities or the obedience of superior orders.[70] The Unionist rhetorical frames often equated victory on the battlefield with truthfulness in the courtroom.

All of this was being decided at the same time prosecutors could argue that the Union generals had "never intended to pardon soldiers who had committed war crimes."[71] Chipman, for example, could read from a letter that he received from James Willet that indicated Wirz had never been promised any implied pardon. Within this Unionist framework, Federal officers did not make the type of promises that would "relieve rebels of every disgrace."[72] By the end of the first week of the trial, Schade and Baker tried to withdraw as legal counsel, but Wirz convinced them they needed to stay on.

Throughout the trial, the defense team watched helplessly as their arguments about prisoner exchanges were tossed aside as irrelevant, and a long procession of former prisoners answered detailed questions about the horrific conditions in Andersonville. Each of the witnesses was asked about the squalor, the overcrowding, the crimes, and the personal acts of barbarity that they may have observed while at Andersonville. A few swore they saw Wirz shoot prisoners at point-blank range, and brought up names that never appeared on the official death register.[73]

Some of the prosecutorial witnesses who appeared in these proceedings tried to adopt a conciliatory tone as they talked about the commandant's situation, but the judge advocate and the rest of commission reconfigured these statements so the focus of attention stayed on the conditions in the camps. The same set of objective facts could be tied to different rhetorical frames, and one's choice of frames influenced one's ideas about natural necessities or legal culpability. For example, when the Wirz commission listened to the evidence from the Southern doctors and commissioners who visited Andersonville in 1864 or 1865, they could ignore the alternative causalities mentioned in these statements. Joseph Jones, a surgeon in the Medical College of Georgia, told the tribunal that at one time he had wanted to learn more about the relationships that existed between the Southern climate and typhus, typhoid, and malarial fevers, but what he found at Andersonville could not be easily diagnosed or remedied:

Scurvy, diarrhea, dysentery, and hospital gangrene were the prevailing diseases. . . . The haggard, distressed countenances of these miserable, complaining, dejected, living skeletons, crying for medical aid and food, and cursing their government for its refusal to exchange prisoners. . . . I heard some of the prisoners go so far as to exonerate the Confederate Government from any charge of inten-

tionally subjecting them to a prolonged confinement, with its necessary and unavoidable sufferings, in a country cut off from all in-
tercourse with foreign nations, and sorely pressed on all sides, whilst
on the other hand they changed [*sic*] their own prolonged captivity
upon their own government, which was attempting to make the ne-
gro [*sic*] equal to the white man.[74]

Jones was supposed to be a prosecution witness at the *Wirz* trial, but
his commentaries on the lack of prisoner exchanges or the problematics
of racial equality were not unique examples of Southern apologetics. Sergeant Oats, in his *Prison Life in Dixie* (1880), told readers that it "was a hard
strain on our patriotism to feel that we were neglected by our own Government. For we believed then, as we learned certainly afterward, that
we could have been exchanged had those in charge of our armies so de-
sired."[75] These critical remembrances reminded observers that not everyone believed in the infallibility of the Union leadership, the martial "necessities" that supposedly ended the exchanges, or the politics of the
Radical Republicans.

Out of fairness it needs to be acknowledged that Baker and Schade
never seemed to understand the special nature of the formalistic rules
used in these military tribunals, and they helplessly tried to apply what
they had learned from work in civil settings. In theory, a great deal of
leeway and discretion was given to those in search of the martial "truth,"[76]
especially in times of war or military necessity. Baker, for example, might
worry about the failure of some of the Andersonville inmates to identify
the exact names of victims, and he might highlight some of the discrepan-
cies that existed in much of the prosecutorial testimony, but prosecutors
were operating under military rules that allowed them to make generous
inferences about some of the activities of the camp commandant.

Unfortunately, the procedural search for the "truth" in this case often
appeared to be a one-sided affair. When potential defense witnesses arrived in Washington, DC, they were often accosted by Union officers who
met them as they got off the trains. These travelers were told that they
could be accused of having violated parole regulations. One critic of the
proceedings was sure that,

testimony lending human attributes to Wirz's character or impugn-
ing the benevolence of Union authorities was disallowed on whatever pretext General Wallace could apply. When defense counsel
tried to impeach the fictions of government witnesses, Chipman
waved the flag, denounced them for daring to insult the veracity of
United States soldiers, but he suffered no qualms about suggesting
that Wirz's Federal witnesses were all deserters, bounty jumpers, or
downright "disloyal."[77]

Critics who have attacked portions of this testimony on procedural
grounds may have a point, but we also need to admit that a balanced reading of the record reveals that occasionally there were times when the
Andersonville commandant *may* have violated some rules of human de-
cency. There is circumstantial evidence that he kicked prisoners, and at
one point he admitted that he gave the orders to his soldiers to shoot
anyone who walked across the infamous "deadline." While few of the
prosecution witnesses could cite the exact names of the alleged victims or
the time of their deaths, some of Wirz's own testimony hurt the defense's
case. The judge advocate ended up claiming he had found at least thirteen
instances where Wirz had maliciously participated in the killing of Union
prisoners.[78]

The arguments presented in a courtroom are only some of the discursive fragments that go into the production of legal cultures, and for sixty-
three days the *Wirz* case became the object of voyeuristic fascination for
the Northern presses. Contributors to and editors of *Harper's Weekly,* for
example, were able to obtain photographs of some of the survivors of
some of the prison releases, and they published them on the front pages
of their publications.[79] The usually subdued Whitman excoriated the commanders at Andersonville for having committed deeds that could not be
forgiven, and he averred that the perpetrators deserved the "blackest,
escapeless, endless damnation."[80] With "millennial zeal" and "conspiratorial vision," some "Union apologists were riveting into American memory"
and chroniclers of these events were left with "interpretation that portrayed Southern Confederates as traitors."[81]

As I argue in the next portion of this chapter, these discursive structures that apportioned blame for the condition of the Civil War prisons spilled over into the broader rhetorical culture, and supplied several generations with what Schwartz has called the "frameworks of memory."[82]

Northern Recollections of Andersonville and the Defense of the *Wirz* Tribunal

With the passage of years, fewer American audiences remembered the name of Henry Wirz, but there was certainly no forgetting "Andersonville." The end of the Reconstruction meant that emancipationist rhetorics now had to compete with regenerative, reconciliationist visions. The performative and ritualistic nature of some of these postwar celebrations altered the historical landscape, as different generations renegotiated the communal boundaries of what would be remembered and what would be forgotten. During the late 1870s, political compromises brought about the election of Rutherford B. Hayes, and the Union troops ended their occupation of the South.[83] Northern crowds now heard about the importance of "reunions," and on these occasions, "historical memory" would be the "prize in a struggle between rival versions of the past."[84]

The potential public acceptance of some of these reconciliationist visions clearly bothered some survivors who fervently believed in the importance of emancipationist rhetorics. In Toledo, Ohio, for example, General Garfield spoke about the "liberty" of the Union soldiers who had survived the "hell of Andersonville."[85] This former officer told his listeners that during one session of Congress he had heard a man claim that "Union soldiers were as well treated and as kindly treated in all the Southern prisons as were the rebel soldiers in all the Northern prisoners." This assertion was greeted with "groans, hisses, and a storm of indignation."[86] Clearly, many victors did not want to hear arguments about conditions in Union prisons, Southern chivalry, or the preeminent importance of the "Glorious Cause."

These commemorative occasions also provided new opportunities for audiences who were still interested in critiquing the motivations and activities of the Southern leadership, and the losers of the Civil War could once again be vilified for maintaining the horrific Civil War prison systems. The passage of years had cut down on some of the potency of these emancipationist visions, but they still resonated with influential segments of the American populace. For example, the presidents and generals of the Old Confederacy may not have shared the fate of Henry Wirz, but this did not mean they could escape the tenacity of martial memory work. For example, during the conclusion of General Garfield's speech at the Andersonville Reunion at Toledo, he indicated that he had not remained silent when he heard colleagues in the post-Reconstruction Congress talk about the moral equivalence of the North and the South:

> [The man who stood by my side in the halls of Congress declared] that no kinder men ever lived than Gen. Winder and his Commander-in-Chief, Jeff Davis. And I took it upon myself to overwhelm him with proof that the tortures you suffered, the wrongs done to you, were suffered and done with the knowledge of the Confederate authorities, from Jeff Davis down—that it was a part of their policy to make you idiots and skeletons, and to exchange your broken and shattered bodies and dethroned minds for strong, robust, well-fed rebel prisoners. . . . I would clasp hands with those who fought against us, make them my brethren and forgive all the past, only on one supreme condition: that it be admitted in practice, acknowledged in theory, that the cause for which we fought and you suffered, was and is and forever more will be right, eternally right.[87]

This fascinating rhetorical fragment, what might be called a hybrid memory, brought together several strands of emancipationist and conciliationist arguments. Here we have less talk of vengeance and retribution, but clearly the Union cause was still considered to be "eternally right." Southerners could now rejoin the Union as citizens, but this egalitarian status was dependent on their admission that their leaders had violated the customary laws of war. Moral prescriptive claims were thus merged with epistemic claims about the "cause."

Forging these hybrid memories therefore involved novel acts of public remembrance and legal commemoration, because these remembrances touched on issues of "social" consciousness, "affinity and identity."[88] Anxious Northerners worried that the arrival of the 1877 "compromise" might mean that future generations would forget about the lasting benefits of abolitionism, the motivations of the antislavery Unionists, and the antebellum origins of the Civil War. Moving toward reconciliation and reunion was an important goal, but for many Americans, this did not mean the total abandonment of emancipationist ideals.

During the last quarter of the nineteenth century and the early twentieth century, some Americans were willing to forgive the ordinary soldiers who fought for the Confederacy, but Wirz was still viewed as a demonic figure who got what he deserved. As a stand-in for the Southern leadership, his actions illustrated just how Southern war policies violated the customary rules of war. John H. Stibbs, perhaps the last surviving member of the Wirz commission, provided some typical commentary when he argued in the *Iowa Journal of History and Politics* (1911) that the passage of years had "practically wiped out" the bitter feelings that had existed between "the North and the South."[89] Stibbs tried to argue that readers needed to differentiate between the honorable "Mister Johnny Reb" who "bared his bosom" to Union bullets, and dastardly "bushwhackers" like Wirz. As far as he was concerned, he was willing to admit that a "spirit of harmony" now existed between many "old veterans,"[90] but there were also times when those who had witnessed these traumatic events had to come forward and set the record straight. As the elder Union army officer reminisced about his role in the *Wirz* trial, he told readers that

> as time passed and one after another of those who served with me passed off the stage, leaving me the sole survivor of the Court, and after a monument was erected to perpetuate the memory of Wirz and he was proclaimed a martyr who had been unfairly tried and condemned, I . . . [decided I would] lay aside all question of propriety and obligation and accede to the request of some of my Iowa friends who were urging me to prepare a paper.[91]

Stibbs admitted that in the fall of 1863 the Richmond prisons were overcrowded and there was a need for a new prison, but he was convinced the Confederates had purposely subjected Union soldiers to "such hardships as would render them unfit for further military service."[92] He asserted that the "lives of more than three-fourths of those who died at Andersonville might have been saved with proper care and treatment."[93]

More moderate Federal veterans were at least willing to consider the possibility that Wirz was only partially to blame for the Civil War prison camp mortality rates. For example, John Ransom, a Union soldier who managed to eventually escape the horrors of Andersonville, would have this to say fifteen years after the hanging:

> It was a righteous judgment, still I think there are others who de-served hanging fully as much. He was but the willing tool of those higher in command. Those who put him there knew his brutal dis-position, and should have suffered the same disposition made of him. Although I believe at this late day those who were in command and authority over Capt. Wirtz [*sic*] have successfully thrown the blame on his soldiers, it does not excuse them in the least as far as I am concerned. They are just as much to blame that thirteen thousand men died in a few months at that worst place the world has ever seen, as Capt. Wirtz, and should have suffered accordingly. I don't blame any of them for being rebels if they thought it right, but I do their inhumane treatment of prisoners of war.[94]

By the beginning of the twentieth century, the complexities of the *Wirz* trial were often forgotten as modern decision-makers began writing about other war crimes, the Hague Convention, and the need for codes that would regulate how warring parties treated combatants, noncombat-ants, and prisoners of war. After the end of World War I, Henry Wirz was once again in the news, but this time his trial was being reconfigured as a part of the evolutionary development of international martial law. For example, American writers for *Outlook* magazine and the *New York Times* began arguing that the execution of Wirz served as "just precedent for the execution of von Tirpitz and the other detested leaders of Germany."[95]

Obviously, this was not the way many Southerners wanted to remem-ber Wirz and Andersonville. In this next section, I explore some of the afterimages that appeared in Southern recollections of the Civil War.

Reconciliationist Visions and Southern Recollections of Andersonville and Wirz

Many Southerners were traumatized by the idea that Wirz would be asso-ciated with international war crimes. In the early post–Civil War years, these social actors adopted variants of the reconciliationist visions that underscored the importance of fairly apportioning blame for the war, the development of "new" Southern leadership, and the healing power of forgetting. "Wirz's trial," contends Marvel, was viewed by Southerners as "deliberately orchestrated to distract attention from the Union role in suspension of the exchange cartel, which in turn led to the lengthy imprisonments that allowed diseases like scurvy and dysentery to take such a toll."[96] For several months, Jefferson Davis and other former Confederate leaders lived in Northern prisons, awaiting a time when they too were going to have to deal with public and legal accusations.[97] Yet eventually these social agents would be given their freedom, and these could be construed as realistic acts that showed the hypocrisy of the Radical Republicans.

Variants of the reconciliationist visions were now resurfacing as communities reminisced about the enduring meaning of the Civil War and antebellum South.[98] Between the late 1870s and the early 1900s, audiences were reading about the ideas of the "Redeemer Democrats" who battled the Radical Republicans in local and state elections. Former white veterans, including John Brown Gordon of Georgia and Wade Hampton of South Carolina, tried to convince voters they were "determined to reclaim" their homeland for their former occupiers.[99] These Redeemers and their allies were not just interested in building back the economic power of the former plantation owners or the Southern working classes; they also wanted to fight the symbolic wars that would preserve the memories of those who had died fighting for the "Lost Cause."[100]

Southern writers must have realized that this renegotiation of public memories and legal histories needed to include a reassessment of the ways future generations wrote and talked about both Federal and Confederate prisons and wartime regulations. In the name of objectivity, reconciliation, and dispassionate justice, they used the *Wirz* trial as an illustration of the problematics of victors' justice. Members of one local community raised funds so that a commemorative plaque could preserve these words for countless generations:

To the best of his ability he tried to obtain food and medicine for Federal prisoners and permitted some to go to Washington in a futile attempt to get prisoners exchanged. He was tried for failure to provide food and medicines for Federals imprisoned there—though his guards ate the same food—and mortality was as high among Confederate guards as among prisoners. Of him [Wirz] Eliza Frances Andrews, Georgia Writer [*sic*] said, "If he had been an angel from heaven, he could not have changed the pitiful tale of privation and hunger unless he had possessed the power to repeat the miracles of the loaves and fishes."[101]

How one characterizes the authors of this plaque, and responds to the arguments that are embedded within the artifact, tells us a great deal about the motivations, feelings, and anxieties of readers who are constantly grappling with the complexities of wars and modern memories. Morgan Peoples, for example, argued as late as 1980 that this plaque was "placed there by the people of the State of Georgia."[102] Now we can understand why Blight once remarked that "the Civil War remains very difficult to shuck from its shell of sentimentalism," because it serves as a "mother lode of nostalgia" and is deeply "embedded in an American mythology of mission."[103]

Conclusion and Assessment

This chapter's critical analysis of the *Wirz* trial shows us how legal forums can become cultural markers in our conversations about military necessities, the history of the Civil War, and the need for military tribunals that try war criminals. Gayla Koerting once argued that reactions "to the trial, whether a contemporary account or a scholarly interpretation, are crucial to understanding its impact on the American consciousness,"[104] and Wirz would be remembered as "the only soldier on either side of the Civil War executed for a war crime."[105]

Interestingly enough, modern commentators continue to debate both the legitimacy and the desirability of the *Wirz* tribunal, and they have selectively appropriated parts of these complex emancipatory or conciliatory rhetorics. Defenders of the trial recirculate some of the same arguments that were presented by Stibbs and other members of the tribunal, and they focus attention on the commandant's personal misdeeds. For example, Robert Morsberger and Katherine Morsberger have argued that although "Andersonville was not the only atrocity of the war," Wirz did

commit acts of omission or commission that cannot be "dismissed as unavoidable under the circumstances."[106] They provided their own permutation of an emancipationist rhetoric as they wrote about how Wirz could
have enlarged the stockade, how he could have allowed prisoners to cut
wood for fuel, and how he might have helped build more shelters. Moreover, Morsberger and Morsberger underscore the fact that his "refusal to
go beyond his literal orders to care for prisoners was a moral failure," and
that there was little question that he had given orders that cost lives.[107]

Critics of these *Wirz* proceedings assert that systematic irregularities
were a central part of this affair, and that Union officers abused their
discretion when they misapplied the rules of evidence that should have
governed martial trials.[108] Shelby Foote, for example, advanced the contentious claim that Union officers and soldiers had used trumped up testimony so they could document the commandant's deliberate cruelty.[109]
In 1994, William Marvel described the proceedings as a "shameless cha-
rade,"[110] a meaningless postwar inquiry that allowed the victors the opportunity of offering up Wirz's life to "appease the public hysteria."[111]
Other observers were quick to point out the equally abhorrent conditions
of Northern prisons, exigencies of war, and the caring attitudes of some
prison doctors and commissioners. These are conscious or unconscious
reproductions of variants of the reconciliationist visionary tales.

Southern apologists or interested scholars have not been the only critics of the *Wirz* commission. For example, James Page of Pennsylvania, a
former Federal lieutenant who spent some seven months in Andersonville,
wrote in 1919 that "the trial of Wirz was the greatest judicial farce enacted
since Oliver Cromwell instituted the Commission to try and condemn
Charles I."[112] More than eighty years later, and thousands of miles away,
Julian Lewis told Australian readers how "Captain Henry Wirz holds the
dubious distinction of being the only person executed in the United States
for war crimes," and that "his trial set the precedent that military personnel could be accountable for following orders that violated the rules of
war or common law of humanity."[113]

Some scholars and laypersons have complained that Andrew Johnson's
administration, and the Radical Republicans in Congress, simply had too
much power in the wake of President Lincoln's untimely death. Darrett
Rutman intoned that Wirz had been unfairly maligned by Northern news-

papers as a "foreign, ugly, cruel, hulking," "cringing and cowardly" ward of Union prisoners.[114] He claimed that until "the day of his arrest he [Wirz] was to exert every effort to alleviate the conditions within the camp and stem the ever-rising death toll."[115] This former journalist turned Civil War historian was convinced that newspapers such as the *New York Tribune, Frank Leslie's Illustrated Newspaper,* and the *New York Times* had contributed to the creation of a "mass psychosis which gripped the triumphant Union."[116] Captain Glen LaForce, a member of the South Carolina and Confederate States bar associations, wrote in 1988 that the trial "was a national disgrace."[117]

A proponent of critical rhetorical analysis, who critiques both the emancipationist and the reconciliationist visions of the Civil War, realizes that even the clearest of legal records can be written "in anticipation of future needs," and that a "trial transcript is as much about what is denied, repressed, or excluded as what is said."[118] When we take into consideration the polysemic and polyvalent interpretations of the trial, we can see how these forums reflected and refracted how various publics thought about individual and group culpability during wartime.

Obviously critics could argue that there are problems with both of these rhetorical frameworks. The communities who advance reconciliationist narratives have provided us with information on the alternative causes that may have contributed to the Andersonville horrors, but they went overboard when they characterized Wirz as an innocent martyr who saved thousands of lives. In an ironic twist of fate, some modern commentators have adopted a hybrid line that follows the claims of former Union officers, where observers try to shift individual blame so that we interrogate the activities of Wirz's superior officer, General John Winder, who was supposed to be in charge of all of the Confederate prisoner-of-war camps in the region.[119]

Unfortunately, this search for the right culpable party means we end up blaming single individuals for cataclysmic events, and this in turn provides us with only a partial picture of the complexities of wars or military commissions. Critics need to be able to take into account the economic, political, and social problematics of warfare, and they must grapple with the conflicting testimony that comes from both emancipationist and reconciliationist interpretations of the Civil War years. An analysis of the legal and public commentaries on the trial, and an assessment of various generational memories of these proceedings, show us the variegated nature of human responses in catastrophic situations. These Andersonville tales contain subplots where we see some individual acts of kindness on the part of guards, officers, and inspectors. Yet some of these same reports or chronicles also document the shooting of those who crossed the "deadline," the innumerable verbal threats of bodily harm, the callousness of those who did not build shelters, and other evidence of incompetence, indifference, or inefficiency.

When we choose up positions in our modern ideological debates about "military necessity," or the need for martial tribunals, we need to adopt a reflective stance that takes into account some of the other symbolic and material realities that have influenced our own recollections of the *Wirz* precedent. This is especially important in the wake of 9/11, where the American public will witness the trials of both citizens and noncitizens in the prolonged "War on Terrorism."

6

FDR, Wartime Anxieties, and the Saboteurs' Case

[Enemy] belligerents . . . are generally deemed not to be entitled to
the status of prisoners of war, but to be offenders against the law of war
subject to trial and punishment by military tribunals.
                          —Justice Harlan F. Stone, *Ex parte Quirin,* 1942

When some Bush administration officials,[1] or federal judges reviewing modern detentions,[2] sifted through the sands of time to find examples of expansive uses of presidential authority, they soon discovered that Franklin Delano Roosevelt had once had to make decisions about World War II saboteurs, attacks on U.S. war production, and the authorization of military commissions. In the name of "military necessity," Japanese Americans were placed in internment camps,[3] scarce resources were rationed, and war zones were established. On 9/11, history seemed to have repeated itself, and a different president was faced with seemingly analogous situations. A "democratic hero," notes Frank Murray, was used to "justify the use of military courts."[4] When President Bush decided he would characterize the attackers who brought down the World Trade Center as "unlawful combatants," he was said to be faithfully tracking "the path FDR trod to execute World War II saboteurs."[5] Some sixty years later, a "large number of public officials, especially those who hold cabinet-level, and additional upper-echelon Bush administration positions," have "invoked the World War II precedent of *Ex parte Quirin*"[6] in explaining the lawfulness of new military tribunals. In 2003, Donald Downs and Erik Kinnunen averred that "anyone who argues that military tribunals violate the letter or spirit of *Milligan*" need to deal with the *Quirin* case, because in "the end" it is "still the primary constitutional precedent dealing with military tribunals and has been relied upon by federal courts dealing with the Bush administration's detainment of enemy combatants."[7]

Whether these situations were in fact analogous will perhaps always be a major source of academic debate, but even skeptics have to admit there are some interesting parallels. The *Quirin* case[8] was a decision that dealt with some foreign saboteurs who brought to American shores some explosives and other devices. This was a secret trial that stayed primarily within the executive's chain of command because "President Roosevelt was desperate to keep the reason for the invasion's failure a secret."[9]

In the wake of the attack on Pearl Harbor in December of 1941, President Roosevelt understood he was now faced with a war that had to be fought on several fronts, and contemporary news writers wondered what he was going to do to protect the coastlines and interior from the dangers that came from "fifth columnists." On June 13, 1942, four members of the German Marine Infantry landed on a beach at Amagansett, some 125 miles east of New York City. Four days later, another group of four Germans landed at Ponte Vedra Beach, near Jacksonville, Florida. Both groups buried their incendiaries, fuses, and timing devices before traveling to some of America's largest cities.[10]

Newspaper writers would later report that six of the eight visitors—Richard Quirin, Hermann Neubauer, Heinrich Heinck, Werner Thiel, John Kerling, Georg Dasch—were German citizens. They had been assigned the mission of wreaking havoc in enemy territory, and they carried with them a list of American targets—factories, power plants, transportation centers, and water supply facilities. When the FBI finally captured these "belligerents," they had on their person some $175,000. Alpheus Mason wrote that this incident shook the "public confidence in the ability of political leaders to protect those at home."[11] The FBI director tried to assuage the fears of the public by telling them the "confessions" of all of the captured men would make any repetition of sabotage invasions extremely difficult.[12]

Three days after the capture of the German saboteurs, the nation's commander in chief sent a memo to Attorney General Francis Biddle, claiming that these individuals were "as guilty as it is possible to be" and that these offenses were "probably more serious than any offense in criminal law." Roosevelt felt the captured Germans needed to be tried by "court martial" and that the "death penalty" was called for because the saboteurs threatened the existence of the nation.[13] After conferring with several other high-ranking governmental officials, Biddle suggested to the president that perhaps the most expeditious way of proceeding involved the use of military commissions in trying the saboteurs.

In less than a week, President Roosevelt issued two key proclamations—one that outlined the procedures for the establishment of military tribunals in accordance with the laws of war, and another that created a specific military commission. The first proclamation indicated that any of the enemies who entered the United States for the purposes of committing acts of sabotage, espionage, or other hostile acts would be denied access to civilian courts,[14] while the second authorized the prosecution of saboteurs by the attorney general and the judge advocate general. What makes this case even more interesting is the fact that President Roosevelt then sealed the records in *Ex parte Quirin* until the end of the war.[15]

Roosevelt wanted quick closure in this case, and he got it. The military commission that was formed would eventually take just a few months to decide that six of the German invaders would forfeit their lives. They were charged with having violated the "Law of War" that had been drawn from general principles of international law, and the U.S. Articles of War that touched on communication of intelligence and spying.[16] In his memoirs, Attorney General Biddle observed that if these types of indictments had been presented in the nation's civil courts the prosecutors would have had a difficult time establishing the fact that the preparations and landings were "close enough to the planned act of sabotage to constitute attempt."[17] Moreover, some of the German saboteurs wanted an open trial where they could talk about alleged deals and the real reasons for the swiftness of their capture.[18] Key members of the tribunal believed the "nature of the testimony" involved the "security of the United States and the lives of its soldiers, sailors and citizens."[19] Justice William Rehnquist once intoned that this case showed there was "some truth to the maxim *inter arma silent leges*" [in times of war the law is silent].[20]

In this chapter I am interested in unpacking the various texts and contexts that influenced the trajectory of the arguments presented in *Ex parte Quirin,* and I augment these insights with commentaries that come from the broader public sphere. Obviously, given the growing recognition of the precedential value of this case, those who espouse "whig" views of military tribunals have to confront both the propositional logics and rhetorical narratives that surround these trials. Moreover, since the *Ex parte Quirin* case appears to be a key litmus test, I am willing to push the envelope and ask several important questions. Are there ever really times when the "rules of law" are silent, when military necessities demand that military solutions come to the foreground? What role did the contemporary international "laws of war" or the U.S. "Articles of War"[21] play in the rhetorically constructed justifications used by those who supported President Roosevelt's Proclamation[22] and Orders?[23]

These types of questions are important, because the claims that were advanced in parts of the *Ex parte Quirin* decision have resurfaced in contemporary debates over such issues as the scope of executive power, the need for military tribunals, and the limits of habeas corpus relief. In many ways this World War II decision provided new generations with the opportunity of symbolically overturning *Ex parte Milligan,* so that governmental authorities could once again decide the "constitutional power of a military commission to try persons apprehended in the United States when the federal and state courts were open and functioning."[24]

Interest in the *Ex parte Quirin* case has waxed and waned, depending on how various audiences thought about the "civilianization" of military courts, and the possibility of maintaining the precarious balance that existed between "national security" and "civil liberties." David J. Danelski insightfully observed that many of the researchers who analyzed this decision remembered some of the more formalistic rules associated with the idea of military necessity, but they have sometimes missed the fascinating, underlying tales of "intrigue, betrayal, and propaganda."[25] John Bickers is more charitable in his assessment of the case, and he argues that a "less cynical" remembrance of the decision might focus on the U.S. government's concern that an open trial would have allowed Hitler to learn about the ease with which foreign operatives moved to the vicinity of America's military industries.[26] Sound familiar?

With this in mind, the first portion of the chapter provides a brief overview of some pretrial activities in the early 1940s. The second and third sections are complementary segments that outline the prosecutorial and defense positions in the case. The fourth part of the chapter supplies a textual critique that assesses some of the selective choices made by the members of the U.S. Supreme Court when they heard the decision. Finally, in the conclusion, I illuminate the ways these arguments have been appropriated and deployed in our modern debates about the desirability and legitimacy of these tribunals.

Operation Pastorius and the Contextualization of the Case of the German Saboteurs

After war had been declared between Nazi Germany and the United States, Hitler was confident that his espionage organization (the *Abwehr*) could "shake the American public's confidence and upset the production and flow of war materials."[27] The chief of the *Abwehr*, Admiral Wilhelm Canaris, told Colonel Erwin von Lahousen that he needed to find a recruiter who could train the type of saboteurs willing to take on the dangerous mission of working behind the American lines. Lahousen chose Lieutenant Walter Kappe for this task because Kappe had lived in the United States for more than a decade. Kappe, in turn, combed through the files of the Deutsches Ausland-Institut (DAI) in order to find Germans who could speak English and who might have a working knowledge of American customs.[28] These German officers named their mission Operation "Pastorius" (Franz Daniel Pastorius was one of the leaders of the first group of German immigrants who came to the United States).[29]

After looking through the DAI files, Kappe chose eight men for the mission, and each of the trainees was given a new identify and a biography.[30] Joan Miller contends that because of the "importance of the aluminum and magnesium industries to America' production of military airplanes," German intelligence experts wanted these teams to think about targeting plants in Tennessee, Illinois, and New York.[31] During the trial proceedings, some of the defendants claimed they "had changed their minds on the submarine coming over or after reaching America."[32] This type of defensive discursive framing of the situation tried to minimize the actual danger of sabotage.

William Lewis has written about how legal narratives are often filled with romances and tragedies, where human conflict is configured in myths about the "clashes of good and evil,"[33] and in this particular context American publics were presented with tales of individual heroism, FBI organizational skills, and intergovernmental cooperation. According to one of the first newspaper reports that broke the story of the Amagansett landing, a young Coast Guardsman, John Cullen, discovered this "gang" after they had finished burying their equipment. The invaders tried their best to bribe this serviceman, but he "spurned the bribe and they fled."[34] The Coast Guardsman then ran back to his station, where his superior sounded the alarm.

In today's remembrances, it is President Roosevelt who is usually the main figure tied to the *Ex parte Quirin* case, but in the early 1940s it was J. Edgar Hoover who took center stage. His FBI subordinates were considered to be heroes who had prevented major catastrophes. "Despite their training," noted Will Lissner in June of 1942, "the two [German] gangs each fell afoul of special agents of the Federal Bureau of Investigation."[35] The FBI supplied newspapers with pictures of boxes of foreign supplies, and audiences read about how some governmental officials found ten blocks of TNT, safety fuses, and other detonating equipment. Hoover also released a public statement that provided anxious readers with the same biographical material on each of the saboteurs that had been sent to President Roosevelt.[36]

The German saboteurs were characterized as the vanguards of much larger conspiracies that might be operating throughout the country. One editorial writer for the *New York Times* wanted to warn readers that they needed to realize "we may have more of these dangerous visitors."[37] While these particular graduates of Germany's school of sabotage appeared to be a "thick-headed lot," that did not mean that authorities needed to quit worrying about patrolling a 3,000 mile coastline. What if other "dynamiters" came from the ranks of the organizations like the German American Bund? Some surmised that the captured German saboteurs had "expected the help of friendly fifth columnists and planned to corrupt others."[38] Lissner wrote about how these invaders had been former waiters, machinists, and "German-American agitators."[39] The arrests seemed to create the impression that the German embassy in Washington, and the German consulates in New York and San Francisco, were a part of a "pre-war set-up designed to bring home to Germany nationals who could be used for sabotage when war started."[40] A *March of Time* radio broadcast informed

American listeners that these belligerents "would have stilled the ma-
chines and endangered the lives of thousands of defense workers . . . they
came to maim and kill."[41]

Given this wartime cultural milieu, any potential threat to the nation
was obviously going to be magnified, and Roosevelt's administration had
to provide evidence that it was acting prudently and swiftly. Boris Bittker,
a young attorney fresh out of law school, remembered how he was assigned the task of helping defend the Germans, and he had to familiarize
himself with the key issues in the case. "According to the gossip in the
corridors of the Justice Department," Bittker notes, "the White House
hoped that the drama of a military trial would help to convince the public
that we were really at war, and to end the civilian complacency that pre-
vailed even in 1942, six months after the debacle at Pearl Harbor."[42] One
popular cartoonist depicted J. Edgar Hoover physically restraining some
of the prisoners, while Attorney General Biddle stood on a ladder in front
of a row of books, saying, "You hold on to them Edgar, and I'll find something here that we can punish them under."[43] Obviously not all critics were
this skeptical of the political maneuvering in this case, but it does provide some indication that members of the American press and public
wanted at least a modicum of judicial oversight of Roosevelt's military
commission.

The Prosecutorial Case in *Ex Parte Quirin* and
the Transcendent Importance of State Necessities

When President Roosevelt issued his order that established the military
commission in July of 1942, he wanted to make sure the German saboteurs would be tried for violations of both the international "laws of war"
and the American Articles of War. In his memoirs, Biddle claimed that
Roosevelt had told him: "I won't give them up. . . . I won't hand them
over to any United States marshal armed with a writ of habeas corpus.
Understand?"[44] Insightful modern critics, such as Bryant and Tobias, underscored how these types of statements provide us with clues about some of
the external factors that may have influenced the outcome of the *Quirin*
case,[45] but at a time when millions of Americans feared foreign invasions
of the U.S. coastlines, the saboteurs looked like scouts for much larger

operations. If Roosevelt was putting pressure on the commission, he was not alone.

The military commission he created would be made up of three major generals and three brigadier generals, and they would all serve under Major General Frank McCoy. The prosecutorial team would be led by Attorney General Biddle and the Army's Judge Advocate General, Major General Myron Cramer. In June of 1942, one of Cramer's memorandums indicated that he thought the nation needed a military tribunal in this situation, because a federal district would be "unable to impose an adequate sentence."[46] The commission then asked Colonial Cassius Dowell and Colonel Kenneth Royall to be the leading defense counsel members.

A close reading of the proclamations, trial records, military court rules, and the public discourse surrounding Roosevelt's actions provides us with some indication of the rhetorical difficulties that confronted the defense. As noted above, in some ways this was a unique type of American military commission, and it deviated from the traditional Anglo-American Articles of War in that the commission "was authorized to make its own rules," to use any evidence that was considered to have "probative value" to a reasonable person, to "convict or sentence by a two-thirds vote, and to "transmit its findings to the President for final action."[47] Moreover, since this was not a civil proceeding, the usual constitutional guarantees that were associated with grand juries or jury trials were not considered to be applicable in this military situation. These rules were meant to "permit the commission to accept testimony that might not be admitted by civil courts under the rules and traditions which Anglo-Saxon law has developed to protect the accused."[48] It would be the members of the commission who made decisions about the applicability of any procedures from the Articles or War or the *Manual for Courts-Martial*.[49] It was also determined that this trial would be held in the Department of Justice building, "behind an impenetrable veil of secrecy."[50]

The vast majority of Americans, who were already fretting about how the war was being waged overseas, had little problem accepting the idea that the saboteurs were having to deal with these restrictive rules. In those days, sacrosanct notions about habeas corpus relief took a backseat to winning the war.[51] Eugene Rachlis, who later defended the legality of these proceedings, noted in 1961:

The press and public considered the President's action both bold and proper. Most editorials favored a military trial over a civil trial. "There should be no quibbling or fine spun devotion to the nicer technicalities of the law in dealing with these Nazi criminals," and the military will provide "more justice than they really deserve" were some of the phrases which reflected press opinion. Not until the trial was actually under way was there any criticism, and that, understandably . . . was directed at the secrecy of the proceedings.[52]

This type of support is part of the reason the situation of the saboteurs was considered to be so analogous to that of the terrorists in the wake of 9/11.

From a rhetorical perspective, "national security" was considered to be an overriding presidential and congressional priority. Even some of the critics who complained about the trial's secrecy admitted they were bothered by the fact that in civil court the prosecutors might have to settle for using conspiracy laws that only carried a two-year sentence. This seemed to be a disproportionate response, especially if one considered the potential damage to the nation's war-fighting capabilities. Moreover, the use of civilian courts might encourage the defensive use of some "ludicrous offenses," including unlawful entry into the country without valid passports, or failure to register for the draft under the Selective Service Act.[53] In spite of the fact that this "Army trial" was being conducted behind the "barricaded doors at the Department of Justice," the American press reported that the government was demanding the deaths of seven of the eight prisoners.[54]

In early July, the attorney general turned the German prisoners over to the government, and Frank McCoy and six other Army generals were put in charge of hearing the evidence in this case. The defendants each faced four specified charges: 1) they had violated "the laws of war" by passing through the American lines in civilian dress in order to commit sabotage, espionage, and other hostile acts; 2) they had violated Article 81 of the Articles of War, which prohibited any relieving or attempting to relieve, or corresponding with, or giving intelligence to the enemy; 3) they had violated Articles of War, Article 82, by "spying"; and 4) they had conspired to commit the offenses alleged in the foregoing charges.[55] The judge advocate general of the Army provided a nice summary of the prosecution's position:

> In the saboteur cases the Government contended that all seven petitioners (one defendant not having sought the writ) were German nationals, and hence enemy aliens, who had entered into a theatre of operations in the United States by penetrating the lines of the armed forces of the United States, during a time of war, while in the uniform of the German Reich; who brought with them a large amount of money, certain explosives and the knowledge of means of secret communications; who thereafter assumed civil guise for the purpose of spying, giving aid to the enemy and committing hostile acts against armed forces of the United States; and as a result of these alleged facts, the petitioners having violated the law of war and acts of Congress had no right to the issuance of the writ of *habeas corpus.*[56]

As soon as the German saboteurs entered America during time of war, without uniforms or appropriate means of identification, illegal acts had been committed and jurisdiction had been conferred.[57]

Some thirty-two hours passed before the public had any knowledge the trial had even started. The members of the press knew that Army Major General Myron Cramer was one of those "speaking against the Nazis behind the soldier-guarded doors,"[58] but for the time being reporters had to speculate about the exact nature of the arguments and claims that were being made in front of the military commission. One correspondent noted that the "dynamiters" were probably being turned over to a military court because there the "processes would be swifter," and because those type of courts had "wider discretion than the civil courts."[59] We now know the trial lasted three weeks, and that this rush to judgment was considered by many to be expeditious and fair.

What often gets left out of accounts of the *Ex parte Quirin* case is the fact that some of these German visitors seemed to have sabotaged their own mission. Many members of the American press who covered these proceedings either did not know, or did not tell, the story of how George

Dasch—the leader of the Long Island expedition—turned state's evidence. Dasch argued that he became a part of this mission so they could escape from Nazi oppression.[60] Even those who heard this story must have been incredulous, because this rendition of the tale would have contradicted the myths that were being circulated about the prowess of Hoover and his agents. Readers of national newspapers were told that the FBI had already investigated more than 5,000 complaints about sabotage, and although the vast majority were from "disgruntled employe[e]s and cranks," some of them did involve suspicious saboteurs.[61] All of this was circulating in the public sphere at the same time the members of Roosevelt's commission were taking evidence from witnesses like Dasch and Burger. J. Edgar Hoover, who played no official role in this social drama, was allowed to sit at the prosecution's table during most of these closed-door sessions.[62]

Presenting the prosecutorial story in this instance seemed to be a relatively easy matter. Attorney General Biddle was given the responsibility of proving the charges against the saboteurs. Biddle's first witness, John Cullen, helped the attorney general document the fact that the entire east coast of the United States could be considered a "zone of war."[63] This was a cagey rhetorical move because it accomplished several prosecutorial tasks. It helped with the identification of some of the Germans, it implicitly answered the question of why a military proceeding was warranted, and it helped magnify the dangers that came from the landing of the saboteurs.

During the trial, FBI agents certified that they had been given boxes of bombs, fuses, and wires. One explosives expert, D. J. Parsons, testified that he had tested these materials and found that many of them were potentially lethal. Agent Norval Wills reported on statements Dasch made while he was in FBI custody.[64] These were interpreted as confessions rather than evidence of any exaggerated dangers. This military commission also heard about handkerchiefs that contained hidden messages, confessions from Heinck and Quirin, false social security cards, and the existence of other prosecutorial evidence. This was one of the shining moments in the history of the FBI.

After winning some key arguments about the admissibility of defendants' confessions and their links to the overall conspiracy, Biddle rested his case. Now it would be the defense's turn to put their evidence before Roosevelt's military commission.

The Paramount Importance of Civil Law and Defense Interrogations of Military Necessity in *Ex Parte Quirin*

Today there is some dispute about the inherent fairness of these military proceedings, but most commentators admit that Colonel Dowell and Colonel Royall carried out the duties outlined in their *Courts-Martial Manual*—they were supposed to "guard the interests of the accused by all honorable and legitimate means known to law."[65] According to the evidence at hand, it appears as though the defense team did everything they could under the circumstances. They advanced arguments about the unconstitutionality and legitimacy of Roosevelt's order, they tried to gain civilian appellate review, and they initiated habeas corpus proceedings.[66]

Several members of the defense team risked their careers when they sought civil review for their clients at a time when many believed this was strictly a matter that needed to be handled within the executive branch of government. On July 6, 1942, Dowell and Royall sent this letter to President Roosevelt:

> Our investigation convinces us that there is a serious legal doubt as to the constitutionality and validity of the Proclamation and . . . of the Order [setting up the military commission]. It is our opinion that [the accused] should have the opportunity to institute appropriate proceedings to test the constitutionality and validity of the Proclamation and of the Order. In view of the fact that our appointment is made on the same Order which appoints the Military Commission, the question arises as to whether we are authorized to institute the proceedings suggested above. We respectfully suggest that you issue to us or to someone else appropriate authority to that end.[67]

This message let the Army prosecutors know the defense did not intend to keep all of this legal maneuvering behind closed doors, and the saboteurs' team implied that some type of civil action might be considered in the near future. McCoy, the leading decision-maker in the case, later denied similar motions when they were formally made by the defense.

In the coming weeks, Dowell and Royall took a number of controversial legal positions on questions that involved jurisdictional matters, habeas corpus petitions, and the proof of conspiratorial intent. Evidence from the trial records also shows they spent considerable time attacking some of the factual arguments being advanced by Biddle and the prosecutorial witnesses. They questioned whether certain types of evidence could be used against all of the clients, or even whether certain acts were committed in furtherance of a conspiracy. For example, when FBI investigators tried to talk about a waiver of a search warrant that was signed on June 22, 1942, Royall pointed out that the search and arrest of Burger took place on June 20, two days earlier. Was this the type of methodology that would provide "probative value to a reasonable man?" Several days later, the commission ruled in favor of Biddle on the question of the admissibility of Burger's confession.[68]

We still cannot be sure how these prisoners were treated while they were in federal custody.[69] During Biddle's presentation of the evidence against the four Germans who had landed in Florida, Royall was able to argue that perhaps some of the confessions may have been obtained under duress. When Joseph G. Fellner, an FBI agent, took the stand, he admitted during cross-examination that Kerling told him someone had "brushed" him on the side of the face.[70] While he eventually lost on the vast majority of these motions, these types of smaller skirmishes illustrate how Royall was able to leave us with a subtext that highlights some of the differences that existed between the evidentiary and procedural rules governing civilian and military courts. It also leaves us with important memories of some of the difficulties that might attend secretive military tribunals.

Interestingly enough, several years prior to the Nuremberg trials, it appears that some lawyers were beginning to think about the nature and limits of soldiers' responsibilities during wartime. If the entire United States was going to be considered a "war zone," did this mean that the spies or insurgents instantly became "soldiers"? Was the Eastern Defense Command a part of the "theatre of operations"?[71] These are still important questions, because in 2003 federal judges have argued that the U.S. president may lack "inherent constitutional authority as Commander-in-Chief to detain American citizens on American soil *outside* a zone of combat" [my emphasis].[72] Yet if we turn back the hands of time and return to 1942, the entire United States was viewed by many officials as one big zone of combat.

These types of cultural and legal beliefs exacerbated the problems of defense teams in the *Quirin* case. After Biddle finished with the presentation of the prosecution's case, Royall made the traditional motion for an immediate verdict of not guilty for his clients, because he claimed that the prosecutors had not proven their case. He attacked the idea that any one person could be "relieving the enemy," because if this was taken to its logical conclusion, every German soldier could be held accountable for the actions of German citizens who were trying to help Germany. During the same diatribe, Royall tried to argue that the defendants should also be acquitted of at least the "spying" charges, because in this situation there was no false presence, no zone of military operation, and no intent to relay military information to the enemy. The military commission elected not to sustain Royall's motions.[73]

During the second half of the military commission's proceedings, Dasch's lawyer, Carl Ristine, joined Royall in advancing some contentious defense positions. At this stage of the inquiry, Ristine averred that perhaps McCoy and his fellow generals needed to take into consideration the possibility that Dasch may have been trying to leave Germany in order to fight the Nazi tyranny. This counternarrative was supposed to be plausible because Dasch did not kill the young Coast Guardsman, and he voluntarily visited the FBI. Did this not show that Dasch was trying to protect American citizens from Hitler's minions? After Ristine's presentation, Royall argued that Burger should also be separated from the other saboteurs. After all, had he not joined Dasch in providing the prosecution with evidence?[74]

Near the end of this stage in the military proceedings, it appears that the defense attorneys realized their clients were in dire straits. They now began making arguments about how individual soldiers like Haupt never intended to commit sabotage or kill Americans. Haupt supposedly joined the group because he did not want to be viewed as a "rat" or "hoodlum." Haupt testified that he thought if he just went to the FBI and told them about the whole plan, "there would be no reason to be guilty of anything."[75] When it came time to find explanations for the actions of

Neubauer, Thiel, and Kerling, the defense team talked about how these soldiers felt trapped, and how they were simply obeying orders.

Things went from bad to worse when Biddle got Kerling to admit he had written a letter to a friend mentioning how America was falling "prey" to "a small group of Jews," and that Kerling was doing "his duty."[76] This type of cross-examination deflated the hopes of those who wanted to re-characterize the saboteurs as victims of the Nazis. By the time that Heinck and Quirin took the stand, there seemed little hope for acquittal. On Monday, July 27, 1942, Dowell announced to the commission that the defense was going to rest. The trial of the German saboteurs had been in session for sixteen days.

During the last week of the trial, Royall, Dowell, and Ristine had lost many of their arguments, but they still had one hope left—perhaps the U.S. Supreme Court would hear their civil pleas.

Making Choices between Transcendent Values and Competing Ideographic Interpretations

Near the end of these proceedings, the prosecution gained some important allies when the District Court of the District of Columbia denied the defense counsel leave for filing petitions for habeas corpus.[77] This, however, did not end matters, because the defense could still ask for a review of this ruling and leave to appeal. It appears that Colonel Stone first approached Supreme Court Justice Roberts, who then talked to Justices Black and Stone, and then all of the members of the Court got together and discussed this issue.[78] In an extremely unusual move, the defense came forward with petitions for writs of habeas corpus in July of 1942, and the Supreme Court decided to meet in special session. The briefs indicated that the defense attorneys wanted to talk about ex post facto laws, the nonexistence of any common law of crime against the United States, the lack of jurisdiction, violations of specific provisions of the Articles of War, and the petitioners' right to a civil trial.[79]

Some American observers were alarmed when they heard about these Supreme Court activities. Representative Emmanuel Celler explained that "[O]ur people are of the opinion that the eight Nazi saboteurs should be executed with all possible dispatch. . . . They are confident that the military tribunal will decree their death. Any interference with that trial by civil court would strike a severe blow to public morale."[80] This type of remark brings to mind the Minnesotans' lamentations about Lincoln's involvement in the U.S.-Dakota War tribunals (chapter three).

Biddle and Royall once again faced each other in court, but this time the debate was going to take place in a public forum. Since their petition had initially been denied by Justice James Morris of the District Court for the District of Columbia, the defense had only a few days to come up with arguments and briefs that would explain just why the nation's highest appellate court should hear this particular appeal, and why the Circuit Court of Appeals should be bypassed.[81] In a very curious procedural move, the U.S. Supreme Court decided to deal with this situation without having to directly tackle the key question of whether it had "original" jurisdiction to hear the case. The defense attorneys were allowed to carry papers from the "Appeals Court" to the Supreme Court "only a few minutes before Chief Justice Stone started speaking from the bench."[82]

For almost two days, most of the members of the Supreme Court heard the petition for habeas corpus that came from seven of the eight prisoners.[83] Dasch, who would later be vilified in Germany for his role in the case, decided he would not join in this particular legal action.[84] One critical observer remarked that if "any person detained anywhere in the United States for any allegedly unlawful reason could go straight to the Supreme Court for relief," this would open the floodgates for any aggrieved party to issue a writ to any federal, state, or local governmental official.[85]

One of the many fascinating legal points in this case is that both the defense and the prosecution wanted to revisit *Ex parte Milligan*.[86] Royall wanted to use the case as precedent for why civil courts would have been the best forums for trying the German saboteurs, but this was clearly not the position of many Army officers. Contemporaries who supported the prosecution treated *Milligan* as a "production of an obsolete day and outmoded science of war," that was "filled with irrelevant dicta."[87] Charles Fairman, for example, wrote in his revised edition of *Law of Martial Rule* that it "by no means follows that what appeared a salutary restraint upon the tyranny of the Stuarts is today an appropriate limit on power of both executive and legislature in a highly responsible national government."[88] Given the waning power of the ancient "whig" rhetorics, perhaps it was time to acknowledge that in some situations civilianization could be problematic.

Realistic thinking was in the air, and the war seemed to show that Oliver Wendell Holmes Jr. had been right when he talked about the transcendent importance of the "felt necessities" of the times.[89] Treating the rights, liberties, and freedoms of these saboteurs as if they were metaphysical absolutes seemed to be a regressive move that took us back to the time when the state had real tyrants who talked of feigned needs. Who could dispute the visual proof presented by Biddle and Hoover's FBI agents? Some of Royall's colleagues liked to remember the admonition of Charles Evans Hughes, who once defined the war power as "the power to wage war successfully" to the point where it extended to "every matter and activity so related to war as substantially to affect its conduct and progress."[90]

Given this popular view of executive powers, it makes complete sense that President George W. Bush's administrators would see *Ex parte Quirin* as their core precedent. Like Roosevelt and his officers, John Ashcroft and his subordinates could similarly place *Ex parte Milligan* on the periphery of the conversation. President Roosevelt's attorney general, Francis Biddle, needs to receive a great deal of credit for helping instantiate this particular transvaluation of values. During the oral arguments in *Ex parte Quirin,* Biddle invited the Court to rethink their decision in *Ex parte Milligan* so that the judiciary might allow for more expansive presidential wartime powers. As Bickers notes, the Court eventually "declined to overturn the *Milligan* precedent,"[91] even though they did accept many of Biddle's other arguments.

The Supreme Court's involvement in the case captured the nation's attention. One outside observer noted that "various experts" who were polled prior to the Court's decision in *Ex parte Quirin* thought the "judges might confine their coming opinion solely to the theory that the Nazis, landing from warships as invaders, had utterly no civil rights in the United States."[92] A correspondent for the *Baltimore Sun* would write that "people lined up at 9 a.m." and acted like "movie fans" as they waited for the beginning of the oral arguments before the Supreme Court.[93]

Many of the legal arguments presented during these oral proceedings and in the written briefs provided the American public with an inkling of some of the arguments that must have been used by the prosecutorial and defense teams during the earlier secret trial. The government claimed the "saboteurs" attended "a sabotage school near Berlin and came here in U-Boats with specific instructions for sabotage of war industries and other important spots."[94] The defense tried to answer these charges by once again arguing that these former "residents" of the United States had boarded the submarines because this was the only means of fleeing Nazi Germany. Moreover, the defense noted the fact that the sabotage campaign was never actually carried out, and hence they should not receive the maximum sentences.

The defense team hoped they could take advantage of the rhetorical baggage that had accompanied the *Ex parte Milligan* case for almost eighty years—had the post–Civil War jurists not warned their readers about the dangers of confusing true with false necessities? In his written remarks, Royall argued that *Ex parte Milligan* was controlling, and that if the military in 1942 was going to talk about real dangers, they needed to go beyond talking about "threatened invasion." This was one of the very few times this argument would be made in public during wartime. Justice Frankfurter, Royall's former law professor, grilled him about questions involving the flooding of the court with petitions, the definition of an "invading" force, what constituted a "theater of operations," "sabotage," and the extent of the president's powers as commander in chief.[95]

When it came time for the attorney general to present his case, he had few qualms about having "unlawful belligerents" tried before military commissions. Biddle explained to the members of the Supreme Court that World War II would determine whether the United States or Germany was going to survive, and that this "case" was a "part of the business of war." While the attorney general recognized the importance of protecting civil liberties and the writ of habeas corpus, he did not think such remedies were ever intended to be used as constitutional bulwarks that would protect "armed invaders."[96]

In his own analysis of *Ex parte Milligan,* the attorney general took on the role of a pragmatist dealing with an ancient principle that needed to be reshaped to fit modern conditions. Biddle spent a few minutes explaining the differences between the positions of the petitioners in 1942 and the status of Milligan in 1864. Milligan had been a resident of Indiana, he had not crossed through enemy lines, and he had lived at a time when the military dealt with a very different theater of operations.

Biddle was equally persuasive when it came to questions involving the fairness of the procedures used by the military commission. If Royall was going to complain about the two-thirds vote supposedly needed for convictions in military forums, he needed to remember that this applied only to courts-martial, and not to military commissions. Had the president's proclamations not included the authority to set up commissions that could come up with their own reasonable rules of evidence? As far as Biddle was concerned, during times of war, the president had the authority to decide if "natives, citizens, denizens, or subjects of the hostile nation" could be barred from civil courts, apprehended, restrained, secured, or removed.[97] If this deviated from the traditional Articles of War, then so be it.

On July 31, Chief Justice Stone handed down a *per curiam* that validated the president's order that had established the military commission, and the Supreme Court justices could not find any legal rationale that would support the discharge of the defendants. Stone told members of the press that the Court would be writing two opinions, one that would be immediately presented (short in length), and a longer one that would be publicized later on in the year. The shorter *per curiam* opinion took only a few minutes to read, and Lewis Wood of the *New York Times* reported the next day that this was the first time in twenty-two years the Court had felt it needed a "special session." Moreover, even though these justices "gave no indication how deeply it [*sic*] had gone into the Presidential war powers," their actions were "widely construed as tacit approval of steps which might be considered unwise in peace days."[98] This illustrated how the members of the Supreme Court were willing to accept the fact that the petitioners were going to face a "sentence of death by shooting or hanging."[99]

One of the most fascinating illustrations of the polysemic nature of legal decisions comes from the fact that there is some evidence that some of the Justices actually thought their decision would be construed as falling in line with the precedents that placed *limits* on military commissions and executive power! John Bassett Moore, for example, left us with fragments that show how some of the justices were perturbed when American news reporters neglected to talk about how the Court did hear the habeas corpus petitions in the first place, in spite of Roosevelt's order prohibiting the courts from listening to the pleas of the saboteurs.[100] Did this not show that the Court was preserving the separation of powers and maintaining the integrity of the judicial process? These jurists did not want to be re-membered as the judges who eviscerated *Ex parte Milligan,* yet at the same time they also wanted to acknowledge that circumstances occasionally necessitated military solutions. The same Supreme Court decision could therefore by read as either an extension or a limitation of presidential powers during times of war, depending on one's political proclivities and selective reading of the case.

After this brief interlude, the military commission went back to busi-ness as usual and finished hearing testimony in the saboteurs' case, but for all practical purposes many of the participants in this social drama knew the end was drawing near for most, if not all, of the saboteurs. While some observers were still bothered by the secrecy of the military commission, many felt this was a time when the country needed to rally around both President Roosevelt and the Court. One writer for the New York Times interpreted the unanimous decision in *Ex parte Quirin* as an indication that the entire nation could draw a "long breath of relief," because now mem-bers of the German Army could no longer hide behind any "discharge" that could have come from a civil trial.[101]

In early August, the "seven Army Generals" finally reached a verdict, and the president of the United States became "the court of last resort."[102] On a cold Saturday morning, a convoy of three Army automobiles arrived at the district jail housing the defendants. Several Army chaplains, doctors, and a coroner also came to the prison. One by one the six convicted pris-oners were electrocuted, and officials in charge of carrying out the sen-tence were pledged to secrecy. One witness later recalled that each of the unlucky invaders appeared to be in a "stunned, confused, trance-like state."[103] Burger received a life sentence, and Dasch got thirty years of prison time.[104] Moreover, the dead were buried with no names, just num-bers from 276 to 281. Operation Pastorius was at an end, and the law was silent no more.

On October 29, 1942, the nation's highest appellate court released its longer, *per curiam* decision. Harlan Fiske Stone was given the task of writ-ing this opinion, and this document echoed many of the remarks made by Biddle and the other government prosecutors. The Court reasoned that in theory the Constitution granted some war powers to the president, and when Congress declared war the president was expected to exercise his authority so that he could successfully wage war. Since the Articles of War contained explicit provisions for the establishment of military commissions, and the nation's justice system followed the "law of war," the nation's commander in chief could constitutionally carry out these duties.[105]

James Boyd White once argued that authors of legal texts often think about both the "speaker and the materials" of "culture,"[106] and in this particular situation the members of the Court had the unenviable task of explaining their reasoning. From the very beginning of the decision, they made it clear they were not concerned "with any question of guilt or innocence of petitioners,"[107] but rather the procedural questions that were associated with habeas corpus petitions from the district and circuit courts. Were these prisoners subject to the jurisdiction of the president's military commissions, and if so, what type of principles would ensure that these detainees received a full and fair trial? Given the public and legal interest in these deliberations, the justices understood the importance of issuing a unanimous opinion that avoided any concurrences and dissent, which meant they were going to have to work behind closed doors in hammering out their differences on such issues as the limits of executive authority, the nature and scope of the "laws of war," and the applicability of habeas corpus review for aliens and belligerent combatants.

Several of the justices, including Robert Jackson and Hugo Black, initially worried that the president might have overstepped his authority when he used an executive order that set up a military commission without the prior consent of either Congress or the courts.[108] Because of the nonstatutory nature of the precedents that touched on the "law of war," and the historical discretion given to previous military tribunals, these jurists had to walk the fine line between complete deference regarding presidential power, and judicial activism in the realm of military affairs. One key issue was whether Article 50 1/2 of the Articles of War, which provided an examination by a board of review, was violated when President Roosevelt issued a proclamation requiring the trial record of the military commission be sent directly to him for final review. Justice Stone and his colleagues decided the Articles of War allowed the president to create military tribunals that punished offenses "against the law of war not ordinarily tried by court martial,"[109] and that Roosevelt had exercised some of the power "conferred upon him by Congress."[110] From a rhetorical vantage point, this stance created a rebuttal presumption that the nation's commander in chief had broad discretion in the establishment of military commissions during wartime.

At the same time that Justice Stone underscored the importance of maximizing the powers of the president during wartime, he minimized the constitutional protections afforded the German detainees. There was little question that six of the eight saboteurs were "alien" soldiers, and the two others who were claiming U.S. citizenship seemed to have maintained "German allegiance and citizenship."[111] The Court followed Attorney General Biddle's lead and noted that "unlawful combatants" were not really prisoners of war, but rather "belligerents" who had violated the law of war.[112] The rhetorical status of being a "belligerent" meant that even U.S. citizens (like Haupt) could be tried by an executive's military tribunal.

All of the justices seemed to have agreed that when the German saboteurs cast aside their uniforms and concealed their identities, they lost whatever rights they may have been able to claim under the laws of war.[113] Hence, these defendants were not protected by the *Milligan* precedent, because that case had involved a U.S. citizen who had lived in Indiana for some two decades. By distinguishing, rather than overturning, the *Milligan* precedent, the author of the October 29 decision could point out that only "non-belligerents" could avoid being "subject to the law of war."[114]

This second opinion is interesting for a number of reasons, including the fact that Stone and the other jurists wanted to avoid taking up the question of the "ultimate boundaries" of these empowered military tribunals.[115] They candidly admitted they were not interested in providing an opinion that looked into the question of whether Congress could place any restrictions on the power of the commander in chief when he was dealing with enemy belligerents, and they thought that a fair reading of the Articles of War "could not at any stage of the proceeding afford any basis for issuing a writ."[116] This focus on jurisdictional matters showed that the members of the Supreme Court no longer had the right to look into questions of secrecy, the balance of governmental power, or the problems that might be associated with the interpretation of specific provisions of the laws of war.

With the benefit of hindsight, we now know that during the behind-closed-doors machinations that preceded the October 29 pronouncement, both Justice Robert Jackson and Justice Felix Frankfurter had steadfastly defended President Roosevelt's handling of this affair. In one of his memos, Jackson argued that the detention of prisoners was a "part of the work of waging war," and that members of the Supreme Court were exceeding their powers when they tried to review the legality of the president's Order. He admonished his colleagues to remember that the "judicial system" was "unfitted to deal with matters in which we must present a united front to a foreign foe."[117] In an infamous "soliloquy" that circulated among the justices, Frankfurter excoriated his fellow jurists for having even considered looking into the procedural safeguards that were outlined in "Articles 46–50 1/2" of the laws of war.[118] He worried that going in that direction would mean that the Court would be implicitly supporting a congressional takeover of "the business of the President as Commander in Chief in the actual conduct of a war."[119] In this fabricated dialogue, the patriotic Frankfurter characterized the "invading German belligerents" as "scoundrels," "low-down, ordinary, enemy spies" who needed to remain in "present custody and be damned" because they did not have any of the claimed "procedural rights" under the Articles of War.[120]

Obviously, many of these candid commentaries did not become a part of the Court's more formalistic written record, but they do constitute an important part of the interaction that exists between "text and historical context."[121] We can see how Stone's focus on the procedural nature of the Supreme Court review of Roosevelt's commission meant that he and the other justices could avoid a major legal battle over the limits of either executive or congressional power during wartime. These court decisions could also be viewed as pragmatic commentaries on the balancing of civil liberties and necessitous obligations. One editorial writer for the *Washington Post* remarked that "Americans can have the satisfaction of knowing that even in a time of great peril we did not stoop to the practices of our enemies."[122]

These key commentaries on the "law of war" provisions provided the American president with a great deal of implied and explicit power, because Stone and the other members of the Supreme Court were not just looking at the rules that had been codified in statutes or interpreted in the

American courts. The "laws of war" were supplemental and flexible, and several nations' legal traditions and histories made it very clear that many international communities had distinguished between armed forces and peaceful populations, noncombatants and combatants. These rules and regulations were intended to protect "lawful combatants" who might be detained as prisoners of war. Stone, in the longer unanimous opinion, wrote:

> The spy who secretly and without uniform passes the military lines of a belligerent in time of war, seeking to gather military information and communicate it to the enemy, or an enemy combatant who without uniform comes secretly through the lines for the purposes of waging war by destruction of life or property, are familiar examples of belligerents who are generally deemed not to be entitled to the status of prisoners of war, but to be offenders against the law of war subject to trial and punishment by military tribunals.[123]

Now *Ex parte Quirin* could stand for the proposition that military tribunals could legitimately be treated as "law of war" courts. This species of military commission was considered to be constitutional even in settings that did not involve martial law, an occupational military government, or the determination of the guilt or innocence of war criminals.[124] Lawyers and judges may talk about the narrow focus of the decision, or its limitations, but the symbolic value of the case could not always be contained in some formal fashion.

In many subsequent stories told about Dasch, Burger, or the other German saboteurs, they were not remembered as bunglers simply fleeing Nazi Germany.[125] For many future generations, these individuals were transmogrified into "unlawful combatants," who had to face the trials and punishments meted out by military tribunals. Some jurists or commentators may not have liked the protean nature of the common law of the "laws of war,"[126] but Congress seemed to have been satisfied that the chief executive and the military tribunals needed this flexibility.

What was even more disappointing for the defense were the ways the Court dealt with the issues of civilian trials and the *Ex parte Milligan* precedent. Colonel Royall, who was described by one press writer as the "tall

North Carolinian who fought so vigorously for the prisoners," observed that the "court had acted," and that he "knew of no other steps that could be taken in behalf of the saboteurs."[127] Robert Cushman, one of the early experts on the *Ex parte Quirin* case, had this to say about Stone's opinion and the Civil War precedent:

> The *Milligan* case had been the chief bulwark of the defense. . . .
> For seventy-five years, the *Milligan* case has been cited as protecting
> the right of the civilian to a jury trial in time of war[,] except in the
> immediate theatre of action. It will be recalled that during the Civil
> War, Milligan was charged with seditious and treasonable activities
> in Indiana where he lived, and was arrested by a military commission
> set up for the purpose by President Lincoln without the sanction of
> any statute. . . . The Government's position was that the doctrine
> of the *Milligan* case, properly construed, is inapplicable to the Nazi
> saboteurs, but that if it should be held applicable, then it ought to
> be overruled.[128]

"Practically," opined Biddle, "the *Milligan* case" was out of the way and "should not plague us again."[129] He was not the first, or the last, public servant who would express such sentiments.

Appreciating the Continued Rhetorical Significance of *Ex Parte Quirin*

It could be argued that these military officials and the FBI may have exaggerated the "necessities" that were used to justify the speed and martial nature of the trial of the German saboteurs, but this is not the type of argument that has become a part of some of our dominant collective memories of the *Ex parte Quirin* proceedings. Given the inherent polysemic dimensions of both language and cultural expectations, we are now seeing contentious debates that are recycling the claims that were advanced by Royall, Biddle, and Stone. Attorney General John Ashcroft will now play the role of Biddle in the new social dramas involving the trial of modern terrorists.

This is not to say that all observers have agreed with our dominant legal and public remembrances of the *Ex parte Quirin* decision. Edward Corwin, in his *Total War and the Constitution,* wrote about how he had once considered this opinion to be "little more than a ceremonious detour to a predetermined goal intended chiefly for edification."[130] Years later, Danelski recontextualized the saboteurs' case as a "constitutional and propaganda victory," in that it "expanded executive power" and "allayed public fears of subversion."[131] Yet in order to reach this result, the Supreme Court had created an "institutional defeat," where the Court had to depart "from its established rules and procedures." For Danelski, Dasch and the rest of the German saboteurs had been a part of a cautionary tale that reminded us of the susceptibility of the Court "to co-optation by the executive."[132]

In order to support such a position, legal historians and other scholars can point out how participants in these World War II judicial proceedings later had second thoughts about their acquiescence and their ready acceptance of the "necessity" pleas. Critics of military tribunals can show how some of the justices who participated in the *Ex parte Quirin* case worried about the precedents established in 1942. Justice Felix Frankfurter noted in 1953 that this was "not a happy precedent," while Justice William O. Douglas expressed his regret that there had not been a more detailed discussion on the merits of the case.[133] John Frank, a clerk for Justice Black, remembered how the "Court allowed itself to be stampeded."[134] Was this a situation where there was a real—not threatened—danger that would impede the nation's ability "to wage war successfully?"[135] Of course such a stance assumes that some privileged group has the ability to distinguish real from false necessities, pure motives from political propaganda, adherence to the true record, and so forth. Such positions miss the role that negotiation, compromise, and audience expectations play in the acceptance or rejection of these arguments. If we are going to learn anything from our revisiting of cases like *Ex parte Quirin,* we will have to pay attention to both presences and absences, and see the broad range of arguments that were circulating within both the legal and public forums of the times. Instead of complaining about the politics or the abuses of one side or the other, we need to focus our energies on figuring out ways to work on coproducing the texts and contexts that will help all of us become engaged in the process of drawing the lines between civil liberties and military necessities.

7

General MacArthur's Tribunal and the Trial of General Yamashita

If the decision was right and just, it will become a precedent of justice
among nations. If the decision was wrong, it must turn into a curse . . .
unless the wrong is acknowledged to the world.
                                                    —Adolf Frank Reel, 1949

By the 1940s, the evolutionary complexities of "military necessity" and
military tribunals presented the American elite and public audiences with
a host of rationales that justified the existence of military tribunals.[1] As
John Bickers explains, many observers who studied the histories and laws
associated with military justice were often mixing and matching three different "species of military commissions"—the type that involved martial
law in the United States, the type that referred to "military control beyond
the orders of the imposing state" (when occupiers were "unable or unwilling to entrust that role to the courts of the occupied nation"), and the
type that centered around violations of "law of war."[2] These three species
are important, but this chapter primarily focuses on a fourth species of
tribunal—where "violations of the law of war" bring "war crimes" trials.[3]
These proceedings often involve violations of battlefield norms—the
"willful killing of prisoners of war, torture or inhumane treatment of the
wounded, and deliberate targeting of protected places."[4]

When legal theorists and American citizens think about the legitimacy
of and need for war crimes trials, they usually remember Nuremberg. Yet
this dominant focus on the concerns of the West should not obviate the
need for studies of the Far East, where the Allies conducted what would

be known as the "Tokyo War Crimes Trials of 1946–48."[5] Even before this time, some of the Allies had been busy collecting evidence against some of the Japanese military leaders, and General Tomoyuki Yamashita, the commander of the forces in the Philippines, became one of the major targets.[6] "No account of United States, indeed Allied, Eastern war crimes operations would be balanced," argues Philip Piccigallo, "without special treatment of the case of General Tomoyuki Yamashita."[7] Between October 7, 1944, and September 3, 1945, General Yamashita was believed to be the leader of both the Japanese army and navy forces fighting rear-guard actions in that region. Years earlier he had gained national and international fame as the "Tiger of Malaya," for his stunning capture of Singapore from the British in 1942, but today he is often remembered as the first high-ranking Japanese leader tried by the Allied powers.

For the first six months after 9/11, very public few discussions of Yamashita's case were held, but as critics began assailing the constitutionality and validity of President Bush's Military Order, both defenders and detractors realized that *In re Yamashita*[8] could no longer be ignored. Major Jeffrey Spears, writing in June of 2003, notes the importance of this decision:

> General MacArthur's legal staff was left to its own devices to develop the regulations to govern the prosecution of war criminals before military commissions in the Far East. . . . The United States in the Pacific selected a case with importance to an American possession—the Philippines—as the first case tried before military commission. The case of General Yamashita . . . highlights the potential frailty of any system of justice when the court fails to follow the spirit of the law in practice. . . . When viewed with the benefit of history, *In re Yamashita* appears more about a race to conclude a case before Pearl Harbor day than a model for jurists seeking to oversee commissions.[9]

Not everyone would be this critical of the decision, and we will see that many modernists couple this decision with the *Ex parte Quirin* (chapter six) precedent. *In re Yamashita* would be remembered as a case that looked into the applicability of military common law systems by military commissions, the review of decisions made by high military authorities, the availability of habeas corpus relief for prisoners of war, and the interpretative meaning of violation of the "laws of war."[10]

Yet if we go back in time and rhetorically recontextualize this decision, we can better understand some of the motivations that influenced the trajectories associated with this controversial decision. For more that six weeks, newspapers around the world carried stories about the fierce fighting taking place in and around Manila, and tens of thousands of noncombatants lost their property and their lives. One of General MacArthur's military commissions eventually determined that General Yamashita deserved to die because he had failed to prevent the atrocities committed by the forces under his command.

Some American members of his military defense team eventually wrote essays and books that pointed out some of the procedural problematics that tarnished the reputation of MacArthur's military commission, and a vocal community of press agents who witnessed these proceedings complained about the political pressures that seemed to stack the deck against this famous Japanese general. Critics pointed out that the idea of "command responsibility" had little precedent,[11] and that prejudicial press coverage made a fair trial in the Philippines an impossibility.

This was also a decision whose evolutionary path was influenced by a variety of domestic and international anxieties and prefigurations—the notion that the creeds of "Christianity" and "Democracy" were fighting against the propaganda of Asiatic despotism, anger over the bombing of Pearl Harbor, British fury over the loss of Singapore in 1942, and the legitimacy of the American possession of "the Commonwealth" of the Philippines. Moreover, when MacArthur put Yamashita on trial for his alleged violations of the norms of international law, he was performing a key role in post–World War II social dramas, where he could show the world that American prowess, determination, and exceptionalism had overcome the arrogance and violence of the Japanese militants.[12] The Japanese notion of the "Greater East Asia co-prosperity sphere" was ridiculed as a perversion of the idea of benevolent imperialism.

I therefore begin my analysis in this chapter by explaining Yamashita's rise within the Japanese ranks during the war. The second section looks at some of the arguments presented at Yamashita's trial, while the third portion analyzes public reactions to the case. The last segment of the chapter illustrates the selective nature of modern memories of *In re Yamashita*.

The Rise of General Yamashita and
the Fighting in the Pacific, 1941–45

In many ways, some of the early discourses surrounding the Axis-Allied battles in the Pacific configured them as being between imperial powers and intractable foes. Japanese militarists, for example, circulated tracts that explained to readers some of the dangers that accompanied the spread of Western influences. One of Yamashita's colonels, Masanobu Tsuji, left us this example of the arguments that appeared in Japanese military pamphlets:

> The remarkable exploits of Yamada Nagamasa in Siam (the present Thailand) took place more than three hundred years ago, but in the years between then and the 1868 Restoration all overseas expansion by the Japanese was brought to a stop by the rigidly enforced seclusion policy of the Tokugawa shoguns, and in that intervening period the English, the French, the Americans, the Dutch, the Portuguese and others sailed into the Far East as if it was theirs by natural right, terrorized and subjugated [*sic*] the culturally backward natives, and colonized [*sic*] every country in the area. . . . These territories, the riches in natural resources in the Far East, were taken by a handful of white men, and their tens of millions of Asian inhabitants have for centuries, down to our own day, suffered constant exploitation and persecution at their hands.[13]

In the Philippines, for example, "a few thousand Americans" were ruling some "thirteen million Filipinos."[14] Just weeks after the bombing of Pearl Harbor, Japanese troops invaded the Philippines. These recursive Orientalist and Occidental ideologies that circulated in many communities helped to create a climate where resource scarcities, imperial desires, nativism, and nationalist fervor all contributed to war fever.

Before the bombing of Pearl Harbor, General Yamashita had been an obscure division commander who chased guerillas in northern China. In the spring of 1941 he traveled to Germany to learn about larger operations, and in 1942 he was sent "against the citadel of British power in the Orient—Singapore."[15] By the end of January of that year, Yamashita's troops controlled the vast majority of the Malaya peninsula, and on February 15, he accepted the surrender of Singapore from British Lieutenant General A. E. Percival.[16]

Although Yamashita was considered to be a hero in the eyes of his troops and in many Japanese communities, he was not one of the Emperor's favorite generals, and he spent some time in Manchuria before the Allied counteroffensive in 1944.[17] In October of 1944, the Japanese Fourteenth Army was assigned the unenviable task of slowing down the American advances in the Philippines. By February of 1945, American readers were being told about the "Jap Fires in Manila," and the fierce fighting taking place in the region. General Yamashita, who was about to evacuate Manila, was said to have told Japanese correspondents that he had MacArthur in his "iron trap," and that he looked forward to a "face-to-face meeting" with the American general he was "chasing all over the South Seas."[18] A sarcastic contributor to the *New York Times* claimed that some of the Japanese troops who had been captured were reporting that they were left starving while their general was well supplied with whiskey and one hundred head of cattle.[19]

By the time of his capture, Yamashita was no longer remembered as the heroic character who had captured Singapore. Dozens of well-trained members of the War Crimes Division of General MacArthur's Judge Advocate Office were roaming the islands, collecting affidavits and taking pictures that would be used in future war crimes proceedings.[20] In October of 1945, Yamashita was being described as a "200-pound bullet-headed general, wearing a green uniform," with polished "brown boots with spurs."[21] This attire would change in the aftermath of the decision of MacArthur's military commission.

Court Performances during and after the Tomoyuki Yamashita Trial, 1945–46

Many of the researchers and commentators who have looked at the *Yamashita* trial focus primary attention on the technical and legal arguments that appeared in the United States Supreme Court review of these proceedings. This apparently dispassionate and objectivist approach has the unintentional effect of downplaying the rhetorical dimensions of the courtroom dramas that unfolded in the Philippines, and elides some of the subnarratives that operated during this time. As I noted in the introduction to this chapter, this was a decision influenced by the competitiveness of the Allied and Axis generals, the belief in the righteousness of the victors' cause, and the bringing of "independence" to the "Commonwealth" of the Philippines. It was no coincidence that when the charges against Yamashita were made public he was accused of having committed atrocities and other high crimes against the people of "the United States," *and* "the Philippines."[22]

The courtroom dramas that took place in front of MacArthur's military commission and the Filipino Supreme Court served several different functions. They allowed many individuals and communities to expiate their guilt, or perform acts of witnessing against the aggressors. American readers were reassured that while the "five U.S. generals of the trial commission" hoped to give Yamashita "every legal courtesy," they were also "men devoutly" hoping "to see him face a firing squad."[23]

When Yamashita's trial began on October 29, 1945, he became the iconic figure who represented all of the worst flaws that were supposed to exist in the Japanese military character. One contemporary reporter observed that during the "Japanese defense of Manila, Filipinos spoke the name of General Tomoyuki Yamashita as if it was blasphemous."[24] When the onetime "Tiger of Malaya" was brought into a "shell-scarred, balconied Manila ballroom" to stand trial, he now "looked incredibly tame and safe, a froglike [*sic*] man in a green uniform," who occasionally smiled.[25] These remarks of course built on many of the stereotypes of the Japanese that had been circulating since the end of the nineteenth century.

Although Yamashita's lawyers had never denied that atrocities had taken place in Manila and other parts of the Philippines, a great deal of the prosecution's time was spent documenting the personal and communal tragedies that accompanied the Japanese occupation.[26] From a propositional standpoint, the prosecution was trying to prove four major claims:

1. A commander should not carry out what were plainly inhumane orders;
2. Yamashita had been in command of all of the forces in the Philippines, and he therefore could have controlled the Japanese naval forces;
3. The atrocities committed were so widespread and so notorious that Yamashita could not have remained in ignorance of their existence except by taking positive steps to avoid such an awareness;
4. While guerrilla fighters may be summarily executed under the accepted laws of war, there was no civilized concept that excused the torture of these fighters.[27]

These types of claims explain why the case would be remembered as one that "was based in part upon a theory of command responsibility[,] in that he knew or should have known of the atrocities committed under his command because of the scope of his troops' activities."[28] Interestingly enough, the prosecutorial team, led by Robert Kerr, did not think they needed to show that Yamashita had "personally participated in or authorized such crimes."[29] He merely had to be in a commanding position.

What are often lost in the dry, technical discussions of the propositional arguments that survive the case are the discursively created pictorial moments that captured the emotional tenor of these times. For the first several weeks of Yamashita's trial, the prosecution called dozens of witnesses who told stories that underscored the heinous acts committed by drunken Japanese soldiers. One of the first of these testimonials came from the well-known Filipino actress, Corazon Noble, who talked of how these Japanese atrocities were a part of Yamashita's plan. She explained how her ten-month-old baby had been mortally wounded by Japanese bayonets. Another Filipino witness turned to the defendant and told him that he ought "to be cut to pieces."[30] Yamashita was not in the vicinity of these atrocities, but he was considered the culpable commander of those who had committed these acts.

One of the most poignant of these trial moments apparently came in mid-November, when General Yamashita had to sit and listen to the testimony of eleven-year-old Rosalinda Andoy, who explained to MacArthur's military commission just why she was now an orphan. When she took the witness stand, her sandals kept coming off, and her interpreter observed that Rosalinda was saying that her parents had once lived in Intramuros, an older walled part of Manila.[31] When the Japanese troops entered the city, they took her father away to Fort Santiago, and herded her mother and many other women and children into a church, where grenades were lobbed in their midst. Rosalinda had been stabbed thirty-eight times, and reporters recorded:

> As she testified Rosalinda began to cry and tears ran down her cheeks and fell on the pink dress. She turned toward the five U.S. generals sitting as commissioners, and showed them her left arm. There were ten scars. There were four more on her right arm. She stood up and pulled her dress up above her brown bloomers, showing 18 scars on her chest and stomach, one on her back . . . she had stayed close to her mother and the bloody church floor . . . then she crawled away. . . . While Rosalinda testified, the Japanese general Yamashita stared coldly at the table before him. In the audience, many people wept.[32]

After hearing this type of testimony, we can readily understand why one contemporary jotted down that "many in the audience guessed that the verdict would be quick and harsh."[33] A. Frank Reel, a key member of the defense team, and a harsh critic of many parts of the proceeding, admitted that "no ordinary man [sic] could hear that testimony and fail to be moved by a desire for revenge."[34]

Yet a desire for revenge is not always the type of motivation that helps illustrate the justice of a particular proceeding. When it came time for Yamashita's defense team to take center stage, they tried to influence the opinion of both their immediate audience and those watching the trial in the broader court of world opinion. General MacArthur had asked that Lieutenant General Wilhelm Styer organize Yamashita's trial, and Styer in turn assigned Colonel "Bud" Young the task of putting together the defense team.[35] During some of the first interviews, Yamashita told Young that over 300,000 troops had landed at Luzon. Evidently, he had not been given any real control over the air force, over the naval troops, or over some 30,000 soldiers attached to the Supreme Southern command.[36]

Yamashita's narratives were filled with commentaries on the chaos of war, and he told the defense team about his evacuation of Manila. Some 20,000 naval troops made a different choice—they would stay in the city and fight the Americans to the death. Yamashita noted that if the atrocities being reported had been committed, they were acts that went against his express orders. Furthermore, if he had known about these violations he would have punished the perpetrators himself.[37] All of the Japanese witnesses who testified in the defendant's behalf "agreed that Yamashita, miles away from Manila in the hills, had no means of communication with the desperate sailors in Manila, let alone directing them."[38]

At the same time that the defense team was collecting this factual information, they were putting together the legal arguments that would be used throughout the trial. For example, Lieutenant Colonel Walter Hendrix, of Atlanta, Georgia, told reporters that General MacArthur was not authorized to establish a military commission in the Philippines, because this was not considered to be "occupied territory."[39] This claim was connected to the idea that under the traditional military laws associated with the laws of war, some commissions only convened in occupied territories. An unnamed member of the United States Army legal defense team advanced a different complaint when he denounced the "MacArthur system" of "war crimes prosecution before the Philippine Court."[40]

These types of arguments would be presented over and over again throughout the appellate process, but it would the testimony of the Japanese general himself that changed the minds of at least some observers who watched his courtroom demeanor. For hours the prosecutors tried to trap him as they searched for contradictory remarks, but he made it clear to his Nisei interpreter that he wanted to leave behind an accurate record of his own words and deeds. When he took the witness chair, he "denied that he had ever known of Philippine atrocities, much less condoned or ordered them."[41] He explained to the commission members and his listeners that he had arrived just days before the American landing at Leyte, and that he was unfamiliar with the country, the people, and even his own officers. In the fog of war, and the nerve-racking confusion that came with pitched battles, it was easy to lose communication. Yamashita averred that he "was under constant attack by superior American forces."[42] At one crucial point in his testimony, the beleaguered Japanese general made this plea; "I have put forth my maximum effort in order to control my troops. If this is not sufficient then somehow I should have done more. . . . I feel that I did my best."[43]

What once appeared to be a clear-cut case for many spectators had now been transformed into an ambiguous situation filled with "uneasy perplexity."[44] A reporter for *Time* magazine, who tried to capture the spirit of the times, intoned:

> When the defense rested, the task of the trial commission no longer seemed simple. Yamashita's spirited defense had suddenly emphasized the lack of precedent for war crimes trials, the vagueness of the charges—violation of the rules of war. The commission had other problems. What was Yamashita—a consummate liar or a victim of circumstance? What was to be his fate? The rope or the firing squad? Prison? Freedom? Manila waited for the answer.[45]

The Filipino people did not have to wait very long. On December 7, 1945—exactly four years after the bombing of Pearl Harbor—MacArthur's five-person commission condemned Yamashita to be hanged. Many Japanese citizens who heard about the story of his death were incredulous, and spread rumors of how he had actually been spirited away to Washington so they could prepare for the "Soviet-American war."[46]

When General MacArthur was asked to review the findings of the members of the military commission that convicted Yamashita, he upheld their decision and publicized a short memorandum explaining his position. This was once described as a "scathing denunciation of Yamashita."[47] The American general argued that given the "cruel and wanton" record before him, he searched in "vain" for some "mitigating circumstances" that might have helped his defeated adversary. MacArthur claimed this "officer of proven field merit" had nevertheless violated his sacred trust as protector of the weak. He had profaned "his entire cult," and he had threatened "the very fabric of international society."[48] In sum, he had neglected "his duty to his troops, to his enemy and to mankind."[49] MacArthur indicated that he believed that in October of 1944, the Japanese military authorities had been warned that any failure to accord prisoners of war or civilians the proper treatment they deserved would bring repercussions.

Yamashita was blamed for having allowed the "peculiarly callous and purposeless sack of the ancient city of Manila, and its Christian population and its countless historic shrines and monuments of culture and civilization."[50]

MacArthur then defended the idea that commanding officers should be held responsible for the actions of their troops. "Resultant liability," he opined, "is commensurate with resultant crime." The American general claimed this was not a new limitation, and that such principles had always been "subject to due process of law." Since the commanding general could not have absolute or autocratic power, even in times of war, he was "responsible before the bar of justice." Hence, universal practices—"from time immemorial"—allowed "military transgressions" to be tried "by military tribunals." As Commanding General of the United States Forces in the Western Pacific, he felt he had to "execute the sentence."[51]

In many of the Allied interpretations of the *Yamashita* ruling, the executed Japanese leader had violated not only the rules of international law but also the formal and informal rules of a warrior code. General Courtney Whitney, both a subordinate and friend of MacArthur, told readers in 1956:

> Probably nothing during his administration of the occupation gave MacArthur deeper concern than his obligation to act upon the judgment of the International Military Tribunal of the Far East. He quickly approved penalties adjudged against the enemy field commanders or other military personnel who had permitted or committed atrocities against soldiers or civilians who had fallen under their custody during the war. He held to a rigid code delineating the responsibility for fair and humane treatment of the enemy, military or civilian, who fell under the power of a military commander, and he was outraged that this code was wantonly violated. He set forth this code in his review of the trial proceedings against General Tomoyuki Yamashita, who had been the Japanese military commander in the Philippines at the time of the sack of Manila in 1945.[52]

What Whitney did not focus on were the numbers of Allied soldiers or commanders who had also witnessed, "permitted or committed" their own atrocities. In his *Wartime Journals,* Charles Lindbergh explained that "[o]ur men think nothing of shooting a Japanese prisoner or soldier attempted to surrender. They treat the Jap with less respect than they would give to an animal, and these acts are condoned by almost everyone."[53] This was not a common or popular sentiment in American circles, but it nevertheless illustrated the one-sided nature of some of these proceedings.

When the defense attorneys realized MacArthur was not going to challenge the verdict of the five generals of Yamashita's military commission, they began preparing briefs arguing that the "military commission had no authority to act," and that the "Philippine courts were the proper forums" for any appeals. Furthermore, the defense noted that their client had not been "accused of any violations of the laws of warfare."[54] From their vantage point, Yamashita's lawyers believed this commission had allowed evidence to be presented that was based on depositions, affidavits, hearsay, and opinions, and that the defendant was not given the same due process guarantees available to an American soldier who might have been charged with the same offense. The defense team also complained that they had not been provided with sufficient time to thoroughly prepare their case.[55]

As soon as Yamashita's lawyers filed a petition for a writ of certiorari by air mail with the United States Supreme Court, the solicitor general's office allowed the press to see some of the legal arguments that would be used by the prosecutors during the appellate process. J. Howard McGrath told reporters that since the Japanese commander had been tried by a military commission set up by the Army in a combat zone, the five-member military commission had jurisdiction, and the Supreme Court "may not inquire into the evidence or into any alleged procedural irregularities or defects." Thus only the military needed to be involved in any review of the commission's activities. McGrath informed readers of the *New York Times* that since a "military commission was not a court," it should be considered an "agency of the Executive Branch of the Federal Government."[56]

The solicitor general was thus able to provide the American public with a short explanation of what it meant to receive justice under existing military law. Although the commission was interested in protecting the rights of the accused, this did not mean that the defendant had any right to trial by jury, or that the offenses "against the law of war" had to be tried "in the civil courts." A "long recognized procedure of the law of war," argued McGrath, allowed the "military commission" the "right to try enemy belligerents for violations of the law of war committed prior to their capture[,] even after cessation of hostilities and when the civil courts are open."[57] This, of course, implied that the *In re Yamashita* case could be distinguished from the *Ex parte Milligan* precedent (chapter four).

Would these arguments resonate with the members of the U.S. Supreme Court or the American public?

The Legal and Public Commentaries on General Yamashita's Situation

Whenever a highly controversial case reaches the Supreme Court, many of the justices want to avoid having a lot of concurring and dissenting opinions, and in this case Chief Justice Stone searched in vain for that unanimity. Only some of the justices agreed with Stone when he claimed that any errors found in the procedures of military commissions were not subject to civilian judicial review.[58] The chief justice opined that a military commission should be compared to an expert administrative body that had the right to receive all of the relevant evidence with "probative" value. While Stone was not interested in writing an opinion that totally closed off any judicial review for habeas corpus relief, he wanted to make sure that for the most part the judiciary stayed out of military affairs.

After the circulation of many compromising memos, Stone was able to put together a 6-2 majority, and he wrote an opinion that clearly outlined just why the Supreme Court did not have the jurisdiction to review the determinations made by military tribunals established by congressional enactments. This in turn meant that the Court was not going to look into the substantive issue of Yamashita's guilt or innocence.[59] Moreover, in this particular case, they were denying the application for leave to file a writ of habeas corpus for General Yamashita. There would be no stay of the subsequent execution of the sentence handed down by MacArthur's commission.[60] The Court determined that the five-member commission had the lawful authority to proceed with the *Yamashita* trial, and that that body had not violated any military, statutory, or constitutional guidelines.

The majority opinion was written in such a way that it gave the impression the military system did an adequate job of protecting the constitutional rights or privileges of the defendants who fell under military jurisdiction. Stone took the position that the "due process" rights available to defendants who stood before military commissions under international law were just not the same ones that were applicable in domestic forums.[61] The commanding officer who put together the tribunal had to follow the "common law of war," and not all of the written Articles of War:

> Petitioner, an enemy combatant, is therefore not a person made subject to the Articles of War by Article 2, and the military commission before which he was tried, though sanctioned, and its jurisdiction saved, by Article 15, was not convened by virtue of the Articles of War, but pursuant to the common law of war. It follows that the Articles of War, including Articles 25 and 38, were not applicable to the petitioner's trial and imposed no restrictions upon the procedure to be followed. The Articles left the control over the procedure in such a case where it had previously been, with the military command.[62]

The Court could of course also rely on the precedents that had been set by *Ex parte Quirin* (chapter six).

The two dissenting justices in the *In re Yamashita* case, Murphy and Rutledge, "read their dissenting opinions in tones so bitter and in language so sharp that it was readily apparent to all listeners that even more acrimonious expression must have marked the debate behind the scenes."[63] Justice Murphy was clearly worried about the rights of the individuals who came before military commissions and international perceptions:

> The Fifth Amendment guarantee of due process of law applies to "any person" who is accused of a crime by the Federal Government or any of its agencies. No exception is made as to those who are accused of war crimes or as to those who possess the status of an enemy belligerent. Indeed, such an exception would be contrary to the whole philosophy of human rights which makes the Constitution the great living document that it is. The immutable rights of the individual, including those secured by the due process clause of the

Fifth Amendment, belong not alone to the members of those nations that excel on the battlefield or subscribed to the democratic ideology. They belong to every person in the world, victor or vanquished, whatever may be his [*sic*] race, color or beliefs. They rise above any status of belligerency or outlawry. They survive any popular passion or frenzy of the moment.[64]

Justice Murphy's dissent was written in such a way that it attempted to build on those ancient "whig" building blocks used in the ideographic framing of the "civilianization" of the military. He was trying to recontextualize the case in ways that reflected a balancing of idealistic and realistic concerns—after all, the specific wording of the Constitution needed to be interpreted in light of actual circumstances. This was one justice who was unwilling to pretend that passions or racial prejudice could be bracketed out of the legal decision-making process.

The other dissenter in the *Yamashita* case, Justice Rutledge, questioned the degree of the "necessity" that was needed when hostilities had ended.[65] This was one of the arguments raised by Yamashita's defense counsel. Rutledge declared that "there is no law restrictive upon these proceedings other than whatever rules and regulations may be prescribed for their government by the executive authority or the military, and, on the other hand, that the provisions of the Articles of War, of the Geneva Convention, and the Fifth Amendment apply."[66] What Rutledge was particularly concerned about was the *speed* of the military commission proceedings—the process began with arraignments on October 8 and ended with the sentencing on December 7. This put an incredible burden on the defense, and he thought that they had been placed in an "impossible" situation.[67] One contemporary writer argued that from "their dissents arises a gloomy picture of sloppy procedure on the part of the military tribunal," and "a gross violation of Anglo-Saxon principles of law."[68] Perhaps this is one of the reasons why modern defenders of tribunals move quickly toward embracing the *Ex parte Quirin* precedent, and walk gingerly around *In re Yamashita*.

Very few contemporary critics of the *Yamashita* proceedings disputed the fact that tens of thousands of atrocities had been committed by the Japanese forces in the Philippines. What worried them were the selective applications of military justice that assumed Japanese commanders "should" have known about all of the activities of their subalterns. Several writers commented on the fact that Yamashita had not been allowed to choose his own lawyers, that the cross-examinations of his defense team were limited by the tribunal, that he was given little time to prepare his defense, and that the Americans were crafting newly minted violations of the laws of war.[69] Hanson Baldwin, who tried to compare the *Yamashita* proceedings and the Nuremberg trials, noted that the former looked like one of those "kangaroo courts" where the "verdict was forgone and the trial nearly a mockery."[70] Major Eugene Boardman, a member of the United States Marine Corps and interpreter at the *Yamashita* trial, worried about the "considerable latitude" that was "given as regards the admissibility of evidence" during the proceedings.[71] Since the military commission was "in effect neither a court-martial nor a civil body," it needed to follow the rules of procedure that had been created "specifically for the trial of war criminals." According to Major Boardman, the "new concept of command responsibility" meant that "nearly any commander anywhere, Americans included, could be held liable as a war criminal for murder or rape committed by a subordinate, even is he [*sic*] had ordered the punishment of such crimes."[72] He was worried that the "elastic rules of the *Yamashita* trial" would be "made applicable to Nuremberg," and this in turn to would lead to "a blanket indictment and a distortion of the ordinary concepts of Anglo-American justice."[73]

The vast majority of mainstream newspaper writers supported the efforts of the five generals who made up MacArthur's military commission. An editorial in the *New York Times* claimed that "most persons who have followed the testimony will believe that a fair verdict was reached."[74] This writer was convinced that "it was more than General Yamashita who was on trial," in that the "whole Japanese military clique and its twisted warrior code also was in the prisoner's dock." The editorial claimed that some 60,000 unarmed non-combatant Filipinos had been "foully murdered," and that this particular struggle "characterized every Japanese action through three and two-thirds years of war."[75] The *Yamashita* case was viewed as a precedent that might stop future aggressions, because now there "can be no legitimate plea of ignorance," under deliberate programs of systematic atrocities.

Many defenders of the *Yamashita* proceedings were convinced that the critics of the military commissions simply did not understand that there were major differences in the procedural rules of civilian and military courts, and that ancient common laws, recent court cases, and modern statutory provisions helped these tribunals carry out their special mandates. Yamashita's trial was depicted as one that gave him the opportunity to call witnesses, and he was said to have been provided with "practically every legal protection that would have been given a defendant on trial in a criminal court" in America.[76] Supporters of the five American generals noted that the battery of lawyers that defended him would have cost $50,000, and that even Yamashita, in a pre-verdict statement, had "thanked the commission for a fair trial."[77] If the Americans had lost the war, would they have gotten this type of treatment?

In late February of 1946, General Yamashita's appeals were exhausted and newspapers around the globe carried detailed accounts of his death by hanging. In many ways, this event was filled with its own symbols and rituals, and this solemn occasion became a part of the historical memories of Philippine involvement in the war. A writer for *Newsweek* told readers that the "gallows stood hidden by green camouflage and trees in a weed-strewn cane field near Los Baños, southwest of Manila."[78] His wards had taken away his Japanese uniform, and he now wore a GI shirt, trousers, and fatigue cap. Another magazine contributor claimed this outfit was "the symbol of military disgrace ordered by his conqueror, General Douglas MacArthur."[79] Lieutenant Colonel Seichi Ohta, the former head of the Japanese Kempei Tai (thought police), and Takuma Higashigi, a Japanese civilian interpreter, followed Yamashita to the scaffold.[80] His interpreter claimed that he spoke (or wrote in some versions) these last words:

> Until now I am believed that I have tried to do my best throughout the army. As I said in Manila Supreme Court, that I [*sic*] done with all my capacity, so I don't [*sic*] ashame in front of God for what I have done. When I have been investigated in Manila Court, I have had a good treatment, kindful attitude from your good-natured officers, who all the time protect me . . . God bless them . . . I will pray for the emperor's long life and his prosperity forever.[81]

Other renditions of the story had him saying that if he was told that "You do not have any ability to command Japanese Army," he would "say nothing of it, because it is my own nature."[82] Before dying, he personally thanked the members of his defense team—Clarke, Feldhaus, Hendrix, Guy, Sandberg, and Reel. He also told his father and mother that he would soon be joining them, and that he wanted someone to educate his children.

The geographic choice of Los Baños for the execution of General Yamashita was no accident, because this was near the site where a year earlier his soldiers allegedly killed 2,000 civilians in revenge for the release of some Allied nationals at a prison camp.[83] The rhetorical framing of the death of Yamashita allowed the American and Filipino audiences to share a common vision of an alliance against the imperialist foe. His grave would be marked by a white post that would bear no name.

By the 1950s, literally hundreds of essays had been written that justified the existence of the military commissions, and now writers could talk about how *Yamashita*'s case would help preserve the peace and protect noncombatants in the future. During his six-week trial, some 4,000 pages of testimony and evidence had been presented, and some four hundred exhibits collected. These discursive and iconic artifacts were considered to be parts of an archival record that preserved the documentation of Japanese atrocities—and the righteousness of the allied cause. Arthur Kuhn, for example, wrote in the *American Journal of International Law* that this proceeding was just one part of the tribunal system that had been agreed upon by the Allies who signed the London Agreement in August 1945, and that:

> General MacArthur subsequently reviewed the proceeding and approved the sentence. . . . It was doubtlessly intended by Congress to adopt a different procedure in trials of Army personnel but not of enemy combatants for offenses against the customary laws of war. . . . General Yamashita was tried chiefly for crimes against noncombatants committed on a scale so vast that the accomplishment to be hoped for a result of the trial ought to be far removed from any mere satisfaction of vengeance or even of retributive justice[,] but as a deterrent against similar conduct in the future.[84]

There were of course some influential texts that raised key questions about the use of military commissions in general, and MacArthur's tribunal in particular. Reel, who published *The Case of General Yamashita* in 1949, had reached the conclusion that the "most serious defect" in the American system of justice came from the inherent political and hierarchal nature of the process. Judges were "supposed to make a decision based on the evidence," but Reel thought it was "next to impossible to find a military court" that felt free enough to "act independently of the wishes of the appointing authority."[85] Alpheus Mason, in *Harlan Fiske Stone,* averred in 1956 that Chief Justice Stone, in upholding the military, "required a strained interpretation of the Articles of War." Even worse, in Mason's mind, was the idea that the chief justice had "led a divided Court into obscurity, paying the price that one must always pay for artificial unanimity."[86] Reel has similarly remarked that the majority decision was a "patchwork of ideas and statements, patched together to satisfy the divergent views of men [*sic*] who were seeking to find 'good' reasons for a politically expedient result."[87]

Several decades later, in the midst of the Vietnam War, the Americans were facing the question of whether the *Yamashita* discussions of "command" responsibility were going to be applied to all of the officers fighting in the jungles of Vietnam. A. J. Barker, writing in 1973, argued that if Yamashita was guilty of anything, it was "moral turpitude," and not legal culpability. He pointed out that the Japanese general had countermanded many of the orders that emanated from Tokyo, and that Yamashita had occasionally used his influence to prevent the killing of many U.S. prisoners of war who survived in Philippine prisons.[88] What was even more telling was the fact that

> Yamashita was brought to trial for crimes of which he was far more innocent than the majority of other Japanese commanders. And what followed put a permanent stain on the American escutcheon, and created an embarrassing precedent which would be remembered by American legal experts when Lieutenant Calley was cited as a war criminal for his part in the My Lai incident during the Vietnam War.[89]

One wonders what MacArthur would have thought if he had seen one of his co-creations now being applied in a variety of novel combat situations.

Conclusion: Legal Remembering and Forgetting in Modern Discussions of the *Yamashita* Case

When supporters or critics of President Bush's Military Order looked around for historical precedents, the name of Yamashita occasionally appeared in a string of citations of cases. For example, Cass Sunstein talked about it when he testified about military tribunals before the Senate Judiciary Subcommittee on Administrative Oversight and the Courts in first week of December in 2001.[90] A week later, the *Yamashita* case was one of the precedents discussed in a hearing of the Senate Armed Services Committee that was chaired by Senator Carl Levin.[91] Many of these discussions were framed in ways that focused on the inherent power of the chief executive to form tribunals when Congress has declared war.

Some of these formalistic commentaries leave out the contextual and emotive dimensions of the *Yamashita* case.[92] Yes, it is true that we can single out the principle of command responsibility, executive discretion during wartime, or limited habeas corpus review, but as I have argued throughout this book, this should only be a part of our deliberation as we assess the costs and benefits associated with the use of military tribunals. Note, for example, the beliefs of one of the veterans who watched with interest the modern memory work surrounding these cases. Near the end of 2001, Stephen Ives, a Bronze Star recipient for his work on Luzon in 1945, talked with newspaper reporters and radio hosts[93] about the problematics of the *Yamashita* proceedings. Ives told readers of the *Washington Post* that President Bush's November declaration stated that the "United States is free to try terrorist leaders in U.S. courts abroad"; it brought back "memories of just such a trial, held in similar circumstances more than a half century ago."[94] He was convinced that Yamashita had been "railroaded to the gallows in Manila in February of 1946," and that the case showed that military tribunals were sometimes "susceptible to abuse."[95] Ives, who had been an officer in the G-2 Section of the U.S. Sixth Army, had been one of the officers responsible for keeping track of enemy units and analyzing their movements, so he was "troubled that Yamashita was to be held responsible for actions I knew he could not possibly have known of or prevented."[96]

Ives provides all of us with a very different counternarrative from the one that briefly appears before the Senate subcommittee. Here there is no detached talk about Articles I, III, or III, or the exact wording that was used to justify the *Yamashita* decision. Instead, Ives gives us a hint about the rhetorical culture of the times when he recalls that the "winners" were "eager for revenge and scapegoats are readily available." Ives had tried to become a part of the Yamashita defense team, but his commanding officer in Japan told him that the "conviction was already settled," and that all he could do was get himself into trouble. Ives publicly acknowledged he had continually regretted that decision.[97]

In a relatively short article that Ives sent to the *Washington Post,* he gave one of the most devastating critiques of the *Yamashita* decision that has ever appeared in print. Since that time we have more summaries of some of the legalistic dimensions of these decisions,[98] but Ives can perhaps be forgiven for mentioning some taboo subjects. He noted, for example, that none of the five generals who sat on MacArthur's tribunal had much serious command experience, and that during the trial Yamashita's name was rarely even mentioned. Instead, what we were given was a parade of hundreds of witnesses who talked about beatings, rapes, and group killings of Filipinos. This was all presented "without evidence of Yamashita's approval or even knowledge."[99]

Ives makes the interesting argument that the trial evidence presented "failed to establish that the atrocities were carried out by military personnel under Yamashita's control." Since most of the atrocities described to the tribunal had been committed during February and March of 1945, thus had taken place after Yamashita ordered all of the forces withdrawn from the city. The Japanese forces that stayed had disobeyed his express orders. "The southern forces," argued Ives, "were isolated, often stragglers, and completely out of touch with Yamashita's headquarters, more than 150 U.S.-occupied miles to the north."[100]

Ives admonished American readers to remember that the trial seemed put together in ways that moved "relentlessly toward conviction." Defense teams were not provided with access to the "Army's investigative reports, which might have revealed exculpatory materials." At times the court allowed the prosecutors to change specifications at the last minute, and they allowed a lot of erroneous hearsay evidence to be presented. Ives concluded his essay by arguing:

> It is clear that the military tribunal rammed through a conviction at MacArthur's prodding. . . . One motive was surely vengeance, but it seems clear that the conviction was primarily designed to reduce pressure to try the Emperor. . . . The *Yamashita* case is a cautionary tale against the wisdom of victors holding military trials when their people are crying out for revenge. We can't undo what happened. But by drawing attention to this miscarriage of justice, we can perhaps prevent its repetition.[101]

From a rhetorical vantage point, the modern discussions of victims' rights and the observation of terrorist trials sound a lot like the arguments used to justify the trial of Yamashita. In a very short while, we too may be seeing martial cases where very little time is spent talking about the specific acts of an individual, and a vast amount of time is spent on victims' rights and collective traumas.

Unquestionably, the events of 9/11 were emotionally and physically devastating, but this is exactly the time when we need to think prudentially about the efficacy of our judicial actions and the long-term impacts of our decisions. Do we really want to celebrate the anniversaries of this tragic event in the same way that some army officials rushed to have closure with the *Yamashita* case on Pearl Harbor day? The use of these military tribunals may provide us with what appear to be more efficient trials, but the rush to judgment means we forget how our perceptions of the Japanese and the Arab "other" impact the dispensation of that justice. Do we really think that after 9/11 we can have military tribunals that are any fairer than the one that tried General Yamashita? Even the clearest and fairest of civilian or military guidelines provide little protection when the members of the rhetorical culture refuse to give warranted assent to those restraints.

8

The Legal and Public
Debates over the Necessity
of Bush's Military Order

The Constitution of the United States is a law for rulers and people,
equally in war and in peace, and covers with the shield of its protection
all classes of men [*sic*], at all times, and under all circumstances.
———Justice Davis, in *Ex parte Milligan* (1866)

The exigencies of war demand that the administration of that justice be
swift as well as fair.
———Judge Advocate General of the Army Myron Cramer,
September 25, 1942

When key decision-makers within the George W. Bush's administration
looked for precedents or historical narratives that would help them deal
with the post 9/11 exigencies,[1] we now know they had plenty of "tory"
and "whig" versions of necessitous tales from which to choose.[2] On the
one hand, they could use those cases that highlighted the "will" of military
commander, and the need for quick decisions. This would mean quoting
those cases that talked about how the mere *declaration* of an emergency
was enough to constitute a national exigency, the importance of deference
when reviewing the decisions of military leaders, and wartime needs.[3]
On the other hand, Bush administrators could have listened to some of
the critics of broad discretionary powers in times of war, where "whig"
narratives were told about the primacy of civilian courts, the dangers of
martial law, or the abuse of the tyrant's plea of necessity. As we have seen
in previous chapters, the "tory" versions of necessitous situations often

underscored the importance of having a great deal of governmental flexibility and executive discretion, while the "whig" approach would have entailed using rhetorics that highlighted the differences between declared necessities and real necessities, and the benefits of incremental decision-making. Modern commentators may want us to continually make technical distinctions between various rationales related to species of military commissions—some for military systems in foreign lands, some during times when martial law has been declared, and some for trying actors who have violated the "rule of law"—but a rhetorical analysis of some of the histories associated with these tribunals illustrates how various communities mixed and matched many of these arguments.

Lawyers, judges, and ordinary citizens often commingled a host of principles that came from select military cases, and they sometimes crafted narratives that were used in unpredictable ways. Our idealistic and pragmatic discussions of Washington's Board of General Officers, the Dakota trials, the Wirz Commission, *Ex parte Milligan, Ex parte Quirin,* and *In re Yamashita* have left us with many complex ideas about tribunals, and our legal histories are filled with contradictions, ambivalences and dilemmas. We have inherited more than just a single, linear "rule of law" that can be discerned propositionally through some deductive analysis of court precedents, and we need to admit that we have a host of hybrid rhetorical histories that have influenced the discursive and iconic trajectories of *both* the "tory" and "whig" versions of these necessitous tales.

Supporters and detractors of the Bush Military Order oftentimes make the mistake of decontextualizing many of these precedential cases, as they abstract out the pithy phrases that support their positions, leaving behind the rich public commentaries and legal analyses that explain some of the motivations for the choices made in other turbulent times. For example, liberals sometimes forget how the Dakota trials illustrate some of the problematics that can attend civil courts, where Lincoln's discretion may have saved the lives of hundreds of Americans. The purveyors of these whiggish narratives may attack the fairness of military proceedings, but they underestimate the social agency of the military staff members assigned to the *Quirin* and *Yamashita* cases. These members of various defense teams fought valiantly to save their defendants' lives. Moreover, the analysis provided in earlier chapters illustrated how some of these officers were some of the most vociferous critics of these military tribunals.

At the same time, uncritical defenders of all forms of military tribunals forget about the prejudices that motivated the creation of some of these bodies, the dangers associated with the rush to judgment, or the difficulties associated with coming up with written rules or documents that can constrain broad discretionary power. Note, for example, the deference given to Abraham Lincoln or General MacArthur, or the public discussions of the guilt of the defendants that circulated before their trials.

In this chapter I am interested in providing a rhetorical analysis that looks into just how various supporters and critics of President's Bush's Military Order have appropriated some of these historical fragments in their modern debates about "military necessity," and the legitimacy of military tribunals. As I noted in chapter five, after 9/11 many Bush administrators and U.S. congressional leaders treated the attack on the Twin Towers and the Pentagon as another Pearl Harbor, where they now stood in the shoes of then President Franklin D. Roosevelt. American Democrats and Republicans rallied around President Bush, and there were few observers who doubted that this was a time when necessitous measures had to be passed in order to maintain "law and order" or "national security."[4] The relatively easy passage of the Patriot Act[5] provided some symbolic indicators of the apparent unity of the nation. As long as legislators got the sense that they would be heavily involved in the decisions made about these wars, they were willing to go along with many of the president's initiatives. In spite of occasional judicial criticisms of some specific Bush measures, most federal judges also supported the constitutionality and validity of the Patriot Acts, I and II.

This would not be the case when President George W. Bush invoked his executive powers and put forward the "Military Order of November 13, 2001," which dealt with the "Detention, Treatment, and Trial of Certain Non-Citizens in the War against Terrorism."[6] Criticisms of this announcement cut across party lines, as even supporters of the "War on Terrorism" worried that perhaps this went too far. Almost two months before the signing of this executive order, the American president told his listeners the country needed to "bring our enemies to justice or bring justice to our enemies," and Josh Tyrangiel noted that since that speech, "the sharpest legal minds in the White House and Department of Justice have been working to turn the President's poetic abstraction into specific judicial doctrine."[7]

Given the various species of military commissions, there were a number of rhetorical frames that might have been used in the formation of the Bush Military Order. However, this was not a situation involving martial law, and this was not a time when foreign lands needed to be ruled temporarily by military forces. From a theoretical standpoint, the president's legal advisors needed to at least connect the 9/11 acts to alleged violations of the "rules of war." At the same time, the very debates about even the possible use of these military trials had immense symbolic value, in that they illustrated how Americans could dispense justice in forums that need not resemble the Nuremberg proceedings or other traditional venues.

This of course meant that arrival of the Bush Military Order raised the possibility that some terrorists or other belligerents would not appear in American federal court, and that they would not have to stand in the docks of Nuremberg-type tribunals. As Laura Dickinson explained in 2002:

> [The Bush commissions] would be conducted unilaterally by the United States . . . those who have supported the use of the commissions have made it clear—if not in their explicit rhetoric then in the procedures that they have proposed and condoned—that they view law as an inconvenience at moments when real interests are threatened and real action is necessary. . . . Roosevelt limited the substantive offenses triable before the commissions to "sabotage, espionage, or other hostile or warlike acts." The Bush order, by contrast defines the offenses triable before the commissions as including violations of the "laws of war and other applicable law." The Bush order would thus extend the scope of military commissions beyond that which the Court upheld in *Quirin*.[8]

Obviously not all commentators who consider the Bush Order would adopt Dickinson's "whiggish" view of "necessity," *Ex parte Quirin,* or the legal impact of this announcement, but her explanation gives us a good overview of some of the key issues considered relevant in the modern debates over the legitimacy of the Military Order.

During the late fall of 2001, the authors and the supporters of the Bush Military Order were having to comb through the historical archives so that they could study how other wartime presidents had justified the use of their power as commanders in chief of the armed forces. Here one does not hear a great deal about General Pope and the Dakota trials, or General MacArthur and the *Yamashita* trials. The Bush teams needed to find less controversial precedents, which meant resurrecting the old debate between the *Ex parte Milligan* and *Ex parte Quirin*[9] frameworks, and defending "realist" modifications from the harping of critics who were "at best" naive, "and at worst" aiders and abettors of terrorists.[10] Assistant Attorney General Michael Chertoff remarked that when nations are at war,

> military commissions are a traditional way of bringing justice to persons charged with offenses under armed conflict. The Supreme Court has upheld the use of such commissions. The use of such commissions is not only legally proper; there may be sound policy reasons to employ it in individual cases. Proceedings before military commissions may be needed to safeguard classified information at the trial of particular members of Al Qaida. Also, military commissions are equipped to deal with the significant security concerns that can arise from a trial of the terrorists. We are all aware that trying terrorists in our cities could place judges and juries—and, indeed, the cities themselves—at risk. Finally, bear in mind that the attacks of September 11 were launched by a foreign power and [and that they] killed thousands of innocent people. These are war crimes, in addition to domestic crimes.[11]

In this very brief summary, Chertoff is covering a lot of legal and symbolic ground. He is magnifying the danger posed by the criminality of the terrorists, explaining the orthodox nature of these acts, making claims about the Supreme Court's views on the legitimacy of the tribunals, and rationalizing why civilian courts are not the best places to try these belligerents. I would contend that Chertoff's summary was also tapping into genealogical memories dating back hundreds of years, where other jurists, politicians, and military leaders had written about the principles of war that came from battlefield experiences, authoritative textbooks, statutes, and judicial edicts.

At the same time, the assistant attorney general was adapting these remarks to the specific occasion. He implied that he was not talking about the need for international military tribunals—this was something that the Americans could deal with by themselves.[12] Of course Chertoff was right that there had been times when individual nations conducted their own "war crimes" trials—the Adolf Eichmann trial comes quickly to mind[13]— but one of the key issues for many critics involved the question of whether all of the various branches of government had really been involved in the planning of these forums.

As I note in chapter nine, the potential military trial of the Guantánamo detainees exacerbated some of the legal problems that existed in an already complex situation, because many commentators worried that if the American president had declared a "war" on terrorism, then unilateral activity would escalate and the zones of war would proliferate as the U.S. fought protracted battles in Afghanistan and Iraq. By April of 2002, there were some three hundred detainees who faced the very real prospect of being tried for their membership in al-Qaeda,[14] and more wars on terrorism might bring more detentions.

From the very beginning, President Bush made it clear that he believed the alleged terrorists should not be treated as ordinary criminals who deserved the due process rights Americans were used to seeing. This characterization of the 9/11 tragedy as a part of a much larger war, and not as a large-scale policy matter, was just one more reason why civilian courts might be bypassed in these exigent situations. In his January 2002, State of the Union Address, the U.S. commander in chief told Congress that "[T]housands of dangerous killers, schooled in the methods of murder, often supported by outlaw regimes, are now spread throughout the world like ticking time bombs, set to go off without warning."[15] These types of remarks traverse temporal distance, as we are taken back to a time when an anxious President Roosevelt faced the conspiracies of the German saboteurs.

In this chapter I begin my rhetorical analysis by looking at some of the specific textual arguments appearing within the Bush Military Order itself, and then I illustrate how various communities have debated the legality and desirability of these commissions. This is followed by a critique of the "modifications" that were made following this debate.

A Textual Analysis of the Bush Military Order

In many ways, the Bush "Military Order" is a rhetorical fragment that serves a number of persuasive purposes. It announces to the world the nation's grievances, and it explains to readers some of the protections that are gratuitously afforded to defendants who might be tried by military commissions. The Bush administration seemed to be signaling that they were interested in having the type of military tribunals that met the demands of several audiences—readers who might be interested in victims' rights, the dispensation of justice, and the teaching of some moralistic lessons. From a formalistic legal standpoint some of the provisions do not seem to cohere, but as a rhetorical document it resonates with many constituencies.

In the "findings" section of this decree, for example, the nation's commander in chief of the armed forces explained that the members of al-Qaeda, and other international terrorists, had carried out attacks on the United States, and that the scale of attacks led to the proclamation of a national emergency (September 14, 2001).[16] Since there was evidence that both individuals and groups might initiate further attacks against the United States, the government needed to protect itself and its citizens from mass deaths, mass injuries, and mass destruction of property. This type of language obviously builds on many of the ideographic permutations of the concept of "necessity" or "military necessity" that were outlined in chapter one—survival, self-defense, coercion, and so forth.

After noting the factual causes of these exigent circumstances, the authors of the Military Order proceed to explain just why military commissions are the appropriate response in this type of situation. Sections e–g of the Military Order allowed President Bush to provide some of the mandates and the legal reasoning that justified the creation of these military commissions:

(e) To Protect the United States and its citizens, and for the effective conduct of military operations and prevention of terrorist acts, it is

necessary for individuals subject to this order pursuant to section 2
hereof to be detained, and, when tried, to be tried for violations of
the laws of war and other applicable laws by military tribunals.

(f) Given the danger to the safety of the United States and the nature
of international terrorism, and to the extent provided by and under
this order, I find consistent with section 836 of title 10, United States
Code, that it is not practicable to apply in military commissions under this order the principles of law and the rules of evidence generally recognized in the trial of criminal cases in the United States
district courts.

(g) Having fully considered the magnitude of the potential deaths,
injuries and property destruction that would result from potential
acts of terrorism against the United States, and the probability that
such acts will occur, I have determined that an extraordinary emergency exists for national defense purposes, that this emergency constitutes an urgent and compelling government interest, and that is-
suance of this order is necessary to meet the emergency.[17]

Several days after the publication of the Military Order, President Bush
noted: "I would remind those who don't understand the decision I made
that Franklin Roosevelt made the same decision in World War II. Those
were extraordinary times as well."[18]

This claim, that the nation faced an "extra-ordinary" emergency, provided some key reasons why the chief executive needed such unusually
discretionary power. This is no longer a criminal investigation of the acts
of a few dozen terrorists, but a military decision that will help create some
of the scaffolding that might be used in American war crimes trials. At the
same time, this very clear explanation of what some considered to be the
"necessities" of the times was obviously meant to detail just why terrorists
were not going to be allowed to use the civil courts and be shielded by
some of the orthodox procedural and substantive rules that protected ordinary litigants. The Order also implies that the jurists, lawyers, witnesses,
and other participants in civil trials might be putting their lives in danger
when they try dangerous terrorists in open court.

Some of these passages seemed to have been lifted right out of the
Roosevelt texts used by other Americans in earlier emergencies. For ex-

ample, section 7 of the Military Order, entitled "Relationship to Other Law and Forums," noted that any "individual subject to this order" would not be "privileged to seek any remedy or maintain any proceeding, directly or indirectly, or to have any such remedy, or proceeding sought on the individual's behalf, in (i) any court of the United States, or any State thereof, (ii), any court of any foreign nation, or (iii) any international tribunal.[19] Alberto Gonzales, one of the key presidential advisers, later argued that President Bush was simply following the lead of other presidents who had decided to invoke their executive powers as they tried enemy "belligerents" who commit war crimes.[20] Gonzales went on to explain to readers that in some situations, military commissions should be preferred over civilian trials because military forums would prevent the compromising of either intelligence or military efforts. Moreover, since tribunals dispensed "justice swiftly," this could be done "without years of pretrial proceedings or post-trial appeals."[21] Not surprisingly, we hear little about the swiftness of either the Dakota trials or the *Yamashita* proceedings.

Within this particular Order, the use of the term "belligerents" to characterize the alleged terrorists would soon be replaced with the monikers of "unlawful belligerents" or "enemy combatants."[22] According to the definitional and policy portions of this executive order, President Bush had the discretionary authority to decide if any "individual who is not a United States citizen" had violated the other provisions of the Military Order. He also had the right to "determine from time to time in writing if such a person is or was a member of Al Qaida," had engaged in aiding, abetting, or conspiring to commit acts of international terrorism, had acted in preparation for such acts, or had "knowingly harbored one of more" of these individuals.[23] The mere "suspicion" of terrorist activities could lead to detention, or trial before one of the president's military commissions.[24] This obviated the need for any grand juries, international tribunals, or civilian trials.

Later on, the applicability of some of the Geneva Convention principles would be a major point of contention, but the authors of the Order seemed to have anticipated some of these legal niceties when they mentioned in this text that once an "individual subject to this order" was detained, that person was supposed to be treated humanely. Moreover, there would not be any "adverse discrimination based on race, color, religion, gender, birth, wealth, or any similar criteria." The secretary of defense was authorized to make sure that those detained had adequate food, drinking water, shelter, clothing, and medical treatment. Interestingly enough, these detainees were also to be "allowed the free exercise of religion consistent with the requirements of such detention."[25] This provided textual evidence that at least some international guidelines were going to be observed.

Part of the controversial nature of the Bush Order stemmed from the fact that the penalty provisions of this executive act seemed to be an encroachment on juridical powers. One portion of the executive order explained that when individuals were being tried by the authorized military commissions they could be punished in accordance with the penalties provided under applicable law, including death or life imprisonment. Bush's Military Order also followed Roosevelt's early ruling that allowed for the admission of any evidence that had "probative value to a reasonable person." The military commission that tried these individuals was supposed to provide a "full and fair trial," and these were governed by the orders and regulations issued by the secretary of defense. In order to get a conviction, there had to be a two-thirds majority vote of the members of the commission present at the vote.[26] Such provisions made it abundantly clear that it would be the historical fragments and spirit that came from *Ex parte Quirin*—and not *Ex parte Milligan*—that would infuse the new Military Order with meaning.

This did not sit well with critics, who worried that the Order "installs the executive branch as lawgiver as well as law-enforcer, law-interpreter, and law-applier."[27] Other observers remembered a time when another Republican president—Abraham Lincoln—also had subordinates who wanted military commissions. Would the specifics of the Military Order, combined with its genealogical precursors, provide defenders with the suasory arguments that they would need when Congress studied these issues? How would members of the Bush administration, and the supporters of strong executive power, justify these legal choices?

In cases like this, administrators can often come up with a series of popular arguments they can use when trying to justify controversial decisions, and in this particular situation there were a plethora of possible answers that could be used to rationalize the use of military commissions.

For example, William Barr, the former attorney general of the United States, perhaps expressed the mood of the nation when he noted that our "national goal in this instance is not the correction, deterrence and rehabilitation of an errant member of the body politic," but rather, "the destruction of [a] foreign force that poses a risk to our national security."[28]

Many of the president's supporters argued that since the attack on the World Trade Center resembled the Japanese attack on Pearl Harbor, decision-makers needed to pay particular attention to the judicial decisions handed down during World War II. Hence, both elites and laypersons should revisit the case of *Ex parte Quirin,* because that had been a decision that recognized the magnitude of military existence and the need for deference. As I noted in chapter six, some of the jurists involved in the *Ex parte Quirin* case took pride in the fact that they had allowed for habeas corpus relief, but the dominant impression that has been left of this case is that the judiciary stood on the sidelines when war was declared. Gonzales might talk about the retention of habeas corpus relief, but this interpretation seemed to contradict the literal wording of the Military Order.

Obviously there were other cases that would be mentioned and other arguments that would be used in these heated debates over the legitimacy of the Bush Military Order, but given the popularity of the president and his working relationship with Congress, a critical rhetorician might ask just why he and his administrators got so much flack? Was it because of the particular timing of its presentation? The fact that this was an executive order and not a congressional promulgation? Was this a question of maintaining the separation of powers, where defenders of the Order might have had more support if they had come forward with the Order at the same time they were debating the specifics of the Patriot Act?

I contend that some of the political obstacles that confronted governmental officials came from inherited permutations of the "whig" traditions of Anglo-American civil liberties. Since 1866, the nation had jettisoned some, but not all, of the rhetorical baggage that surrounded the *Milligan* decision. "The military justice system," notes Jonathan Turley, "evolved around two strong and opposite poles," and "its history reflects the gravitational pull of constitutional values in the civilian system."[29] Even during times of war there have been those who have claimed that Parliaments and Congresses were the primary decision-making bodies, and that the preservation of individual rights was of paramount importance. For example, Neal Katyal and Laurence Tribe recently worried about the lack of "equality" and "due process." They are convinced that

> These constitutional principles, in conjunction with the provisions for a divided government, *are* our security, and to assert them here is to win at home the war we are waging so effectively abroad. Terrorists have attacked the Federal Building in Oklahoma and the Pentagon and have toppled the towers of the World Trade Center, massacring thousands of innocent civilians in the process. We must not allow them to tear down as well the structures of government, constituted by the separation of powers, that makes our legal and political system—and the liberties it embodies and protects—unique.[30]

In the fall of 2001, congressional leaders became some of the key public actors in the forums that deliberated the legality and desirability of Bush's military tribunals.

The Fall 2001 Congressional Debates and the Legality of the Bush Military Order

In the immediate aftermath of 9/11, there were few senators or representatives who did not back the president's plans for national unity, but the sudden announcement of the Bush Military Order was considered to be a different matter altogether. It was one thing to call for sweeping legislation that would help with the funding of airport security, homeland defenses, and warfare abroad,[31] but quite another to think that the judicial and legislative branches were now going to totally capitulate. Just as British Parliaments had at one time been "jealous" of royal prerogatives, now U.S. congressional leaders wanted some oversight of the proposed military tribunals.

President Bush had advisers who were convinced that the *Ex parte Quirin* decision gave the commander in chief the exclusive right to put together expeditious forums. Before November of 2001, there were very few detailed analyses of the saboteurs' case, but within a matter of weeks the public began reading narratives that told tales of how Franklin Roosevelt had once had the support of a different Supreme Court, and how that judicial body had decided that German saboteurs could be lawfully tried in front of a military commissions. Readers were told that *Ex parte Quirin* was a landmark case that provided historical and legal proof that courts recognized the importance of discretionary executive power.

Detractors of Bush's Military Order responded by crafting some of their own counternarratives that brought together many of the topoi, characterizations, and ideographs that had circulated in the public and legal spheres for centuries. While he did not specifically mention the "tyrant's plea" of necessity, Patrick Downes did claim that George W. Bush's Military Order showed that he was trying to "act as the sole arbiter of who is an accused terrorist," and that this should worry all citizens who remembered that he "was elected president, and not crowned a monarch."[32] In one of the most quoted essays in these early public debates, William Safire excoriated the promoters of the Bush Military Order for setting up "kangaroo courts for people he designates before trial to be terrorists."[33] Safire noted that even "military attorneys are silently seething," because they knew the Uniform Code of Military Justice contained procedural protections that did not appear in the president's Military Order. These included the need for public trials, proof beyond reasonable doubt, input from the accused in the selection of juries and right to counsel, unanimity in cases where death sentences were being handed out, and appellate review by "civilians confirmed by the Senate." "Bush's fiat," averred Safire, "turns back the clock on all advances in military justice, through three wars, in the past half-century."[34]

Given the cultural milieu of the times, few critics questioned the magnitude of the attacks on the World Trade Center, or the impact they had on the national psyche. Yet many wondered how the particular act of establishing military commissions was going to help the general goal of fighting terrorism. If the president's subordinates were going to bring up cases of where military commissions had done their job, then they had the moral, political, and legal obligation to tell the public about the problematic nature of some of these same military tribunals. Laurence Tribe, for example, wrote in the *New Republic* that the Bush Military Order lacked "the ritualistic solemnity of a declaration of war," that the order did not contain any specific definition of "international terrorism." He felt the

Ex parte Quirin precedent was one of the cases that actually showed that the Supreme Court often "caved in to puffed-up claims of military necessity."[35] Tribe was convinced that congressional leaders should get involved, because "the necessary and proper" clause of the Constitution indicated that they were the ones who had the national government's "enumerated powers." As far as he was concerned, if "Congress uses those prerogatives to trim the order's sails, then President Bush's extraordinary tribunals may be a permissible response to an extraordinary war."[36]

Yet this hybrid narrative of partial support for the Bush Military Order would not be the only one that circulated in America's rhetorical culture during the fall of 2001. Other critics delved into the nation's history, and they were convinced the studies of earlier usages of military commissions presented very different pedagogical lessons. What is fascinating about these criticisms is that they too were often selective and truncated in their presentation. While they often disagreed with the particular interpretation of a given legal case, they allowed the Bush administrators to maintain the overall tenor of the controversy by framing this as a debate between the principles of *Ex parte Milligan* and *Ex parte Quirin*. Although occasionally one read about the case of Major André (chapter two), Henry Wirz (chapter five), or General Yamashita (chapter seven), but to my knowledge few detailed public or legal commentators looked into the contexts of these decisions. This binary structuring that focused on two apparently polar Court decisions narrowed the range of plausible options that were often considered in these legal and public debates. Decision-makers were expected to vote in favor or against tribunals, with little discussion of other possibilities.

In the weeks that preceded some of the most intense congressional discussions of the new tribunals, the president's administrators and outside supporters tried to head off controversy by clarifying some of the definitional and functional parts of Bush's Military Order. For example, some of the president's defenders noted that the Order only mentioned that "non-citizens" could be the subjects of the edict, and that the tribunals would be used to try suspected terrorists who might have been captured overseas.[37] Vice President Dick Cheney implied that some of the key targets of the Order were the people who came into the United States illegally, so that they could conduct large-scale terrorist operations.[38] A growing number of supporters of the Military Order could now recite the familiar refrains that Roosevelt's staff used in their defenses of earlier tribunals.

These explanations did not satisfy all of the critics. Duke University law professor Scott Silliman, a former Air Force attorney, admitted that Bush's tribunals might be "convenient," but thought this was "a step back for American criminal justice."[39] There were those who were still convinced that the Bush Military Order contained "subversions" of some fundamental constitutional safeguards.[40] In a typical commentary, Joseph Hoffmann wrote:

> The historic precedents argument in favor of the military tribunals is specious, at best. The trials following Lincoln's assassination and the trials of the German saboteurs during World War II were related to acts of enemy agents in times of war declared by Congress, situations very different from today's combat activities. Furthermore, it's important to note that the guarantees of the Fifth and Sixteenth Amendments are not limited to citizens, but extend to "any person."[41]

During these first few months after 9/11, readers did not know if the Order would allow for the trial of citizens, if the Geneva Convention restrictions were relevant, or if the White House was even contemplating trying any particular enemy belligerents. Audiences were hearing different tales about the applicability of the writ of habeas corpus or the dangers associated with civil trials.

Congressional leaders decided they would hold a series of hearings to study how they could combat terrorism while preserving civil liberties. Senator Patrick Leahy, a democrat from Vermont, led some of these hearings, which were supposed to bring together the best civilian and military experts on the subject of congressional oversight. These hearings also became public events that served as catalytic moments for the already growing modern interest in military tribunals.

From the very beginning, congressional leaders realized they had to carefully word the questions they would ask the experts and Bush's subordinates, because the polls showed that the American public supported both the president and the use of military tribunals.[42] The *New York Times*/CBS surveys taken in the fall of 2001 showed that the president sometimes had a 90 percent approval rating, and that almost 80 percent of Americans were willing to "give up some of their personal freedoms in order to make the country safe from terrorist attacks."[43] At the same time, the senators and representatives needed to make sure they were not giving the impression that they were abdicating their constitutional responsibilities.

During the Senate judiciary hearings held on November 28, 2001, congressional leaders took up the topic of "Preserving Our Freedoms While Defending against Terrorism." Neal Katyal informed his listeners that he worried that the "current course of conduct" was leading to "an unprecedented aggrandizement of power," that "not only" threatened "the constitutional prerogatives" of Congress, but also risked "jeopardizing the criminal convictions of those responsible for the September 11 attacks."[44] He was joined by a colleague who argued that the Military Order allowed the "President to decide when a threatened form of group crime becomes a war, justifying detention and military tribunals."[45]

When high-ranking officials or other guests are summoned to speak in front of Congress, they usually adopt a strategy based on respect and conciliation, but the tenor of these debates showed that Bush's subordinates understood that they were playing out a historical role in the public debates over just who should be in charge in cases of national security and military necessities. An admiring Philip Gailey wrote that politicians "can read the polls," and that this "may help explain why the Senate Judiciary Committee was more lamb than lion when" they had to deal with Bush administrators.[46] For example, Vice President Dick Cheney, showed no fear when he told reporters that the terrorists who were responsible for the September 11 attacks "don't deserve the same guarantees and safeguards that we use for an American citizen. . . . They will have a fair trial under the procedures of the military tribunal."[47] Foreign observers might not like America's intransigence and unilateral actions, but the majority of Americans seemed to equate support of the tribunals with allegiance to a wartime president.

One of the major ideographic issues occupying the attention of many audiences revolved around the question of how to define the notion of "full and fair" treatment of the alleged terrorists. What type of procedural and substantive due process rights were going to be given to those who participated in the planning and carrying out of the 9/11 attacks, or who fought against the international coalition in Afghanistan? For defenders of the president's policies, the fact that these "unlawful belligerents" had "pursued their deadly purpose in a training camp in Afghanistan or a flight school in Florida" meant they had "cast their lot by waging war against the United States," and therefore "are properly judged by the laws of war."[48] The attorney general of the United States, John Ashcroft, elaborated on *NBC News* just why he thought the nation needed military commissions:

> Can you imagine the . . . apprehending [of] . . . a soldier, terrorist, or foreign prisoner in Afghanistan and having a circus atmosphere in a televised trial that might send signals to other terrorists around the world? The President should have a right to try alien war criminals in the military commission. It's something that's happened in previous settings, Franklin Roosevelt did it. This President has issued an order which makes it open, not secret, like the Roosevelt order.[49]

These types of remarks added to the confusion and ambiguity surrounding some of these debates, because some of the interpretations being presented in these public forums conflicted with the textual evidence that appeared within the Military Order itself. Moreover, it was unclear just which "modifications" were actually going to be implemented, and what parties would be involved in the modification process. Ashcroft, like many other commentators who looked at *Ex parte Quirin,* simply assumed that the U.S. Supreme Court had spoken with one voice, and that Roosevelt had been given the requisite powers during wartime. One Bush supporter derisively characterized skeptics as members of the "civil rights lobby" that simply would not accept the fact that a majority of Americans had "no problem with bringing terrorists before military tribunals."[50]

Some of the Bush administrators may have hoped their presence would mute some of the criticism of the Bush Order, but their commentaries often opened up new lines of inquiry. Did the attacks on the World Trade Center and the Pentagon turn the United States, or parts of America, into a "war zone"? If this was a war that involved "belligerents," did this mean the nation's civil and military courts had to take into account various

Geneva Conventions and the protocols that protected combatants? If Congress has not technically declared war on any nation, did this mean that we could still be at war with al-Qaeda? Was Bush's Military Order the type of text that provided the best balance of civil liberties and national necessities?

Congressional leaders were caught between the rock and the hard place—they wanted to publicly perform their roles as defenders of legislative prerogatives, and yet they did not want to come across as obstructionists interfering with wartime preparedness. They therefore needed to find a way of asking questions that displayed their concerns while offering their qualified support of the U.S. commander in chief. For example, there was some precedent for the idea that only Congress had the right to establish these military tribunals.[51] These critical narratives built on the old Anglo-American distinctions made between an executive simply asserting that an emergency existed ("feigned"), and really necessitous circumstances. Did Congress not have the right to authorize the use of military force against individuals, organizations, or nations that were involved in the 9/11? Several members of the House and Senate Judiciary Committees—including Patrick Leahy of Vermont,[52] John Conyers of Michigan, Arlen Specter of Pennsylvania, and Bob Barr of Virginia—indicated that their support of the Patriot Act did not automatically mean they were buying the arguments and rationales being used by the president and his advisers in the conversations about the military commissions.

Interestingly enough, many of these congressional leaders waffled on the question of whether the nation needed *modified* military tribunals, or whether the country needed to be content with federally conducted civil trials. After all, there was some evidence that other terrorists—including those involved in the 1993 World Trade Center bombing attack, the conspiracy to attack the New York City tunnels, and the embassy bombings in 1998—had been tried successfully in open, civil courts. The defenders of the tribunals needed to come up with tangible proof of the deterrence effect, the savings, or other benefits that would come from trying these same individuals in extraordinary military courts. Even the Patriot Act had at least held out the possibility that detainees would have access to the federal courts to ensure the protection of their rights.[53] If this was the case, then why were Pentagon officials being given the discretion to conduct secret trials?

During these debates on Capitol Hill, congressional leaders indicated they wanted more information on just who would be the target of these tribunals—were the military tribunals going to be used in the trials of a few dozen high-ranking al-Qaeda leaders, the 20 million alien residents in the United States, or all "non-citizens" who harbored terrorists? Although the Bush Military Order mentioned "non-citizens," the decree was written in such a way that authorities could prosecute anyone who had any tangential relation to known or unknown terrorists. This was not the type of executive order that only addressed the problems that had been created by a narrow class of al-Qaeda leaders or members, although supporters of the Order often argued that these were the primary culprits who needed to be apprehended. Administrators may have talked about the need for "options" and "flexibility," but critics worried that when these words were put into practice, the polysemic nature of these executive fragments could be used to broaden the scope of military investigations. For example, dissenters in other lands, who might be engaged in nonviolent protest activities, could be characterized as individuals who are involved in "acts of international terrorism,"[54] and they could be detained indefinitely.

Imagine a scenario where a U.S. citizen—or American resident—was accused of "harboring" a terrorist. Since the specific wording of the Bush Military Order allowed the secretary of defense to use or establish rules that did not have to follow either the courts-martial rules of the Uniform Code of Military Justice[55] or civilian courts, writers like Timothy Edgar opined that the president's Order threatened the civil liberties of all persons, regardless of their status. After all, the same *Ex parte Quirin* case that was specifically referred to by Bush administrators had court members who decided that the status of being a U.S. citizen did "not relieve him" from trial before a military commission.[56] Occasionally one read about how there was evidence that J. Edgar Hoover was more worried about "his own image," and that he was not about to tell the American public about Dasch's defection during the *Quirin* affair. Such tales purportedly illustrated how a "military trial" had not really protected any "national security" interests.[57] These commentaries highlighted the importance of tracing both the texts and contexts of these key legal precedents.

Some of the critics who read about these congressional debates took the position that the nation could not afford to treat the *Ex parte Quirin* case as the last word in the evolution of American civil liberties. For example, the decision-makers and publics who were supportive of the military commissions of the 1940s were not having to deal with the progressive changes coming from cases like *Gideon v. Wainwright* (1963), which ensured that defendants had the Sixth Amendment and Fourteenth Amendment due process rights of assistance of counsel in state trials.[58] Moreover, in 1942, "international human rights law was in its infancy," and *Ex parte Quirin* was decided before the United States become a party to a series of international covenants that protected certain civil and political rights.[59] In the post–World War II eras, there had been several Geneva Conventions that had commented on the rights of several types of prisoners and detainees.

Some of the most effective and influential experts who appeared before Congress were the moderates who understood the importance of drawing a pragmatic and "legal" line between national security interests and individual civil liberties. These critics could explain how they were in favor of constitutional martial frameworks, and yet voice their opinions that Bush's subordinates had not put together an adequate "case" in defending the legitimacy of the Military Order. For example, Neal Katyal stated that if certain policies were "carefully crafted and appropriately circumscribed," there could be times when the United States would profit from the creation of some types of military tribunals.[60] Katyal admitted that Bush's present Military Order was so sweeping it could cover the Basque Separatist who killed an American citizen in Madrid, or a member of the Irish Liberation Army who threatened the members of the American embassy in London. "At most," noted Katyal, "the reach of a military tribunal can reach a theater of war, not Spain, Great Britain, Montana, or the range of other locations not currently in armed conflict."[61] As I noted in earlier chapters, this subissue of the proper "zone of war" was one that preoccupied earlier generations, and it is still a major point of contention in our modern debates.

In order for congressional leaders to be able to effectively evaluate the

Bush Military Order, they also had to be able to establish some rhetorical distance between that particular text and the much larger Patriot Act. They needed to hear from witnesses who would be able to put into the record some of the differences that existed between these two discursive fragments. For example, Philip Heymann, who thought the Patriot Act had been reasonable and "overdue," told the Senate Judiciary Committee that he did not have "the same reaction to the president's order on military trials."[62] The only benefit that Heymann could see from holding these military tribunals was that they could convict "without even the evidence that a jury of angry, patriotic Americans would demand."[63] He worried that the implementation of the Bush Military Order would deprive the United States of its historic claim to moral leadership, and that it would create resentment, fear, and suspicion of the military. Heymann advanced the specific argument that the Order might violate Article 102 of the Geneva Convention, and that it would apply a law that could cover some 18 million U.S. noncitizens and the "citizens of every nation."[64]

More radical critics of the Military Order who watched these debates worried about potential violations of the Freedom of Information Act (FOIA), the problems with secret detentions, "the trumpeting" of numbers of arrests as a part of an effort to reassure the public, imprisonment without probable cause, the denial of the constitutional right of bail, and the intimidation of immigrants.[65] One anonymous writer for *Progressive* magazine described the Bush Order as an "extra-constitutional" authorization that was "one of the scariest orders ever issued by any President."[66] This writer speculated that the Order amounted to the "gravest assault on our Constitution at least since Richard Nixon's Saturday Night Massacre and perhaps since FDR's order to put Japanese Americans in internment camps or John Adams's Alien and Sedition Acts of 1798."[67]

This type of hyperbole carried little weight with those Americans who totally supported both the letter and the spirit of Bush's Military Order. This was obviously a president who was willing to admit that part of his duties included his role as commander in chief, and his advisers willingly defended the notion of broad executive power.

In this next segment of the chapter I look at some of the modifications made in the Bush Order, and some of the contemporary legal and public debates that have taken place since the publicizing of that text.

Contemporary Critiques of the Bush Military Order, and Remembrances of *Ex parte Milligan* and *Ex parte Quirin*

In many formalistic legal discussions of a case or statute, a chronological history is presented in a manner that gives the impression that all "rules of law" develop in some progressive and linear fashion. If we consistently applied this orthodox way of looking at military commissions we might expect that congressional and public commentators would talk about the presence or absence of military tribunals in a series of post–World War II conflicts—the Korean War, Vietnam, the Gulf War, and such. Yet from a symbolic standpoint, it seems as though many Americans felt quite comfortable with the idea that sometimes history is not linear but cyclical, that legal history seemed to be repeating itself, as this newest generation read about the exploits of Abraham Lincoln or Franklin Roosevelt.

When supporters of the Bush Order recalled the events that took place during the American Civil War, they did not focus on the thousands of imprisonments, the taking of property, or the words used by members of the *Milligan* case—it was President Lincoln's wartime power that captured their attention. Moreover, the passage of years had provided multiple illustrations of how all of the various branches had looked the other way in the face of real and perceived necessities. For more than a hundred years legal experts had been talking about the need for more realism in reassessing the balance that needed to exist between individual rights and communal exigencies, and *Ex parte Milligan* always seemed to be at the center of these controversies. Justice William Rehnquist, in his *All the Laws but One,* argued that "*Quirin,* decided during the darkest days of World War II, actually cut down on some of the extravagant dicta favorable to civil liberty in *Milligan.*"[68] This type of statement, written three years before 9/11, would have resonated with many members of Congress and the American public. One pollster told the *St. Petersburg Times* that "people just don't want terrorists to take advantage of a legal system that already bends over backwards too much for defendants."[69] The officials of the Bush administration who argued with some congressional leaders were obviously not the first or the last public servants who questioned the wisdom and precedential value of *Ex parte Milligan.*

As noted earlier in this chapter, these congressional debates involved more than simply a retrieval of the past—they allowed modern day Americans to identify with the trials and tribulations of those who lived through the bombing of Pearl Harbor up through V-J Day. FDR's announcement of his own military order was viewed as an example of how leaders were supposed to react when they faced the dangers that came from spies and saboteurs. Representative Ike Skelton, a Democrat from Missouri, remembered how Dasch's lawyer, Carl Ristine, had come from Skelton's hometown and had been a mentor to Skelton's father. Skelton was sure the "due process" rights that had protected Dasch and Ernest Burger would now be remembered by President Bush in any expeditious modern forum put together by the chief executive.[70]

By early December 2001, the members of the Senate Judiciary Committee had become familiar with the arguments on both sides of the controversy. Senator Orrin Hatch quipped that after the president has asked the secretary of defense to draft the procedures that would be employed in future military tribunals, it seemed as though "this committee, the Armed Services Committee, numerous law professors, and just about every pundit with a microphone or a typewriter" had "expressed their opinion of how those procedures should be written."[71] Now they looked forward to hearing from one of the key defenders of the Bush Military Order—Attorney General John Ashcroft. Senator Leahy, who led the discussion, complained that "with all of the changes and switchbacks," it was hard to find any consistency in the answers given by other Bush administrators.[72] Leahy was a congressional leader who wanted clarification so that America could avoid the appearance of having pursued "victor's justice."[73] In his introductory remarks, Leahy got to the heart of the matter when he noted there were some "Democrats, Republicans, moderates, conservatives," and liberals who had expressed concern that the administration was trying to bypass Congress and the courts.[74]

When Attorney General Ashcroft began his presentation, he mixed together ideographs and iconographs as he held up a captured al-Qaeda "how-to guide" for terrorists as he talked about President's Bush's leadership in the war against terrorism. This visual gesture was supposed to punctuate the fact that Senators could not ignore the reality that the terrorists were trying to use "America's freedom as a weapon against us."[75] Ashcroft then rattled off the various achievements of his department, including the identification of dozens of terrorist networks, the beefing up of border patrols, and the screening of immigrants. He lashed out at critics who came at him with "charges of kangaroo courts," and he vilified the commentators who were "shredding the Constitution" in ways that "gave new meaning to the term 'fog of war.' "[76] Nat Hentoff later described this as the attorney general's way of trying to "intimidate American critics who say his and the president's war on terrorism is causing collateral damage to civil liberties on the home front."[77]

Some of the attorney general's former colleagues tried to get him to admit that the president had exceeded his authority when he unilaterally set up plans for the military tribunals, but Ashcroft responded that these needed to be thought of as "war crimes commissions"[78] that were authorized under the commander in chief's war powers. When Leahy asked him if the administration was thinking about applying this Military Order to cover some 20 million people living legally in the United States,[79] the attorney general retorted that the Defense Department had been assigned the task of spelling out the specific procedures that would be followed in any future military tribunals. Later on, in an answer to one of the questions posed by Senator Dianne Feinstein, Ashcroft did concede that "legal aliens" were "subject to this order."[80]

At this point it was evident that tempers were beginning to flare, and Senator Hatch tried to step in so that he could defuse the situation by talking about the *Yamashita* decision, but Leahy wanted to go back and discuss *Ex parte Milligan,* while Ashcroft stuck with *Quirin.* The attorney general argued that he thought that the president had an "inherent authority and power to conduct war," and that the Uniform Code of Military Justice contained provisions based on these precedents.[81] In order to move the senators away from a legal framework that focused on domestic defendants and ordinary criminal ways of thinking about due process rights, Ashcroft asked his listeners to keep in mind that it was "not uncommon" for "international commissions to litigate "war crimes." Under the *Ex parte Quirin* precedent and the "laws of war," the president also had the authority to try "unlawful belligerents."[82] This appeared to provide multiple and independent rationales for supporting the Bush administration's take on the inherent powers of the nation's commander in chief. While answering some of Senator Charles Grassley's questions, Ashcroft wanted the record to reflect that

> It is my view that the [*sic*] Congress has recognized the power inherent in the president, both in the articles of war that supported the Roosevelt administration's establishment of a commission most recently. I might add that these presidents are not alone. From George Washington to Abraham Lincoln, to George Bush and to Franklin Delano Roosevelt, presidents have undertaken these responsibilities, and they have done so both with and without the specific language of the Uniform Code of Military Justice found in the law today.[83]

To give Ashcroft his due, this is probably a fair statement—many presidents have made claims about their inherent powers, and many of these presidents have not been shy about using that power. This dodges the question, however, of whether the use of that power was legitimate.

Obviously the attorney general did not talk about all executive tribunals, the amorphous nature of these supposedly inherent military powers, the specific contexts of each of the cases that he did mention, or the controversial nature of some of these very decisions.

Near the end of his questioning by the Senate Judiciary Committee, Ashcroft voiced the opinion that he was dealing with savages who had no respect for the "rule of law," and that the only way to deter these war crimes was through the passage of harsh penalties for violators. Since the "constitutional founders didn't expect us to have war conducted by committee," they had vested the president with some very substantial powers.[84] This was one attorney general who did not mind letting his former colleagues know he felt that there were some questions being asked that he did not have to answer. For hours, he adamantly defended the position that the formation of Bush tribunals was a military—and not civilian—matter.

In the following days other witnesses came before the Senate Judiciary Committee, but the confrontation between Leahy and Ashcroft became the focal point of public commentary for many members of the broader rhetorical culture. Charles Lane, a *Washington Post* staff writer, insightfully observed how the "debate seemed to peak at a confrontational Dec. 6 hearing in which Democratic members of the Senate Judiciary Committee grilled Attorney General John D. Ashcroft on the commissions—and Ashcroft suggested that unnamed critics of the administration's anti-terror policies were providing 'ammunition' to terrorists."[85] "It took awhile," notes Hentoff, but despite "this threat by the nation's chief law enforcement officer, choruses of dissent began to rise from bar associations, constitutional scholars, journalists, civil liberties groups, and citizens across the political spectrum."[86] The inheritors of "whig" ideologies could perhaps take solace from the fact that the unmodified Bush Military Order was drawing such heavy fire.

Conclusion

With the benefit of hindsight, we now know that the Department of Defense was given the task of coming up with the "modifications" needed to assuage some of the fears of those who complained that Bush's Military Order. In the next chapter I will deal with the political and legal maneuvers that helped garner support for these discursive compromises. In this concluding section, I am interested in explicating how readers might think about evaluating the congressional debates that took place in front of the Senate Judiciary Committee in the fall of 2001.

For those who believe in the existence of immutable, apolitical, or foundational "rules of law," the rhetorical wrangling that took place during these hearings has to be evaluated by comparing these interpretations of the law with the written laws themselves. Both liberals and conservatives who believe in the absolutism of parts of the constitutional nomenclature are sometimes bothered when decisions are made that appear to deviate from the intentions of the Founders, or the "clear" ideas of those who pass particular legislative acts. This is not as problematic from a rhetorical framework, where critics are much more comfortable with tensions, ambiguities, and political compromises. Given these paradigmatic frameworks, traditionalists might ask whether the supporters of the *Ex parte Milligan* or *Ex parte Quirin* decisions were accurately representing our extant "rules of law" on questions involving the legitimacy of military tribunals.

This sometimes implies that we have to make a choice between *Milligan* or *Quirin,* or that we have not been influenced by the rhetorics and contexts of both opinions. Whether we like it or not, there simply are no apolitical rules that came from the Founders, and we are always involved in the renegotiating of these mythic rules of law. Given the vast array of precedents and prior usages of military commission, we need to openly admit that our own generation is selectively accepting or rejecting particular storylines in the vast network of the "whig" and "tory" narratives that circulate in our legal histories and collective memories. As John Reid explained, our public perceptions of these "necessities" are an important part of the choices that we make in the sanctioning of particular renditions of "competing legal cultures."[87] Hence, we should be paying attention to the entire range of policy alternatives we have in front of us, and not narrow our vision to the point where we talk only about "American" civil or military trials, or the precedent that can be found in a single case.

In many ways this supposed 2001 congressional "debate" over the legality of the military tribunals was a truncated one, because few participants were debating the existence of the "necessity," the problematics of military tribunals, or the need for international solutions to this problem. There were few detailed commentaries on prior criticisms of these tribunals, and many participants used labels that treated potential defendants as "terrorists" who already had their day in court. Moreover, given the time constraints of the congressional question and answer sessions, all that we find in the legislative transcripts are tiny summaries of some very complex legal cases. When Senator Leahy tried to talk about J. Edgar Hoover's mistakes in the *Ex parte Quirin* case (the fact that much of the evidence in the case came from "two of the saboteurs" and the "cover up" that may have been involved) he was cut off by colleagues who reminded him that three hours had already passed.[88]

When we are asked to choose between *Ex parte Quirin* and *Ex parte Milligan,* we end up taking polarizing positions that miss the role that negotiation, compromise, and audience expectations play in the acceptance or rejection of these commentaries on military necessity and the need for military commissions. We leave behind all of the work of people like Reverend Whipple in the Dakota trials, the military defense teams that

represented Dasch and Yamashita, or the other figures from the past who
had their own experiences with tribunals. If we are going to learn anything
from our revisiting of cases like *Ex parte Milligan* or *Quirin,* it can only
come from appreciating the broad range of selective arguments circulated
by many communities within both the legal and public forums of the
times. Instead of complaining about the politics or the abuses of one side
or the other, we need to focus our energies on figuring out the most pragmatic approaches that can be applied in dealing with terrorism. Any meaningful executive, legislative, or judicial discussions have to take into account the possibility that the use of our own forums will always be viewed
as examples of "victor's justice."

The locus of the debate during the fall hearings in front of the Senate
Judiciary Committee centered on the dispute over the power of Congress
or the president, rather than on extending our range of options in apparently exigent situations. When Ashcroft began talking about The Hague,
Nuremberg, Bosnia, and Rwanda, no one wanted to hear extended discussion of any international alternatives. These were used as examples
of places where war crimes had been recognized—or unilateralism accepted.

As critics look back through the mists of time and the fog of an undeclared war, they may find ample justification for providing broad presidential powers and executive authority during necessitous times, but this
does not mean that the simple declaration of war should translate into the
closing off of civil jurisdiction in all cases. Do the events of 9/11 create the
type of danger to the public safety, health, and well-being of the nation
that justifies the creation of military tribunals? If we do capture Osama bin
Laden or other members of terrorist organizations, we should follow the
lead of those who suggest we look into the possibility that they be tried
by international tribunals. Diane F. Orentlicher and Robert Goldman ad-
monish us to remember:

> When active duty military officers assume the role of judges, they
> remain subordinate to their superiors in keeping with the estab-
> lished military hierarchy. The manner by which they fulfill their
> assigned task might well play a role in their future promotions, as-
> signments, and professional rewards. It is because of this inherent

dependence that these tribunals are not suited to try civilians. . . . Similar considerations have led the Inter-American Commission and Court of Human Rights, as well as the U.N. Human Rights Committee, to find that the use of military courts to try civilians in Guatemala, Peru, Chile, Uruguay, and elsewhere violated fundamental due process rights. Moreover, no human rights supervisory body has yet found the exigencies of a genuine emergency situation, such as that now faced by the U.S., to justify suspending basic fair trial safeguards on a temporary basis.[89]

One might respond that "terrorists" do not deserve these protections, but this type of argument begs the very questions that need to be put in front of international communities.

Do we want legal edicts that confuse the "role of legislator, policeman [sic], prosecutor, judge, and court" of appeal?[90]

That being said, I do not want to give readers the impression that the congressional debates that took place in the fall of 2001 did not accomplish some key public tasks. They did at least provide the forum for talking about the success or failure of the civil trials in cases like the 1993 World Trade Center attack, or the 1998 embassy bombings trials. Moderate critics could remind Americans about the arguments made about open courts in *Ex parte Milligan*. Congressional leaders also encouraged us to think about the relative power of the executive, legislative, and judicial branches of government. As I argue in the next chapter, these hearings also served as catalyzing moments that forced the "modification" of the rules that would govern any future use of military tribunals.

In the years ahead, how we remember the rhetoric surrounding these congressional debates—from many different sides—will tell us a great deal about how we are going to draw the line between state necessities and civil liberties. When we see the recirculation of the claims deployed during World War II, we can see how some familiar patterns of argumentation are being appropriated or domesticated to justify some extremely contentious claims. As critics and laypersons we need to be aware of what is being said and left unsaid in the new tales we are hearing about Bush's Military Order. In one the most concise and moving commentaries on our present dilemma, Katyal noted:

The issues raised by the Military Order concern not only today, but tomorrow. You can already hear how our treatment of the Nazi saboteurs in 1942 has become the guidepost for our treatment of individuals today. What will the present course of conduct mean for situations down the road? Once the President's power to set up military tribunals is untethered to the locality of war or explicit congressional authorization, and given to the President by dint in the office he holds, there is nothing to stop future Presidents from using these tribunals in all sorts of ways. In this respect, it is important to underscore that the precedent the Bush administration seeks to revitalize, the Nazi saboteur case of *Ex parte Quirin,* 317 U.S. 1, 20, 37–38 (1942), explicitly goes so far as to permit military tribunals to be used against American citizens. We must be extraordinarily careful when revitalizing an old and troubling court decision, for doing so will set a new precedent for future Presidents that can come back to haunt citizens and aliens alike.[91]

If we do end up taking the military commissions route, hopefully we will have gained an appreciation of the historical and contemporary roadblocks that might stand in our way.

9

The Future Use of
Military Tribunals

Many think it not only inevitable but entirely proper that liberty give
way to security in times of national crises—that, at the extremes of
military exigency, *inter arma silent leges.* . . . that view has no place in
the interpretation and application of a Constitution.

——Justice Scalia, joined by Justice Stevens, dissenting in
Hamdi et al. v. Rumsfeld et al. (2004)

During the summer of 2004, just days before the Iraqi people regained
their "sovereignty,"[1] the members of the U.S. Supreme Court determined
that an American citizen by the name of Yaser Esam Hamdi could legally
contest his detention as an "enemy combatant."[2] Several other detention
cases would be decided that day,[3] but the *Hamdi* case became the focal
point of controversy because it provided the most detailed discussion of
the rights of American citizen detainees. For more than two and a half
years both conservative and liberal critics of the Bush administration had
been complaining about this "imperial presidency,"[4] but now it appeared
as though a plurality of the nation's highest appellate court would help
defend the principle that "a state of war is not a blank check for the President when it comes to the rights of the Nation's citizens."[5]

Many civil libertarians treated the *Hamdi* case as a decision that would
safeguard essential constitutional liberties, but I would argue that in many
ways this decision helped legitimate the notion that during times of war
many types of detentions are warranted in the name of "military necessity." Moreover, this case contained the assertion that military tribunals
may provide the type of hearings that can segregate "the errant tourist,
embedded journalist or aid worker" from the "enemy combatant" de-

tainee.[6] The historical voices that had once complained about the Unionist prejudices in the *Wirz* trial, or the hasty hangings of the Dakota warriors, were now conveniently muted, and one's mere "affiliation" with a Taliban unit or an al-Qaeda network could bring a life sentence.

In the interim years since the passage of Bush's Military Order (chapter eight), the key topoi in the legal and public debates regarding military tribunals had shifted away from the legality and desirability of these tribunals toward "access" issues during times of war. After constant interrogation, isolation, and coercion, many detainees' lawyers are writing briefs asking for variants of the very hearings that were once characterized as unconstitutional and problematic. Approximately six hundred detainees were still being held in Guantánamo, Cuba, and many more were being questioned in Afghanistan and Iraq. To be fair, the handing down of the *Hamdi* decision now enabled many of these detainees and their relatives to demand that the U.S. government provide some type of "basic process," but the circulation of some befuddling and contradictory opinions (one plurality, one concurring, and two dissenting) complicated an already complex situation. While Justice David Souter and Justice Ruth Bader Ginsburg were writing about the *Ex parte Milligan* limitations on the "emergency power of necessity" or the protections afforded by traditions dating back to the time of the "Magna Carta,"[7] Justice Clarence Thomas was sure that Hamdi had already "received all the process to which he was due under the circumstances."[8] These commentaries, however, did not stop military authorities from assuring members of the press that they already had procedures in place that would probably pass constitutional muster.

In many ways Justice Sandra Day O'Connor—the author of the plurality opinion in *Hamdi*—was apparently sending a message to military authorities that she believed the nation needed "enemy combatant proceedings" that could be "tailored" in ways that would not "burden the Executive at a time of ongoing conflict."[9] Militarist templates overshadowed criminalized frameworks in an opinion that refused to second-guess many of the American commander in chief's prerogatives during times of war. In writing a decision that explicitly tried to balance the rights of the individual with the interests of the state, O'Connor implied that these minimalist hearings did not have to be elaborate affairs—hearsay evidence would be admissible, and the "Constitution wouldn't be offended by a presumption in favor" of the Government's "credible evidence."[10] Not surprisingly, O'Connor also found that the *Quirin* decision was the "most apposite precedent that "postdates and clarifies *Milligan.*"[11] The *Hamdi* case was remanded back to the lower courts, and the Supreme Court advised district judges that they needed to allow for a "fact-finding process that is both prudent and incremental."[12]

Within a matter of hours, representatives of the American military establishment began reading the *Hamdi* decision, and one of them told a reporter for the *St. Louis Post-Dispatch* that governmental authorities were busy preparing the trials that "would be the first military tribunals convened by the United States since the end of World War II."[13] The U.S. military ended a great deal of speculation when it was announced that an Australian and two alleged bodyguards of Osama bin Laden would be the first detainees tried in front of a five-member military tribunal. David Matthew Hicks would be charged with conspiracy to commit war crimes, attempted murder by an unprivileged belligerent, and aiding the enemy,[14] while Ali Hamza Ahmad Sulayman al Bahlul and Ibrahim Ahmed Mahmoud al Qosi faced conspiracy charges. As John Mintz and Michael Powell explained, the *Hamdi, al Odah,* and *Padilla* rulings "did not address the legality of the military tribunals that the government has planned," nor was it clear whether the ruling would affect the Pentagon's plans for an annual review procedure for the detainees.[15] In all likelihood, as long authorities put together some rudimentary type of administrative hearing for detainees, that will suffice.[16]

In this chapter I argue that a rhetorical analysis of these June 2004 decisions illustrates how the American judiciary has once again abdicated its constitutional responsibilities. As critics review the choice of arguments used in these debates about jurisdiction and the merits of detainee cases, they will notice how select legal characterizations and narratives are used in defenses of American unilateral actions, and how entire conversations about the problematics associated with historical cases are ignored or summarily dismissed. The "whig" arguments that once constrained tyrants have now been domesticated and melded together with more authoritarian "tory" fragments. In the name of necessity, American presidents and their subordinates can now declare wars that are recognized by the federal judiciary, they can make uncontested assertions about the duration of military conflicts, they can talk about the need for secrecy and coercive interrogations, and they can have a great deal of say in formulating the substantive and procedural rules that will guide the formation of tribunals.

With this in mind, this chapter has been organized into four major segments. The first portion highlights the range of plausible legal positions on military tribunals that were circulating in various public circles in the years following the registration of Bush's military orders. The second section extends this analysis by looking at how this range was narrowed as various federal courts began hearing some of the first detainee cases, and the third segment looks at the selective nature of the oral and written arguments presented in the *Hamdi, Padilla,* and *Odah* cases. The final segment presents some of the reasons why we need to rethink the unilateral nature of these tribunal proceedings, and how we can all profit from a recontextualization of some of these historic cases.

The Early Post-9/11 Critiques

Before the declared "end" of the second Iraqi war, many legal and public commentators avidly dissected the governmental arguments used in general defenses of military tribunals. In late 2001 and early 2002, hundreds of essayists were writing short commentaries on *Ex parte Quirin* and the need for collateral habeas corpus review. Philip Allen Lacovara, a former solicitor general, remarked that "public opinion mandates that the tribunals be used sparingly," and that the government should not "prosecute every low-level peripheral character."[17] At this evolutionary stage in the debate, the topoi centered around the notion that civil courts should be preferred over military tribunals, and America's laws were sometimes compared with international rules of law. For example, an anonymous writer for *Progressive* noted in January of 2002 that the tribunal rules defended by President Bush and Donald Rumsfeld were examples of how "Peru works, not the United States!"[18] Geoffrey Robertson, a human-rights attorney, reminded readers that Vice President Cheney, with his comments on enemies who "don't deserve the same guarantees and safeguards that would be used for an American citizen," was forgetting about "a presidentially ordained tribunal used to convict General Yamashita," who "historians now believe was innocent."[19] These types of remarks indicated that many critics were critiquing both the legality and the desirability of various military tribunal schemes.

During these turbulent times, the *Milligan*-type arguments became a part of what Charles Lane called the "template" that helped with the "managing" of the "trade-off between safety and freedom."[20] Lane went on to argue that both liberal and conservative "civil libertarians" had learned from the problematics of the Civil War cases, and that President Bush would have "gone even further in cracking down on terrorism" if he had not been "constrained by a legal and political culture" that favored civil liberties.[21] Michal Belknap, writing in the *San Diego Union-Tribune,* assured readers that *Ex parte Milligan* had not been overturned, and that the decision "held that a military trial of someone who is not a member of the armed forces in an area where the civilian courts are open and functioning violates the Fifth and Sixth Amendments and Article III's guarantee of a jury trial in criminal cases."[22]

Yet these types of critiques did not become a part of the dominant discourses during this period because the focus of debate shifted away from the legitimacy of these tribunals and toward issues related to the shape and form of these proceedings. For example, in March of 2002, Secretary of Defense Donald Rumsfeld did not need any more apologetics as he unveiled the "groundbreaking" rules that were going to provide for a new system of "fair and impartial" tribunals.[23] The public announcement of these rules did not mean the president was automatically thinking about using these rules or even having tribunals—he and his administrators were simply espousing their view that they had the authority to do this, and they were just putting together the "blueprint" that might be used in necessitous situations. Rumsfeld told reporters the new tribunals would provide the "flexibility" needed to ensure "the safety and security of the American people."[24]

Some of these tribunal modifications looked salutary—now defendants would be considered innocent until proven guilty, prosecutors would have to cope with a standard of proof that had to be "beyond a reasonable doubt," and no defendant could be tried twice for the same offense.[25] The trials would now be partially open, although they could be closed at the discretion of the presiding officer. The suspected terrorists were going to be given the right to choose counsel, and they could see the prosecution's evidence.[26] If the tribunal decided on a verdict of not guilty, this couldn't be changed or modified by the President.

Yet these "modifications" did not change all of the rules and standards that appeared in the original Bush Military Order, and they did not alter the dominant militarist templates that framed the key public and legal debates. A great deal of hearsay evidence was still going to be allowed to be heard in the courtroom, and the modified rules do not provide for any multistep review outside of a "relatively narrow sphere of military officers"—"the Secretary of Defense, the appointed authority, and the President."[27] This could easily mean these military tribunals could be turned into show trials that propagated the American versions of the causes of terrorism since the time of the Afghan or Iraqi wars. In the same way that the Dakota Indians had to listen to general tales of massacres in 1862 (chapter three), and Yamashita had to hear about the pillaging of Manila at the end of World War II (chapter seven), the al-Qaeda defendants would most likely have to listen to hundreds of American survivors talk about the loss of their loved ones in the attacks on the World Trade Center and the Pentagon.[28] Given the nature of "conspiracy" charges, any potential defendants would have a difficult time proving that the prosecutorial evidence had no "probative value to a reasonable person." For example, Rumsfeld has explained that military tribunals may need more inclusive rules of evidence than are used in Article III criminal trials, because in "wartime, it may be difficult to locate witnesses or establish chains of custody for documents." He concluded that "evidence that could protect the American people from dangerous terrorists should not be excluded simply because it was obtained under conditions of war."[29]

In sum, even with these modifications, the president and his subordinates were still provided with a great deal of discretionary power in the formation and maintenance of these tribunals. Perhaps the most troublesome aspect of these modifications is that they still highlight the importance of having military, and not civilian, review of these decisions. The new rules only allow for an appellate procedure that uses panels of judges appointed to, or by, the military, which "means no truly independent review."[30]

I share the concerns of those observers who worry that we risk going back to the time when the "will" of the sovereign becomes the measure of one's due process rights. Jonathan Turley had this to say about the extent of the president's powers under the modified defense plans:

> [the review panel] will not be permitted to apply the U.S. Constitution or federal law. This creates the mere presence of legal process. . . . The framers expressly denied the president the right to create and mete out his own form of justice. It takes more than a few rule changes to remove the "kangaroo" from the court. One can shampoo and pedicure a kangaroo, but it does little to change the appearance of a president's own private menagerie of justice.[31]

From a technical standpoint, one of the most worrisome parts of this entire debate over the modified Bush orders is the fact that Congress sat on the sidelines as defense experts put together legal arguments buttressing the president's claims about inherent or authorized executive powers. In many ways, the discretion now afforded President Bush appears to undo the half-century of ideological work of "whig" rhetorics that came in the aftermath of World War II, the Korean War, and Vietnam. It is amazing how quickly public fears and anxieties over terrorism have altered the political landscape in ways that bring so many cultural amnesias. Many American audiences conveniently forget the dangers that come from executive fiat, or that Congress was the institution that helped create the Uniform Code of Military Justice and the Court of Appeals for the Armed Forces.[32]

Yet perhaps I am being too pessimistic, and I need to provide a rhetorical review that looks at how federal jurists dealt with this balancing of rights and interests between 2001 and 2004. In this next segment, I analyze some of the legal discourse about citizens' rights that circulated before the U.S. Supreme Court's decision in *Hamdi* and the other detainee cases.

Narrowing of the Nature and Scope of Judiciary Review of Military Tribunals

In our post-9/11 world, two names have become symbolically tied to the rights of all detained citizens—Padilla and Hamdi. Jose Padilla (Abdullah al-Muhajir) was often characterized as a Brooklyn-born American citizen detained by authorities for more than two years.[33] The early press accounts reported that thirty-one-year-old Padilla was believed to have had ties to al-Qaeda as he traveled around the world between 1998 and 2001, and for several years his name appeared alongside Milligan's, Quirin's, and Yamashita's.

Wearing the moniker of the "dirty bomber," Padilla was labeled a modern "enemy combatant," a nominal U.S. citizen. Attorney General John Ashcroft accused Padilla of having conspired with the enemy during times of war, and he purportedly planned to set off a low-level radiological bomb somewhere in the United States. In theory, governmental authorities foiled this attempt, in the same way that J. Edgar Hoover's FBI stopped the World War II German saboteurs.

Critics of the Bush administration turned the *Padilla* case into a litmus test that supposedly provided us with some concrete indicators of how various American communities felt about civil liberties, military tribunals, and the powers of chief executives. As Tom Brune explained, for "many attorneys and libertarians, the *Padilla* case is the most extreme example of executive overreach by the president."[34] Commentators used this case as a prism for writing about American unilateralism, the duration of emergency detentions, the meaning of "full and fair" trials for both citizens and noncitizens, and the possible suspension of habeas corpus.

In both the traditional legal forums and the broader public spheres, Padilla has become an iconic symbol loaded with a host of valences. For many of those who want a strong chief executive, he is the typical example of the dangerous terrorist hiding behind the legal protections that are supposed to be afforded to only deserving American citizens. As early as December 6, 2001, John Ashcroft asked this of congressional leaders: "Are we supposed to read [terrorist] suspects their Miranda rights" and allow the hiring of "a flamboyant defense" lawyer? Are we going to bring "them back to the United States to create a new cable network of 'Osama TV,'" that will "provide a worldwide platform for propaganda?"[35] Not to be outdone in the public rhetorical marketplace, Defense Secretary Donald Rumsfeld excoriated some of America's critics who complained about the treatment of detainees at Guantánamo, characterizing them as "isolated pockets of international hyperventilation."[36] Bill Keller maintained these types of remarks treated civil courts as "criminal-coddling, secret-spilling, procedure-clogging terrorist pulpits."[37]

When Jose Padilla entered this prefigured discursive battle over the nature, scope, and limits of executive power, he became the perfect test case, given his Islamic conversion, his supposed connections to al-Qaeda, and his status as an American citizen. After all, as John Murphy points out, the war on terrorism had been framed by President Bush as a "war between citizens and barbarians, between American values and those of a horde rushing the gates of civilization from the Middle East and Afghanistan."[38] Padilla symbolically represented many of the misguided thugs living in the undeveloped world, and he could be characterized as a trained terrorist who did not really understand the West.

Not surprisingly, government officials who captured Padilla at Chicago's O'Hare airport claimed that the *Ex parte Quirin* precedent allowed for the detention of "enemy combatants," and that these captured prisoners should not be shielded by their fortuitous status as nominal citizens. Although in recent months government officials[39] and members of the federal judiciary have underscored the importance of having legal counsel, detainees like Padilla lived for years in a gray zone, where they were neither charged nor arrested. One liberal federal court, the Second Circuit Court, decided in December of 2003 that Padilla had to be released from military detention within a month,[40] but when the U.S. Supreme Court reviewed this decision they did not reach the merits of the decision because of jurisdictional technicalities.

Throughout 2002 and 2003, many different public and legal communities helped move the debates about military tribunals away from the legality of these types of proceedings and toward the security interests associated with the detention of both citizens and noncitizens. Readers were told that the interrogation of these detainees was helping win the military battles being waged in Afghanistan, Iraq, and the United States. Here one finds few commentaries that focus on the "civilianization" of the military, or the importance of criminal guidelines. Instead, rights are trivialized and military scenarios take center stage. Take, for example, the claims advanced by Ruth Wedgwood, a former federal prosecutor and professor of international law at Yale and Johns Hopkins universities. In an article in the *Wall Street Journal,* Wedgwood argued that:

U.S. Marines may have to burrow down an Afghan cave to smoke out the leadership of al-Qaeda. It would be ludicrous to ask that they pause in the *dak* to pull an Afghan language Miranda card from their kit bag. This is war, not a criminal case. . . . The detention of combatants is a traditional prerogative of war. We have all seen movies about captured soldiers in World War II. After surrender or capture, a soldier can be parked for the rest of the war, in humane conditions, to prevent him from returning to the fight. His [*sic*] detention does not depend on being charged with a crime.[41]

Many months later, University of Chicago law professor Cass Sunstein told readers of the *Chicago Tribune* that when "national security is threatened, the nation's highest priority is to eliminate the threat, not to grant the most ample procedural safeguards to those who have created the threat."[42] This type of foregrounding of military concerns indicates that we have fewer conversations about those ancient "whig" ideas considered to be bulwarks against tyrannical forces.

It will be my contention that during this period the vast number of jurists in this country followed the lead of several U.S. attorney generals and solicitor generals in their recycling of the propositional logics and narratives that are used in rhetorical defense of tribunals. Once in a while they might grant that a particular detainee needed to have access to a lawyer, or they afforded a defendant some minor constitutional privilege, but for the most part American federal jurists assiduously avoided dealing with some of the larger constitutional issues that needed to be tackled— the proper authorities and the responsibilities associated with declarations of emergency, the problematics associated with military tribunals, or potential violations of many different types of treaties and international agreements.

Take, for example, the legal fragments that appeared in the rhetorics provided by Michael Mukasey, of the Southern District of New York. In December of 2002, he had to hear the case of *Jose Padilla v. George W. Bush, Donald Rumsfeld, and Commander M. A. Marr.*[43] Padilla's lawyers, Donna Newman and Andrew Patel, complained that Padilla was an American citizen who was detained without formal charges. Padilla's legal team was petitioning Mukasey for judicial relief in the nature of habeas corpus, and was challenging the lawfulness of his detention. Mukasey concluded that the U.S. president was indeed authorized under the Constitution and "by law" to direct the military to detain enemy combatants, and that Padilla's detention was not per se unlawful. This district court judge granted that Padilla needed legal counsel, but as long as the president and his subordinates had "some" evidence that Padilla might be an "enemy combatant," the courts were supposed to defer to the judgment of the members of the executive branch.[44]

When Judge Mukasey framed his lower court opinion, he did not begin by talking about the condition of the detainees who were being held by the American authorities, and he did not focus on the fundamental nature of key individual liberties. Instead he presented a chronological narrative that punctuated time by reminding us that the president declared a state of national emergency on September 14, 2001. Readers of the opinion are informed that four days later Congress passed a joint resolution (AUMF) that authorized the American president to use "all necessary and appropriate force against those nations, organizations, or persons he determines planned, authorized, committed, or aided the terrorist attacks . . . or harbored such organizations or persons."[45] This is an incredibly powerful fragment, because it magnifies the social agency of the president. The nation's commander in chief, and his subordinates, have the power to decide just who will be designated a terrorist, and Congress has supposedly ratified those choices.

Obviously, one of the key issues involved in these debates is the question of how this particular narrative fits within the rhetorical frameworks that have circulated within legal and public spheres in our post-Vietnam era. Mukasey makes it clear that other parts of the joint resolution were enacted to get around any potential problems with the War Powers Act, which was enacted in 1973 over Nixon's presidential veto.[46] This district court judge went on to argue that in June of 2002, President Bush determined that Padilla should be designated an "enemy combatant," and that he was "closely associated with al-Qaeda." Furthermore, the court accepted factual claims that the defendant had engaged in "hostile and warlike acts," that he possessed important information, and that he represented "a continuing, present and grave danger to the national security of the United States."[47] Mukasey accepted many of the assertions that circulated in a memo claiming that Padilla was sent to the "United States to conduct reconnaissance and/or conduct other attacks on their behalf."[48]

In all fairness, Judge Mukasey does try to point out some of the problems with the Bush administration's handling of the *Padilla* case. For example, he notes that even though the president himself had declared that American citizens would not be tried by tribunals, it seemed as though some governmental officials had other ideas. During a news briefing in June of 2002, Secretary of Defense Rumsfeld had this to say about Padilla's detention:

> Here is an individual who has intelligence information . . . [who] will be submitted to a military court, or something like that—our interest really in his case is not law enforcement, it is not punishment because he was a terrorist or working with the terrorists. Our interest at the moment is to try and find out everything he knows so that hopefully we can stop other terrorist acts.[49]

The New York district judge described this as an "inartful [*sic*] reference to trial before military tribunal."[50]

Pages later, Mukasey begins to focus on the plight of Padilla, and here he is sure that the Posse Comitatus Act, which bars the detention of American citizens "except pursuant to an Act of Congress,"[51] is not a legal hurdle, because Padilla is not being accused of having violated any *civilian* laws. The defendant is being detained because of his affiliation with terrorist organizations. Moreover, Mukasey is convinced that the president had both congressional authority and inherent executive power to declare war, and that the international "laws of war" provided additional justification for his actions. This district court judge did not want to speculate about the endpoint for this war on terrorism, and he was convinced the Third Geneva Convention did not protect "unlawful combatants."[52] The ideas presented in *Ex parte Quirin,* and not *Ex Parte Milligan,*[53] would be controlling. "Padilla," argued Mukasey, "like the saboteurs [*Quirin* case]" was "alleged to be in active association with an enemy with whom the United States is at war."[54]

Obviously, given the controversial nature of the *Padilla* case, many legal scholars and judicial actors played the part of Cassandras, warning us of the dangers that awaited those who fell under the spell of a strong chief executive. For example, in December of 2003, American readers were informed that "two of the nation's most liberal appellate courts weighed in," and that a New York appeals court ruled that Jose Padilla had to be released from military detention within a month.[55] Other federal courts disagreed with these statutory and constitutional interpretations, and many of the jurists who sat on more conservative courts underscored the importance of judicial deference in extraordinary situations. For example, in *Hamdi v. Rumsfeld,* the Fourth Circuit Court of Appeals noted:

> Thus, in *Quirin,* the Supreme Court stated in no uncertain terms that detentions "ordered by the President in the declared exercise of his powers as Commander-in-Chief of the Army in time of war and of grave public danger" should not "be set aside by the courts without the clear conviction that they are in conflict with the Constitution or laws of Congress constitutionally enacted.[56]

By the time that the U.S. Supreme Court announced it was going to hear several appellate cases dealing with civilian detention issues, the Department of Defense had already been working on the procedures for the military tribunals and the selection of the personnel who would oversee these proceedings.

Some of the military lawyers who defended many of these detainees would become some of the harshest critics of the Bush policies, and they took the extraordinary step of challenging the legality of the newest tribunals. In late 2003 and early 2004, several of these military officers received their assignments from the Office of Military Commissions in the Office of General Counsel of the U.S. Department of Defense, and they were "under orders to defend named or yet-to-be-named individuals" who were "targets of investigations by military commissions that are to take place at Guantánamo Bay, Cuba."[57] In one of the amicus curiae briefs that was written for the United States Court of Appeals for the District of Columbia Circuit, Lieutenant Colonel Sharon Shaffer, Lieutenant Commander Charles Swift, Lieutenant Commander Philip Sundel, Major Mark Brides, and Major Michael Mori claimed that the nation's chief executive was trying to "oust Article III courts of jurisdiction over the military prosecution of individuals whom the President deems 'enemy combatants.'"[58] These attorneys acknowledged the importance of having a military that could "wage war," but they worried that some members of the executive branch were forgetting about many of the principles that could be found in the post–World War II Uniform Code of Military Justice (UCMJ), the 1949 Geneva Convention, and "domestic extensions of criminal and habeas law." Given the fact that the "struggle against terrorism is potentially never-ending," the Bush administration was said to be moving away from "case-by-case reviews." This created an intolerable situation, because the "Constitution cannot countenance an open-ended executive power, with no civilian review whatsoever."[59]

In their "whiggish" critique of the Bush detentions, Shaffer and the other authors of the *Odah* amicus brief appropriated some of the rhetorical figurations that had been circulated in the public sphere for quite some time as they wrote about the creation of "a legal black hole," where a "simulacrum of Article III justice is dispensed but justice in fact depends on the mercy of the executive."[60] The potential acceptance of military commission rules crafted by the executive's subalterns meant that the detainees could not contest the jurisdiction, competency, or the constitutionality of the tribunals, and this violated the constitutional provisions that provided for habeas corpus relief. Moreover, this alleged "monarchial regime" had officials defending legal arguments that flew in the face of the "competent tribunal" provisions of the Geneva Convention. In the same way that American colonists complained about King George's attempt to "render the Military independent of and superior to the Civil Power,"[61] the detainees were worried about a president who was trying to proclaim himself the "superior or sole expositor of the Constitution in matters of justice."[62] While the lawyers admitted that the president might be able to detain enemy combatants as prisoners of war, as soon as he moved into the actual *adjudication* of their guilt, he was no longer simply waging war.

When these military lawyers reviewed the *Ex parte Milligan, Ex parte Quirin,* and *In re Yamashita* precedents, they treated these as access cases that underscored the importance of having habeas corpus relief. In one of the most fascinating sections of their amicus brief, Shaffer and her colleagues noted that even these cases did not provide the most "direct precedent," because in their opinion this was the first time that an American government had consciously created a trial process and courtroom that was outside of the battlefield and "housed" in an "area calculated to divest civilian jurisdiction."[63] The military officers surveyed the dusty tomes of Anglo-Saxon jurisprudence as they searched for that "direct" precedent, and their investigations took them back to the 1660s, when Lord Clarendon was shipping prisoners off to military garrisons so that they could "evade habeas corpus." Clarendon was impeached for his actions, and the English Parliament eventually passed the 1679 Habeas Corpus Act. This type of "direct" precedent supposedly stood as a bulwark that stopped "sham trials" and the "absolute" positions of the president.[64]

Some of these military officers wrote their own separate briefs that contained even stronger language, and there is even one relatively unknown detainee case (*Hamdan*) that has served as a vehicle for defense lawyers who want to argue that all forms of military proceedings should be considered unconstitutional and against international law. Note how the briefs of Navy Lieutenant Commander Charles Swift and his assistants contain passages that discuss the president's seizure of legislative and judicial powers that brought back memories of "the conduct of King George III."[65] Swift was representing Salim Ahmed Hamdan, a former driver for Bin Laden, and this Naval officer's commentaries were part of a civil suit filed in a Seattle federal district court on Hamdan's behalf. Swift, with Georgetown University law professor Neal Katyal's help, put out a petition filled with several "whiggish" rhetorical fragments that provide some of the strongest rationales for why we still need *Milligan*-type reviews of military tribunals that are outside the military chains of command.[66] In Katyal's memorandum in support of several writs, he averred that these military tribunals lacked both personal and subject matter over the defendant. In one of the strongest segments of the memorandum, Katyal claimed the Bush Military Order violated the "separation of Powers, Equal Protection, the Suspension Clause, the Uniform Code of Military Justice and 42 U.S.C. section 1981."[67] Bush's military subordinates were said to have placed "Mr. Hamdan in solitary confinement without charge," and this act was viewed as "an arbitrary and illegally imposed sentence that is incompatible with fundamental guarantees of due process recognized by all civilized people."[68]

Many of the other lawyers who represent other detainees have assiduously avoided this type of commentary—they put together briefs that advanced more moderate positions. For example, they might ask for congressional intervention, some form of military trial, or a change of venue. The Swift-Katyal position is the first direct attack on the constitutionality and desirability of military tribunals, and Hamdan's legal representatives were asking U.S. District Court Judge Robert Lasnik for civil reviews that would look into a host of factual and legal issues.[69] For example, they wanted civilian investigations that would review the factual accuracy of the detainee's claims that he was an innocent civilian, caught in the wrong place at the wrong time.

Without question Swift and Katyal were fighting an uphill battle, because their interpretations of *Ex parte Milligan, Ex parte Quirin,* and *In re Yamashita* provided a nondeferential critique of the Bush Military Order. They pointed out that all of these cases involved federal review of military court proceedings, and that throughout "our" Anglo-American "history," federal courts had stood as bulwarks "against unilateral overreaching by the Executive Branch." Within their radical storyline, the Bush administration was engaging in the types of "arbitrary" acts that resembled the despotisms of other ages, and the authors of the Hamdan memorandum quoted extensively from Alexander Hamilton's critiques of William Blackstone's treatise passages on unlawful imprisonment.[70] Swift told reporters that Mr. Hamdan was merely a poorly educated functionary who worked for Bin Laden out of desperation. This detainee was characterized as a father of two "beautiful kids—one's 4 and one's 2," and Swift's client was said to have left Yemen in the mid-1990s. Hamdan was portrayed as an anticommunist freedom fighter who was trying to reach Tajikistan, but "weather and politics" worked against him.[71]

These discursive attacks were rarely taken seriously in most legal circles,[72] and many newspaper accounts of this controversy have simply repeated the governmental assertions that have been made about Hamdan's terrorist activities. At the same time, official documents contain reports that claim "that there was reason to believe that Hamdan was an Al Qaeda member or otherwise involved in terrorism directed at the United States and therefore designated for trial before a military commission."[73] The "tory" narratives in this case highlighted the importance of presidential and military discretion during times of war, and emphasized the fact that Allied forces in Afghanistan had captured Hamdan. When defense attorneys asked federal judges for at least some type of evidentiary hearing, governmental lawyers responded that the military now had various screening processes in place that helped separate dangerous enemies from other Guantánamo detainees at Camp Delta. Within this scenario, Hamdan's status as a U.S. citizen was viewed as irrelevant, given the fact that he was caught in a zone of war.

The U.S. Supreme Court never heard the radical arguments presented in the *Hamdan* case, because in May of 2004 Judge Lasnik granted the government's motion to hold this petition in abeyance until the nation's highest appellate court heard the other detainee cases.

Of "Enemy" Citizens and "Ticking" Time Bombs

In the spring of 2004, military leaders had informed several members of the press that the Guantánamo tribunals were now a reality, and the defense teams who prepared for the oral presentations in the *Hamdi*,[74] *Padilla*,[75] and *Rasul/al Odah*[76] cases were desperately seeking some type of habeas corpus relief for these detainees. Tania Cruz was right on the mark when she observed that in the *Hamdi* case, the governmental designation of "enemy combatants" was being used to ensure that some U.S. citizens were not even receiving a "scaled down version" of important constitutional liberties.[77] Yaser Esam Hamdi was born in St. Louis and grew up in Saudi Arabia, and was said to have been captured on the battlefield by Northern Alliance Forces fighting in Afghanistan. This alleged fighter was then turned over to the Americans, who took him to Guantánamo and then transferred him to a Norfolk Naval Station brig.[78] For more than two years, Hamdi stayed in government custody, and his father filed a habeas corpus brief as Hamdi's "next friend." In some of the lower court briefs, his counsel argued that he was not enjoying the full protection of the Constitution because he was being held without charges, access to a civil trial, or counsel. This supposedly violated his due process rights under the Fifth and Fourteen Amendments of the U.S. Constitution.[79]

In December of 2003, representatives of the Department of Defense surprised public and legal observers when they announced that Hamdi was going to be provided some type of access to a lawyer. One DOD news release made it clear that this should not be viewed as military precedent, because this was simply a policy decision.[80] Several days later, Neil Lewis of the *New York Times* surmised that this was simply a "calculated gesture" from an administration that was trying to "shield its policies from criticism and reversal by the courts."[81]

During the hour-long oral argument in the *Hamdi* case, many of the justices asked questions that clearly showed they believed Congress had specifically authorized some type of detention when they passed legislation indicating the president could take "all necessary and appropriate force." At one point during these oral presentations, Hamdi's lawyer, Frank Durham, asked the Court to remember that the "Great Writ" [habeas corpus] came into being because of the inherit distrust of centralized authority. As far as he was concerned, this decision involved the rights of one "citizen," and not "thousands," and Durham's client had simply been "caught up in a problem in Afghanistan."[82] In this instance:

> The Government is saying trust us . . . and driving a truck right through the right of habeas corpus and the Fifth Amendment. . . . I would urge the court to find that citizens can only be detained by law. And here there is no law. If there is any law at all, it is the executive's own secret definition of whatever enemy combatant is. And don't fool yourselves into thinking that that means somebody coming off a battlefield because they've used it in Chicago, they've used it in New York and they've used it in Indiana.[83]

Durham later implied that many of his arguments must have resonated with most of the members of the Supreme Court, but I would agree with Tony Mauro's observation that at "one time or another, most of the justices sounded sympathetic to the government's wartime stance."[84]

This was clearly underscored in the oral debates in the *Padilla* case, where the Second Circuit Court of Appeals handed down an opinion questioning the inherent constitutional authority of the American commander in chief to detain American citizens on "American soil *outside* a zone of combat" [my emphasis]. Circuit Judges Pooler and Parker had argued that Congress had not provided any specific authorization for the president's detention of "enemy combatants."[85] Paul Clement, who argued the government's case, fielded a lot of questions about venue and jurisdiction, but it would be the queries about the merits of the *Padilla* case that gave us hints about the ways these jurists felt about executive prerogatives and the separation of powers.

A rhetorical analysis of these oral arguments leaves the impression that this is was a Court trying to respect what Antonin Scalia has called the "George Washington power" of a president who leads military forces.[86] When Clement talked about the congressional authorization of force, prior military histories, and the *Quirin* precedent, he did not field many questions focusing on the legitimacy of the tribunals or the circumstances surrounding the president's designation of this "war" on terrorism—the trajectory of the arguments seemed to take for granted that battlefield conditions did exist and that at least some detentions of both citizens and noncitizens were prudent and necessary.

In many ways, the governmental insistence that this was not a case involving traditional criminal behavior framed the overarching narratives presented in these detention cases, and Clement and his colleagues tried to always cite legal precedents that justified the expansive use of a president's wartime powers. During oral argumentation, the deputy solicitor general opined that Padilla had the same rights as other "belligerents" who were caught on the battlefield, and he told Justice Anthony Kennedy that this detainee needed to be treated as if he had been caught in Afghanistan.[87] As soon as a citizen was captured on the battlefield and then brought to "safety," Clement averred the "rules of engagement" demanded that the "appropriate force" be used. Hence, even unlawful belligerents would be considered less of a threat and treated accordingly.[88]

A few justices worried about the abandonment of *Milligan*-type principles. For example, Justice Stephen Breyer questioned Clement about the scope of Congress's Use of Force Act, and he asked:

So why would it be necessary and proper in a country that has its courts open, that has regular criminal proceedings, that has all the possibility of adjudicating a claim that I'm the wrong person? Why is it a necessary and appropriate thing to do once you have a person who is a citizen in this country to proceed by other than a normal court procedure?[89]

Clement seized this opportunity and claimed that in this "war on terror-ism," the country did not need to have a host of federal courts looking into these statutes in such a way that they were viewing this as an "invitation for a sort of judicial management of the executive's war-making power."[90]

Many commentators who listened to the audio versions of these oral arguments, or who read the written transcripts, noted that there were moments during these proceedings when observers got some hint that these jurists were not particularly enamored with the government's posi-tion on the topic of "indefinite" detention. Capturing a citizen fighting against his or her nation was one thing, but Padilla had been picked up in Chicago, on the basis of a "material witness" warrant. Were these the types of activities that justified nonintervention on the part of either Congress or the judiciary?

In the last several years, Bush officials used a host of rationales as they tried to justify these indefinite detentions (these "enemies" could not re-turn to the battlefield, the detainees provided essential information that helped stop future terrorist attacks, the detainees served as material witnesses in other proceedings, etc.), and at this point in time the mem-bers of the Court wanted to hear more about the meaning of the ideo-graph "necessary and appropriate." When Justice Anthony Kennedy asked Clement about his "vision" of how the military process would work in this situation, the deputy solicitor general answered that the goal of preventing "future terrorist attacks" was so important the "military ought to have the option of proceeding" in ways that got them "actionable intelligence." Moreover, Clement maintained that the Bush administration should not be forced into a situation where choices had to be made about proceeding with trials for "past acts."[91]

Perhaps prompted by an argument that appeared in some of the respon-dent or amicus curiae briefs, several members of the Court pressed the government's counsel on the issue of "unchecked" executive power. For example, Ginsburg asked Clement about the constraints that would be in place in situations where the executive or his subordinates felt *torturing* Padilla was "necessary and appropriate." Would the deputy solicitor gen-eral still want to keep everything within the military chains of command if the orders for "mild torture" came from "an executive command"?[92] When Clement responded that the United States still had its "treaty obligations," he had a defensible response, but when he talked of how this form of torture would have violated "our own conception of what's a war crime," he was on much weaker ground.

At this point in the proceedings, the government seemed to take the position that the torturing of civilian prisoners would be the type of situation that might trigger habeas corpus jurisdiction, but Clement tried to qualify these concessions when he noted that federal courts also needed to remember these were "quintessential military judgments." The deputy solicitor general opined that Congress had authorized the use of force, and by "negative implication" authorized "military commissions."[93] In theory, congressional silence on the issue of tribunals meant that congressional leaders were supporting the use of these military forums.

Jennifer Martinez, who presented Padilla's case in front of the Supreme Court, explicitly contested the government's interpretation of the applicable law when she argued that Congress had never explicitly authorized the indefinite detention of American citizens. At the beginning of her presentation she noted that she was asking for a very narrow ruling in this case, and that she would not be dealing with the very broad question of whether the entire U.S. constitutional "system" permitted these types of detentions. Interestingly enough, as soon as Martinez tried to invoke a moderate variant of the "whiggish" arguments by commenting on the "Founding Fathers" experiences with a "British Crown" that "locked up citizens," Justice William Rehnquist interjected and wanted to go back to the topic of congressional force authorization.[94]

The issue of congressional authorization seemed to be one of the core concerns of most of the justices listening to the Padilla oral arguments, and Martinez remarked that,

> There is simply no indication that when Congress passed the authorization for use of military force which enabled us to deploy our troops overseas, the Congress also thought that they were authorizing the indefinite military detention without trial of American citizens on American soil. There was no debate of such a dramatic departure from our constitutional traditions. And just a few weeks later when Congress passed the Patriot Act, it extensively debated a provision that allowed the detention of aliens for seven days.[95]

Minutes earlier, Justice Ginsburg had asked if the Due Process Clause protected both citizens and noncitizens, and Martinez responded by talking about the vagueness of government's position. She reminded the Court that those who adopted the government's position were agreeing that "anyone who is associated with Al Qaeda" could be detained by American forces.[96] When Padilla's counsel argued that Congress needed to take a more active role in designing the legal frameworks for "preventive detention," Justice Kennedy responded that declarations of war are not written in that type of specific terminology.

In the weeks that preceded these oral arguments, observers wondered how the Court would characterize Padilla, and some of those queries were implicitly answered when Justice Breyer began asking Martinez about her "vision" of the law when the nation faced a "ticking time bomb." The deputy solicitor general's written brief had commented on the need for discretion in cases where evidentiary revelations would hurt intelligence gathering, and Breyer wanted to know how this was "supposed to play out under an ordinary criminal system." Martinez admitted the government might need to be engaged in short periods of interrogation, but she stood by her earlier claims that congressional hearings could follow the example of Israel and the United Kingdom and temporally regulate the detentions. An incredulous Sandra Day O'Connor retorted that perhaps the respondents were asking the Court to "turn loose a ticking time bomb."[97] Justice Breyer chimed in and exclaimed that in situations where the nation faced "the real emergency, the real ticking time bomb," Martinez was suggesting that decision-makers were going to have to keep going back to Congress.[98] This characterization of Padilla as a "ticking time bomb" could now be used in legal narratives that rationalized the transcendent importance of swift executive decisions during times of war, and it also created the impression that congressional intervention was either unnecessary or counterproductive.

By now the lawyers for the detainees appeared to be on the defensive, and Martinez was forced to admit that in battlefield situations the American president was authorized to use either his inherent powers or his authority under the AUMF "to seize an individual in the case of imminent violent activity." Yet the defense argued that this was not the situation in this case, because Padilla was supposedly a custodial inmate who was no longer being interrogated by the government. Martinez noted that once this type of person was taken into custody, the Bush administration had to treat him "in accordance with our positive laws."[99] Without these positive laws, government officials could hypothetical lock up Padilla's "mother, because she is associated with her son," who in turn was accused of associating with al-Qaeda.[100]

Clement had saved a few minutes of rebuttal time in the *Padilla* case, and he wanted to make sure this Court was aware that the *Quirin* case, and not *Milligan,* was the "relevant line" that needed to be followed. The deputy solicitor general did not have the time to go into very much factual detail about the *Milligan* case, but he did note that Lambdin Milligan had never left the state of Indiana. Padilla, conversely, was someone who went abroad, associated with the enemy, took weapons training, and then returned to the United States "with the intent to commit hostile and warlike acts as the direction of the enemy."[101]

After I reviewed all of these competing claims in the *Rasul, al-Odah, Hamdi,* and *Padilla* cases, I got the sense that most of these Supreme Court jurists were leaning toward a position that would grant that the president and his subordinates needed short-term detention powers. While some appeared to be suspicious of the "inherent" and open-ended nature of some forms of executive power, a majority appeared to be quite comfortable with the idea that Congress may have authorized at least the *temporary* detention of persons based on reasonable suspicions that came from confidential intelligence sources.[102] From an ideographic perspective, the "necessary and appropriate" force language that appeared in key congressional legislation (AUMF) seemed to provide the American military with some leeway, especially in battlefield situations.

In early June 2004, the DOD shocked reporters when it declassified and released copies of another "summary" that allegedly provided more information on the nefarious activities of Jose Padilla. Deputy Defense Secretary Paul Wolfowitz authored the summary, and the document synthesized material that came from Padilla's interrogations, other senior al-Qaeda detainees, and various American intelligence sources.[103] This new information claimed that Padilla had completed a training camp application for one of the al-Qaeda camps, and that he had associated with Abu Zubaydah, Adnan G. el-Shukrijumah, Muhammed Atef, and other high-ranking "enemy" operatives. Wolfowitz surmised that Padilla may have been directed to return to the United States to conduct "reconnaissance" on behalf of al-Qaeda,[104] but what was even more worrisome was the evidence that tended to indicate Padilla and an accomplice were going to try and detonate some apartment buildings using natural gas.[105]

This newly disclosed information about Padilla—circulated just weeks before the end of the Supreme Court's term—was viewed as an "egregious" governmental act by members of his legal defense team. Newman, one of Padilla's court-appointed lawyers, complained that the military was trying to influence public opinion at a time when they "zip up our lips by saying everything is classified."[106] It is obviously difficult to assess whether these types of pronouncements impacted the decision-making of the nation's highest appellate court, but they provide us with even more clues that Bush administrators must have understood the symbolic value of these detainee cases.

When the Supreme Court finally announced its rulings in these detainee cases, it was the *Hamdi* case that garnered the most attention, and one of al Qosi's lawyers, Lieutenant Colonel Sharon Shaffer, claimed that ruling meant that once prisoners exhausted their military avenues of relief, the federal "courts are open to them."[107] This was certainly not the dominant interpretation of the case that barely mentioned the topic of military tribunals. In the eyes of many observers, the *Hamdi* plurality opinion stood for the principle that Congress had indeed empowered the American president to "use all necessary and appropriate force" against "nations, organizations, or persons," and that this power included the legal "detention of a man whom the Government alleges took up arms with the Taliban during the conflict."[108] In fact, in this case the detainee's lawyers were demanding that the courts provide for at least some type of rudimentary hearing before some neutral decision-maker. In one key passage that appeared in the *Hamdi* decision, Justice O'Connor opined that there "remains the possibility that the standards we have articulated could be met by an appropriately authorized and properly constituted military tribunal."[109]

For more than two years, Hamdi and many other detainees in Afghanistan, Iraq, and Cuba were fighting for the right to be heard, for the chance to rebut the American government's designations and factual narrations.

Since hundreds of detainees were still being interrogated or held without charges, we can readily understand how cases like *Ex parte Quirin* and *In re Yamashita* were now being used by *defense* teams trying to take advantage of the polysemic nature of these texts. The government used these cases as illustrative precedents of the military's power during wartime, but now they were being appropriated for the proposition that both citizens and noncitizens deserved some form of judicial due process.

When many members of the national and international presses heard about Justice O'Connor's decision in *Hamdi,* they often described this case as a victory for civil libertarians, an example of how the Supreme Court can often curb the aspirations of an empowered American executive. Joan Biskupic and Toni Locy, for example, argued in *USA Today* that the Court had "sharply rebuked President Bush's claim that he has unfettered power to lock up people without given them hearings."[110] Eight of the nine justices were said to have sided with Hamdi. Steven Shapiro, the legal director of the American Civil Liberties Union, affirmed that the decision was a "very stinging and watershed defeat" for the administration, because now the Court was saying that Congress had some say in the war on terrorism, and that at least some of the commander in chief's decisions were going to be second-guessed by some members of the federal judiciary.[111] Hamdi's federal public defender, Frank W. Durham Jr., told reporters that "We cleaned their clocks."[112] In many ways, the case would be hailed as the latest in a long line of decisions, where at least some of the judges who decided the case were writing about the whiggish ideas associated with the Magna Carta and the ancient habeas corpus writs.

A vocal minority of reporters who wrote about the *Hamdi* case were a bit more cautious, and wondered about the pragmatic impact of these detainee decisions. The Supreme Court, after all, seemed to be certifying that the attacks on 9/11 were indeed the catalysts for a "war," and several members of the Court must have accepted that position that Congress had provided the president with a great deal of authorized force. None of the detainees were going to be immediately released, and as long as the government could come up with some substantial evidence that supported the "enemy combatant" designation, the lawyers for the detainees would have the burden of proof in any future factual disputation. Nowhere in the opinion was there any indication that President Bush had acted illegally when "he ordered certain prisoners to be held without charge,"[113] and Louise Christian argued that the "*Hamdi* ruling" was "very depressing" because it still condoned indefinite detention of both U.S. citizens and foreigners.[114]

Obviously I share the skepticism of this second group, and I argue that the U.S. Supreme Court has assiduously avoided any meaningful interrogation of the power of America's commander in chief. In the same way that chapter eight illustrated some of the constraints that stood in the way of congressional oversight of Bush's military orders, this chapter traces the rhetorical figurations that display the U.S. Supreme Court's weakness and deference. O'Connor and many of the other justices who wrote opinions in the *Hamdi* case went out of their way to claim they were preserving many of our traditional notions about "separation of powers," but a closer review of their choice of arguments illustrates how they accepted martial frameworks of analyses that provided citizens and noncitizens with few protections, and how the few rights that were preserved stayed primarily within military chains of command. As one commentator astutely observed, far "from the defeat that was portrayed in the media, Monday's raft of Supreme Court decisions reaffirmed the basic tenets of the Bush administration's legal approach to the war on terror."[115]

Consciously or unconsciously, the governmental defenders of the Bush administration policies were deploying variants of "tory" rhetorics that emphasized the importance of military discretion, swift decision-making, battlefield exigencies, and circumscribed individual rights (chapter one). By asking for unfettered power and discretion during times of war, any slight loss of power had to be magnified by opponents searching for any glimmer of hope. A whole range of public and legal arguments could have been deployed in stronger critiques of military tribunals, but these were swiftly swept aside as audiences accepted the idea that any type of trial was better than indefinite detention. Over time, fewer and fewer participants in these public debates were willing to defend the idea that these detainees were "prisoners of war," deserving a non-militant, "competent tribunal" under the whiggish principles of the Third Geneva Convention.[116]

By focusing their attention on the American tribunal cases, both the petitioner and respondent teams were deflecting attention away from an important topic—the need for international or multinational tribunals. If critics of these proceedings could not halt the evolutionary development of tribunals, they needed to demand that many international communities participate in this coalition-led "war on terrorism."

The Path Not Taken:
International Law and Multilateral Tribunals

In the *Hamdi* decision, there is very little commentary on the applicability of the Articles of the Geneva Convention, and when those principles are cited, they are used to buttress allegations that "the law of war" allows for detentions during times of active hostilities.[117] International communities are supposed to accept the legitimacy of American military proceedings, but they are constantly being bombarded with unilateralist rhetorics filled with tales of how these detainees cannot be treated as prisoners of war, or how "war crimes" have been committed against the United States. The very nation that once asked for international justice before the Nuremberg tribunals was now steadfastly defending the use of more nationalistic legal venues. This creates distrust and cynicism. As William Safire insightfully observed in March of 2002, if "the war on terror is supposed to be a unified effort," than "why go it contemptuously alone in setting up an extraordinary military judiciary?"[118]

I argue that we need to recognize the fact that the Guantánamo detainees come from more than forty nations, and that these countries need to be actively involved in the formation and implementation of these legal proceedings. If we are going to claim that these prisoners have ties to the international problem of terrorism, we need international solutions.

It is also imperative that scholars, lawyers, and laypersons who are worried about the potential loss of civil liberties continue the work of challenging the taken-for-granted rhetorics used by today's authoritative figures. When Attorney General John Ashcroft talks about "the people" of this country and the "safety and security of its citizens,"[119] we need to be attentive to the fact that there are many different ways of handling these threats. For example, we need to maintain the presumptions that many of these defendants can be tried in criminal court, and we need to hear more substantive arguments from governmental officials when they argue about the need for tribunals. At the same time, we need to support the positions of jurists on the federal courts who have demanded that Padilla be tried or set free, or who have asked for detailed government documents in detainee classification cases.[120] We need to make sure that those who cite *Ex parte Quirin* are not summarily dismissing the whiggish principles instantiated in *Ex parte Milligan*. As a pragmatic matter, the popularity of the tribunals may mean that most American citizens and jurists will defend the use of these forums, but this does not mean we cannot help shape the contours of these governmental bodies.

Moreover, we need to continually recover and have worldwide circulation of some of the stories that have been forgotten, like the Dakota trials that serve as cautionary tales about some of problematics of these tribunals. Other generations have felt the need for hurried judicial decisions, and we have national and international paper trials of regret and contrition that indicated a rush to justice often precludes the possibility of a full and fair trial. Mark Osiel recently wrote that even "legal advocates," who know how to find the "historical record to support a particular interpretation of the law," are "almost entirely blind to how our legal interpretations, and the records they create in a given dispute, may favor—subtly but decisively—one of the competing historical interpretations of a period."[121]

My rhetorical analyses of these seminal tribunal decisions also indicate that national and international communities should be debating these key issues when they discuss the costs and benefits associated with the use of unilateral or multilateral military tribunals:

- The jurisdictional questions that are raised by these military commissions
- The potential loss of traditional procedural and substantive due process rights
- The difficulty of defining acts connected with "terrorism," or the potential violation of international rules of law and martial codes
- The potential loss of the presumption of innocence and other burdens of proof
- The nature and scope of the review processes involved
- The disruptive impact these decisions would have on the separation of powers

• The impact these military commissions may have on international diplomatic relations
• The ease with which many rhetors blur the distinctions that exist between the necessities created by crises, and the alleged necessities of the tribunals

In all likelihood, civil libertarians and concerned military lawyers will not be able to prevent the arrival of American tribunals, but we need to participate in the dissemination of cautionary tales that come from the clash and mixture of "whig" and "tory" heritages. As noted above, we need to begin by presuming that civil courts can effectively and safely try any potential criminals, and that in camera proceedings[122] can help ensure that information is not covertly being leaked to other criminal parties. Gerald Clark provides a synthesis of this reasoning when he intones:

> Close analysis of the President's order sanctioning military tribunals signals not a lack of faith in the President, the military or the federal enforcement apparatus, but the Constitutional prejudice that aggregated power is dangerous if unchecked . . . extreme enforcement measures that introduce indefinite detention, abrogation of the rules of evidence, the exclusion of the legislative branch in the development of the rules, and the exclusion of the judicial branch in the trials should occur, if ever, in only the most extreme case in which traditional methods of law enforcement and trial are clearly inappropriate. Trials conducted on the field of battle come to mind. . . . As sinister as the attacks of September 11 were, they did not cause a general declaration of martial law and they ought not dictate a suspension of the powers of Article III courts or the application of the United States Constitution.[123]

In the very, very rare cases of extreme necessity, when *Congress* and the United Nations have decided we need to impose martial law or have commissions in occupied lands, we may have situations where all of the civil courts are closed and where the military may need more discretion. Yet these "tory" assertions of power need to be held in check by recognizing that most of the time we should begin with the baseline "whig" assumption that we want to maintain the civilianization of the military, and not the other way around.

As I review these chapters, I firmly believe that on balance the use of military tribunals has not been justified, and that in many cases their very existence exacerbated the problems they were supposed to solve. For example, those who defend Lincoln's use of tribunals have a difficult time showing how the use of these commissions helped end the war or dispense justice. Pope's formation of military tribunals during the Dakota wars was a rushed affair, a proceeding where former fighters now judged their former enemies. Moreover, the Dakota trials helped legitimate the movement of entire Native American communities out of Minnesota. Even the famous *Ex parte Quirin* case that involved the potential dangers of espionage conspiracies was an affair held in secret, where citizens and enemy belligerents received few due process rights.

A cursory review of the "modified" rules of the Department of Defense provides us with few assurances that these "new" guidelines will be implemented in ways that guarantee these combatants will receive their full rights under domestic and international law. The now infamous memo from Alberto R. Gonzales to the Department of Justice, which put together a collage of arguments on why the Geneva Convention III on the Treatment of Prisoners of War does not apply to the conflict with al-Qaeda, reminds us of the dangers that attend claims that "the war on terrorism is a new kind of war."[124] We need to keep in mind both the spirit and letter of our vaunted rules of law.

Even if consider ourselves to be realists who look beyond the idealistic principles of the law, we have to take into consideration the media atmosphere that would be a part of these tribunal spectacles. Given the dominant feelings of most Americans in the aftermath of the 9/11 tragedies, even the fairest of formulaic guidelines will provide precious little protection for those who have already been labeled as "killers" by several officials within the Bush administration.

Obviously, we have to make some difficult choices. Are we interested in having military tribunals that cater to the traumatic needs of the families of the victims? Do we want trials that have rules that allow for prosecutions in the absence of "specific evidence" that defendants "engaged in war crimes?"[125] Do we really believe these trials will deter future acts of terrorism, and are we willing to take the risk that holding these tribunals may have the opposite effect?

I argue that all of these issues should be factors in helping steer us away from defenses of unilateral military tribunals. From a critical vantage point, we need to be thinking about long-term solutions to the problems of terrorism. If we ever truly want to get at the root causes of violence around the world, we will need to provide trials that appear to be legitimate in the eyes of both friends and enemies. It "is in America's interest," argues Aryeh Neier, "that verdicts against those tried for terrorism should be credible to shopkeepers in Cairo or Jakarta or civil servants in Marrakech, Islamabad, or Dacca."[126] Military tribunals may be considered legitimate forums by local communities within the United States, but we risk losing the moral capital we have gained from our previous critiques of other nationalistic usages of similar military tribunals. Michael Ignatieff recently noted that in the wake of the Abu Ghraib revelations, Americans need a strong dose of humility, and we all need to remember that the nation "paid the price for American exceptionalism, the idea that America is too noble, too special, too great to actually obey international treaties like the Torture Convention or international bodies like the Red Cross."[127]

Building the symbolic and material realities needed for an effective international tribunal will not be an easy task, but if we are going to talk about real necessities and concrete actions, we have to avoid the path of swift and vengeful justice. Ironically, I would argue that it was the U.S. quest for an "international" coalition in the war against worldwide terrorism that placed us in a situation where we now have a moral obligation to at least attempt to be a part of multilateral solutions to these longitudinal problems. An analysis of the commentary surrounding the recent defenses of the modified Defense Department rules indicates officials are trying to sit on both sides of the fence—they want to provide nationalistic trials that try to minimize the rights of detainees and maximize the rights of "victims," while at the same time claiming that commissions that follow courts-martial rules can also cover the principles of various Geneva Conventions. Diane F. Orentlicher and Robert Goldman aver that Bush "seeks to detain suspected *terrorists* on the basis of his authority to prosecute *war criminals*" [emphasis in the original].[128]

The military trials of these alleged terrorists in American forums will provide ample ammunition for world critics who are already calling these tribunals "kangaroo" courts. Whether we like it or not, in the eyes of billions of other denizens of this world, Americans do not live in an "exceptional" nation, and we are explicitly or implicitly blamed for helping exacerbate the problems associated with terrorism. United States citizens can argue about how they traveled to Saudi Arabia to protect the sovereignty of Kuwait, or intervened in Afghanistan in the name of self-defense, but many international communities view us as interlopers, bullies, tyrants, and imperialists. For example, one Afghan merchant told William Vollmann: "First you created one Osama. Now you are creating many, many Osamas."[129] Will trials of "foreign" enemies really decrease the risks of terrorism?

In the ideal world I firmly believe we would not have any military tribunals, but as a prudential matter we need to think about U.S. participation in international tribunals. Allowing some of foreign skeptics to have a representative voice in the dispensation of justice in these terrorist cases would help ameliorate our present situation. Anne-Marie Slaughter made these comments in October of 2001:

> Even assuming that Osama bin Laden is more likely to be captured dead than alive, many others will be apprehended over the coming months and years. Where will they be tried? George W. Bush appears to assume that the next step would be trial in U.S. courts. Such a course would be swift but it would have enormous legitimacy problems for many other countries—not to mention security problems for the U.S. In effect, it would proclaim the U.S. to be not only the world's policeman but also the world's judicial system. A better alternative is some kind of international tribunal to work in conjunction with national courts around the world.[130]

Given the social construction of figures like "terrorists," we also need to admit that terrorism is not an individuated problem that will go away when we have tried key leaders or destroyed local "cells." This is a multifaceted problem that has multicausal origins. Military tribunals appear to provide quick solutions to visceral problems. Patriotic grandstanding did not help legitimate the *Wirz* proceedings from a legalistic standpoint, and these types of arguments do not resonate with international audiences.

If the creation of the *appearance* of justice involves the coproduction of legal knowledge, we need to have as many international communities as possible involved in these trials of the alleged terrorists. Vivian Curran, in her investigation of the semiotics of French Vichy trials, had this to say about the possibilities and limitations of these public spectacles:

> The trial can be an ideal medium for representing memory, so long as the concern is to control meaning according to present perspectives, to concretize a normative position. . . . Judicially imposed strictures limit both the questions posed and the answers permitted. Even the nature of the lawyers' questions to witnesses and parties becomes defined by the presiding judge's interpretations, for a judge's directions presuppose the judge's unimpeachable understanding of the questions . . . the emergent version of reality is determined by the judge's array of presuppositions and perspectives, operating within the particular formative framework of the judicial setting. . . . Trials offer resolution by purporting to supply the answer, while in fact producing merely one of many possible answers.[131]

Can we risk resolving our immediate public relations issues at a time when we are dealing with a host of terrorist threats? Let us hope the past does not become prologue as we preserve our histories and memories of military tribunals. It is no coincidence that Judge Rutledge, one of the dissenters in *In re Yamashita,* quoted these words from Thomas Paine: "He [*sic*] that would make his own liberty secure must guard even his enemy from oppression; for if he violates this duty he establishes a precedent that will reach to himself."[132] In the name of necessity, we risk losing many of our cherished civil liberties.

Notes

Chapter 1

1. *Epigraph*. Thomas Jefferson, quoted in Kirk L. Davies, "The Imposition of Martial Law in the United States," *Air Force Law Review* 49 (2000): 112.

2. See, for example, Julie Scott's claim that those who petitioned for peace and engaged in antiwar protests did not understand that this "strike on Iraq" was "the result of the government fulfilling its most fundamental responsibility of taking necessary military action of a defensive, not aggressive, nature against a foul dictator who stands gleefully on the brink of wreaking murderous havoc on America." Julie G. Scott, "Action against Iraq a Military Necessity," *[Greensboro] News and Record,* February 19, 2003, A-8, paragraph 1, http://proquest.umi.com/pdqweb?index (July 5, 2004).

3. Rick Atkinson and Thomas E. Ricks, "War's Military, Political Goals Begin to Diverge," *Washington Post,* March 30, 2003, A-1, paragraph 1, web.lexis-nexis.com/universe (July 5, 2004).

4. George W. Bush, quoted in Peter Charlton, "POW Double Standards," *[Queensland] Courier Mail,* March 25, 2003, 15, paragraph 2, web.lexis-nexis.com/universe (July 5, 2004).

5. George W. Bush, quoted in Zachary Coile, "President Defends Military Tribunals," *San Francisco Chronicle,* November 30, 2001, A-1, paragraph 4, web.lexis-nexis.com/universe (February 7, 2004).

6. George P. Fletcher, "Black Hole in Guantánamo Bay," *Journal of International Criminal Justice* 2 (2004): 130.

7. The U.S. State Department has at various times complained about political repression and military trials in Burma, China, Colombia, Egypt, Kyrgyzstan, Malaysia, Nigeria, Peru, Russia, Sudan, and Turkey. See Human Rights Watch, *Fact Sheet: Past U.S. Criticism of Military Tribunals,* June 2003, http://www.hrw.org/press/2001/11/tribunals1128htm (July 2, 2004).

8. Neil A. Lewis, "Bush's Power to Plan Trial of Detainees Is Challenged," *New York*

Times, January 16, 2004, A-16, paragraph 6, http:web.lexis-nexis.com/universe (January 26, 2004).

9. See Peter Grier, "Bush Team and the Limits of Torture," *Christian Science Monitor,* June 10, 2004, 1, paragraph 5, http:proquest.umi.com/pdqweb?index (July 5, 2004).

10. Michael Ignatieff, "Is the Human Rights Era Ending?" *New York Times,* February 5, 2002, A-25, paragraph 1, http:proquest.umi.com/pqdweb?index (July 5, 2004).

11. Anne English French, "Trials in Times of War: Do the Bush Military Commissions Sacrifice Our Freedoms?" *Ohio State Law Journal* 63 (2003): 1282.

12. Hugo Black, *Duncan v. Kahanamoku,* 327 U.S. 305, 317 (1946).

13. Civilian-military concerns and relationships have always been an important part of our Anglo-American cultures. For an overview of some of the schisms in many civil-military relationships, see Peter D. Feaver and Richard H. Kohn, eds., *Soldiers and Civilians: The Civil-Military Gap and American National Security* (Cambridge, MA: MIT Press, 2001).

14. Security Council Resolution, quoted in Ratna Kapur, "Collateral Damage: Sacrificing Legitimacy in the Search for Justice," *Harvard International Review* 24 (Spring 1992): 43.

15. President Bush, quoted in Kenneth R. Bazinet, "Bush OKs Secrecy in Terror Trials," *[New York] Daily News,* November 14, 2001, 9, paragraph 3, http://proquest.umi.com/pdqweb?index (July 5, 2004).

16. Fighting terrorism is obviously one key branch of this necessitarian discourse. For some of the best overviews of how domestic and policy makers are theorizing about these new terrorist attacks, see Kurt M. Campbell and Michèle A. Flournoy, *To Prevail: An American Strategy for the Campaign against Terrorism* (Washington, DC: Center for Strategic and International Studies, 2001); James F. Hoge Jr. and Gideon Rose, eds., *How Did This Happen? Terrorism and the New War* (New York: PublicAffairs, 2001); Strobe Talbott and Nayan Chanda, eds. *The Age of Terror: America and the World after September 11* (New York: Basic Books, 2001).

17. Kapur, "Collateral," 43.

18. *Authorization for Use of Military Force,* Public Law Number 1-7–40, 107 Cong., 1st sess., (October 11, 2002), sections one and two.

19. Kapur, "Collateral," 43.

20. Ibid.

21. See William C. Smith, "Lawyers at War: JAGS Hammer Out Agreements, Advice Top Brass on Rules of Engagement," *American Bar Association Journal* 89 (2003): 14.

22. Harvey C. Mansfield, quoted in Jeffrey Rosen, "The Nation: What Price Security?" *New York Times,* November 11, 2001, sec. IV, p. 1, paragraph 17, web.lexis-nexi.com/universe/document (July 5, 2004).

23. Charles Fairman, "The Law of Martial Rule and the National Emergency," *Harvard Law Review* 55 (1942): 1253.

24. Barry Kellman, "Catastrophic Terrorism: Thinking Fearfully, Acting Legally," *Michi-*

gan Journal of International Law 20 (Spring 1999): 537–64. For an excellent overview of how the doctrine of "necessity" can be revitalized by nations that would like to combat terrorism, see John-Alex Romano, "Combating Terrorism and Weapons of Mass Destruction: Reviving the Doctrine of a State of Necessity," *Georgetown Law Journal* 87 (April 1999): 1023–57.

25. Throughout this book, I will be using the term "military tribunals," but readers should know that other writers use other terms. John Bickers, for example, explains that "these military commissions" in the "early years of American history" were "not called military commissions" but "Board of Officers." General Winfield Scott would later be credited with convening "military commissions" when he tried Mexican citizens who were accused of committing ordinary crimes. John M. Bickers, "Military Commissions Are Constitutionally Sound: A Response to Professors Katyal and Tribe," *Texas Tech Law Review* 34 (2003): 908.

26. See Peter Maguire, "Bush Can't Have Justice Both Ways," *Newsday,* December 28, 2003, A-29, http://proquest.umi.com/pqdweb?index (July 5, 2004).

27. For a seminal discussion on just why Bin Laden needs to be tried by some ad hoc international tribunal, see Geoffrey Robertson, "Trial by Fury," *Harvard International Review* 24 (Spring 2002): 48–53.

28. David Cole and James X. Dempsey, *Terrorism and the Constitution: Sacrificing Civil Liberties in the Name of National Security* (New York: The New Press, 2002).

29. "The Pentagon Releases a Proposed List of War Crimes to Be Judged by Tribunals," *New York Times,* March 1, 2003, A-11, paragraph 1, http://proquest.umi.com/pdqweb?TS (April 1, 2003).

30. "Pentagon Releases," paragraph 5.

31. Circuit judges Pooler, Parker, and Wesley, *Jose Padilla v. Donald Rumsfeld,* 2003 U.S. App. Lexis 25616 (2003).

32. For key legal commentators that analyze these various rationales, see Keith S. Alexander, "In the Wake of September 11th: The Use of Military Tribunals to Try Terrorists," *Notre Dame Law Review* 885 (2003): 885–916; Laura A. Dickinson, "Using Legal Process to Fight Terrorism: Detentions, Military Commissions, International Tribunals, and the Rule of Law," *Southern California Law Review* 75 (2002): 1407–92.

33. One of the best overviews of some of these problematic histories can be found in Louis Fisher, "Military Tribunals: A Sorry History," *Presidential Studies Quarterly* 33 (2003): 484–508.

34. Davies, "Imposition of Martial Law," 68–69.

35. Bickers, "Military Commissions," 926.

36. Heather Anne Maddox, "After the Dust Settles: Military Tribunals for Terrorists after September 11, 2001," *North Carolina Journal of International Law and Commercial Regulation* 28 (2002): 430.

37. Kenneth Burke, *A Grammar of Motives* (New York: George Braziller, 1955), 74.

38. Gregory A. Raymond, "Necessity in Foreign Policy," *Political Science Quarterly* 113 (Winter 1998): 673.

39. See the arguments that were cobbled together by Supreme Court jurists in *Jacobsen v. Massachusetts,* 197 U.S. 11 (1905).

40. Michel Foucault, quoted in Nancy Fraser, "Struggle over Needs: Outline of a Socialist-Feminist Critical Theory of Late-Capitalist Political Culture," in *Women, the State, and Welfare,* ed. Linda Gordon (Madison: University of Wisconsin Press, 1990), 199.

41. John Milton, *Paradise Lost,* ed. Alastair Fowler (New York: Longman, 1971), 218.

42. See, for example, Lawrence M. Friedman, *History of American Law* (New York: Simon and Schuster, 1985).

43. Shoshana Felman, *The Juridical Unconscious: Trials and Traumas in the Twentieth Century* (Cambridge, MA: Harvard University Press, 2002), 11.

44. Peter Fitzpatrick, ed., *Dangerous Supplements: Resistance and Renewal in Jurisprudence* (Durham, NC: Duke University Press, 1991).

45. Stuart Hall once claimed that "historically-elaborated [*sic*] discourses" have left us a "reservoir of themes." Stuart Hall, "The Rediscovery of 'Ideology': Return of the Repressed in Media Studies," in *Culture, Society, and the Media,* ed. Michael Gurevitch, Tony Bennett, James Curran, Janet Woollacott (London: Methuen, 1982), 73.

46. Langdell, who became the first dean of the Harvard Law School in 1870, is often credited with having invented the "case" method, where legal forums are treated as if they were laboratories for the discovery of legal "truth." Grant Gilmore, *The Ages of American Law* (New Haven, CT: Yale University Press, 1977), 43.

47. Elmer J. Mahoney, "Civil Rights versus Military Necessity," in *Civil-Military Relations: Changing Concepts in the Seventies,* ed. Charles L. Cochran (New York: The Free Press, 1974), 77.

48. Pooler, Parker, and Wesley, *Padilla v. Rumsfeld,* 50.

49. For just some of the recent work on ideographs, see Dana L. Cloud, "The Rhetoric Of: Scapegoating, Utopia, and the Privatization of Social Responsibility," *Western Journal of Communication* 62 (1998): 387–419; Fernando Delgado, "The Rhetoric of Fidel Castro: Ideographs in the Service of Revolutionaries," *Howard Journal of Communications* 10 (1999): 1–14; Janis L. Edwards and Carol K. Winkler, "Representative Form and the Visual Ideograph: The Iwo Jima Image in Editorial Cartoons," *Quarterly Journal of Speech* 83 (1997): 289–310; Robert L. Ivie, "The Ideology of Freedom's 'Fragility' in American Foreign Policy Argument," *Journal of the American Forensic Association* 24 (1987): 27–36; Xing Lu, "An Ideological/Cultural Analysis of Political Slogans in Communist China," *Discourse and Society* 10 (1999): 487–508.

50. See Michael C. McGee, "The 'Ideograph': A Link between Rhetoric and Ideology," *Quarterly Journal of Speech* 66 (1980): 1–16.

51. An excellent discussion of the early meanings of "liberty" can be found in John T.

Agresto, "Liberty, Virtue, and Republicanism," *Review of Politics* 39 (1977): 473–504. For related discussions of other significant terms, see Burke, *Grammar of Motives,* 322–401.

52. Extending the work of historians R. G. Collinswood and Herbert J. Muller, McGee has argued that words like "freedom" and "progress" are examples of ideographs that are cherished parts of our discursive heritage. McGee, "The 'Ideograph,'" 11. See R. G. Collinswood, *The Idea of History* (1946; reprint London: Oxford University Press, 1972), 302–34; Herbert J. Muller, *The Uses of the Past* (New York: Oxford University Press, 1952), 37–38.

53. "Negative" ideographs are still evocative—they simply are meant to appeal to a different order of commitment. For example, many of us are willing to pay higher taxes, surrender some of our civil, social, or political rights, or restrict the movement of other citizens in order to maintain the "rule of law" or the "social order."

54. Celeste M. Condit, "Democracy and Civil Rights: The Universalizing Influence of Public Argumentation," *Communication Monographs* 54 (March 1987): 3.

55. Celeste M. Condit and John L. Lucaites, *Crafting Equality: America's Anglo-African Word* (Chicago: University of Chicago Press, 1993), xii.

56. Celeste Condit, "Rhetorical Criticism and Audience: The Extremes of Leff and McGee," *Western Journal of Speech Communication* 54 (1990): 332.

57. Condit, "Democracy," 2.

58. Maurice Blanchot, *The Writing of the Disaster,* trans. Ann Smock (Lincoln: University of Nebraska Press, 1995), 3.

59. This approach has affinities with projects that assess the role of "hegemony" in mass media studies. See, for example, Hall, "Rediscovery of 'Ideology,'" 56–90.

60. Dominick LaCapra, *History and Criticism* (Ithaca, NY: Cornell University Press, 1985), 11.

61. For example, note the attitude toward the masses of someone like Walter Bagehot, who envisioned a public that is composed of an ignorant mass who are constantly being duped by an intellectual elite. Andrew King, "The Rhetoric of Power Maintenance: Elites at the Precipice," *Quarterly Journal of Speech* 62 (1976): 127.

62. Ana Maria Alonso, "The Effects of Truth: Re-Presentations of the Past and the Imagining of Community," *Journal of Historical Sociology* 1 (March 1988): 33–57.

63. See Burrus M. Carnahan, "Lincoln, Lieber and the Laws of War: The Origins and Limits of the Principle of Military Necessity," *American Journal of International Law* 92 (1998): 213–31.

64. Condit "Universalization," 1–5.

65. The concept of the "fragment" is developed in Michael C. McGee, "Text, Context, and the Fragmentation of Contemporary Culture," *Western Journal of Speech Communication* 54 (1990): 274–89.

66. For perhaps the most biting criticism of what he calls "archive fever," the "irre-

pressible desire to return to the origin" (p. 91), see Jacques Derrida, *Archive Fever* (Chicago: University of Chicago Press, 1996).

67. *Ex parte Milligan,* 71 U.S. 2 (1866).

68. *Ex parte Quirin,* 317 U.S. 1 (1942). Commonly called the Nazi Saboteurs' case.

69. *In re Yamashita,* 327 U.S. 1 (1946).

70. Military Order—Detention, Treatment, and Trial of Certain Non-Citizens in the War against Terrorism, November 16, 2001, 66 Fed. Reg. 57833 (2001), Part IV. See *Weekly Compilation of Presidential Documents* 47 (November 13, 2001), 1665–68.

71. Austin Sarat, "Rhetoric and Remembrance: Trials, Transcription, and the Politics of Critical Reading," *Legal Studies Forum* 23 (1999): 355–56.

72. Howard R. Patch, "Necessity in Boethius and the Neoplatonists," *Speculum* 10 (1935): 394.

73. David M. Robinson, "The Wheel of Fortune," *Classical Philology* 41 (1946): 207–16.

74. Ross G. Woodman, "Shelley's Changing Attitude to Plato," *Journal of the History of Ideas* 21 (1960): 503.

75. Thucydides, *History of the Peloponnesian War,* ed. Paul Woodruff (Indianapolis: Hackett Publishing, 1993), 30, quoted in Raymond, "Necessity," 673.

76. Woodman, "Shelley's," 502–3.

77. Patch, "Necessity in Boethius," 397.

78. Thomas Hobbes, quoted in Sheldon S. Wolin, "Hobbes and the Culture of Despotism," in *Thomas Hobbes and Political Theory,* ed. Mary G. Dietz (Lawrence: University Press of Kansas, 1990): 28.

79. J. Samuel Prues, "Spinoza, Vico, and The Imagination of Religion," *Journal of the History of Ideas* 50 (1989): 92.

80. Fairman, "Law of Martial," 1256.

81. *Case of Armes, English Reports* 79 (1597): 1227, quoted in Fairman, "Law of Martial," 1256.

82. Fairman, "Law of Martial," 1257.

83. John Phillip Reid, "In a Defensive Rage: The Uses of the Mob, the Justification in Law, and the Coming of the American Revolution," *New York University Law Review* 49 (1964): 1043–91.

84. Matthew Hale, *History of the Common Law* (London: H. Butterworth, 1820), 40–44, quoted in George M. Dennison, "Martial Law: The Development of a Theory of Emergency Powers, 1776–1861," *American Journal of Legal History* 18 (January 1974): 52–79.

85. Matthew Hale, quoted in Dennison, "Martial Law," 53. For an illustration of how folks in the 1940s were still talking about this phrase, see Fairman, "Law of Martial," 1259.

86. Nathan Rosenberg, "Mandeville and Laissez-Faire," *Journal of the History of Ideas* 24 (1963): 185.

87. Oliver Cromwell, *The Writings and Speeches of Oliver Cromwell,* vol. 4, ed. Wilbur Cortez Abbott (Cambridge, MA: Harvard University Press, 1947), 460, quoted in Victoria Kahn, "Revising the History of Machiavellianism: English Machiavellianism and the Doctrine of Things Indifferent," *Renaissance Quarterly* 46 (Autumn 1993), 538. For a critique of Cromwell's use of his power, see Christopher Hill, *God's Englishman: Oliver Cromwell and the English Revolution* (New York: Dial Press, 1970).

88. Kahn, "Revising," 538.

89. Note, for example, the necessitous world that was fabricated by Bernard Mandeville. He was sure that "a national frugality there never was nor never will be without a national necessity." Bernard Mandeville, *The Fable of the Bees, or Private Vices, Public Benefits,* ed. Douglas Garman (London: Wishart and Company, 1934), 194.

90. Lord Chancellor, *Vernon v. Bethell* (1762), *English Reports,* vol. 28 (Edinburgh: William Green and Sons, 1903), 839. F. D. R. would later argue that "We have come to a clear realization of the fact that true individual freedom cannot exist without economic security and independence. 'Necessitous men [sic] are not free men.'" Franklin D. Roosevelt, "Unless There Is Security Here at Home, There Cannot Be Lasting Peace in the World," Message to the Congress on the State of the Union. January 11, 1944, in *The Public Papers and Addresses of Franklin D. Roosevelt,* ed. Samuel I. Rosenman (New York: Harper and Brothers, 1950), 13: 41.

91. J. H. Plumb, *England in the Eighteenth Century* (Baltimore, MD: Penguin Books, 1950), 134.

92. Richard Epstein, "Proceedings of the Conference on Takings of Property and the Constitution," *University of Miami Law Review* 41 (1986): 50.

93. *The Declaration of Independence* (1776), paragraphs 15–17; Davies, "Imposition of Martial Law," 75.

94. Stephen E. Lucas, "Justifying America: The Declaration of Independence as a Rhetorical Document," in *American Rhetoric: Context and Criticism,* ed. Thomas W. Benson (Carbondale: Southern Illinois University Press, 1989), 75.

95. Dennison, "Martial Law," 56.

96. William Rehnquist, *All the Laws but One: Civil Liberties in Wartime* (New York: Knopf, 1998).

97. John Stuart Mill, "Of Liberty and Necessity," in *A System of Logic, Ratiocinative and Inductive,* ed. J. M. Robson (Toronto: University of Toronto Press, 1974), 814.

This notion of compulsion has also influenced the ways that legal theorists talk about "necessity" and criminal culpability. John T. Parry, "The Virtue of Necessity: Reshaping Culpability and the Rule of Law," *Houston Law Review* 36 (Summer 1999): 397–469.

98. *The Queen v. Dudley,* 14 Q.B.D. 273 (1884). See Parry, "Virtue," 405.

99. Lord Coleridge, *The Queen v. Dudley,* 287–88.

100. Chief Justice Waite, *United States v. Diekelman,* 92 U.S. 520, 526 (1876).

101. *Id.*

102. Fairman, "Law of Martial," 1254.

103. Duke of Wellington, "Affairs of Ceylon," The House of Lords, *Hansard's Parliamentary Debates* 115 (1851): cols. 880–81.

104. *Ex parte Milligan,* 4 Wall. 2 (U.S. 1866).

105. For an overview of how military authorities in the nineteenth and twentieth centuries treated the *Ex parte Milligan* case, see Davies, "Imposition of Martial Law," 97–107.

106. See Jill Elaine Hasday, "Civil War as Paradigm: Reestablishing the Rule of Law at the End of the Cold War," *Kansas Journal of Law and Public Policy* 5 (Winter 1996): 135–36.

107. Gerald F. Crump, "Part I: History of the Structure of Military Justice in the United States, 1775–1920," *Air Force Review* 16 (1974): 54.

108. G. Norman Lieber, "What Is the Justification of Martial Law?" *North American Review* 163 (November 1896): 548.

109. Lieber, "What Is the Justification," 549.

110. Ibid.

111. See *Moyer v. Peabody,* 212 U.S. 78 (1909).

112. Edward F. Sherman, "The Civilianization of Military Law," *Maine Law Review* 22 (1970): 5–27.

113. For some key commentaries on the promises and perils of this "civilianization," see Samuel Huntington, *The Soldier and the State* (Cambridge, MA: Belknap Press of Harvard University Press, 1957); Michael S. Sherry, "The Military," *American Quarterly* 35 (Spring–Summer 1983): 64–65.

114. Fairman, "Law of Martial," 1254–55.

115. Ibid.

116. See Davies, "Imposition of Martial Law," 87–88.

117. Sherman, "Civilianization," 3.

118. *Solorio v. United States,* 107 S. Ct. 2924 (1987).

119. Gary L. Hoffman, "Court-Martial Jurisdiction and the Constitution: An Historical and Textual Analysis," *Creighton Law Review* 21 (1987–88): 46.

120. Davies, "Imposition of Martial Law," 111–12.

121. Major John Smith, quoted in John Mintz, "Lawyer Criticizes Rules for Tribunals," *Washington Post,* January 22, 2004, A-3, paragraph 6, http:web.lexis-nexis.com/universe/document (January 26, 2004).

122. Sherry, "Military," 65.

Chapter 2

1. *Epigraph.* James K. Paulding, *A Life of Washington* (New York: Harper and Brothers, 1835), 71.

2. Elbridge Gerry, quoted in James Kirby Martin and Mark Edward Lender, *A Respect-*

able Army: The Military Origins of the Republic, 1763–1789 (Arlington Heights, IL: Harlan Davidson, 1982), 119–20.

3. For an overview of the importance of civil virtue in the maintenance of a republic, note the commentary that is provided in John T. Agresto, "Liberty, Virtue, and Republicanism, 1776–1787," *Review of Politics* 39 (1977): 473–504.

4. George Washington, quoted in Maurer Maurer, "Military Justice under General Washington," *Military Affairs* 28 (Spring 1964): 8.

5. Michael O. Lacey, "Military Commissions: A Historical Survey," *Army Lawyer* 350 (2002): 42.

6. For an excellent discussion of some of the colonial debates that surrounded the use of standing armies, executive discretion, and military tribunals, see Jonathan Turley, "Tribunals and Tribulations: The Antithetical Elements of Military Governance in a Madisonian Democracy," *George Washington Law Review* 70 (2002): 649–768.

7. Ibid., 719–20.

8. Gerald J. Clark, "Military Tribunals and the Separation of Powers," *University of Pittsburgh Law Review* 63 (2002): 838.

9. Turley, "Tribunals," 719.

10. James Madison, quoted in Heather Anne Maddox, "After the Dust Settles: Military Tribunal Justice for Terrorists after September 11, 2001," *North Carolina Journal of International Law and Commercial Regulation* 28 (2002): 433.

11. For some of the best analyses of the capture and trial of Major André, see Isaac N. Arnold, *The Life of Benedict Arnold* (Chicago: Jensen McClurg, 1990); Anthony Bailey, *Major André* (New York: Farrar, Straus and Giroux, 1987); John Bakeless, *Turncoats, Traitors, and Heroes* (Philadelphia: J. B. Lippincott, 1959); Charles J. Biddle, "The Case of Major André," *Memoirs of the Historical Society of Pennsylvania* 6 (1858): 317–416; Clare Brandt, *The Man in the Mirror: A Life of Benedict Arnold* (New York: Random House, 1994), Richard C. Brown, "Three Forgotten Heroes," *American Heritage* 26 (1975): 25–29; Robert E. Cray Jr., "Major John André and the Three Captors: Class Dynamics and Revolution Memory Wars in the Early Republic, 1780–1831," *Journal of the Early Republic* 17 (1997): 371–97; Henry B. Dawson, *Papers Concerning the Capture and Detention of Major John André* (Yonkers, NY: The Gazette, 1866); Robert A. Ferguson, "Becoming American: High Treason and Low Invective in the Republic of Laws," in Austin Sarat and Thomas R. Kearns, eds., *The Rhetoric of Law* (Ann Arbor: University of Michigan Press, 1994): 103–33; Robert McConnell Hatch, *Major John André: A Gallant in Spy's Clothing* (Boston: Houghton Mifflin, 1986); J. E. Morpurgo, *Treason at West Point: The Arnold-André Conspiracy* (New York: Mason/Charter, 1975); Willard Sterne Randall, *Benedict Arnold: Patriot and Traitor* (New York: Morrow, 1990); Larry J. Reynolds, "Patriots and Criminals, Criminals and Patriots: Representations of Major André," *South Central Review* 9 (1992): 57–84; Charles Harvey Roe, "André's Captors: A Study in Values," *Westchester Historian* 42 (1966):

61–66; Charles Royster, "'The Nature of Treason': Revolutionary Virtue and American Reactions to Benedict Arnold," *William and Mary Quarterly* 36 (1979): 163–93; Winthrop Sargent, *The Life and Career of Major John André* (1861; reprint New York: Garrett Press, 1969); Joshua Hett Smith, *An Authentic Narrative of the Causes Which Led to the Death of Major André* (New York: New York Times, 1969); Carl Van Doren, *Secret History of the American Revolution* (New York: Viking, 1941); Frances Vivian, "The Capture and Death of Major André," *History Today* 7 (1957): 813–19.

12. Timothy C. MacDonnell, "Military Commissions and Courts-Martial: A Brief Discussion of the Constitutional and Jurisdictional Distinctions between the Two Courts," *Army Lawyer* (March 2002): 26.

13. The proceedings of Washington's commission have been published in several places. See "Proceedings of a Board of General Officers," *New York Gazette and Weekly Mercury,* November 6, 1780, 1; "Proceedings of a Board of General Officers, Held by Order of General Washington, Respecting Major John André, Adjutant General of the British Army, Who Was Apprehended as a Spy," *Gentleman's Magazine* 50 (1780): 610–16.

14. Mark J. Osiel, "Ever Again: Legal Remembrance of Administrative Massacre," *University of Pennsylvania Law Review* 144 (1995): 464–65.

15. On the role that Benedict Arnold played in the crafting of American identities during the time of the Founders, see Lori J. Ducharme and Gary Alan Fine, "The Construction of Nonpersonhood and Demonization: Commemorating the Traitorous Reputation of Benedict Arnold," *Social Forces* 73 (1995): 1309–31; James Kirby Martin, "Benedict Arnold's Treason as Political Protest," *Parameters* 11 (September 1981): 63–64; James Kirby Martin, *Benedict Arnold, Revolution Hero: An American Warrior Reconsidered* (New York: New York University Press, 1997); E. L. Morris, "Should We Despise Benedict Arnold?" *New England Magazine* 35 (1904): 638–48; William Gilmore Simms, "Arnold, the Traitor, as a Subject for Dramatistic Fiction," *Southern and Western Magazine* 1 (1845): 257.

16. Reynolds, "Patriots and Criminals," 57. Note here the popularity of James Fenimore Cooper's *The Spy: A Tale of Neutral Ground,* ed. Charles Swain Thomas (Boston: Houghton Mifflin, 1911). For more visually oriented impressions of Major André, see Michael Wynn Jones, *The Cartoon History of the American Revolution* (New York: Putnam, 1975), 147.

17. MacDonnell, "Military Commissions" 27. Influential American jurists have also looked back at this case. For example, see how some of the Supreme Court justices during World War II talked about how the Founding Fathers were aware that military commissions did not use trial by jury, and that they had been used to try unlawful belligerents. *In re Quirin,* 317 U.S. 1, 41 (1942), quoted in Anne English French, "Trials in Times of War: Do the Bush Military Commissions Sacrifice Our Freedoms?" *Ohio State Law Journal* 63 (2003): 1242.

18. Martin and Lender, *Respectable Army,* 90.

19. For an investigation of the role that some of these tales played in the collection of pensions, see Edward Tang, "Writing the American Revolution: War Veterans in the Nineteenth-Century Cultural Memory," *Journal of American Studies* 32 (April 1998): 63–80.

20. Bakeless has argued that André was actually an important part of Sir Henry Clinton's intelligence network in several states, including Rhode Island, Connecticut, New York, New Jersey, Pennsylvania, Maryland, and Delaware. Bakeless, *Turncoats,* 266.

21. Vivian, "Capture and Death," 816.

22. Some British loyalists were convinced that it may have been Smith who had "betrayed André to the rebels." Anonymous, "Circumstances Respecting the Betraying of Major André," *Political Magazine* 2 (February 1781): 62.

23. For an overview of the eyewitness accounts of these three captors, see Pennypacker, *George Washington's Spies,* 160–83.

24. Peleg W. Chandler, "Major John André," *American Criminal Trials* (1844; reprint New York: AMS Press, 1970), 163.

25. Lord Mahon, *History of England: From the Peace of Utrecht to the Peace of Versailles, 1713–1783* (London: John Murray, 1858), 62. For an explicit response to some of Mahon's claims, see Charles J. Biddle, "The Case of Major André," *Memories of the Historical Society of Pennsylvania* 6 (1858): 400–401.

26. James Thomas Flexner, *The Traitor and the Spy: Benedict Arnold and John André* (New York: Harcourt, Brace, 1953), 358. Several decades later, Larry J. Reynolds would challenge the "elitist ideology" that seemed to be embedded in Flexner's account of the capture. Reynolds, "Patriot and Criminals," 57.

27. Vivian, "Capture and Death," 816.

28. Ferguson, "Becoming," 110.

29. Martin and Lender, *Respectable Army,* 159.

30. Vivian, "Capture and Death," 813.

31. Ibid., 814.

32. Benedict Arnold, quoted in Martin and Lender, *Respectable Army,* 159.

33. Saul K. Padover, ed., *The Washington Papers: Basic Selections from the Public and Private Writings of George Washington* (New York: Harper and Brothers, 1955), 367.

34. Nathaniel Greene, quoted in Morton Pennypacker, *George Washington's Spies on Long Island and in New York* (Brooklyn, NY: Long Island Historical Society, 1939), 181.

35. Martin, "Benedict Arnold's," 63.

36. Alexander Hamilton, quoted in John C. Hamilton, *The Life of Alexander Hamilton* (New York: Appleton, 1840), 274.

37. Robert D. Arner, "The Death of Major André: Some Eighteenth-Century Views," *Early American Literature* 11 (Spring 1976): 52.

38. Carroll L. Judson, *The Sages and Heroes of the American Revolution* (1851; reprint Port Washington, NY: Kennikat Press, 1970), 39.

39. Judson, *Sages and Heroes,* 34.

40. Lacey, "Military Commissions," 42.

41. Turley, "Tribunals," 725.

42. For a general overview of how the British forces during the war put these rules into practice, see Stephen Conway, "To Subdue America: British Army Officers and the Conduct of the Revolutionary War," *William and Mary Quarterly* 43 (July 1986): 381–407.

43. Maurer, "Military Justice," 8.

44. Some British officers were willing to administer close to five hundred lashes, while other leaders thought that one hundred lashes would suffice.

45. Maurer, "Military Justice," 9.

46. William Tudor, quoted in Maurer, "Military Justice," 9.

47. Maurer, "Military Justice," 9.

48. Ibid.

49. Ibid., 9–10.

50. Anonymous, "Life of Major André," *North American Review* 93 (1861): 83–99.

51. For example, see "Proceedings of a Board of General Officers," *New York Gazette and Weekly Mercury,* November 6, 1780, 1.

52. Alexander Hamilton, quoted in Vivian, "Capture and Death," 817.

53. Benedict Arnold, quoted in Edward C. Boynton, *History of West Point, and Its Military Importance during the American Revolution, and the Origin and Progress of the United States Military Academy* (New York: D. Van Nostrand, 1863), 145–46.

54. MacDonnell, "Military Commissions," 27.

55. Vivian, "Capture and Death," 817.

56. Hamilton, *Life,* 263.

57. Frederick William Von Steuben, quoted in Friedrich Kapp, *The Life of Frederick William Von Steuben* (New York: Mason Brothers, 1859), 290.

58. For more on the strategic importance of these "neutral" areas, see Martin and Lender, *Respectable Army,* 61.

59. Note, for example, Alexander Hamilton's characterization of the captors as "three simple peasants." Hamilton, *Life,* 274.

60. Maurer, "Military Justice," 8.

61. Alexander Hamilton, quoted in Anonymous, "Life of Major," 83.

62. Vivian, "Capture and Death," 818.

63. James Fenimore Cooper, *Notions of the Americans: Picked Up by a Travelling Bachelor,* introduction by Robert E. Spiller (New York: Ungar, 1963), 1:219. Cooper tried to contrast the emotional outburst of the British with the dispassionate inquiry of the Americans:

It was necessary to show the world that he who dared to assail the rights of the infant and struggling republics, incurred a penalty as fearful as he [sic] who worked his treason against the majesty of the king. The calmness, the humanity, the moderation, and the inflexible firmness, with which this serious duty was performed, are worthy of praise. While the English general [Clinton] was vainly resorting to menaces, the American authorities were proceeding with deliberation to their object.

Cooper, *Notions,* 219.

64. William B. Willcox, ed., *The American Rebellion: Sir Henry Clinton's Narrative of His Campaigns, 1775–1782* (New Haven, CT: Yale University Press, 1954), 460.

65. Willcox, *American Rebellion,* 460–61. Vivian was sure that from a legal standpoint, "it is difficult to dispute the verdict." Vivian, "Capture and Death," 817.

66. John Hart, "Letter From an Eyewitness of the Execution of André," *Genealogical Register* 69 (1915): 226.

67. Boynton, *History,* 132; Willcox, *American Rebellion,* 459.

68. In Willcox, *American Rebellion,* 459.

69. Ibid.

70. This retaliatory type of argument is still being used by some critics of the Bush tribunals, who worry that other nations will begin trying American soldiers and civilians. See John Mintz, "Lawyer Criticizes Rules for Tribunals," *Washington Post,* January 22, 2004, A-3, paragraph 8, http://.web.lexis-nexis.cin/universe (July 6, 2004).

71. Colonel B. Robinson, quoted in Boynton, *History,* 137.

72. Vivian, "Capture and Death," 817.

73. Lieutenant General James Robertson, quoted in Boynton, *History,* 142; Sargent, *Life and Career,* 362.

74. Philip Davidson, *Propaganda and the American Revolution, 1763–1783* (New York: W. W. Norton, 1973), 326–27.

75. Benedict Arnold, "A Proclamation," *Political Magazine* 1 (1780): 767.

76. "Postscript," *London Evening News,* November 14, 1780, 4.

77. Milton M. Klein and Ronald W. Howard, eds., *The Twilight of British Rule in Revolutionary America: The New York Letter Book of General James Robertson, 1780–1783* (Cooperstown, NY: New York State Historical Association, 1983), 157.

78. Lord Mahon, *History,* 70.

79. Anonymous, "Life of Major," 98.

80. Lord Mahon, *History,* 659.

81. Reynolds, "Patriot and Criminals," 67.

82. B. A. Henisch and H. K. Henisch, "Major André," *Journal of General Education* 28 (1976): 241.

83. Flexner, *Traitor and the Spy,* 356.

84. "Trial of Joshua Hett Smith," *Historical Magazine,* 10 Supplement (1866): 71.

85. For example, John Hamilton, Alexander's son, would focus attention on the fact that André had used "feigned signatures" and "mercantile" disguises. Hamilton, *Life,* 264.

86. Cooper, *Notions,* 210.

87. Ibid., 217.

88. Cray, "Major John André," 371.

89. Anonymous, "Life of Major," 83.

90. J. Dykman, "The Last Days of Major John André," *Magazine of American History* 22 (1889): 156–57.

91. Roe, "André's Captors," 61.

92. David Golove, "Military Tribunals, International Law, and the Constitution: A Franckian-Madisonian Approach," *Journal of International Law and Politics* 35 (2003): 381.

93. Mintz, "Lawyer Criticizes," paragraph 3.

94. Ibid.

95. Ibid.

Chapter 3

1. *Epigraph.* In Thomas C. Blegen, *Minnesota: A History of the State* (St. Paul: University of Minnesota Press, 1975), 276.

2. President George W. Bush, Military Order of November 13, 2001, *Detention, Treatment, and Trial of Certain Non-Citizens in the War against Terrorism,* 66 F.R. 57833, November 16, 2001.

3. Department of Defense, Fact Sheet, Department of Defense Order on Military Commissions, March 21, 2002.

4. See Bruce Zagaris, "U.S. Defense Department Issues Orders on Military Commissions," *International Law Enforcement Law Reporter* 18 (May 2002), paragraphs 5–6, http://web.lexis-nexis.com/universe (April 27, 2002).

5. "Review and Outlook: Due Process for Terrorists," *Wall Street Journal,* March 22, 2002, A-14.

6. *Ex parte Milligan,* 71 U.S. (4 Wall.) 2 (1866).

7. Within legal circles, *Ex parte Quirin,* 317 U.S. 1 (1942) is known as the World War II German "saboteurs' case."

8. For a rhetorical analysis of some of these other tensions and amnesias, see Richard Morris, Richard Wander, and Philip Wander, "Native American Rhetoric: Dancing in the Shadows of the Ghost Dance," *Quarterly Journal of Speech* 76 (1990): 164–91.

A more general discussion of the rhetorical power of "cultural amnesia" can be found in Nathan Stormer, "In Living Memory: Abortion as Cultural Amnesia," *Quarterly Journal of Speech* 88 (2002): 265–83.

9. Heather Anne Maddox, "After the Dust Settles: Military Tribunal Justice for Terrorists after September 11, 2001," *North Carolina Journal of International Law and Commerce Regulation* 28 (2002): 426—27.

10. Carol Winkler, "Manifest Destiny on a Global Scale: The U.S. War on Terrorism," *Controversia* 1 (2002): 86.

11. Ellen Farrell, "'The Most Terrible Stories': The 1862 Dakota Conflict in White Imagination," *Journal of the Indian Wars* 1 (2000): 33.

12. Charles S. Bryant and Abel S. Murch, *A History of the Great Massacre of the Sioux Indians in Minnesota, Including the Personal Narratives of Many Who Escaped* (Cincinnati, OH: Rickey and Carroll, 1864), 458.

13. Bryant and Murch, *History,* 458.

14. See, for example, "The Moussaoui Problem," *Washington Post,* April 27, 2002, A-20.

15. William Lee Miller, *Lincoln's Virtues: An Ethical Biography* (New York: Knopf, 2002).

16. See, for example, Nelson A. Miles, "The Indian Problem," *North American Review* 128 (March 1879): 304—14.

17. Carol Chomsky, "The United States–Dakota War Trials: A Study in Military Injustice," *Stanford Law Review* 43 (November 1990): 13—98; Michael Clodfelter, *The Dakota War: The United States Army versus the Sioux, 1862—1865* (Jefferson, NC: McFarland, 1998); Kenneth Carley, *The Sioux Uprising of 1862* (St. Paul: Minnesota Historical Society Press, 1976); Paul N. Beck, "'Firm but Fair': The Minnesota Volunteers and the Coming of the Dakota War of 1862," *Journal of the Indian Wars* 1 (2000): 1—19.

I appreciate the symbolic importance of Chomsky's usage of the term "Dakota War." This provides some deference in discussing tribal self-identification and alternative historiographies. Yet as a communication scholar I am also aware of how the very naming of these communities and these conflicts is itself a part of the politics of these rhetorical histories. I therefore occasionally use the terms that became a part of the dominant discourse surrounding the contemporaneous and historiographical reconstruction of these events.

Angie Debo has argued that the Dakota War was the "most disastrous Indian uprising white Americans had experienced since the attacks of Opechancanough and Philip on the Virginia and Massachusetts frontiers two centuries before." Angie Debo, *A History of the Indians of the United States* (1970; reprint Norman: University of Oklahoma Press, 1974), 189.

18. Farrell, "'Most Terrible,'" 21—37.

19. C. M. Oehler, *The Great Sioux Uprising* (New York: Oxford University Press, 1959).

20. Isaac V. D. Heard, *History of the Sioux War and Massacres of 1862 and 1863* (New York: Harper and Brothers, 1863); Marion P. Satterlee, *A Detailed Account of the Massacre by the Dakota Indians of Minnesota in 1862* (Minneapolis: Marion P. Satterlee, 1923); Ralph K. Andrist, "Massacre!" *American Heritage* 13 (April 1962): 8—11, 108—11.

21. For example, The Union General-in-Chief, Henry Halleck, had to deal with a situation where his army had suffered more than 45,000 casualties in battles like Antietam and Second Bull Run. Clodfelter, *Dakota War,* 45.

22. Chomsky, "U.S.-Dakota," 14.

23. Ibid.

24. Farrell, "'Most Terrible,'" 21.

25. For some general overviews of the legal and military issues involved in the Wounded Knee controversies, see Roxanne Dunbar Ortiz, "Wounded Knee 1890 to Wounded Knee 1973: A Study in United States Colonialism," *Journal of Ethnic Studies* 8(2) (1980): 1–15; Peter R. DeMontravel, "General Nelson A. Miles and the Wounded Knee Controversy," *Arizona and the West* 28 (1986): 23–44.

26. See Robert H. Jones, "The Northwestern Frontier and the Impact of the Sioux War," *Mid-America* 41(3) (1959): 131–53.

27. Miles, "Indian Problem," 305.

28. Charles Flandrau, "The Indian War of 1862–1864, and Following Campaigns in Minnesota," in The Board of Commissioners, *Minnesota in the Civil and Indian Wars, 1861–1865* (St. Paul: Pioneer Press, 1890), 748–49.

29. Ibid., 749.

30. Blegen, *Minnesota,* 167.

31. Heard, *History,* 18.

32. Ibid.

33. Gerald S. Henig, "A Neglected Cause of the Sioux Uprising," *Minnesota History* 45 (Fall 1976): 107.

34. Heard, *History,* 25.

35. Ibid.

36. Ibid., 26–27.

37. Ibid., 27.

38. Chomsky, "U.S.-Dakota," 16–17.

39. By the summer of 1862, some 7,000 members of four Dakota tribes were living on a reservation that bordered the Minnesota River.

40. Clodfelter, *Dakota War,* 40; Minnesota Board of Commissioners, *Minnesota in the Civil and Indian Wars, 1861–1865: Official Reports and Correspondence* (St. Paul: Pioneer Press, 1899).

41. Blegen, *Minnesota,* 262.

42. For a skeptical look at the Myrick tale, see Gary Clayton Anderson, "Myrick's Insult: A Fresh Look at Myth and Reality," *Minnesota History* 48(5) (1983): 198–206.

43. Chomsky, "U.S.-Dakota," 17; Roy W. Meyer, *History of the Santee Sioux: United States Indian Policy on Trial* (Lincoln: University of Nebraska Press, 1967), 116; "Big Eagle's Account," in Gary Clayton Anderson and Alan R. Woolworth, eds., *Through Dakota Eyes:*

Narrative Accounts of the Minnesota Indian War of 1862 (St. Paul: Minnesota Historical Society, 1988), 55–56.

44. Blegen, *Minnesota,* 260.

45. Ibid., 260–61.

46. Editorial, "Indian Murders," *New York Daily Tribune,* August 25, 1862, 4.

47. Blegen, *Minnesota,* 274.

48. The Minnesota conflict was often considered to be an event that threatened to spill over into Kansas and the Dakotas. This provided just one of the justifications for asking the frontier to be militarized under the federal command of Major General John Pope. See Robert H. Jones, "The Northwestern Frontier and the Impact of the Sioux War," *Mid-America* 41 (1959): 131–53.

49. Clodfelter, *Dakota War,* 48.

50. Harry T. Williams, *Lincoln and the Radicals* (Madison: University of Wisconsin Press, 1941).

51. Major General John Pope, quoted in Blegen, *Minnesota,* 274.

52. Blegen, *Minnesota,* 278.

53. Gary Clayton Anderson and Alan R. Woolworth, eds. Introduction, *Through Dakota Eyes: Narrative Accounts of the Minnesota Indian War of 1862* (St. Paul: Minnesota Historical Society, 1988), 1.

54. For an overview of the town reactions to the Dakota uprising, see Don Heinrich Tolzmann and Louis Albert Fritsche, *Memories of the Battle of New Ulm: Personal Accounts of the Sioux Uprising* (Bowie, MD: Heritage Books, 2001).

55. Clodfelter, *Dakota War,* 52–53.

56. Chomsky, "U.S.-Dakota," 21.

57. For illuminating summaries of some of the schisms that existed within the Sioux camps, see Priscilla Ann Russo, "The Time to Speak Is Over: The Onset of the Sioux Uprising," *Minnesota History* 45 (1976): 97–106.

58. Henry Sibley, quoted in Chomsky, "U.S.-Dakota," 22.

59. See "The Minnesotians Ferocious," *[St. Paul] Pioneer and Democrat,* December 12, 1862, 2.

60. Blegen, *Minnesota,* 275.

61. Clodfelter, *Dakota War,* 57.

62. John Pope, quoted in Chomsky, "U.S.-Dakota," 23.

63. Heard, quoted in Karin Thiem, *The Minnesota Sioux War Trials* (thesis; Mankato: Minnesota State University–Mankato, 1979), 95.

64. Chomsky, "U.S.-Dakota," 23.

65. Carley, *Sioux Uprising,* 68. Heard would serve as recorder, and he would leave us one of the first histories of the uprising and these trials. See Heard, *History.* One of Sibley's contemporaries, J. Fletcher Williams, claimed that the "Hon. I. V. D. Heard" served as

"Judge Advocate" during these proceedings. J. Fletcher Williams, "Henry Hastings Sibley: A Memoir," *Collections of the Minnesota Historical Society* 6 (1894): 290.

66. See James Garfield Randall, *Constitutional Problems under Lincoln* (Urbana: University of Illinois Press, 1951), 174–87.

67. Thiem, *Minnesota Sioux,* 39.

68. Ibid.

69. William W. Winthrop, *A Digest of Opinions of the Judge Advocates General of the Army between September 1862 and July 1867* (Washington, DC: Government Printing Office, 1901), 411; Thiem, *Minnesota Sioux,* 40.

70. Thiem, *Minnesota Sioux,* 41. See also William W. Winthrop, *Military Law and Precedents* (Washington, DC: Government Printing Office, 1887).

71. Thiem, *Minnesota Sioux,* 48.

72. Flandrau, "Indian War," 748.

73. See Chomsky's discussion of the correspondence between Pope and Halleck. Chomsky, "U.S.-Dakota," 26.

74. Chomsky, "U.S.-Dakota," 26.

75. Henry Sibley, "Letter from Colonel Henry Sibley to Colonel Charles Flandrau," September 28, 1862, quoted in Chomsky, "U.S.-Dakota," 23.

76. Chomsky, "U.S.-Dakota," 25.

77. The six acquittals were case numbers 7, 16, 17, 20, 21, 27.

78. "H. [Heard]," "The Indian Expedition," *[St. Paul] Pioneer and Democrat,* November 15, 1962, 2.

79. See *Records of the Military Commission That Tried Sioux-Dakota Indians for Barbarities Committed in Minnesota, 1862* (Washington, DC: National Archives and Record Administration, 1988), case #1; Carley, *Sioux Uprising,* 68.

80. See *Records,* case #2, 1.

81. See *Records,* case #2, 3.

82. See *Records,* case #2, 4.

83. Thiem, *Minnesota Sioux,* 57–58.

84. Heard, *History,* 254–55; Chomsky, "U.S.-Dakota," 46.

85. Thiem, *Minnesota Sioux,* 52.

86. Nancy McClure, "The Story of Nancy McClure, Captivity among the Sioux," *Minnesota Historical Society Collections* 6 (1894): 456.

87. Thiem, *Minnesota Sioux,* 49–50.

88. Ibid., 47–48.

89. Andrist, "Massacre!" 111. Interestingly enough, Andrist believed that "most" of the Indians "deserved their fate," even though "at least one or two of those executed were the wrong men."

90. Nancy McClure Faribault Huggan, "Narrative 8: Nancy McClure Faribault Huggan's Account," Anderson and Woolworth, *Through Dakota,* 267.

91. Peter Maguire, "Questions Hang Over Military Tribunals," *Newsday,* November 21, 2001, paragraph 3, http://proquest.umi.com/pdqweb?index (July 6, 2004).

92. See Isaac Heard, "The Indian Trials," *[St. Paul] Pioneer and Democrat,* December 11, 1862, 1; Blegen, *Minnesota,* 279.

93. Reverend S. R. Riggs, quoted in "Trial of the Indian Prisoners," *[St. Paul] Pioneer and Democrat,* December 12, 1862, 4.

94. Chomsky, "U.S.-Dakota," 27.

95. Carley, *Sioux Uprising,* 69.

96. See *Records of the Military Commission That Tried Sioux-Dakota Indians for Barbarities Committed in Minnesota, 1862* (1862; reprint Washington, DC: National Archives and Records Administration, 1988).

97. Blegen, *Minnesota,* 279.

98. See, for example, "The Execution of the Condemned Indians," *[St. Paul] Pioneer and Democrat,* December 5, 1862, 2; "What Shall Be Done with the Indians," *[St. Paul] Pioneer and Democrat,* December 12, 1862, 2.

99. Carley, *Sioux Uprising,* 70.

100. Heard, *History,* 31; Farrell, "'Most Terrible,'" 35.

101. Blegen, *Minnesota,* 262–63.

102. William P. Dole, quoted in Francis Paul Prucha, *Documents of United States Indian Policy* (1975; reprint Lincoln: University of Nebraska Press, 1990), 96–97.

103. Clodfelter, *Dakota War,* 60.

104. Bryant and Murch, *History,* 470–71.

105. Bryant and Murch, *History,* 471.

106. Williams, "Memoirs of Henry," 290–91.

107. Ibid., 291.

108. Anderson and Woolworth, Introduction, *Through Dakota,* 3–5.

109. Kenneth Carley, "Account of George Quinn," *Minnesota History* 38 (September 1962): 147–49; Anderson and Woolworth, *Through Dakota,* 94.

110. Snana, quoted in Anderson and Woolworth, *Through Dakota,* 257–58.

111. Samuel J. Brown, quoted in Anderson and Woolworth, Introduction, *Through Dakota,* 228.

112. Charles R. Crawford, quoted in Anderson and Woolworth, *Through Dakota,* 260.

113. Anderson and Woolworth, Introduction, *Through Dakota,* 5.

114. Urania White, "Captivity among the Sioux, August 18 to September 26, 1862," *Minnesota Historical Collections* 9 (1901): 395–426; Anderson and Woolworth, *Through Dakota,* 267.

115. See, for example, Mark E. Neely Jr., *The Fate of Liberty: Abraham Lincoln and Civil Liberties* (New York: Oxford University Press, 1991).

116. Note, for example, the several cursory paragraphs on the Sibley commission that are discussed in Solon J. Buck, "Lincoln and Minnesota," *Minnesota History* 6 (December 1925): 359.

117. Carley, *Sioux Uprising,* 69.

118. Clodfelter, *Dakota War,* 58.

119. Chaska, whose Dakota name was We-chan-hpe-was-tay-do-pee, was listed as no. 20 and characterized as the savior of Wakefield and her children in a St. Paul newspaper. See "Mrs. Wakefield and Her Children," *[St. Paul] Daily Press,* December 28, 1862, cited in Sarah F. Wakefield and June Namias, *Six Weeks in the Sioux Tepees: A Narrative of Indian Captivity* (Norman: University of Oklahoma Press, 1997), 152.

120. See Wakefield and Namias, *Six Weeks,* 3–42.

121. Sarah F. Wakefield, *Six Weeks in the Sioux Tepees (Little Crow's Camp): A Narrative of Indian Captivity* (Shakopee, MN: Job Printing Office, 1864), 53–59; Clodfelter, *Dakota War,* 58.

122. Robert Hariman, "Performing the Laws: Popular Trials and Social Knowledge," in Robert Hariman, ed., *Popular Trials: Rhetoric, Mass Media, and the Law* (Tuscaloosa: University of Alabama Press, 1990), 5.

123. For intriguing accounts of various local, contemporaneous discussions of the Dakota conflict, see Larry Lundblad, "The Impact of Minnesota's Dakota Conflict of 1862 on the Swedish Settlers," *Swedish-American Historical Quarterly* 51(3) (2000): 209–21.

124. Bryant and Murch, *History,* 475; Clodfelter, *Dakota War,* 58–59.

125. Donald Bloxham, *Genocide on Trial* (New York: Oxford University Press, 2001), 2.

126. The Uniform Code of Military Justice (UCMJ), which was passed by Congress in the spring of 1950, was intended to provide a codified set of regulations that would provide some rights to those individuals who appeared in military courts. See William T. Generous Jr., *Swords and Scales: The Development of the Uniform Code of Military Justice* (Port Washington, NY: Kennikat, 1973).

127. Maguire, "Questions Hang," paragraphs 1–3.

Chapter 4

1. *Epigraph.* Justice Davis, *Ex parte Milligan,* 71 U.S. 2, 121 (1866).

2. Robert Cover, "The Supreme Court, 1982 Term-Foreword: Nomos and Narrative," *Harvard Law Review* 97 (1983): 4–5.

3. George P. Fletcher, quoted in Donald A. Downs and Erik Kinnunen, "Civil Liberties in a New Kind of War," *University of Wisconsin Law Review* 2003 (2003): 398.

4. Jonathan Turley, "Trials and Tribulations: The Antithetical Elements of Military Governance in a Madisonian Democracy," *George Washington Law Review* 70 (2002): 733.

5. Gerald J. Clark, "Military Tribunals and the Separation of Powers," *University of Pittsburgh Law Review* 63 (2002): 847.

6. Ibid., 848.

7. Turley, "Trials," 733.

8. Anthony Lewis, "Civil Liberties in a Time of Terror," *University of Wisconsin Law Review* 2003 (2003): 260.

9. Anne English French, "Trials in Times of War: Do the Bush Military Commissions Sacrifice Our Freedoms?" *Ohio State Law Journal* 63 (2003): 1228–29.

10. Downs and Kinnunen, "Civil," 394–97.

11. Allan Nevins, for example, writing in the early 1960s, was sure that the primacy of the civil authority would "remain absolute and unquestionable," and that the "heart" of the *Milligan* decision "is the heart of the difference between the United States of America and Nazi Germany or Communist Russia." Allan Nevins, "The Case of the Copperhead Conspirator," in *Quarrels That Have Shaped the Constitution,* ed. John A. Garraty (1962; reprint New York: Harper and Row, 1964), 108.

12. Liam Braber, "Comment: *Korematsu*'s Ghost: A Post–September 11th Analysis of Race and National Security," *Villanova Law Review* 47 (2002): 452.

13. Jill Elaine Hasday, "Civil War as Paradigm: Reestablishing the Rule of Law at the End of the Cold War," *Kansas Journal of Law and Public Policy* 5 (Winter 1996): 129.

14. Turley, "Trials," 733.

15. *Hamdi v. Rumsfeld,* 316 F.3d 450, 459 (4th Cir. Va. 2003), known within the legal community as *Hamdi III.*

16. See Joy J. Jackson, "Keeping Law and Order in New Orleans under General Butler, 1862," *Louisiana History* 34 (Winter 1993): 51–67.

17. G. R. Tredway, *Democratic Opposition to the Lincoln Administration in Indiana* (Indianapolis: Indiana Historical Bureau, 1973), 265.

18. Mark E. Neely Jr., *The Fate of Liberty: Abraham Lincoln and Civil Liberties* (New York: Oxford University Press, 1991), 232.

19. William Rehnquist, *All the Laws but One: Civil Liberties in Wartime* (New York: Knopf, 1998), 224–25.

20. Nevins, "Case," 107–8.

21. Milligan, quoted in Emma L. Thornbrough, *Indiana in the Civil War Era, 1850–1880* (Indianapolis: Indiana Historical Bureau, 1965), 213; Frank L. Klement, "The Indianapolis Treason Trials and *Ex Parte Milligan,*" in Michal R. Belknap, ed., *American Political Trials* (Westport, CN: Greenwood Press, 1981), 104.

22. Nevins, "Case," 101.

23. Joseph G. Gambone, "*Ex Parte Milligan:* The Restoration of Judicial Prestige?" *Civil War History* 16 (1970): 246.

24. *Ex parte Milligan,* 121.

25. Kathleen M. McCarroll, "With Liberty and Justice for All," *University of Detroit Mercy Law Review* 80 (2003): 236.

26. For some excellent general discussions of many of the civil rights issues that were at issue during the Civil War, see Belknap, *American Political Trials;* Robert S. Harper, *Lincoln and the Press* (New York: McGraw-Hill, 1951); Samuel Klaus, *The Milligan Case* (New York: Da Capo Press, 1929); Frank L. Klement, *The Limits of Dissent* (Lexington: University Press of Kentucky, 1970).

27. Eugene H. Berwanger, "Book Review: *The Fate of Liberty,*" *Presidential Studies Quarterly* 22 (Winter 1992): 177.

28. Neely, *Fate,* 224–35.

29. Abraham Lincoln, quoted in French, "Trials," 1231.

30. French, "Trials," 1232.

31. William H. Rehnquist, "Civil Liberty and the Civil War: The Indianapolis Treason Trials," *Indiana Law Journal* 72 (1997): 927.

32. James Speed, "Opinion of the Honorable James Speed," *Opinions of the Attorney General* 11 (July 1865): 5–6.

33. Rehnquist, "Civil Liberty," 933.

34. James Randall, "Civil and Military Relationships under Lincoln," *The Pennsylvania Magazine of History and Biography* 69 (1945): 200.

35. Judge Advocate Major H. L. Burnett, quoted in Benn Pitman, *The Trials for Treason at Indianapolis* (Cincinnati, OH: Moore, Wilstach and Baldwin, 1865), 68.

36. Carleton explained that the Democratic Party during the war contained three factions—the War Democrats, the Majority Democrats, and the Peace Democrats. William G. Carleton, "Civil War Dissidence in the North: The Perspective of a Century," *South Atlantic Quarterly* 65 (Summer 1996): 392.

37. Randall, "Civil and Military," 199–205.

38. Horace Greeley, quoted in Elbert J. Benton, *The Movement for Peace without a Victory during the Civil War* (Cleveland, OH: Western Reserve Historical Society, 1918), 2.

39. *Ex parte Merryman,* 17 F. Cas.144 (C. Cir. Md.1861).

40. Lorraine A. Williams, "Northern," 336.

41. Taney, *Merryman,* 150.

42. *Id.,* 152.

43. *Id.*

44. *Id.*

45. Horace Binney, *The Privilege of the Writ of Habeas Corpus under the Constitution* (Philadelphia: C. Sherman and Sons, 1862).

46. [Joel Parker], "Habeas Corpus and Martial Law," *North American Review* 93 (October 1861): 471–518.

47. Williams, "Northern," 337.

48. Parker, "Habeas Corpus," 500–501.

49. Ibid., 512.

50. Harper, *Lincoln and the Press,* 172.

51. Ibid., 232.

52. Williams, "Northern," 341.

53. Harper, *Lincoln and the Press,* 178.

54. Ibid., 176.

55. Ibid., 178.

56. French, "Trials," 1232; Williams, "Northern," 340.

57. Some military theorists at the time sometimes described "military law" as that body of rules and regulations that were promulgated by legislatures, while "martial law" involved the more prudential and localized rules that were made by the "will of the commanding officer of an armed force," or the decisions of a "geographically military department." AG Speed and Butler, "Argument for the United States: The Merits or Main Question," *Ex parte Milligan,* 71 U.S. 2, 14 (1866).

58. Charles Stille, *Northern Interests and Southern Independence: A Plea for United Action* (Philadelphia: W. S. and A. Martien, 1863), 48.

59. Williams, "Northern," 341.

60. Curtis, "Lincoln," 122.

61. Harper, *Lincoln and the Press,* 242.

62. Abraham Lincoln, "To Erastus Corning and Others," June 12, 1863, in Abraham Lincoln and Don. E. Fehrenbacher, *Speeches and Writings, 1859–1865: Speeches, Letters, and Miscellaneous Writings, Presidential Messages and Proclamations* (New York: Viking, 1989), 455.

63. Lincoln, "To Erastus," 456.

64. Ibid.

65. Ibid., 457.

66. Ibid.

67. Ibid., 460.

68. Nat Hentoff, *The First Freedom: The Tumultuous History of Free Speech in America* (New York: Dell, 1981), 95.

69. Hentoff, *First Freedom,* 96.

70. "Statement of the Case," *Ex parte Milligan,* 6.

71. *Id.*

72. Alvin v. Sellers, "The Historic Case of *Milligan et al.,*" in *Classics of the Bar,* vol. 2 (Washington, DC: Washington Law Book Company, 1942), 174.

73. Rehnquist, "Civil Liberty," 933.

74. James Garfield later became president of the United States, and David Dudley Field would be remembered as one of the luminaries who served as a leading member of the New York bar. Rehnquist, "Civil Liberty," 933.

75. AG Speed and Butler, "Argument for the United States: The Merits or Main Question," *Ex parte Milligan*, 71 U.S. 2 (1866), 12.

76. Speed and Butler, "Argument," 14.

77. *Id.*

78. *Id.*, 20.

79. Benjamin Butler, quoted in Sellers, "Historic Case," 175.

80. David Dudley Field, "One the Side of the Petitioner," 22–23.

81. Field, "One the Side of the Petitioner," 29.

82. *Id.*

83. *Id.*, 29–30.

84. *Id.*, 33.

85. *Id.*, 35.

86. *Id.*, 36.

87. *Id.*

88. *Id.*, 36–37.

89. *Id.*, 37–38.

90. *Id.*, 38.

91. Garfield, "On the Side of the Petitioner," 43.

92. *Id.*, 47.

93. Jeremiah Black, quoted in Sellers, "Historic Case," 178–79.

94. Black, quoted in Sellers, "Historic Case," 181.

95. Ibid., 182.

96. Ibid., 186.

97. Ibid., 191–92.

98. Ibid., 194–99.

99. Ibid., 205.

100. See, for example, French, "Trials," 1234–35.

101. David Davis was joined by Stephen Field, Samuel Nelson, Robert Grier, and Nathan Clifford.

102. Justice Davis, *Ex parte Milligan*, 109.

103. *Id.*, 110.

104. *Id.*, 114–15.

105. Rehnquist, "Civil Liberty," 934.

106. Justice Davis, *Ex parte Milligan*, 118.

107. *Id.*, 121.

108. *Id.*

109. *Id.*, 123.

110. *Id.*, 124.

111. *Id.*, 127.

112. *Id.*, 128.

113. *Id.,* 130.

114. Rehnquist, *All the Laws,* 223.

115. Ibid.

116. Randall, "Civil and Military," 200.

117. Hentoff, *First Freedom,* 94.

118. Neely, *Fate,* 233.

119. Rehnquist, "Civil Liberty," 933.

120. Craig Smith and Stephanie Makela, "Lincoln and Habeas Corpus," in *Silencing the Opposition: Government Strategies of Suppression,* ed. Craig R. Smith (Albany: State University of New York Press, 1996), 25.

121. Lorraine A. Williams, "Northern Intellectual Reaction to Military Rule during the Civil War," *Historian* 27 (May 1965): 334–35. See also James G. Randall, *Constitutional Problems under Lincoln* (Urbana: University of Illinois Press, 1951), 49–50.

122. Randall, "Civil and Military," 200.

123. Ibid.

Chapter 5

1. *Epigraph.* John H. Stibbs, "Andersonville and the Trial of Henry Wirz," *Iowa Journal of History and Politics* 9 (1991): 53.

2. Michael Griffin, "The Great War Photographs: Constructing Myths of History and Photojournalism," in *Picturing the Past: Media, History, and Photography,* ed. Bonnie Brennen and Hanno Hardt (Urbana: University of Illinois Press, 1999), 129.

3. Robert Hariman and John Louis Lucaites, "Performing Civil Identity: The Iconic Photograph of the Flag Raising on Iwo Jima," *Quarterly Journal of Speech* 88 (2002): 364.

4. Hanno Hardt and Bonnie Brennen, Introduction, *Picturing the Past,* ed. Brennan and Hardt, 1

5. For some of the best overviews of the *Wirz* trial, see Gayla Marie Koerting, *The Trial of Henry Wirz and Nineteenth-Century Military Law* (PhD diss., Kent State University, 1995,); Christopher Mahoney, "Redecorating the Beast: The Life and Death of Captain Henry Wirz, CSA," *Alabama Heritage* 36 (1995): 26–41; Darrett B. Rutman, "The War Crimes and Trial of Henry Wirz," *Civil War History* 6(2) (1960): 117–33.

6. Martha Minow, *Between Vengeance and Forgiveness* (Boston: Beacon Press, 1998), 118.

7. For an interesting commentary on the erasure of public memories and the rise of scholarly histories, see Pierre Nora, "Between Memory and History: Les lieux de mémoire," *Representations* 26 (Spring 1989): 7–25.

8. David W. Blight, *Race and Reunion: The Civil War in American Memory* (Cambridge, MA: Belknap of Harvard University Press, 2001).

9. Lawrence Douglas, *The Memory of Judgment: Making Law and History in the Trials of the Holocaust* (New Haven, CT: Yale University Press, 2001), 2.

10. For general overviews of this infamous prison, see Ovid Futch, *History of Anderson-*

ville Prison (Gainesville: University Press of Florida, 1968); William B. Hesseltine, *Civil War Prisons: A Study in War Psychology* (Columbus: University of Ohio Press, 1930); John McElroy, *This Was Andersonville* (New York: Bonanza Books, 1957).

11. See House of Representatives, *Trial of Henry Wirz,* 40th Cong., 2nd sess., H. Exec. Doc. 23, Ser. 1331 (Washington, DC: Government Printing Office, 1880).

12. James D. Horan, *Mathew Brady, Historian with a Camera* (New York: Bonanza Books, 1955), 67.

13. Robert E. Morsberger and Katherine M. Morsberger, *Lew Wallace: Militant Romantic* (New York: McGraw-Hill, 1980), 192.

14. William Marvel, *Andersonville: The Last Depot* (Chapel Hill: University of North Carolina Press, 1994), 308.

15. For example, see the excellent overview of the importance of the *Wirz* case for issues of "command responsibility" that appears in Matthew Lippman, "Humanitarian Law: The Uncertain Contours of Command Responsibility," *Tulsa Journal of Comparative and International Law* 9 (2001): 1–93.

16. David W. Blight, "'For Something beyond the Battlefield': Frederick Douglass and the Struggle for the Memory of the Civil War," *Journal of American History* 75 (1989): 1161.

17. See, for example, Amos E. Stearns and Leon Basile, *The Civil War Diary of Amos E. Stearns, A Prisoner at Andersonville* (Rutherford, NJ: Fairleigh Dickinson University Press, 1981); John W. Northrop, *Chronicles from the Diary of a War Prisoner in 1864* (Wichita, KS: John W. Northrop, 1904).

18. Francis Trevelyan Miller, *Prisons and Hospitals: The Photographic History of the Civil War* (New York: Castle Books, 1957); Mark D. Katz, *Witness to an Era: The Life and Photographs of Alexander Gardner* (New York: Viking, 1991).

19. See MacKinlay Kantor, *Andersonville* (Cleveland, OH: World Publishing, 1955).

20. One of the most popular of these plays was by Saul Levitt, *The Andersonville Trial, a Play* (New York: Random House, 1960).

21. David Rachels and Robert Baird, "Andersonville Goes to Hollywood—Courtesy of Ted Turner," *Film and History* 25 (1995): 54.

22. One of the most exhaustive collections of wartime memos appears in United States War Department, *War of the Rebellion: A Compilation of the Official Records of the Union and Confederate Armies,* Ser. I, II, III (Washington, DC: Government Printing Office, 1880–901).

23. Griffin Bell, "Panel II of a Hearing of the Senate Judiciary Committee; Preserving Freedoms While Defending against Terrorism," *Senate Judiciary Hearings,* November 29, 2001, paragraph 25, http://web.lexis-nexis.com/congcomp/printdoc (July 7, 2004).

24. Evan J. Wallach, "Afghanistan, Quirin, and Uchiyama: Does the Sauce Suit the Gander?" *Army Lawyer* (November 2003): 30.

25. James B. Insco, "Defense of Superior Orders before Military Commissions," *Duke Journal of Comparative and International Law* 13 (2003): 402.

26. Blight, *Race and Reunion,* 2–4.

27. Maurice Halbwachs, *On Collective Memory,* trans. Lewis A. Coser (Chicago: University of Chicago Press, 1992).

28. See, for example, Peter Burke, "History as Social Memory," in *Memory: History, Culture, and the Mind,* ed. T. Butler (Oxford: Basil Blackwell, 1990), 97–113.

29. E. Culpepper Clark and Raymie E. McKerrow, "The Rhetorical Construction of History," in *Doing Rhetorical History: Concepts and Cases,* ed. Kathleen J. Turner (Tuscaloosa: University of Alabama Press, 1998), 35.

30. Kathleen J. Turner, "Rhetorical History as Social Construction: The Challenge and the Promise," in *Doing Rhetorical History,* ed. Turner, 2.

31. Nancy Wood, *Vectors of Memory* (New York: Berg, 1999), 1.

32. For other usages of these "strategies of remembrance," see Michael L. Bruner, *Strategies of Remembrance: The Rhetorical Dimensions of National Identity Construction* (Columbia: University of South Carolina Press, 2002).

33. Devin O. Pendas, " 'I Didn't Know What Auschwitz Was': The Frankfurt Auschwitz Trial and the German Press, 1963–1965," *Yale Journal of Law and Humanities* 12 (2000): 431–432, 424, 397.

34. Cecilia Elizabeth O'Leary, "Clasping Hands over the Bloody Divide: Memory, Amnesia, and Racism," *American Quarterly* 54 (March 2002): 159.

35. Wood, *Vectors,* 10–11.

36. Kirk Savage, *Standing Soldiers, Kneeling Slaves: Race, War, and Monument in Nineteenth-Century America* (Princeton, NJ: Princeton University Press, 1997), 3.

37. Eric Foner, "Selective Memory," *New York Times Book Review,* March 4, 2001, sec. VII, 28.

38. Blight, *Race and Reunion,* 32.

39. Barry Schwartz, *Abraham Lincoln and the Forge of National Memory* (Chicago: University of Chicago Press, 2000), 45.

40. Donald Bloxham, *Genocide on Trial: War Crimes Trials and the Formation of Holocaust History and Memory* (New York: Oxford University Press, 2001), vii.

41. Bloxham, *Genocide on Trial,"* 89, 2.

42. Griffin, "Great War," 131–32.

43. Susan Sontag, quoted in Rea S. Hederman, *Anthology: Selected Essays from Thirty Years of the New York Review of Books* (New York: New York Review of Books, 2001), 106.

44. Louis Untermeyer, ed., *The Poetry and Prose of Whitman* (New York: Simon and Schuster, 1949), 320.

45. These prisoner exchanges, or cartels, began in July of 1862, and were modeled after agreements that had been reached by the United States and England during the

Revolutionary War. Lewis L. Laska and James M. Smith, "Captain Henry Wirz, C.S.A., 1865," *Military Law Review* 68 (1975): 79.

46. Ulysses S. Grant, quoted in Tyler, "Major Henry Wirz," 148.

47. S. W. Ashe, *The Trial and Death of Henry Wirz* (Raleigh, NC: Uzell, 1908), 17, quoted in Glen W. LaForce, "The War-Crimes Trial of Major Henry Wirz, C.S.A.: Justice Served or Justice Denied?" *Journal of Confederate History* 1 (Fall 1988): 290.

48. Koerting, *Trial,* 53–55.

49. John L. Ransom, *John Ransom's Diary* (1881; reprint New York: Paul S. Eriksson, 1963).

50. LaForce, "War-Crimes," 296.

51. Marvel, *Andersonville,* 243.

52. Laska and Smith, "Captain Henry," 77.

53. Henry Wirz, quoted in "The Trial of Wirz," *New York Daily Tribune,* August 25, 1865, A-1.

54. House of Representatives, *Trial of Henry Wirz,* H.R. Exec. Doc. No. 23, 40th Cong., 2nd sess. (Washington, DC: Government Printing Office, 1868): 8.

55. Blight, *Race and Reunion,* 21.

56. Laska and Smith, "Captain Henry," 77.

57. Marvel, *Andersonville,* 243. It is Marvel's contention that many "ex-prisoners had been spinning exaggerated tales of torture and deliberate attrition since the Thanksgiving exchanges at Savannah [1864]" (243).

58. The traumatic feelings of many Northerners following the assassination have been documented in Thomas Reed Turner, *Beware the People Weeping: Public Opinion and the Assassination of Abraham Lincoln* (Baton Rouge: Louisiana State University Press, 1982).

59. Koerting, *Trial,* 7.

60. LaForce, "War-Crimes," 298. Koerting echoes these remarks by noting that the "Wirz trial served as an expedient way to implicate former high ranking Confederates in a conspiracy to kill Union prisoners." Koerting, *Trial,* 4.

61. Koerting, *Trial,* 49.

62. For Chipman's own account of these proceedings, see Norton P. Chipman, *The Tragedy of Andersonville; Trial of Captain Henry Wirz, the Prison Keeper* (Sacramento, CA: Norton P. Chipman, 1911).

63. Major General John White Geary would later become a governor. Koerting, *Trial,* 78.

64. Koerting, *Trial,* 7.

65. This lack of knowledge about military jurisprudence was not unusual for the times. See "Military Courts," *United States Service Magazine* 5 (March 1866): 214–19.

66. Koerting, *Trial,* 102.

67. Ibid., 111–12.

68. LaForce, "War-Crimes," 299.

69. Marvel, *Andersonville,* 243.

70. "The very name 'Andersonville,'" notes Robert Jenkins, "has come to stand for the blind obedience to military orders that leads not just to cruelty, but to needless death." Robert N. Jenkins, "Shame and Strength," *St. Petersburg Times,* March 31, 2002, paragraph 3, http://lexis-nexis.com/universe (July 7, 2004).

71. LaForce, "War-Crimes," 300.

72. Koerting, *Trial,* 111–15.

73. Marvel, *Andersonville,* 244.

74. Joseph Jones, quoted in *John Ransom's Diary,* 266–69.

75. Sergeant Oats, *Prison Life in Dixie* (Chicago: Central Book Concern, 1880), 167.

76. See Stephen V. Benét, *A Treatise on Military Law and the Practice of Courts-Martial* (New York: D. Van Nostrand, 1866).

77. Marvel, *Andersonville,* 245–46.

78. Koerting, *Trial,* 137.

79. LaForce, "War-Crimes," 288.

80. Walt Whitman, quoted in Robert E. Morsberger and Katherine M. Morsberger, "After Andersonville: The First War Crimes Trial," *Civil War Times Illustrated* (July 1974): 30–31.

81. Blight, commenting on the remarks of Jubal Early, *Race and Reunion,* 79.

82. Barry Schwartz, *Abraham Lincoln and the Forge of National Memory* (Chicago: University of Chicago Press, 2000), xi.

83. For more on Hayes and his treatment of the South, see Kirt H. Wilson, *The Reconstruction Debate: The Politics of Equality and the Rhetoric of Place, 1870–1875* (East Lansing: Michigan State University Press, 2002): 189–90.

84. Blight, "For Something," 1159.

85. Garfield, quoted in Oats, *Prison Life,* 203.

86. Oats, *Prison Life,* 202–3.

87. Garfield, quoted in Oats, *Prison Life,* 203–5.

88. Schwartz, *Abraham Lincoln,* 10.

89. Stibbs, "Andersonville," 56.

90. Ibid.

91. Ibid., 34.

92. Ibid., 35.

93. Ibid., 44–45.

94. Ransom, *John Ransom's Diary,* 246–47.

95. Tyler, "Major Henry Wirz," 145.

96. Marvel, *Andersonville,* 247.

97. For the former Confederate president's own views on these subjects, see Jefferson Davis, *Andersonville and Other War Prisons* (New York: Belford, 1890).

98. See, for example, Mildred L. Rutherford, *Facts and Figures vs. Myths and Misrepresentations: Andersonville Prison and Captain Henry Wirz* (Athens, GA: United Daughters of the Confederacy, Georgia Chapter, 1921).

99. Edward L. Ayers, *The Promise of the New South: Life after Reconstruction* (New York: Oxford University Press, 1993), 8.

100. See Blight, *Race and Reunion,* 263–69.

101. Futch, *Andersonville,* 121.

102. Peoples, "The Scapegoat," 14.

103. Blight, *Race and Reunion,* 4.

104. Koerting, *Trial,* 1.

105. Insco, "Defense," 402.

106. Morsberger and Morsberger, *Lew Wallace,* 194.

107. Ibid.

108. The question of how Northern leaders dealt with their wartime powers is taken up in Mark E. Neely, *The Fate of Liberty: Abraham Lincoln and Civil Liberties* (New York: Oxford University Press, 1991).

109. Shelby Foote, quoted in Levitt, "Literary Trials," 72.

110. Marvel, *Andersonville,* 246.

111. Ibid., 247.

112. [Lyon G. Tyler], "Major Henry Wirz," *William and Mary Quarterly Historical Magazine* 27(3) (January 1919): 149.

113. Julian Lewis, "Convenient Monster," *[Sydney] Daily Telegraph,* August 27, 2001, paragraphs 1–3, http://web.lexis.nexis.com/universe (July 7, 2004).

114. Rutman, "War Crimes," 118.

115. Ibid., 119.

116. Ibid., 117–18.

117. LaForce, "War-Crimes," 312.

118. Austin Sarat, "Rhetoric and Remembrance: Trials, Transcription, and the Politics of Critical Reading," *Legal Studies Forum* 23 (1999): 359.

119. An overview of Winder's role in the Civil War appears in Arch Frederic Blakey, *General John H. Winder, C.S.A.* (Gainesville: University Press of Florida, 1990).

Chapter 6

1. *Epigraph.* Justice Stone, *Ex parte Quirin,* 317 U.S. 1, 31 (1942).

2. See Judge Reinhardt's comments in *Galen Gherebi v. George Walker Bush and Donald H. Rumsfeld,* 2003 U.S. App. Lexis 25625, 15. Reinhardt noted that the Supreme Court in

Ex parte Quirin decided that Roosevelt had statutory and constitutional authority to have the "enemy alien prisoners" tried before a military commission.

3. Clarke Rountree, "Instantiating 'the Law' and Its Dissents in *Korematsu v. United States:* A Dramatistic Analysis of Judicial Discourse," *Quarterly Journal of Speech* 87 (2001): 1–23.

4. Frank J. Murray, "Justice to Use FDR Precedent for Military Tribunals," *Washington Times,* December 5, 2001, paragraph 4, http://proquest.umi.com/pdqweb?index (July 7, 2004).

5. Ibid., paragraph 5.

6. A. Christopher Bryant and Carl Tobias, "*Quirin* Revisited," *University of Wisconsin Law Review* 2003 (2003): 316. See *Ex parte Quirin,* 317 U.S. 1 (1942).

7. Donald A. Downs and Erik Kinnunen, "Civil Liberties in a New Kind of War," *University of Wisconsin Law Review* 2003 (2003): 397.

8. For an influential interpretation of *Quirin* as precedent for strong executive power, see Spencer J. Crona and Neal A. Richardson in "Justice for War Criminals of Invisible Armies: A New Legal and Military Approach to Terrorism," *Oklahoma City University Law Review* 21 (1996): 349–407.

9. John M. Bickers, "Military Commissions Are Constitutionally Sound: A Response to Professors Katyal and Tribe," *Texas Tech Law Review* 34 (2003): 910.

10. "German Saboteur Case," RG 153, Records of the Office of the Judge Advocate General (Army), Court-Martial Case Files, CM334178, National Archives, College Park, Maryland, 106–11 (hereafter Trial Transcript); Louis Fisher, *CRS Report for Congress: Military Tribunals: The Quirin Precedent* (Washington, DC: Congressional Research Service, 2002), 23–32, http://www.fpc.state.gov/documents/organization/9188.pdf (July 7, 2004); Robert E. Cushman, "The Case of the Nazi Saboteurs," *American Political Science Review* 36 (1942): 1082.

11. Alpheus T. Mason, *Harlan Fiske Stone, Pillar of the Law* (New York: Viking, 1956), 653.

12. *Times* correspondent in New York, "German Saboteurs Seized in U.S." *[London] Times,* June 29, 1942, 3.

13. Franklin Roosevelt, quoted in Bryant and Tobias, "*Quirin* Revisited," 319.

14. President Franklin Roosevelt's Proclamation of July 2, 1942, titled "Denying Enemies Access to the Courts of the United States" indicated that "all persons" who acted as enemies or aided enemies of the U.S. would be "subject to the law of war and to the jurisdiction of military tribunals," *U.S. Statutes at Large* 56 (1942): 1964.

15. The entire record of the trial would later be impounded until the end of the conflict.

16. For an interesting overview of pre–*Ex parte Quirin* national and international precedents and commentaries on the laws of war and enemy belligerents, see Charles F. Barber, "Trial of Unlawful Enemy Belligerents," *Cornell Law Quarterly* 29 (1943): 53–85.

17. Francis Biddle, *In Brief Authority* (Garden City, NY: Doubleday, 1962), 328.

18. During the trial proceedings, one of the FBI agents admitted that one of the saboteurs, Dasch, had been told about the possibility of pardon. *Trial Transcript*, 541; Fisher, *Military Tribunals*, 3.

19. Fisher, *Military Tribunals*, 7.

20. William H. Rehnquist, *All the Laws but One: Civil Liberties in Wartime* (New York: Knopf, 1998), 221.

21. While some of the Articles of War do mention military commissions, there was some question of how they gave guidance on questions of procedure during a military trial. See F. Granville Munson, "The Arguments in the Saboteur Trial," *University of Pennsylvania Law Review* 91 (1942): 251.

22. Presidential Proclamation No. 2561, *Federal Register* 7 (1942): 5101.

23. Executive Order No. 9185, *Federal Register* 7 (1942): 5103.

24. Boris I. Bittker, "The World War II German Saboteurs' Case and Writs of Certiorari before the Judgment by the Court of Appeals: A Tale of Nunc Pro Tunc Jurisdiction," *Constitutional Commentary* 14 (1997): 422.

25. David J. Danelski, "The Saboteurs' Case," *Journal of Supreme Court History* 1 (1996): 61.

26. Bickers, "Military Commissions," 910.

27. Joan Miller, "Nazi Invasion!" *American History Illustrated* 21 (1986): 42.

28. Ibid.

29. Franz Daniel Pastorius brought several groups of German immigrants to America during the seventeenth century.

30. For an overview of Kappe's recruiting strategies, see Danelski, "Saboteurs' Case," 61–65.

31. Miller, "Nazi Invasion!" 43.

32. Fisher, *Military Tribunals*, 12–13.

33. William Lewis, "Of Innocence, Exclusion, and the Burning of Flags: The Romantic Realism of the Law," *Southern Communications Journal* 60 (1994): 15.

34. "Spy Crew Escaped from a Coast Guard," *New York Times*, June 28, 1942, A-1.

35. Will Lissner, "FBI Seizes 8 Saboteurs Landed by U-Boats," *New York Times*, June 28, 1942, A-1.

36. "How Spies Were Recruited," *New York Times*, June 28, 1942, A-30.

37. Editorial, "War on Our Own Shores," *New York Times*, June 29, 1942, 14.

38. "War on Our," 14.

39. Lissner, "FBI Seizes," A-1.

40. Ibid., A-30.

41. J. Edgar Hoover, quoted in Eugene Rachlis, *They Came to Kill* (New York: Random House, 1961), 1.

42. Bittker, "World War II," 434.

43. Rachlis, *They Came to Kill,* 172–73; Bittker, "World War II," 435.

44. Roosevelt, quoted in Biddle, *In Brief Authority,* 331.

45. Bryant and Tobias, "*Quirin* Revisited," 331.

46. Judge Advocate General of the Army, Major General Myron C. Cramer, quoted in Fisher, *Military Tribunals,* 4.

47. Cushman, "Case," 1083. For legal commentary on how these alterations were themselves violations of the Articles of War, see Bryant and Tobias, "*Quirin* Revisited," 320.

48. Rachlis, *They Came to Kill,* 176.

49. Fisher, *Military Tribunals,* 8.

50. Cushman, "Case," 1084.

51. For an excellent explanation of some of the changes that have taken place in the legal arenas associated with habeas corpus since the *Ex parte Quirin* decision, see Bryant and Tobias, "*Quirin* Revisited," 350–55.

52. Rachlis, *They Came to Kill,* 176–77.

53. Bittker, "World War II," 434.

54. Lewis Wood, "Army's Spy Trial Upheld by Court: Case Nears Close," *New York Times,* August 1, 1942, A-1.

55. George T. Schilling, "Constitutional Law—Saboteurs and the Jurisdiction of Military Commissions," *Michigan Law Review* 41 (1942): 483.

56. Cramer, "Military Commissions," 253–54.

57. Cushman, "Case," 1086.

58. Wood, "Army's Spy Trial," A-3.

59. "Decision on Trial of 8 Nazis Today," *New York Times,* July 1, 1942, A-6.

60. See *Trial Transcript,* 541–48, 2582–87.

61. Statement of Clyde A. Tolson, quoted in "Decision on Trial," 6.

62. Fisher, *Military Tribunals,* 7.

63. Rachlis, *They Came to Kill,* 190.

64. Ibid., 190–99.

65. Ibid., 181.

66. Bryant and Tobias, "*Quirin* Revisited," 320–21.

67. Rachlis, *They Came to Kill,* 182; *Military Transcript,* 2102.

68. Rachlis, *They Came to Kill,* 195–98.

69. This is just one of those eerie parallels between the alleged treatment of the saboteurs in 1942 and the al-Qaeda detainees in this century.

70. Rachlis, *They Came to Kill,* 205.

71. *Trial Transcript,* 2746–51; Fisher, *Military Tribunals,* 13.

72. Federal Circuit Judges Pooler, Parker, and Wesley, *Jose Padilla v. Donald Rumsfeld,* United States Court of Appeals for the Second Circuit, 2003 U.S. App. Lexis 25616 (2003), 46.

73. Rachlis, *They Came to Kill,* 212–13.

74. Ibid., 214.

75. Ibid., 219.

76. Ibid., 226.

77. *Ex parte Quirin,* 47 F. Supp. 431 (D.D.C. 1942). Here the district judge had decided that the text of the president's proclamation closed the civil courts to the petitioners.

78. Mason, *Harlan Fiske Stone,* 654.

79. Danelski, "Saboteurs' Case," 69.

80. Emmanuel Celler, quoted in Mason, *Harlan Fiske Stone,* 654.

81. Cushman, "Case," 1084.

82. Wood, "Army's Spy Trial," A-3.

83. Justice Murphy was on temporary leave, because at that time he was in the Army and could not sit.

84. *Times* correspondent in Washington, "German Agents in U.S.: Habeas Corpus Plea," *[London] Times,* July 30, 1942, 3.

85. Bittker, "World War II," 437.

86. *Ex parte Milligan,* 71 U.S. 2 (1866).

87. John P. Frank, "*Ex Parte Milligan* v. The Five Companies: Martial Laws in Hawaii," *Columbia Law Review* 44 (1944): 638.

88. Charles Fairman, *The Law of Martial Rule* (Chicago: Callaghan and Company, 1943), 163, quoted in Frank, "*Ex Parte Milligan,*" 639.

89. Oliver Wendell Holmes Jr., quoted in G. Edward White, *Justice Oliver Wendell Holmes: Law and the Inner Self* (New York: Oxford University Press, 1993), 121.

90. Charles Evans Hughes, quoted in Sidney Fine, "Mr. Justice Murphy and the *Hirabayashi* Case," *Pacific Historical Review* 33 (1964): 197.

91. Bickers, "Military Commissions," 911.

92. Wood, "Army's Spy Trial," A-3.

93. Rachlis, *They Came to Kill,* 253.

94. Wood, "Army's Spy Trial," A-3.

95. Rachlis, *They Came to Kill,* 256–60.

96. Ibid., 256–64.

97. Ibid., 264.

98. Wood, "Army's Spy Trial," A-1, A-3.

99. Ibid., A-1.

100. Mason, *Harlan Fiske Stone,* 664.

101. Editorial, "Motions Denied," *New York Times,* August 1, 1942, 10.

102. Wood, "Army's Spy Trial," A-1.

103. Rachlis, *They Came to Kill,* 286–87.

104. Cushman, "Case," 1085.

105. Ibid., 1086.

106. James Boyd White, *When Words Lose Their Meaning: Constitutions and Reconstitutions of Language, Character, and Community* (Chicago: University of Chicago Press, 1984), 9.

107. Stone, *Ex parte Quirin,* 25.

108. For an excellent summary of some of the memos that were circulated by Jackson and some of the other Justices, see Fisher, *CRS Report,* 23–32.

109. Stone, *Ex parte Quirin,* 27.

110. *Id.,* 28.

111. *Id.,* 20.

112. *Id.,* 37.

113. George Rutherglen explains that the Court reasoned that when these prisoners acted as "belligerents not in military uniform, the prisoners lost the protection that would ordinarily be afforded to military combatants under the Geneva Convention on treatment of prisoners of war." George Rutherglen, "Structural Uncertainty over Habeas Corpus and the Jurisdiction of Military Tribunals," *Green Bag* 5 (2002): 401.

114. Stone, *Ex parte Quirin,* 45.

115. *Id.,* 46.

116. *Id.,* 47.

117. Justice Robert Jackson, quoted in Michal R. Belknap, "A Putrid Pedigree: The Bush Administration's Military Tribunals in Historical Perspective," *California Western Law Review* 38 (2002): 476.

118. Felix Frankfurter, "From the Bag: F. F.'s Soliloquy," *Green Bag* 5 (2002): 438–40. This is a reprint of the "soliloquy" that was circulated by Justice Frankfurter on October 23, 1942.

119. Frankfurter, "From the Bag," 439.

120. Ibid., 438–40.

121. Eileen A. Scallen, "Classical Rhetoric, Practical Reasoning, and the Law of Evidence," *American University Law Review* 44 (1995): 1746.

122. "Justice Is Done," *Washington Post,* August 9, 1942, 6, quoted in Fisher, *Military Tribunals,* 35.

123. Stone, *Ex parte Quirin,* 31.

124. Bickers, "Military Commissions," 901–2.

125. Note here, however, the recent insights provided in Michael Dobbs, *Saboteurs: The Nazi Raid on America* (New York: Knopf, 2004).

126. Barber, for example, wondered whether the "so-called 'rules of war' are more than philosophers' reveries." "Trial of Unlawful," 53.

127. Wood, "Army's Spy Trial," A-1.

128. Cushman, "Case," 1086.

129. Danelski, "Saboteurs' Case," 79.

130. Edward S. Corwin, *Total War and the Constitution* (New York: Knopf, 1947), 118.

131. Danelski, "Saboteurs' Case," 80.

132. Ibid.

133. Ibid.

134. Tony Mauro, "Historic High Court Ruling Is Troublesome Model for Modern Terror Trials," *American Lawyer Media,* November 19, 2001, http://www.law.com (July 7, 2004).

135. Fairman, "Law of Martial," 1287.

Chapter 7

1. *Epigraph.* Adolf Frank Reel, *The Case of General Yamashita* (Chicago: University of Chicago Press, 1949), 1.

2. John M. Bickers, "Military Commissions Are Constitutionally Sound: A Response to Professors Katyal and Tribe," *Texas Tech Law Review* 34 (2003): 901–5.

3. Bickers, "Military Commissions," 923.

4. Ibid., 922.

5. Tim Maga, *Judgment at Tokyo: The Japanese War Crimes Trials* (Lexington: University Press of Kentucky, 2001), ix.

6. For some interesting overviews of the *Yamashita* case, see Ann Marie Prévost, "Race and War Crimes: The 1945 War Crimes Trial of General Tomoyuki Yamashita," *Human Rights Quarterly* 14 (1992): 303–38; Lawrence Taylor, *A Trial of Generals: Homma, Yamashita, MacArthur* (South Bend, IN: Icarus Press, 1981).

Insightful discussions of Yamashita's life and his military activities prior to his arrest appear in A. J. Barker, *Yamashita* (New York: Ballantine, 1973); John Dean Potter, *The Life and Death of a Japanese General* (New York: Signet, 1962). Contemporary writers sometimes called Yamashita the "Beast of Bataan." See "The Philippines: Quiet Room in Manila," *Time,* November 12, 1945, 21.

7. Philip R. Piccigallo, *The Japanese on Trial: Allied War Crimes Operations in the East, 1945–1951* (Austin: University of Texas Press, 1979), 48.

8. *In re Yamashita,* 327 U.S. 1 (1946); Quincy Wright, "Due Process and International Law," *American Journal of International Law* 40 (April 1946): 398–406.

9. Major Jeffrey L. Spears, "Sitting in the Dock of the Day: Applying Lessons Learned from the Prosecution of War Criminals and Other Bad Actors in Post-Conflict Iraq and Beyond," *Military Law Review* 176 (2003): 140–43.

10. Gerald J. Clark, "Military Commissions and the Separation of Powers," *University of Pittsburgh Law Review* (2002): 857.

11. For discussions of the relative novelty and importance of the "command responsibility" standards, and the legality of both the *Yamashita* and *Homma* cases, see Bruce D. Landrum, "The *Yamashita* War Crimes Trial: Command Responsibility Then and Now,"

Military Law Review 149 (Summer 1995): 293–301; Michael L. Smidt, "*Yamashita, Medina, and Beyond*: Command Responsibility in Contemporary Military Operations," *Military Law Review* 164 (June 2000): 155–234; Kurt Steiner, "War Crimes and Command Responsibility: From the Bataan Death March to the My Lai Massacre," *Pacific Affairs* 58 (Summer 1985): 293–98.

12. The topoi of Japanese arrogance and vengeance was something that was commented on by MacArthur and many members of his staff. Douglas MacArthur, *Reminiscences* (New York: McGraw-Hill, 1964); 221–99; See Courtney Whitney, *MacArthur: His Rendezvous with History* (New York: Knopf, 1956), 161.

13. Masanobu Tsuji, *Singapore: The Japanese Version* (New York: St. Martin's, 1961), 300–301.

14. Ibid., 301.

15. "Yamashita Hanged near Los Baños Where Americans Were Tortured," *New York Times*, February 23, 1946, 1.

16. Ibid., 4.

17. Ibid.

18. "If He Catches Me," *Time*, February 19, 1945, 31.

19. "Yamashita Hanged," 4.

20. Reel, *Case*, 6.

21. "Yamashita Hanged," 4.

22. Reel, *Case*, 32.

23. "Philippines: Quiet," 22.

24. "The Philippines: The Gentleman or the Tiger?" *Time*, December 10, 1945, 21.

25. "Philippines: Quiet," 21.

26. Barker, *Yamashita*, 151.

27. Potter, *Life and Death*, 154.

28. Spears, "Sitting in the Duck," 141.

29. Alpheus Thomas Mason, *Harlan Fiske Stone: Pillars of Law* (New York: Viking, 1956), 666.

30. "Philippines: Quiet," 22.

31. "The Philippines: The General and Rosalinda," *New York Times*, November 19, 1945, 22.

32. Ibid., 22.

33. Ibid.

34. Reel, *Case*, 2.

35. Ibid., 7. The members of the defense team included James Feldhaus, a former tax expert from South Dakota, Colonel Harry Clarke from Altoona, Pennsylvania, Lieutenant Colonel Walter C. Hendrix of Atlanta, Lieutenant Colonel Leigh Clark, Milton Sandberg, and Major George Guy.

36. Reel, *Case,* 18.

37. Ibid., 25.

38. Barker, *Yamashita,* 151.

39. Colonel Walter Hendrix, quoted in "Blockade Slashed Luzon[,] Foes Rice," *New York Times,* November 24, 1945, 3.

40. "Blockade Slashed," 3.

41. "The Philippines: The Gentleman," 22.

42. Ibid.

43. Ibid.

44. Ibid.

45. Ibid.

46. "Shanghaied," *Newsweek,* March 11, 1946, 48.

47. "Yamashita Hanged," 4.

48. Whitney, *MacArthur,* 279–80.

49. Reel, *Case,* 4.

50. Whitney, *MacArthur,* 280.

51. MacArthur, *Reminiscences,* 298.

52. Whitney, *MacArthur,* 279.

53. Charles A. Lindbergh, *The Wartime Journals of Charles A. Lindbergh* (New York: Harcourt Brace Jovanovich, 1970), 875. It should also be noted that there were those who attempted to overcome their prejudices. For example, during some of the fighting in the Marianas, American soldiers offered to give blood to a wounded Japanese soldier who would have died without a transfusion. "Thicker Than Water," *Time,* February 19, 1945, 31.

54. "Yamashita Files New Plea in U.S.," *New York Times,* December 8, 1945, 6.

55. Wright, "Due Process," 400.

56. "Yamashita Files," 5.

57. Ibid.

58. Mason, *Harlan Fiske Stone,* 667.

59. Ibid., 669.

60. Arthur H. Kuhn, "International Law and National Legislation in the Trial of War Criminals—the *Yamashita* Case," *American Journal of International Law* 44 (July 1950): 559.

61. Wright, "Due Process," 399.

62. Stone, *In re Yamashita,* 327 U.S. 1, 20.

63. Mason, *Harlan Fiske Stone,* 671.

64. Justice Murphy, *In re Yamashita,* 327 U.S. 1, 26.

65. Justice Rutledge, *In re Yamashita,* 327 U.S. 1, 46.

66. *In re Yamashita,* 327 U.S. 1, 81; Mason, *Harlan Fiske Stone,* 669–70.

67. Justice Rutledge, *In re Yamashita,* 327 U.S. 1, 60. For example, even under the

Nuremberg rules of court, there had to be thirty days between the lodging of an indictment and the beginning of a trial. Wright, "Due Process," 406.

68. "Two Japanese War Generals," *New Republic* 114 (February 25, 1946): 269.

69. See, for example, "Two Japanese," 269.

70. Hanson W. Baldwin, "Nuremberg Trial Upholds Our Justice," *New York Times,* October 2, 1946, 20.

71. Major Eugene Boardman, quoted in Baldwin, "Nuremberg," 20.

72. Ibid. For more detailed discussions of some of the debates that surround the defense of superior orders, see James B. Insco, "The Defense of Superior Orders before Military Commissions," *Duke Journal of Comparative and International Law* 13 (2003): 389–532.

73. Major Eugene Boardman, quoted in Baldwin, "Nuremberg," 20.

74. "Japan Is the Criminal," Editorial, *New York Times,* December 8, 1945, 16.

75. Ibid.

76. Ibid.

77. Ibid.

78. "Yamashita: By the Neck," *Newsweek,* March 4, 1946, 45.

79. "Philippines: I Thank You!" *Time,* March 4, 1946, 23.

80. "Yamashita Hanged," 1.

81. "Yamashita: By," 45.

82. "Philippines: I Thank," 23.

83. "Yamashita Hanged," 1.

84. Kuhn, "International," 562.

85. Reel, *Case,* 40.

86. Mason, *Harlan Fiske Stone,* 671.

87. Reel, *Case,* 216; Mason, *Harlan Fiske Stone,* 671.

88. Barker, *Yamashita,* 152–53.

89. Ibid., 153.

90. Senate Judiciary Subcommittee on Administrative Oversight and the Courts, "Prepared Statement of Cass R. Sunstein, Karl N. Llewellyn Distinguished Professor of Jurisprudence at the Law School and the Department of Political Science at the University of Chicago," *Preserving Freedoms While Defending against Terrorism: Hearings before the Senate Judiciary Committee Subcommittee on Administrative Oversight and the Courts,* 107 Cong., 1st sess., December 4, 2001, paragraph 4, Federal News Service, http://web.lexis.nexis.com/congcomp/form/cong (July 8, 2004).

91. *The President's Order on Trials by Military Tribunal: Hearings of the Senate Armed Services Committee,* 107th Cong., 1st sess., December 12, 2001, Federal News Service, http://web.lexis.nexis.com/congcomp/form/cong (July 8, 2004).

92. For an exception to this general claim, see Peter Maguire, "Questions Hang Over

Military Tribunals," *Newsday,* November 21, 2001, http:proquest.umi.com/p1dweb?index (July 8, 2004). Maguire argues that following *Yamashita* would mean acting unilaterally at a time when we need to be thinking of "more internationalist war-crimes policies," paragraph 7.

93. See Bob Edwards and Nina Totenberg, "War Crimes Tribunal against a Japanese General after World War II," *National Public Radio* (NPR), December 27, 2001, http://web.lexis-nexis.com/universe (July 8, 2004).

94. Stephen B. Ives Jr., "Vengeance Did Not Deliver Justice," *Washington Post,* December 30, 2001, paragraph 1, http://web.lexi-nexis.com/universe (July 8, 2004).

95. Ibid., paragraph 2.

96. Ibid., paragraph 4.

97. Ibid., paragraph 5.

98. See for example, Thomas P. Reel, "History's Guide to Tribunals," *Washington Post,* January 28, 2004, A-20.

99. Ives, "Vengeance," paragraph 8.

100. Ibid., paragraphs 9–10.

101. Ibid., paragraphs 11, 17.

Chapter 8

1. *Epigraph.* Justice Davis, in *Ex parte Milligan,* 71 U.S. 120–21 (1866).

2. *Epigraph.* Myron C. Cramer, "Military Commissions: Trial of the Eight Saboteurs," *Washington Law Review and State Bar Journal* 17 (November 1942): 255.

3. Although Katyal and Tribe do not use the word "tory" to describe this one polar extreme, they do provide us with an excellent summary of some of its basic tenets:

> Indeed, if the UCMJ were stretched to give the President the power to create tribunals purportedly authorized by this Order, then it would risk making the statute an unconstitutional delegation of power. Such an interpretation would leave the President free to define a "time of war," grant him the discretion to set up military tribunal at will, bestow upon him the power to prosecute whomever he selects in a military tribunal, vest him with the authority to label something an offense and to try an offender for it, give him the power to try those cases before military judges that serve as part of the executive branch, and perhaps even empower him to dispense with habeas corpus review by an Article III court.

Neal K. Katyal and Laurence H. Tribe, "Waging War, Deciding Guilt: Trying the Military Tribunals," *Yale Law Journal* 111 (April 2002): 1290.

4. For an insightful discussion of Bush's rhetorical strategies during these turbulent times, see John M. Murphy, "'Our Mission and Our Moment': George W. Bush and September 11th," *Rhetoric and Public Affairs* 6 (2003): 607–32.

5. United and Strengthening America by Providing Appropriate Tools Required to Intercept and Obstruct Terrorism Act of 2001, Public Law, 107–56, 107th Cong., 1st sess., (October 2001).

6. Military Order—Detention, Treatment, and Trial of Certain Non-Citizens in the War against Terrorism, 66 Fed. Reg. 57833 (November 16, 2001), Part IV. A copy of this also appears in *Weekly Compilation of Presidential Documents* 47 (November 13, 2001): 1665–68.

7. Josh Tyrangiel, "And Justice for All," *Time,* November 26, 2001, 66.

8. Laura A. Dickinson, "Using Legal Process to Fight Terrorism: Detentions, Military Commissions, International Tribunals, and the Rule of Law," *University of California Law Review* 75 (2002): 1410, 1420–21.

9. *Ex parte Quirin,* 317 U.S. 1 (1942).

10. Dickinson, "Using Legal," 1407.

11. *Review of Military Terrorism Tribunals: Hearings before the Senate Judiciary Committee,* 107th Cong., 1st sess., 28 November 2001, paragraph 30, Federal Document Clearing House, http://web.lexis-nexis.com/congcomp (July 8, 2004).

12. Of course the case could be made that courts that look into violations of the "laws of war" can look at how the Bush Military Order stacks up against the Charter for the International Military Tribunals or the Rome Statute of the ICC. See Robert John Araujo, "A Judicial Response to Terrorism: The Status of Military Commissions under Domestic and International Law," *Tulane Journal of International and Comparative Law* 11 (2003): 117–40.

13. For an engaging defense of Israel's actions during the capture and trial of Eichmann, see Jacob Robinson, *And the Crooked Shall Be Made Straight: A New Look at the Eichmann Trial* (New York: Macmillan, 1965).

14. "Winging It at Guantánamo," Editorial, *New York Times,* April 23, 2002, paragraph 1, http://proquest.umi.com/pqdweb?index (July 8, 2004).

15. President Bush, "Text of President Bush's State of the Union Address to Congress, *New York Times,* January 30, 2002, A-22, quoted in Katyal and Tribe, "Waging War," 1276.

16. George W. Bush, *Declaration of National Emergency by Reason of Certain Terrorist Attacks,* September 14, 2001, http://www.whitehouse.gov/news/releases/2001/09/2001914-4.html (July 8, 2004).

17. Detention, Treatment, and Trial of Certain Non-Citizens in the War against Terrorism, Part IV, 66 Fed. Reg. 57833, 57833–57834 (2001).

18. George W. Bush, quoted in Mike Allen, "Bush Defends Order for Military Tribunals," *Washington Post,* November 20, 2001, paragraph 7, http://proquest.umi.com/pqdweb?index (July 8, 2004).

19. Detention, section 7. Relationship to Other Law and Forums, 66 Fed. Reg. 57835–57836.

20. Alberto R. Gonzales, "Martial Justice, Full and Fair," *New York Times,* November 30, 2001, A-27.

21. Ibid.

22. See, for example, "Due Process for Terrorists," Editorial, *Wall Street Journal,* March 25, 2002, http://proquest.umi.com (July 9, 2004).

23. Detention, section 2. Definition and Policy, 66 Fed. Reg. 57834.

24. In theory this could impact the lives of millions of residents, but there were some officials who argued that the Military Order was really passed in order to prepare for the trial of only a few key people. See *Review of Military Terrorism Tribunals: Hearings before the Senate Judiciary Committee,* 107th Cong., 1st sess., November 28, 2001, paragraph 22, *Federal Document Clearing House,* http://web.lexis-nexis.com/congcomp (July 8, 2004) [Barr testimony].

25. Detention, section 3. Detention Authority of the Secretary of Defense, 66 Fed. Reg. 57834.

26. Detention, section 4. Authority of the Secretary of Defense Regarding Trials of Individuals Subject to this Order, 66 Fed. Reg. 57834–57835.

27. Katyal and Tribe, "Waging War," 1265.

28. William P. Barr, *Review,* paragraph 1. Like many other conservatives, Barr worried about how "artificial restrictions on our powers of self defense" were being created by those who "gratuitously expanding constitutional guarantees beyond their intended office." William P. Barr, *Review,* paragraph 27.

29. Jonathan Turley, "Trials and Tribulations: The Antithetical Elements of Military Governance in a Madisonian Democracy," *George Washington Law Review* 70 (2002): 654.

30. Katyal and Tribe, "Waging War," 1310.

31. One interesting question is whether America's armed response in self-defense against Osama bin Laden and al-Qaeda can be construed as violations of international law, but not violations of "the law of war." This is commented on by Silliman, the Executive Director for the Center on Law, Ethics and National Security. See *Review of Military Terrorism Tribunals: Hearings before the Senate Judiciary Committee,* 107th Cong., 1st sess., November 28, 2001, paragraph 6, *Federal Document Clearing House,* http://web.lexis-nexis.com/congcomp (July 8, 2004).

32. Patrick A. Downes, "Letters," *Newsday,* November 20, 2001, A-39.

33. William Safire, "Essay: Kangaroo Courts," *New York Times,* November 26, 2001, paragraph 5, http://web.lexis-nexis.com/universe (July 9, 2004).

34. Ibid.

35. Laurence H. Tribe, "Trial by Fury," *New Republic* (December 10, 2001): 18–19.

36. Ibid., 18.

37. David Savage, "Response to Terror," *Los Angeles Times,* November 15, 2001, paragraph 6, http://web.lexis-nexis.com/universe (July 9, 2004).

38. Dick Cheney, quoted in Savage, "Response," paragraph 7.

39. Scott Silliman, quoted in Savage, "Response," paragraph 3.

40. For a much more detailed discussion of how organizations like the ACLU feel about Bush's military order, see Timothy H. Edgar, ACLU Memorandum, *President Bush's Order Establishing Military Trials in Terrorism Cases,* November 29, 2001, http://www.aclu.org/congress/112901b.html (July 9, 2004).

41. Joseph H. Hoffman, "Letter to the Editor," *San Francisco Chronicle,* November 20, 2001, paragraphs 3–4, http://web.lexis-nexis.com/universe (July 9, 2004).

42. Dan Eggen noted in December of 2001 that the Bush administration's "measures have proven popular with the public, which, polls show, overwhelmingly favors military tribunals and aggressive detention policies." Dan Eggen, "Ashcroft Defends Anti-Terrorism Steps," *Washington Post,* December 7, 2001, paragraph 15, http://web.lexis-nexis.com/universe (July 9, 2004).

43. "A Nation Challenged: Civil Liberties," *New York Times,* January 3, 2002, A-14.

44. Neal Katyal, *Review of Military Terrorism Tribunals: Hearings before the Senate Judiciary Committee,* 107th Cong., 1st sess., November 28, 2001, paragraph 1, *Federal Document Clearing House,* http://web.lexis-nexis.com/congcomp (July 8, 2004).

45. Philip B. Heymann, *Review of Military Terrorism Tribunals: Hearings before the Senate Judiciary Committee,* 107th Cong., 1st sess., 28 November 28, 2001, paragraph 25, *Federal Document Clearing House,* http://web.lexis-nexis.com/congcomp (July 8, 2004).

46. Philip Gailey, "Perspective on Security vs. Liberties," *St. Petersburg Times,* December 16, 2001, paragraph 6, http://web.lexis-nexis.com/universe (July 9, 2004).

47. Vice President Dick Cheney, quoted in Ann Gearan, "Legal Issues: Military Trial Details Sketchy," AP release, November 15, 2001, paragraph 5, http:www.freep.com/news/nw/terror2001/probe15_20011115.htm (July 9, 2004).

48. Barr, "Testimony," paragraph 1.

49. John Ashcroft, quoted in "Leading the News," *Bulletin's Frontrunner,* November 20, 2001, http://web.lexis-nexis.com/congcomp (December 3, 2001).

50. Gailey, "Perspective," paragraph 3.

51. Under Article I, section 8 of the U.S. Constitution, it is Congress that has the power to declare war and the power to "define and punish . . . Offences against the Law of Nations." See Edgar, *Memorandum,* paragraph. 7.

52. Patrick Leahy, *Review of Military Terrorism Tribunals: Hearings before the Senate Judiciary Committee,* 107th Cong., 1st sess., November 28, 2001, *Federal Document Clearing House,* http://web.lexis-nexis.com/congcomp (July 8, 2004).

To illustrate how debates within the broader "rhetorical culture" (Condit and Lucaites) can spill over into the legal sphere, note how Leahy quotes from William Safire's column in the *New York Times,* which described the Bush Military Order as "fiat" that "turns back the clock on all advances in military justice, through three wars, in the past half-century." Leahy, *Review,* paragraph 13.

53. Edgar, *Memorandum,* paragraph 7.

54. Ibid., paragraph 17.

55. This would be one of the places where significant modifications were made.

56. *Ex parte Quirin,* at 38, quoted in Edgar, *Memorandum,* paragraph 7. Crona and Richardson, the authors of an influential article on *Ex parte Quirin* and modern terrorism, pointed out in 1996 that the citizenship "of the accused poses no obstacle." "Justice for War Criminals," 372.

57. Edgar, *Memorandum,* paragraph 43.

58. *Gideon v. Wainwright,* 372 U.S. 335 (1963); Edgar, *Memorandum,* paragraph 56.

59. Edgar, *Memorandum,* paragraph 49.

60. Katyal, *Review,* paragraph 1.

61. Ibid., paragraph 3.

62. Philip B. Heymann, *Review of Military Terrorism Tribunals: Hearings before the Senate Judiciary Committee,* 107th Cong., 1st sess., 28 November 2001, paragraph 1, *Federal Document Clearing House,* http://web.lexis-nexis.com/congcomp (July 8, 2004).

63. Ibid., paragraph 6.

64. Ibid., paragraphs 11–22.

65. See Kate Martin, *Review of Military Terrorism Tribunals: Hearings before the Senate Judiciary Committee,* 107th Cong., 1st sess., November 28, 2001, *Federal Document Clearing House,* http://web.lexis-nexis.com/congcomp (July 8, 2004).

66. "Assault on the Constitution," *Progressive* 66 (January 2002): 8.

67. "Assault," 8.

68. Rehnquist, *All the Laws,* 221.

69. Andrew Kohut, quoted in Gailey, "Perspective," paragraph 5.

70. Libby Quaid, "Skelton: History of Military Tribunals Have Missouri Link," AP and local wire, November 27, 2001, paragraphs 8–9, http://web.lexis-nexis.com/universe (July 9, 2004).

71. Orrin Hatch, *The Department of Justice and Terrorism: Hearings of the Senate Judiciary Committee,* December 6, 2001, Federal News Service, paragraph 29, http://web.lexis-nexis.com/congcomp (July 9, 2004).

72. Leahy, *Review,* paragraph 95.

73. Ibid., paragraph 12.

74. Ibid., paragraph 13.

75. John Ashcroft, in Hatch, *Department,* paragraphs 49–50.

76. Ibid., paragraph 63.

77. Nat Hentoff, "Spinning the Military Tribunals," *Village Voice,* April 2, 2002, 27.

78. Ashcroft, in Hatch, *Department,* paragraph 182.

79. Leahy, *Review,* paragraph 82.

80. Ashcroft, in Hatch, *Department,* paragraph 180. The attorney general also conceded that 20 million people were "eligible for prosecution here," although he liked

to think of them as being protected by the laws of the United States as well. Paragraph 182.

81. Ibid., paragraph 93.

82. Ibid., paragraphs 130–32.

83. Ibid., paragraph 138.

84. Ibid., paragraph 327.

85. Charles Lane, "Bush Calls Draft on Tribunals 'Preliminary,'" *Washington Post,* December 29, 2001, paragraph 5, http://web.lexis-nexis.com/congcomp (July 9, 2004).

86. Hentoff, "Spinning," 27.

87. John Philip Reid, "In a Defensive Rage: The Uses of the Mob, the Justification in Law, and the Coming of the American Revolution," *New York University Law Review* 49 (1974): 1090.

88. Leahy, *Review,* paragraphs 391–93.

89. Diane F. Orentlicher and Robert Kogod Goldman, "When Justice Goes to War: Prosecuting Terrorists before Military Commissions," *Harvard Journal of Law and Public Policy* 25 (Spring 2002): 660.

90. Katyal and Tribe, "Waging War," 1265.

91. Katyal, *Review,* paragraph 7.

Chapter 9

1. *Epigraph. Hamdi et al. v. Rumsfeld, Secretary of Defense, et al.,* Slip Opinion, 542 U.S. ___ (2004), Scalia dissent, 27.

2. John Mintz and Michael Powell, "Attorneys for Detainees Plan Fast Action," *Washington Post,* June 29, 2004, paragraph 5, http://web.lexis-nexis.com/universe (July 2, 2004).

3. The other two decisions involved the rights of "alien" Guantánamo detainees *Rasul et al. v. Bush, President of the United States, et al.,* Slip Opinion, 542 U.S. ___ (2004), and *Rumsfeld, Secretary of Defense v. Padilla et al.,* Slip Opinion, 542 U.S. ___ 2004)—a jurisdictional case that reviewed whether Rumsfeld was the proper respondent in a case where the detainee was being held in a Navy brig in Charleston, South Carolina.

4. Anthony Lewis, "The Silencing of Gideon's Trumpet," *New York Times,* April 20, 2003, paragraph 35, http://web.lexis-nexis.com/universe (July 9, 2004).

5. *Hamdi et al. v. Rumsfeld, Secretary of Defense, et al.,* Slip Opinion, 542 U.S. ___ (2004), Opinion of Justice O'Connor, 29.

6. O'Connor, *Hamdi* Slip Opinion, 27.

7. *Hamdi et al. v. Rumsfeld, Secretary of Defense, et al.,* Slip Opinion, 542 U.S. ___ (2004), Concurring opinion of Justice Souter, joined by Justice Ginsburg, 14–15.

8. *Hamdi et al. v. Rumsfeld, Secretary of Defense, et al.,* Slip Opinion, 542 U.S. ___ (2004), Dissenting Opinion of Justice Thomas, 17.

9. O'Connor, *Hamdi,* Slip Opinion, 27.

10. *Id.*

11. *Id., 15.*

12. Sandra Day O'Connor, quoted in Editorial, "Prudent Check on Detentions," *Christian Science Monitor,* June 30, 2004, paragraph 9, http://web.lexis-nexis.com/universe (July 9, 2004).

13. Paisley Dodds, "U.S. Forms Tribunal for First Trials at Guantánamo," *St. Louis Post-Dispatch,* June 30, 2004, paragraph 3, http://proquest.umi.com (July 2, 2004).

14. U.S. Department of Defense News Release, "Guantánamo Detainee Charged," June 10, 2004, http://www.defenselink.mil (July 2, 2004).

15. Mintz and Powell, "Attorneys," paragraph 14.

16. See, for example, U.S. Department of Defense News Transcript, "Final Administrative Review Procedures for Guantánamo Detainees," May 18, 2004, http://www.defenselink.mil/transcripts/2004/tr20040518–0784.htm l (July 2, 2004).

17. Philip Allen Lacovara, quoted in Molly McDonough, "Tribunals v. Trials," *American Bar Association Journal* 88 (2002): 20.

18. "Assault on the Constitution," *Progressive,* January 2002, 9.

19. Geoffrey Robertson, "Trial by Fury?" *Harvard International Review* 24 (2002): 50.

20. Charles Lane, "Liberty and the Pursuit of Terrorists," *Washington Post,* November 25, 2001, paragraph 5, http://web.lexis-nexis.com/universe (July 7, 2004).

21. Lane, "Liberty and the Pursuit," paragraph 14.

22. Michal Belknap, "Military Tribunals: Legal, but Dubious," *San Diego Union-Tribune,* November 25, 2001, paragraph 3, http://web.lexis-nexis.com/universe (July 7, 2004).

23. Richard A. Serrano, "Rumsfeld Vows 'Fair and Impartial' Anti-Terrorism Trials," *Los Angeles Times,* March 22, 2002, paragraph 1, http://web.lexis-nexis.com/universe (March 29, 2002).

24. Secretary of Defense Donald H. Rumsfeld, quoted in Editorial, "Procedures on Parade," *Pittsburgh Post-Gazette,* March 27, 2002, paragraph 3, http://web.lexis-nexis.com/universe (April 2, 2002).

25. "Procedures," paragraph 1.

26. William Safire, "Military Tribunals Modified," *New York Times,* March 21, 2002, paragraph 2, http://web.lexis-nexis.com/universe (April 24, 2002).

27. Maddox, "After the Dust," 471.

28. "The Defense Department," noted Robertson, "presumably will decide whether relatives will be permitted to attend an event that will not be different in essence from the Taliban's soccer-field executions." "Trial by Fury," 50.

29. Secretary of Defense Donald H. Rumsfeld, *United States Department of Defense News Transcript, DOD News Briefing on Military Commissions,* http://www.defenselink.mil/news/

Mar2002/to3212002_to321sd. html (March 21, 2002), quoted in Maddox, "After the Dust," 470–71.

30. Safire, "Military Tribunals," paragraph 6.

31. Jonathan Turley, quoted in Nat Hentoff, "Spinning the Military Tribunals," *Village Voice,* April 2, 2002, 27.

32. Safire, "Military Tribunals," paragraphs 4, 7.

33. Perhaps the best cursory overview of some of the facts surrounding Padilla's detention within the popular press can be found in Jodi Wilgoren and Jo Thomas, "Traces of Terror: The Bomb Suspect; From Chicago Gang to Possible Al Qaeda Ties," *New York Times,* June 11, 2002, http://web.lexis-nexis.com/universe (July 9, 2004).

34. Tom Brune, "Courts Tackling Bush Policy; Judges Weigh In on 'Enemy Combatants,'" *Newsday,* December 19, 2003, paragraph 9, http://proquest.umi.com (July 9, 2004).

35. John Ashcroft, quoted in Harold Hongju Koh, "The Case against Military Commissions," *American Journal of International Law* 96 (April 2002): 341.

36. Donald Rumsfeld, quoted in Thom Shanker and Katharine Q. Seelye, "A National Challenged: Captives," *New York Times,* February 22, 2002, paragraph 14, http://web.lexis-nexis.com/universe (December 17, 2003).

37. Bill Keller, "Trials and Tribulations," *New York Times,* December 15, 2001, paragraph 1, http://web.lexis-nexis.com/universe (July 10, 2004).

38. John M. Murphy, "'Our Mission and Our Moment': George W. Bush and September 11th," *Rhetoric and Public Affairs* 6 (2003): 621.

39. In December of 2003, the Bush administration reversed course and decided that some detainees (including Yaser Esam Hamdi) would perhaps be allowed access to lawyers. "After 2-Year Wait, Terror Suspect to See Lawyer," *Newsday,* December 4, 2003, http://web.lexis-nexis.com/universe (December 8, 2003).

40. Brune, "Courts Tackling," paragraphs 2, 11.

41. Ruth Wedgwood, quoted in "The Case for Military Tribunals," *Wall Street Journal,* December 3, 2001, paragraphs 1, 3, http://proquest.umi.com (July 10, 2004). For those who want a more legalistic explanation of Wedgwood's views on tribunals, see Ruth Wedgwood, "Al Qaeda, Terrorism, and Military Commissions," *American Journal of International Law* 96 (2002): 328–37.

42. Cass Sunstein, quoted in "Military Tribunals, the Right Way," *Chicago Tribune,* January 2, 2002, paragraph 4, http://proquest.umi.com (July 10, 2004).

43. *Padilla v. Bush,* 233 F. Supp. 564, 569 (S.D.N.Y., 2002).

44. *Id.,* 569–570.

45. *Authorization for Use of Military Force* [AUMF] Public Law No. 107–40, sec. 2a, 115 Stat. 224 (2001), quoted in *Padilla v. Bush,* 570.

46. *War Powers Resolution,* Public Law No. 93–148, 87 Stat. 555 (1973), codified at 50 U.S.C. section 1541 et seq.

47. *Padilla v. Bush,* 572.

48. Michael Dobbs Memorandum, quoted in *Padilla v. Bush,* 573.

49. Donald Rumsfeld, quoted in *Padilla v. Bush,* 573–74.

50. Note 6, *Padilla v. Bush,* 573–74.

51. Posse Comitatus Act, 18 U.S.C. section 1385, section 4001 (a) (2000), quoted in *Padilla v. Bush,* 588.

52. *Padilla v. Bush,* 590–94.

53. *Ex parte Milligan,* 71 U.S. 2 (1866).

54. *Padilla v. Bush,* 594.

55. Brune, "Courts Tackling," paragraph 3.

56. *Hamdi v. Rumsfeld,* 316 F. 3d 450, 472 (4th Cir. 2003), 472, quoting *Quirin,* 317 U.S. 1, 25, quoted in Downs and Kinnunen, "Civil Liberties," 397. Bryant and Tobias contend that "the Bush administration or lower federal courts have read *Quirin* as expressing a mood of near prostrate deference by the judiciary to Executive Branch detention decisions in times of perceived crisis." A. Christopher Bryant and Carl Tobias, "*Quirin* Revisited," *University of Wisconsin Law Review* 2003 (2003): 363.

57. Lieutenant Colonel Sharon A Shaffer, Lieutenant Commander Charles Swift, Lieutenant Commander Philip Sundel, Major Mark A. Bridges, Major Michael D. Mori, and Neal Katyal, *Fawzi al Odah, et al. v. United States et al., No. 03-343, On Writ of Certiorari to the United States Court of Appeals for the District of Columbia Circuit, Brief of the Military Attorneys Assigned to the Defense in the Office of Military Commissions as Amicus Curiae in Support of Neither Party* [*Odah* brief] (Washington, DC: n.p., 2004), 1.

58. Shaffer, Swift, Sundel, Bridges, Mori, and Katyal, *Odah* brief, 3.

59. *Id.,* 3–4.

60. *Id.,* 5. For an example of public commentaries on these "black holes," see Editorial, "The Defense Speaks," *Washington Post,* January 18, 2004, B-6.

61. Declaration of Independence, paragraph 11.

62. Shaffer, Swift, Sundel, Bridges, Mori, and Katyal, *Odah* brief, 5–6.

63. *Id.,* 18.

64. *Id.,* 19–20.

65. Paul Shokovsky, "Navy Lawyer Defends Driver for Bin Laden," *Seattle Post-Intelligencer,* May 7, 2004, paragraph 3, http://proquest.umi.com (July 10, 2004).

66. During an interview, Katyal made specific comparisons between these eras when he told reporters that the Bush administration position "flouts what the American system of justice has been since the Civil War, if not before." Neal Katyal, quoted in Maureen O'Hagan, "Presidential Power in Question," *Seattle Times,* May 19, 2004, paragraph 20, http://proquest.umi.com (July 10, 2004).

67. Neal Katyal, Charles Swift, Perkins Coie, *Case No. CV04-0777L, Memorandum in Support of Petition for Writ of Mandamus Pursuant to 28 U.S.C. section 1361 or, In the Alternative, Writ of Habeas Corpus* (Seattle: Perkins Cole, 2004), 16.

68. Katyal, Swift, and Coie, *Memorandum,* 36.

69. Some of the documents that would be requested purportedly described some alleged mistreatment of Hamdan, and the DOD moved to classify some of these documents. Paul Shokovsky, "U.S. Moves to Classify Abuse Suit Documents," *Seattle Post-Intelligencer,* June 24, 2004, http://proquest.umi.com (July 10, 2004).

70. Katyal, Swift, and Coie, *Memorandum,* 1.

71. Jess Bravin, "Defending the Enemy: Critics of Tribunal Gain Unlikely Allies," *Wall Street Journal,* March 18, 2004, paragraphs 3, 33, http://proquest.umi.com (July 10, 2004).

72. Several members of the press have picked up on the radical nature of these legal positions. For example, Jess Bravin, a writer for the *Wall Street Journal,* contends that the Katyal-Swift approach "could force the administration to answer in open court or risk undercutting its longstanding promise that the tribunals will be 'full and fair.'" Bravin, "Defending," paragraph 6.

73. Robert S. Lasnik, *Case No. CV04-0777L, Order Granting Motion to Hold Petition in Abeyance, United States District Court for the Western District of Washington* (Seattle: Western District of Washington, 2004), 2.

74. *Yaser Esam Hamdi and Esam Fouad Hamdi v. Donald H. Rumsfeld,* Oral Argument before the Supreme Court of the United States (Washington, DC: Alderson Reporting, 2004).

75. *Donald H. Rumsfeld v. Jose Padilla and Donna R. Newman,* Oral Argument before the Supreme Court of the United States (Washington, DC: Alderson Reporting, 2004).

76. *Shafiq Rasul et al. v. George W. Bush and Fawzi Khalid Abdullah Fahad al Odah et al. v. United States et al.,* Oral Argument before the Supreme Court of the United States (Washington, DC: Alderson Reporting, 2004).

77. Tania Cruz, "Executive Restrictions of Civil Liberties 'When Fears and Prejudices Are Aroused,'" *Seattle Journal for Social Justice* 2 (Winter 2004): 158.

78. *Hamdi v. Rumsfeld,* 316 F.3d 450, 460 (4th Cir. 2003), petition for certiorari filed, October 1, 2003, No. 03-5596.

79. *Hamdi,* 460.

80. Department of Defense News Release Number 908-03, *DOD Announces Detainee Allowed Access to Lawyer,* December 2, 2003, http://www.dod.gov/releases/2003/nr20031202–0717html (July 4, 2004).

81. Neil A. Lewis, "Sudden Shift on Detainee, *New York Times,* December 4, 2003, paragraph 2, http://web.lexis-nexis.com/universe (July 10, 2004).

82. Durham, *Hamdi v. Rumsfeld* Oral Argument, 55.

83. *Id.*

84. Tony Mauro, "Court Struggles with Terrorism Cases: Justices Seem Sympathetic to Government and in Search of Compromise in Debating U.S. Power to Detain Citizens," *Legal Times,* May 3, 2004, paragraph 2, http://web.lexis-nexis.com/universe (July 10, 2004).

85. *Jose Padilla and Donna R. Newman v. Donald Rumsfeld,* No. 03-2235, 20003, U.S. App. Lexis 25616, December 18, 2003, http://web.lexis-nexis.com/universe (July 10, 2004).

86. Scalia, Oral Argument in *Rumsfeld v. Padilla and Newman,* 26.

87. Clement, Oral Argument in *Rumsfeld v. Padilla and Newman,* 20.

88. *Id.,* 21–22.

89. Breyer, Oral Argument in *Rumsfeld v. Padilla and Newman,* 16–17.

90. Clement, Oral Argument in *Rumsfeld v. Padilla and Newman,* 17.

91. *Id.,* 23–24.

92. Ginsburg, Oral Argument in *Rumsfeld v. Padilla and Newman,* 22.

93. Clement, Oral Argument in *Rumsfeld v. Padilla and Newman,* 28.

94. Martinez, Oral Argument in *Rumsfeld v. Padilla and Newman,* 29. During the last seconds of her oral argument, Martinez returned to this topic and told the court that the Founders had learned about the "history of the British Crown," and were trying to constitutionally place limits on "an unchecked executive using excuses based on national security, using the military power to render that superior to civilian authorities," 56.

95. Martinez, Oral Argument in *Rumsfeld v. Padilla and Newman,* 43.

96. *Id.,* 29.

97. *Id.,* 36–37.

98. Breyer, Oral Argument in *Rumsfeld v. Padilla and Newman,* 48.

99. Martinez, Oral Argument in *Rumsfeld v. Padilla and Newman,* 49.

100. *Id.,* 53.

101. Clement, Oral Argument in *Rumsfeld v. Padilla and Newman,* 58–59.

102. See, for example, the position of Justice Stevens, Oral Argument in *Rumsfeld v. Padilla and Newman,* 51.

103. Deputy Defense Secretary Paul Wolfowitz to Deputy Attorney General James B. Comey, May 28, 2004, *Department of Defense Summary Interrogations* [Summary] (Washington, DC: Pentagon, 2004), http://news.findlaw.com/wp/docs/padilla/pad52804dodsum.html (July 10, 2004).

104. Wolfowitz, *Summary,* 1.

105. *Id.,* 6.

106. Donna Newman, quoted in Eunice Moscoso, "Terror Suspects' Lawyers Cry Foul," *Atlanta Journal-Constitution,* June 20, 2004, paragraph 8, http://web.lexis-nexis.com/universe (July 10, 2004).

107. Frank W. Durham Jr., quoted in Richard B. Schmitt and John Hendren, "The

Courtrooms Are Open, Now It's Up to the Lawyers," *Los Angeles Times,* June 29, 2004, paragraph 20, http://web.lexis-nexis.com/universe (July 10, 2004).

108. *Hamdi et al. v. Rumsfeld et al.,* 1–2.

109. Justice O'Connor, *Hamdi* Slip Opinion, 31.

110. Joan Biskupic and Toni Locy, "Detainees Still Will Face Many Hurdles to Freedom," *USA Today,* June 29, 2004, paragraph 1, http://web.lexis-nexis.com/universe (July 10, 2004).

111. Steven Shapiro, quoted in Zachary Coile and Bob Egelko, "Justices Affirm Rights of Detainees," *San Francisco Chronicle,* June 29, 2004, paragraph 6, http://web.lexis-nexis.com/universe (July 10, 2004).

112. Schmitt and Hendren, "Courtrooms," paragraph 4.

113. Andrew Buncombe, "Court Defies White House with Ruling on Prisoners," *[London] Independent,* June 29, 2004, paragraph 24, http://web.lexis-nexis.com/universe (July 10, 2004).

114. Louise Christian, quoted in Buncombe, "Court Defies," paragraph 14.

115. "Toward a Terrorist Nuremberg," *Wall Street Journal,* July 2, 2004, paragraph 4, http://proquest.umi.com (July 10, 2004).

116. For an insightful discussion of how the Supreme Court should have applied some international laws as it studied these citizen and non-citizen detentions, see George P. Fletcher, "Black Hole in Guantánamo Bay," *Journal of International Criminal Justice* 2 (2004): 121–32.

117. *Hamdi,* O'Connor Slip Opinion, 12.

118. Safire, "Military Tribunals," paragraph 8.

119. John Ashcroft, quoted in Sullivan, "U.S. to Seek," paragraph 10.

120. Note here, for example, the efforts of U.S. District Judge Robert Doumar, who has battled the Justice Department and extensively critiqued the short memos used to justify Hamdi's detention. Tom Jackman, "U.S. Defies Judge on Enemy Combatant," *Washington Post,* August 2, 2004, A-1.

121. Mark Osiel, *Mass Atrocity, Collective Memory, and the Law* (New Brunswick, NJ: Transaction Publishers, 1997), 105.

122. For a discussion of how defenders of military commissions have also talked about how certain military proceedings can be held in camera, see Robert John Araujo, "A Judicial Response to Terrorism: The Status of Military Commissions under Domestic and International Law," *Tulane Journal of International and Comparative Law* 11 (2003): 140.

123. Gerald J. Clark, "Military Tribunals and the Separation of Powers," *University of Pittsburgh Law Review* 63 (2002): 866–67.

124. Alberto R. Gonzales, *Decision Re Application of the Geneva Convention on Prisoners of War to the Conflict with Al Qaeda and the Taliban,* January 25, 2002, 2, http://www.msnbc.msn.com/id/4999148/site/newsweek (July 10, 2004).

125. Neil A. Lewis, "Legal Doctrine Would Ease War Prisoner Prosecutions," *Milwaukee Journal Sentinel,* April 21, 2002, paragraph 1, http://proquest.umi.com (July 10, 2004).

126. Aryeh Neier, "The Military Tribunals on Trial," *New York Review of Books* 49 (February 14, 2002): 14.

127. Michael Ignatieff, "Mirage in the Desert," *New York Times Magazine,* June 27, 2004, sec. IV, 15.

128. Diane F. Orentlicher and Robert Kogod Goldman, "When Justice Goes to War: Prosecuting Terrorists before Military Commissions," *Harvard Journal of Law and Public Policy* 25 (Spring 2002): 654.

129. An Afghan merchant, quoted in William T. Vollmann, "Letters from Afghanistan: Across the Great Divide," *New Yorker,* May 2000, 72.

130. Anne-Marie Slaughter, "Terrorism and Justice," *[London] Financial Times,* October 21, 2001, paragraphs 1–3, http://web.lexis-nexis.com/universe (July 10, 2004).

131. Curran, "Legalization," 86–87.

132. Thomas Paine, quoted in Rutledge, *In re Yamashita,* 327 U.S. 1, 81; Neal K. Katyal and Laurence H. Tribe, "Waging War, Deciding Guilt: Trying the Military Tribunals," *Yale Law Journal* 111 (April 2002): 1310.

Bibliography

Books

Anderson, Gary Clayton, and Alan R. Woolworth, eds. *Through Dakota Eyes: Narrative Accounts of the Minnesota Indian War of 1862.* St. Paul: Minnesota Historical Society Press, 1988.

Blanchot, Maurice. *The Writing of the Disaster.* Trans. Ann Smock. Lincoln: University of Nebraska Press, 1995.

Blight, David W. *Race and Reunion: The Civil War in American Memory.* Cambridge, MA: Belknap Press of Harvard University Press, 2001.

Bloxham, Donald. *Genocide on Trial: War Crimes Trials and the Formation of Holocaust History and Memory.* New York: Oxford University Press, 2001.

Brennen, Bonnie, and Hanno Hardt, eds. *Picturing the Past: Media, History and Photography.* Urbana: University of Illinois Press, 1999.

Bryant, Charles S, and Abel S. Murch. *A History of the Great Massacre of the Sioux Indians in Minnesota, Including the Personal Narratives of Many Who Escaped.* Cincinnati, OH: Ricky and Carroll, 1864.

Burke, Kenneth. *A Grammar of Motives.* New York: George Braziller, 1955.

Campbell, Kurt M., and Michèle A. Flournoy. *To Prevail: An American Strategy for the Campaign against Terrorism.* Washington, DC: Center for Strategic and International Studies, 2001.

Chipman, Norton P. *The Tragedy of Andersonville, Trial of Captain Henry Wirz, the Prison Keeper.* Sacramento, CA: Norton P. Chipman, 1911.

Cole, David, and James X. Dempsey. *Terrorism and the Constitution: Sacrificing Civil Liberties in the Name of National Security.* New York: The New Press, 2002.

Condit, Celeste M., and John L. Lucaites. *Crafting Equality: America's Anglo-African Word.* Chicago: University of Chicago Press, 1993.

Douglas, Lawrence. *The Memory of Judgment: Making Law and History in the Trials of the Holocaust.* New Haven, CT: Yale University Press, 2001.

Feaver, Peter D., and Richard H. Kohn, eds. *Soldiers and Civilians: The Civil-Military Gap and American National Security.* Cambridge, MA: MIT Press, 2001.

Fitzpatrick, Peter, ed. *Dangerous Supplements: Resistance and Renewal in Jurisprudence.* Durham, NC: Duke University Press, 1991.

Foucault, Michel. *Discipline and Punish: The Birth of the Prison.* Trans. Alan Sheridan. New York: Vintage, 1979.

Friedman, Lawrence M. *A History of American Law.* New York: Simon and Schuster, 1985.

Gilmore, Grant. *The Ages of American Law.* New Haven, CT: Yale University Press, 1977.

Hariman, Robert, ed. *Popular Trials: Rhetoric, Mass Media, and the Law.* Tuscaloosa: University of Alabama Press, 1990.

Hoge, James F., Jr., and Gideon Rose, eds. *How Did This Happen? Terrorism and the New War.* New York: PublicAffairs, 2001.

Huntington, Samuel. *The Soldier and the State.* Cambridge, MA: Belknap Press of Harvard University Press, 1957.

Koerting, Gayla Marie. Dissertation, *The Trial of Henry Wirz and Nineteenth-Century Military Law.* Kent, OH: Kent State University, 1995.

LaCapra, Dominick. *History and Criticism.* Ithaca, NY: Cornell University Press, 1985.

Martin, James Kirby, and Mark Edward Lender. *A Respectable Army: The Military Origins of the Republic, 1763–1789.* Arlington Heights, IL: Harlan Davidson, 1982.

Marvel, William. *Andersonville: The Last Depot.* Chapel Hill: University of North Carolina Press, 1994.

Neely, Mark E., Jr. *The Fate of Liberty: Abraham Lincoln and Civil Liberties.* New York: Oxford University Press, 1991.

Rachlis, Eugene. *They Came to Kill.* New York: Random House, 1961.

Randall, James Garfield. *Constitutional Problems under Lincoln.* Urbana: University of Illinois Press, 1951.

Reel, Adolf Frank. *The Case of General Yamashita.* Chicago: University of Chicago Press, 1949.

Rehnquist, William. *All the Laws but One: Civil Liberties in Wartime.* New York: Knopf, 1998.

Sarat, Austin, and Thomas R. Kearns, eds. *The Rhetoric of Law*. Ann Arbor: University of Michigan Press, 1994.

Talbott, Strobe, and Nayan Chanda, eds. *The Age of Terror: America and the World after September 11*. New York: Basic Books, 2001.

Taylor, Lawrence. *A Trial of Generals: Homma, Yamashita, MacArthur*. South Bend, IN: Icarus Press, 1981.

Thiem, Karin. Thesis, *The Minnesota Sioux War Trials*. Mankato: Minnesota State University–Mankato, 1979.

Tredway, G. R. *Democratic Opposition to the Lincoln Administration in Indiana*. Indianapolis: Indiana Historical Bureau, 1973.

Turner, Kathleen J., ed. *Doing Rhetorical History: Concepts and Cases*. Tuscaloosa: University of Alabama Press, 1998.

Wilson, Kirk H. *The Reconstruction Debate: The Politics of Equality and the Rhetoric of Place, 1870–1875*. East Lansing: Michigan State University Press, 2002.

Journal Articles

Alexander, Keith S. "In the Wake of September 11th: The Use of Military Tribunals to Try Terrorists." *Notre Dame Law Review* 78 (2003): 885–916.

Araujo, Robert John. "A Judicial Response to Terrorism: The Status of Military Commissions under Domestic and International Law." *Tulane Journal of International and Comparative Law* 11 (2003): 117–40.

Belknap, Michal R. "A Putrid Pedigree: The Bush Administration's Military Tribunals in Historical Perspective." *California Western Law Review* 38 (2002): 433–80.

Bickers, John M. "Military Commissions Are Constitutionally Sound: A Response to Professors Katyal and Tribe. *Texas Tech Law Review* 34 (2003): 899–932.

Biddle, Charles J. "The Case of Major André. *Memories of the Historical Society of Pennsylvania* 6 (1858): 317–416.

Bryant, A. Christopher, and Carl Tobias. "Civil Liberties in a Time of Terror: *Quirin* Revisited." *University of Wisconsin Law Review* 2003 (2003): 309–64.

Carnahan, Burrus M. "Lincoln, Lieber and the Laws of War: The Origins and Limits of the Principle of Military Necessity." *American Journal of International Law* 92 (1998): 213–31.

Chomsky, Carol. "The United States–Dakota War Trials: A Study in Military Injustice." *Stanford Law Review* 43 (November 1990): 13–98.

Clark, Gerald J. "Military Tribunals and the Separation of Powers." *University of Pittsburgh Law Review* 63 (2002): 837–71.

Condit, Celeste M., and John L. Lucaites. "The Rhetoric of Equality and the Expatriation of African-Americans, 1776–1826." *Communication Studies* 42 (1991): 1–21.

Conway, Stephen. "To Subdue America: British Army Officers and the Conduct of the Revolutionary War." *William and Mary Quarterly* 43 (July 1986): 381–407.

Cover, Robert. "The Supreme Court, 1982 Term-Foreword: *Nomos* and Narrative." *Harvard Law Review* 97 (1983): 4–68.

Cramer, Myron C. "Military Commissions: Trial of the Eight Saboteurs." *Washington Law Review and State Bar Journal* 17 (November 1942): 247–55.

Cray, Robert E., Jr. "Major John André and the Three Captors: Class Dynamics and Revolutionary Memory Wars in the Early Republic, 1780–1831." *Journal of the Early Republic* 17 (1997): 371–97.

Crona, Spencer J., and Neal A. Richardson. "Justice for War Criminals of Invisible Armies: A New Legal and Military Approach to Terrorism." *Oklahoma City University Law Review* 21 (1996): 349–407.

Cruz, Tania. "Executive Restrictions on Civil Liberties 'When Fears and Prejudices Are Aroused.'" *Seattle Journal for Social Justice* 2 (Winter 2004): 129–72.

Davies, Kirk. L. "The Imposition of Martial Law in the United States." *Air Force Law Review* 49 (2000): 67–112.

Dennison, George M. "Martial Law: The Development of a Theory of Emergency Powers, 1776–1861." *American Journal of Legal History* 18 (January 1974): 52–79.

Dickinson, Laura A. "Using Legal Process to Fight Terrorism: Detentions, Military Commissions, International Tribunals, and the Rule of Law." *University of California Law Review* 75 (2002): 1407–92.

Downs, Donald A., and Erik Kinnunen. "Civil Liberties in a New Kind of War." *University of Wisconsin Law Review* 2003 (2003): 385–412.

Fairman, Charles. "The Law of Martial Rule and the National Emergency." *Harvard Law Review* 55 (June 1942): 1253–302.

Fisher, Louis. "Military Tribunals: A Sorry History." *Presidential Studies Quarterly* 33 (2003): 484–508.

Fletcher, George P. "Black Hole in Guantánamo Bay." *Journal of International Criminal Justice* 2 (2004): 121–32.

French, Anne English. "Trials in Times of War: Do the Bush Military Commissions Sacrifice Our Freedoms?" *Ohio State Law Journal* 63 (2003): 1225–83.

Gambone, Joseph G. "*Ex Parte Milligan:* The Restoration of Judicial Prestige?" *Civil War History* 16 (1970): 246–59.

Golove, David. "Military Tribunals, International Law, and the Constitution: A Franckian-Madisonian Approach." *Journal of International Law and Politics* 35 (2003): 363–94.

Hariman, Robert, and John Louis Lucaites. "Performing Civil Identity: The Iconic Photograph of the Flag Raising on Iwo Jima. *Quarterly Journal of Speech* 88 (2002): 363–92.

Hasday, Jill Elaine. "Civil War as Paradigm: Reestablishing the Rule of Law at the End of the Cold War." *Kansas Journal of Law and Public Policy* 5 (Winter 1996): 129–43.

Insco, James B. "Defense of Superior Orders before Military Commissions." *Duke Journal of Comparative and International Law* 13 (2003): 389–418.

Kapur, Ratna. "Collateral Damage: Sacrificing Legitimacy in the Search for Justice." *Harvard International Review* 24 (Spring 1992): 42–46.

Katyal, Neal K, and Laurence H. Tribe. "Waging War, Deciding Guilt: Trying the Military Tribunals." *Yale Law Journal* 111 (April 2002): 1259–310.

Koh, Harold Hongju. "The Case against Military Commissions." *American Journal of International Law* 96 (April 2002): 337–44.

Kellman, Barry. "Catastrophic Terrorism: Thinking Fearfully, Acting Legally." *Michigan Journal of International Law* 20 (Spring 1999): 537–64.

Lacey, Michael O. "Military Commissions: A Historical Survey." *Army Lawyer* 350 (March 2002): 41–47.

Landrum, Bruce D. "The *Yamashita* War Crimes Trial: Command Responsibility Then and Now." *Military Law Review* 149 (Summer 1995): 293–301.

Lewis, Anthony. "Civil Liberties in a Time of Terror." *University of Wisconsin Law Review* 2003 (2003): 257–72.

Lippman, Mathew. "Humanitarian Law: The Uncertain Contours of Command Responsibility." *Tulsa Journal of Comparative and International Law* 9 (2001): 1–93.

Maddox, Heather Anne. "After the Dust Settles: Military Tribunals for Terrorists after September 11, 2001." *North Carolina Journal of International Law and Commerce Regulation* 28 (2002): 421–76.

MacDonnell, Timothy C. "Military Commissions and Courts-Martial: A Brief

Discussion of the Constitutional and Jurisdictional Distinctions between the Two Courts." *Army Lawyer* 350 (March 2002): 19–40.

McDonough, Molly. "Tribunals vs. Trials." *American Bar Association Journal* 88 (January 2002): 20.

McGee, Michael C. "The 'Ideograph': A Link between Rhetoric and Ideology." *Quarterly Journal of Speech* 66 (1980): 1–16.

Murphy, John M. "'Our Mission and Our Moment': George W. Bush and September 11th." *Rhetoric and Public Affairs* 6 (2003): 607–32.

Nora, Pierre. "Between Memory and History: Les Lieux de Mémoire." *Representations* 26 (Spring 1989): 7–25.

Orentlicher, Diane F., and Robert Kogod Goldman. "When Justice Goes to War: Prosecuting Terrorists before Military Commissions." *Harvard Journal of Law and Public Policy* 25 (Spring 2002): 653–63.

Osiel, Mark J. "Ever Again: Legal Remembrance of Administrative Massacre." *University of Pennsylvania Law Review* 144 (1995): 463–704.

[Parker, Joel]. "Habeas Corpus and Martial Law." *North American Review* 93 (October 1861): 471–518.

Parry, John T. "The Virtue of Necessity: Reshaping Culpability and the Rule of Law." *Houston Law Review* 36 (Summer 1999): 397–469.

Randall, James. "Civil and Military Relationships under Lincoln." *Pennsylvania Magazine of History and Biography* 69 (1945): 199–206.

Robertson, Geoffrey. "Trial by Fury." *Harvard International Review* 24 (Spring 2002): 48–53.

Romano, John-Alex. "Combating Terrorism and Weapons of Mass Destruction: Reviving the Doctrine of a State of Necessity." *Georgetown Law Journal* 87 (April 1999): 1023–57.

Rutman, Darrett B. "The War Crimes and Trial of Henry Wirz." *Civil War History* 62 (1960): 117–33.

Sarat, Austin. "Rhetoric and Remembrance: Trials, Transcription, and the Politics of Critical Reading." *Legal Studies Forum* 23 (1999): 355–56.

Sherman, Edward F. "The Civilianization of Military Law." *Maine Law Review* 22 (1970): 5–27.

Tang, Edward. "Writing the American Revolution: War Veterans in the Nineteenth-Century Cultural Memory." *Journal of American Studies* 32 (April 1998): 63–88.

Turley, Jonathan. "Tribunals and Tribulations: The Antithetical Elements of Military Governance in a Madisonian Democracy." *George Washington Law Review* 70 (2002): 649–768.

Wedgwood, Ruth. "Al Qaeda, Terrorism and Military Commissions." *American Journal of International Law* 96 (2002): 328–37.

Williams, Lorraine A. "Northern Intellectual Reaction to Military Rule during the Civil War." *Historian* 27 (May 1965): 334–49.

Wright, Quincy. "Due Process and International Law." *American Journal of International Law* 40 (April 1946): 398–406.

Key Orders, Statutes, Resolutions, and Bills

Military Order-Detention, Treatment, and Trial of Certain Non-Citizens in the War against Terrorism, 66 Federal Regulation 57833, November 16, 2001.

Uniting and Strengthening America by Providing Appropriate Tools Required to Intercept and Obstruct Terrorism Act of 2001. Public Law 107–56. 107th Cong., 1st sess., October 2001.

Congressional Documents, Reports, and Testimony

Fisher, Louis. *Military Tribunals: The Quirin Precedent.* Washington, DC: Congressional Research Service, 2002.

U.S. House. *Trial of Henry Wirz.* 40th Cong., 2nd sess. H. Exec. Doc. 23, ser. 1331. Washington, DC: Government Printing Office, 1880.

U.S. Senate. Senate Judiciary Subcommittee on Administrative Oversight and the Courts. *Preserving Freedoms While Defending against Terrorism.* 107th Cong., 1st sess., 2001.

U.S. Senate. Senate Judiciary Committee. *Review of Military Terrorism Tribunals.* 107th Cong., 1st sess., 2001.

Index